PRAISE FOR *HOW MUSIC WORKS*

"David Byrne is a brilliantly original, eccentric rock star, and he has written a book to match his protean talents... What's best about [it] is that Byrne concentrates on his own experience, from a teenage geek splicing layers of guitar feedback on his father's tape recorder (he had a mild self-diagnosed case of Asperger's syndrome, he writes) to arty if neo-primitive rock star with the early Talking Heads at CBGB to increasingly sophisticated, globe-wandering art-rocker, happily collaborating with all manner of world musicians and pop-technological innovators."
—John Rockwell, *The New York Times Book Review*

"From the former Talking Heads frontman, a supremely intelligent, superbly written dissection of music as an art form and way of life... Byrne touches on all kinds of music from all ages and every part of the world... Highly recommended—anyone at all interested in music will learn a lot from this book."
—*Kirkus* (Starred Review)

"In this fascinating meditation, Talking Heads frontman Byrne (Bicycle Diaries) explores how social and practical context, more than individual authorship, shaped music making in history and his own career... his chapters on Heads recording sessions are some of the most insightful accounts of musical creativity yet penned. The result is a surprising challenge to the romantic cliché of musical genius... Byrne's erudite and entertaining prose reveals him to be a true musical intellectual, with serious and revealing things to say about his art."
—*Publishers Weekly* (Starred Review)

"Endlessly fascinating, insightful, and intelligent."   —June Sawyers, *Booklist* (Starred Review)

"David Byrne has written several good books, but his latest, *How Music Works*, is unquestionably the best of the very good bunch, possibly the book he was born to write. I could make a good case for calling this *How Art Works* or even *How Everything Works*."   —Cory Doctorow, *BoingBoing*

"Byrne explores a whole symphony of argument in this extraordinary book with the precise, technical enthusiasm you'd expect from the painfully bright art school-educated son—born in Scotland, raised in the States—of an electrical engineer, occasionally mopping his fevered brow in the crestfallen manner of a 19th-century poet... It's fascinating." —Mark Ellen, *The Guardian*

"*How Music Works*, is as engaging as it is eclectic: a buoyant hybrid of social history, anthropological survey, autobiography, personal philosophy, and business manual, sometimes on the same page... Even for the most ardent explorers (and Byrne is one) this is some seriously unknowable territory."
—Joan Anderman, *The Boston Globe*

"By all accounts, Byrne's style and energy are as apparent on the page as on the stage."
—Kathryn Schulz, *New York Magazine*

"Truly dazzling, covering a staggering scope of topics... Almost every page [is] a song."
—Jason Heller, *The Onion A.V. Club*

"In the course of *How Music Works*, Byrne integrates his discussion of all the issues of recording and live performance into a personal account of his own career. Although this book stops short of turning into a memoir or autobiography, fans seeking a behind-the-scenes account of Byrne's life and times won't be disappointed... An essential guide to performance and recording, honest and up-to-date, and filled with both practical advice and insightful commentary."
—Ted Gioia, *The San Francisco Chronicle*

"Bob Dylan, Keith Richards, Jay Z, even Daniel Lanois have all given us books in recent years. And they've all been interesting and worth reading. But none of them is as good as David Byrne's book... He weaves his account of the evolution of music from animals to humans and the history of changes in the way music studios work into the most accessible and unpretentious narrative of such a story that I have yet come across." —David Rothenberg, *The Globe and Mail*

"A decidedly generous book—welcoming, informal, digressive, full of ideas and intelligence—and one has the pleasant sense that Byrne is speaking directly to the reader, sharing a few confidences he has picked up over the years." —Tim Page, *The Washington Post*

"An accomplished celebration of an ever-evolving art form that can alter how we look at ourselves and the world... A meticulously researched and hugely absorbing history of music."
—Fiona Sturges, *The Independent*

"An entertaining and erudite book, from a figure who has spent his career proving that those two adjectives can happily coexist... The chapter on the economics of music should be required reading for all 16-year-olds tinkering with their GarageBand software and dreaming of dollar signs, while the section on 'How to Make A Scene' is nothing less than a manual for urban regeneration through pop culture... A serious, straightforward account of an art form that also manages to be inspiring. You could do a lot worse than use it as a thinking-outside-the-box management manual or a college primer. Art and Society 101: Stop Making Sense."
—Peter Aspden, *Financial Times*

"David Byrne deserves great praise for *How Music Works*. It is as accessible as pop yet able to posit deep and startlingly original thoughts and discoveries in almost every paragraph... This book will make you hear music in a different way." —Oliver Keens, *The Telegraph*

*To Emma and Tom Byrne, who put up with
my adolescent musical expressions and
even helped out from time to time.*

CONTENTS

I've been involved in music all my adult life. I didn't plan it that way, and it wasn't even a serious ambition at first, but that's the way it turned out. A very happy accident, if you ask me. It's a little strange, though, to realize that a large part of my identity is tied to something that is completely ephemeral. You can't touch music—it exists only at the moment it is being apprehended—and yet it can profoundly alter how we view the world and our place in it. Music can get us through difficult patches in our lives by changing not only how we feel about ourselves, but also how we feel about everything outside ourselves. It's powerful stuff.

Early on, though, I realized that the same music placed in a different context can not only change the way a listener perceives that music, but it can also cause the music itself to take on an entirely new meaning. Depending on where you hear it—in a concert hall or on the street—or what the intention is, the same piece of music could either be an annoying intrusion, abrasive and assaulting, or you could find yourself dancing to it. How music works, or doesn't work, is determined not just by what it is in isolation (if such a condition can ever be said to exist) but in large part by what surrounds it, where you hear it, and when you hear it. How it's performed, how it's sold and distributed, how it's recorded, who performs it, whom you hear it with, and, of course, finally, what it sounds like: these are the things that determine not only if a piece of music works—if it successfully achieves what it sets out to accomplish—but what it is.

Each chapter in this book focuses on a distinct aspect of music and its context. One asks how technology has affected the way music sounds and the way we think of it. Another considers the influence of the places in which we listen to it. The chapters are not chronological or sequential. You can read them in any order, though I do think the order my editors and I arrived at has a flow to it—it isn't entirely random. For this paperback edition, I've added sections to several chapters; updates gleaned from my experience on the book tour for the hardcover, recent correspondences, emerging technologies, and a couple new collaborations. My thinking on all of the topics herein are constantly evolving as I learn more.

This is not an autobiographical account of my life as a singer and musician, but much of my understanding of music has certainly been accrued over many years of recording and performing. In this book I draw on that experience to illustrate changes in technology and in my own thinking about what music and performance are about. Many of my ideas about what it means to go on stage, for instance, have changed completely over the years, and my own history of performance is a way of telling the story of a still-evolving philosophy.

Others have written insightfully about music's physiological and neurological effects; scientists have begun to peek under the hood to examine the precise mechanisms by which music works on our emotions and perceptions. But that's not really my brief here; I have focused on how music might be molded before it gets to us, what determines if it gets to us at all, and what factors external to the music itself can make it resonate for us. Is there a bar near the stage? Can you put it in your pocket? Do girls like it? Is it affordable?

I have, for the most part, avoided the ideological aspects of music making and production. That music can be made to bolster nationalistic urges or written in the service of rebellion and overthrowing an established culture—whether the motive is political or generational—those are beyond the scope of this book. I'm not much interested in specific styles and genres either, as it seems to me that certain models and modes of behavior often recur across wildly different scenes. I hope that you will find something to enjoy here even if you have no interest in my own music. I'm also uninterested in the swollen egos that drive some artists, although the psychological makeup of musicians and composers shapes music at least as much as any of the phenomena I'm fascinated by. I have rather looked for patterns in how music is written, recorded, distributed, and received—and then asked myself if the forces that fashioned and shaped these patterns have guided my own work... and maybe the work of others as well. One hopes I'm not just talking about myself here! In most cases the answer is yes; I'm no different than anyone else.

Does asking oneself these questions in an attempt to see how the machine works spoil the enjoyment? It hasn't for me. Music isn't fragile. Knowing how the body works doesn't take away from the pleasure of living. Music has been around as long as people have formed communities. It's not going to go away, but its uses and meaning evolve. I am moved by more music now than I have ever been. Trying to see it from a wider and deeper perspective only makes it clear that the lake itself is wider and deeper than we thought.

CHAPTER ONE

Creation in Reverse

I had an extremely slow-dawning insight about creation. That insight is that context largely determines what is written, painted, sculpted, sung, or performed. That doesn't sound like much of an insight, but it's actually the opposite of conventional wisdom, which maintains that creation emerges out of some interior emotion, from an upwelling of passion or feeling, and that the creative urge will brook no accommodation, that it simply must find an outlet to be heard, read, or seen. The accepted narrative suggests that a classical composer gets a strange look in his or her eye and begins furiously scribbling a fully realized composition that couldn't exist in any other form. Or that the rock and roll singer is driven by desire and demons, and out bursts this amazing, perfectly shaped song that had to be three minutes and twelve seconds—nothing more, nothing less. This is the romantic notion of how creative work comes to be, but I think the path of creation is almost 180 degrees from this model. I believe that we unconsciously and instinctively make work to fit preexisting formats.

Of course, passion can still be present. Just because the form that one's work will take is predetermined and opportunistic (meaning one makes something because the opportunity is there), it doesn't mean that creation must be cold, mechanical, and heartless. Dark and emotional materials usually find a way in, and the tailoring process—form being tailored to fit a given context—is largely unconscious, instinctive. We usually don't even notice it. Opportunity and availability are often the mother of invention. The emotional story—"something to get off my chest"—still gets told, but its form is guided by prior contextual restrictions. I'm proposing that this is not entirely the bad thing one might expect it to be. Thank goodness, for example, that we don't have to reinvent the wheel every time we make something.

In a sense, we work backward, either consciously or unconsciously, creating work that fits the venue available to us. That holds true for the other arts as well: pictures are created that fit and look good on white walls in galleries just as music is written that sounds good either in a dance club or a symphony hall (but probably not in both). In a sense, the space, the platform, and the software "makes" the art, the music, or whatever. After something succeeds, more venues of a similar size and shape are built to accommodate more production of the same. After a while the form of the work that predominates in these spaces is taken for granted—of course we mainly hear symphonies in symphony halls.

In the photo below you can see the room at CBGB where some of the music I wrote was first heard.[A] Try to ignore the lovely decor and think of the size and shape of the space. Next to that is a band performing.[B] The sound in that club was remarkably good—the amount of crap scattered everywhere, the furniture, the bar, the crooked uneven walls and looming ceiling made for both great sound absorption and uneven acoustic reflections—qualities one might spend a fortune to re-create in a recording studio. Well, these qualities were great for this particular music. Because of the lack of reverberation, one could be fairly certain, for

example, that details of one's music would be heard—and given the size of the place, intimate gestures and expressions would be seen and appreciated as well, at least from the waist up. Whatever went on below the waist was generally invisible, obscured by the half-standing, half-sitting audience. Most of the audience would have had no idea that the guy in that photo was rolling around on the stage—he would have simply disappeared from view.

This New York club was initially meant to be a bluegrass and country venue—like Tootsie's Orchid Lounge in Nashville. The singer George Jones knew the number of steps from the stage door of the Grand Ole Opry to the back door of Tootsie's—thirty-seven. Charley Pride gave Tootsie Bess a hatpin to use on rowdy customers.

Below is a photo of some performers at Tootsie's.[C] Physically, the two clubs are almost identical. The audience behavior was pretty much the same in both places, too.[D]

The musical differences between the two venues are less significant than one might think—structurally, the music emanating from them was pretty much identical, even though once upon a time a country music audience at Tootsie's would have hated punk rock, and vice versa. When Talking Heads first played in Nashville, the announcer declaimed, "Punk rock comes to Nashville! For the first, and probably the last time!"

Both of these places are bars. People drink, make new friends, shout, and fall down, so the performers had to play loud enough to be heard above that—and so it was, and is. (FYI: the volume in Tootsie's is much louder than it usually was in CBGB.)

Looking at this scant evidence, I asked myself, to what extent was I writing music specifically, and maybe unconsciously, to fit these places? (I didn't know about Tootsie's when I began to write songs.) So I did a little digging to see if other types of music might have also been written to fit their acoustic contexts.

WE'RE ALL AFRICANS

Percussive music carries well outdoors, where people might be both dancing and milling about. The extremely intricate and layered rhythms that are typical of this music don't get sonically mashed together as they would in, say, a school gymnasium. Who would invent, play, or persevere with such rhythms if they sounded terrible? No one. Not for a minute. This music doesn't need amplification, either—though that did come along later.

The North American musicologist Alan Lomax argued in his book *Folk Song Style and Culture* that the structure of this music and others of its type—essentially leaderless ensembles—emanates from and mirrors egalitarian societies, but suffice it to say that's a whole other level of context.[1] I love his theory that music and dance styles are metaphors for the social and sexual mores of the societies they emerge from, but that's not the story I aim to focus on in this book.

Some say that the instruments being played in the photo[E] at the top of the next page were all derived from easily available local materials, and therefore it was convenience (with a sly implication of unsophistication) that determined the nature of the music. This assessment implies that these instruments and this music were the best this culture could do given the circumstances. But I would argue that the instruments were carefully fashioned, selected, tailored, and played to best suit the physical, acoustic, and social situation. The music perfectly fits the place where it is heard, sonically and structurally. It is absolutely ideally suited for this situation—the music, a living thing, evolved to fit the available niche.

That same music would turn into sonic mush in a cathedral.[F] Western music in the Middle Ages was performed in these stone-walled gothic cathedrals, and in architecturally similar monasteries and cloisters. The reverberation time in those spaces is very long—more than four seconds in most cases—so a note sung a few seconds ago hangs in the air and becomes part of the present sonic landscape. A composition with shifting musical keys would inevitably invite dissonance as notes overlapped and clashed—a real sonic pileup. So what evolved, what sounds best in this kind of space, is modal in structure—often using very long notes. Slowly evolving melodies that eschew key changes work beautifully and reinforce the otherworldly ambience. Not only does this kind of music work well acoustically, it helps establish what we have come to think of as a spiritual aura. Africans, whose spiritual music is often rhythmically complex, may not associate the music that originates in these spaces with spirituality; they may simply hear it as being blurry and indistinct. Mythologist Joseph Campbell, however, thought that the temple and cathedral are attractive because they spatially and acoustically re-create the cave, where early humans first expressed their spiritual yearnings. Or at least that's where we think they primarily expressed these feelings, as almost all traces of such activities have disappeared.

It's usually assumed that much Western medieval music was harmonically "simple" (having few key changes) because composers hadn't yet evolved the use of complex harmonies. In this context there would be no need or desire to include complex harmonies, as they would have sounded horrible in such spaces. Creatively they did exactly the right thing. Presuming that there is such a thing as "progress" when it comes to music, and that music is "better" now than it used to be, is typical of the high self-regard of those who live in the present. It is a myth. Creativity doesn't "improve."

Bach did a lot of his playing and writing in the early 1700s in a church that was smaller than a gothic cathedral.[G]

E

F

G

As you can imagine, there was already an organ there, and the sound was reverberant, though not as much as in the giant gothic cathedrals.

The music Bach wrote for such spaces sounded good in there; the space made the single instrument, the pipe organ, sound larger, and it also had the nice effect of softening any mistakes as he doodled up and down the scales, as was his wont. Modulating into different keys in the innovative way he did was risky business in these venues. Previously, composers for these rooms stayed in the same key, so they could be all washy and droney, and if the room sounded like an empty swimming pool, then it posed no problem.

I recently went to a Balkan music festival in Brooklyn in a hall that was almost identical to the church pictured on the previous page. The brass bands were playing in the middle of the floor, and folks were dancing in circles around them. The sound was pretty reverberant—not ideal for the complicated rhythms of Balkan music, but then again, that music didn't develop in rooms like the one I was in.

In the late 1700s, Mozart would perform his compositions at events in his patrons' palaces in grand but not gigantic rooms.[H,I] At least initially, he didn't write expecting his music to be heard in symphony halls, which is where they're often performed today, but rather in these smaller, more intimate venues. Rooms like these would be filled with people whose bodies and elaborate dress would deaden the sound, and that, combined with the frilly decor and their modest size (when compared to cathedrals and even ordinary churches) meant that his similarly frilly music could be heard clearly in all its intricate detail.

People could dance to it too. My guess is that in order to be heard above the dancing, clomping feet, and gossiping, one might have had to figure out how to

make the music louder, and the only way to do this was to increase the size of the orchestra, which is what happened.

Meanwhile, some folks around that same time were going to hear operas. La Scala was built in 1776; the original orchestra section comprised a series of booths or stalls, rather than the rows of seats that exist now.[J] People would eat, drink, talk, and socialize during the performances—audience behavior, a big part of music's context, was very different back then. Back in the day, people would socialize and holler out to one another during the performances. They'd holler at the stage, too, for encores of the popular arias. If they liked a tune, they wanted to hear it again—now! The vibe was more like CBGB than your typical contemporary opera house.

La Scala and other opera venues of the time were also fairly compact—more so than the big opera houses that now dominate much of Europe and the United States. The depth of La Scala and many other opera houses of that period is maybe like the Highline Ballroom or Irving Plaza in New York, but La Scala is taller, with a larger stage. The sound in these opera houses is pretty tight, too (unlike today's larger halls). I've performed in some of these old opera venues, and if you don't crank the volume too high, it works surprisingly well for certain kinds of contemporary pop music.

Take a look at Bayreuth, the opera house Wagner had built for his own music in the 1870s.[K] You can see it's not that huge. Not very much bigger than La Scala. Wagner had the gumption to demand that this venue be built to better accommodate the music he imagined—which didn't mean there was much more seating, as a practical-minded entrepeneur might insist on today. It was the orchestral

accommodations themselves that were enlarged. He needed larger orchestras to conjure the requisite bombast. He had new and larger brass instruments created too, and he also called for a larger bass section, to create big orchestral effects.

Wagner in some ways doesn't fit my model—his imagination and ego seemed to be larger than the existing venues, so he was the exception who didn't accommodate. Granted, he was mainly pushing the boundaries of pre-existing opera architecture, not inventing something from scratch. Once he built this place, he more or less wrote for it and its particular acoustic qualities.

As time passed, symphonic music came to be performed in larger and larger halls. That musical format, originally conceived for rooms in palaces and the more modest-sized opera halls, was now somewhat unfairly being asked to accommodate more reverberant spaces. Subsequent classical composers therefore wrote music for those new halls, with their new sound, and it was music that emphasized texture, and sometimes employed audio shock and awe in order to reach the back row that was now farther away. They needed to adapt, and adapt they did.

The music of Mahler and other later symphonic composers works well in spaces like Carnegie Hall.[L] Groove music, percussive music featuring drums—like what I do, for example—has a very hard time here. I've played at Carnegie Hall a couple of times, and it can work, but it is far from ideal. I wouldn't play that music there again. I realized that sometimes the most prestigious place doesn't always work out best for your music. This acoustic barrier could be viewed as a subtle conspiracy, a sonic wall, a way of keeping the riffraff out—but we won't go there, not yet.

At the same time that classical music was tucking itself into new venues, so too was popular music. In the early part of the last century, jazz developed alongside later classical music. This popular music was originally played in bars, at funerals, and in whorehouses and joints where dancing was going on. There was little reverberation in those spaces, and they weren't that big, so, as in CBGB, the groove could be strong and up front.[M]

It's been pointed out by Scott Joplin and others that the origin of jazz solos and improvisations was a pragmatic way of solving a problem that had emerged: the "written" melody would run out while the musicians were playing, and in order to keep a popular section continuing longer for the dancers who wanted to keep moving, the players would jam over those chord changes while maintaining the same groove. The musicians learned to stretch out and extend whatever section of the tune was deemed popular. These improvisations and elongations evolved out of necessity, and a new kind of music came into being.

By the mid-twentieth century, jazz had evolved into a kind of classical music, often presented in concert halls, but if anyone's been to a juke joint or seen the Rebirth or Dirty Dozen brass bands at a place like the Glass House in New Orleans, then you've seen lots of dancing to jazz. Its roots are spiritual dance music. Yes, this is one kind of spiritual music that would sound terrible in most cathedrals.

The instrumentation of jazz was also modified so that the music could be heard over the sound of the dancers and the bar racket. Banjos were louder than acoustic guitars, and trumpets were nice and loud, too. Until amplification and microphones came into common use, the instruments written for and played were adapted to fit the situation. The makeup of the bands, as well as the parts the composers wrote, evolved to be heard.

Likewise, country music, blues, Latin music, and rock and roll were all (originally) music to dance to, and they too had to be loud enough to be heard above the chatter. Recorded music and amplification changed all that, but when these forms jelled, such factors were just beginning to be felt.

QUIET, PLEASE

With classical music, not only did the venues change, but the behavior of the audiences did, too. Around 1900, according to music writer Alex Ross, classical audiences were no longer allowed to shout, eat, and chat during a performance. One was expected to sit immobile and listen with rapt attention. Ross hints that this was a way of keeping the hoi polloi out of the new symphony halls and opera houses.[2] (I guess it was assumed that the lower classes were inherently noisy.) Music that in many instances used to be for all was now exclusively for the elite. Nowadays, if someone's phone rings or a person so much as whispers to their neighbor during a classical concert, it could stop the whole show.

This exclusionary policy affected the music being written, too—since no one was talking, eating, or dancing anymore, the music could have extreme dynamics. Composers knew that every detail would be heard, so very quiet passages could now be written. Harmonically complex passages could be appreciated as well. Much of twentieth-century classical music could only work in (and was written for) these socially and acoustically restrictive spaces. A new kind of music came into existence that didn't exist previously—and the future emergence and refining of recording technology would make this music more available and ubiquitous. I do wonder how much of the audience's fun was sacrificed in the effort to redefine the social parameters of the concert hall—it sounds almost masochistic of the upper crust, curtailing their own liveliness, but I guess they had their priorities.

Although the quietest harmonic and dynamic details and complexities could now be heard, performing in these larger, more reverberant halls meant that rhythmically things got less distinct and much fuzzier—less African, one might say. Even the jazz now played in these rooms became a kind of chamber music. Certainly no one danced, drank, or hollered out "Hell, yeah!" even if it was Goodman, Ellington, or Marsalis playing—bands that certainly swing. The smaller jazz clubs followed suit; no one dances anymore at the Blue Note or Village Vanguard, though liquor is very quietly served.

One might conclude that removing the funky, relaxed vibe from refined American concert music was not accidental. Separating the body from the head seems to have been an intended consequence—for anything to be serious, you couldn't be seen shimmying around to it. (Not that any kind of music is aimed exclusively at either the body or head—that absolute demarcation is somewhat of an intellectual and social construct.) Serious music, in this way of thinking, is only absorbed and consumed above the neck. The regions below the neck are socially and morally suspect. The people who felt this way and enforced this way of encountering music probably didn't take the wildly innovative and sophisticated arrangements of mid-century tango orchestras seriously either. The fact that it was wildly innovative and at the same time very danceable created, for twentieth-century sophisticates, a kind of cognitive dissonance.

RECORDED MUSIC

With the advent of recorded music in 1878, the nature of the places in which music was heard changed. Music now had to serve two very different needs simultaneously. The phonograph box in the parlor became a new venue; for many people, it replaced the concert hall or the club.

By the thirties, most people were listening to music either on radio or on home phonographs.[N] People probably heard a greater quantity of music, and a greater variety, on these devices than they would ever hear in person in their lifetimes. Music could now be completely free from any live context, or, more properly, the context in which it was heard became the living room and the jukebox—parallel alternatives to still-popular ballrooms and concert halls.

The performing musician was now expected to write and create for two very different spaces: the live venue, and the device that could play a recording or receive a transmission. Socially and acoustically, these spaces were worlds apart. But the

compositions were expected to be the same! An audience who heard and loved a song on the radio naturally wanted to hear that same song at the club or the concert hall.

These two demands seem unfair to me. The performing skills, not to mention the writing needs, the instrumentation, and the acoustic properties for each venue are completely different. Just as stage actors often seem too loud and demonstrative for audiences used to movie acting, the requirements of musical mediums are somewhat mutually exclusive. What is best for one might work for the other, but it doesn't always work that way.

Performers adapted to this new technology. The microphones that recorded singers changed the way they sang and the way their instruments were played.[O] Singers no longer had to have great lungs to be successful. Frank Sinatra and Bing Crosby were pioneers when it came to singing "to the microphone." They adjusted their vocal dynamics in ways that would have been unheard of earlier. It might not seem that radical now, but crooning was a new kind of singing back then. It wouldn't have worked without a microphone.

Chet Baker even sang in a whisper, as did João Gilberto, and millions followed. To a listener, these guys are whispering like a lover, right into your ear, getting completely inside your head. Music had never been experienced that way before. Needless to say, without microphones this intimacy wouldn't have been heard at all.

Technology had turned the living room or any small bar with a jukebox into a concert hall[P]—and often there was dancing. Besides changing the acoustic context, recorded music also allowed music venues to come into existence without stages and often without any live musicians at all. DJs could play at high school dances, folks could shove quarters into jukeboxes and dance in the middle of the bar, and in living rooms the music came out of furniture. Eventually venues evolved that were purposefully built to play only this kind of performerless music—discos.[Q]

O

P

Music written for contemporary discos, in my opinion, usually *only* works in those social and physical spaces—it really works best on the incredible sound systems that are often installed in those rooms. It feels stupid to listen to club music at its intended volume at home, though people do it. And, once again, it's for dancing, as was early hip-hop, which emerged out of dance clubs in the same way that jazz did—by extending sections of the music so the dancers could show off and improvise. Once again the dancers were changing the context, urging the music in new directions.[R]

In the sixties the most successful pop music began to be performed in basketball arenas and stadiums, which tend to have terrible acoustics—only a narrow range of music works at all in such environments. Steady-state music (music with a consistent volume, more or less unchanging textures, and fairly simple pulsing rhythms) works best, and even then rarely. The roar of metal works fine. Industrial music for industrial spaces. Stately chord progressions might survive, but funk, for example, bounced off the walls and floors and became chaotic. The groove got killed, though some funky acts persevered because these concerts were social gatherings, bonding opportunities, and rituals as much as music events. Mostly the arenas were filled with white kids—and the music was usually Wagnerian.

The gathered masses in sports arenas and stadiums demanded that the music perform a different function—not only sonically but socially—from what it had been asked to do on a record or in a club. The music those bands ended up writing in response—arena rock—is written with that in mind: rousing, stately

Q R

anthems. To my ears it's a soundtrack for a gathering, and listening to it in other contexts re-creates the memory or anticipation of that gathering—a stadium in your head.

CONTEMPORARY MUSIC VENUES

Where are the new music venues? Are there venues I'm still not acknowledging that might be influencing how and what kind of music gets written? Well, there is the interior of your car.[S] I'd argue that contemporary hip-hop is written (or at least the music is) to be heard in cars with systems like the one below. The massive volume seems to be more about sharing your music with everyone, gratis![T] In a sense, it's a music of generosity. I'd say the audio space in a car with these speakers forces a very different kind of composition. The music is bass heavy, but with a strong and precise high end as well. Sonically, what's in the middle? It's the vocal, allocated a vacant sonic space where not much else lives. In earlier pop music, the keyboards or guitars or even violins often occupied much of this middle territory, and without those things, the vocals rushed to fill the vacuum.

Hip-hop is unlike anything one could produce with acoustic instruments. That umbilical cord has been cut. Liberated. The connection between the recorded music and the live musician and performer is now a thing of the past. Although this music may have emerged from dance-oriented early hip-hop (which, like jazz, evolved by extending the breaks for dancers), it's morphed into something else entirely: music that sounds best in cars. People do dance in their cars, or they try to. As big SUVs become less practical I foresee this music changing as well.

One other new music venue has arrived.^U Presumably the MP3 player shown below plays mainly Christian music. Private listening really took off in 1979, with the popularity of the Walkman portable cassette player. Listening to music on a Walkman is a variation of the "sitting very still in a concert hall" experience (there are no acoustic distractions), combined with the virtual space (achieved by adding reverb and echo to the vocals and instruments) that studio recording allows. With headphones on, you can hear and appreciate extreme detail and subtlety, and the lack of uncontrollable reverb inherent in hearing music in a live room means that rhythmic material survives beautifully and completely intact; it doesn't get blurred or turned into sonic mush as it often does in a concert hall. You, and only you, the audience of one, can hear a million tiny details, even with the compression that MP3 technology adds to recordings. You can hear the singer's breath intake, their fingers on a guitar string. That said, extreme and sudden dynamic changes can be painful on a personal music player. As with dance music one hundred years ago, it's better to write music that maintains a relatively constant volume for this tiny venue. Dynamically static but with lots of details: that's the directive here.

If there has been a compositional response to MP3s and the era of private listening, I have yet to hear it. One would expect music that is essentially a soothing flood of ambient moods as a way to relax and decompress, or maybe dense and complex compositions that reward repeated playing and attentive listening, maybe intimate or rudely erotic vocals that would be inappropriate to blast in public but that you could enjoy privately. If any of this is happening, I am unaware of it.

We've come full circle in many ways. The musical techniques of the African diaspora, the foundation of much of the contemporary world's popular music, with its wealth of interlocking and layered beats, works well acoustically in both the context of the private listening experience and as a framework for much contemporary recorded music. African music sounds the way it does because it was meant to be played out in the open (a form of steady-state music loud enough to

be heard outdoors above dancing and singing), but it turns out to also work well in the most intimate of spaces— our inner ears. Yes, people do listen to Bach and Wagner on iPods, but not too many people are writing new music like that, except for film scores, where Wagnerian bombast works really well. If John Williams wrote contemporary Wagner for *Star Wars,* then Bernard Herrmann wrote contemporary Schoenberg for *Psycho* and other Hitchcock movies. The symphony hall is now a movie theater for the ears.

BIRDS DO IT

The adaptive aspect of creativity isn't limited to musicians and composers (or artists in any other media). It extends into the natural world as well. David Attenborough and others have claimed that birdcalls have evolved to fit the environment.[3] In dense jungle foliage, a constant, repetitive, and brief signal within a narrow frequency works best—the repetition is like an error-correcting device. If the intended recipient didn't get the first transmission, an identical one will follow.

Birds that live on the forest floor evolved lower-pitched calls so they don't bounce or become distorted by the ground as higher-pitched sounds might. Water birds have calls that, unsurprisingly, cut through the ambient sounds of water, and birds that live in the plains and grasslands, like the Savannah Sparrow, have buzzing calls that can traverse long distances.

Eyal Shy of Wayne State University says that birdsongs vary even within the same species.[4] The pitch of the song of the Scarlet Tanager, for example, is different in the East, where the woods are denser, than it is in the West.[V]

And birds of the same species adjust their singing as their habitat changes, too. Birds in San Francisco were found to have raised the pitch of their songs over forty years in order to be better heard above the noises of the increased traffic.[5]

It's not just birds, either. In the waters around New Zealand, whale calls have adapted to the increase in shipping noise over the last few decades—the hum of engines and thrash of propellers. Whales need to signal over huge distances to survive, and one hopes that they continue to adapt to this audio pollution.

So musical evolution and adaptation is an interspecies phenomenon. And presumably, as some claim, birds enjoy singing, even though they, like us, change their tunes over time. The joy of making music will find a way, regardless of the context and the form that emerges to best fit it. The musician David Rothenberg claims that "life is far more interesting than it needs to be, because the forces that guide it are not merely practical."[6]

Finding examples to prove that music composition depends on its context comes naturally to me. But I have a feeling that this somewhat reversed view of creation—that it is more pragmatic and adaptive than some might think—happens a lot, and in very different areas. It's "reversed" because the venues—or the fields and woodlands, in the case of the birds—were not built to accommodate whatever egotistical or artistic urge the composers have. We and the birds adapt, and it's fine.

What's interesting to me is not that these practical adaptations happen (in retrospect that seems predictable and obvious), but what it means for our perception of creativity.

It seems that creativity, whether birdsong, painting, or songwriting, is as adaptive as anything else. Genius—the emergence of a truly remarkable and memorable work—seems to appear when a thing is perfectly suited to its context. When something works, it strikes us as not just being a clever adaptation,

but as emotionally resonant as well. When the right thing is in the right place, we are moved.

In my experience, the emotionally charged content always lies there, hidden, waiting to be tapped, and although musicians tailor and mold their work to how and where it will be best heard or seen, the agony and the ecstasy can be relied on to fill whatever shape is available.

We do express our emotions, our reactions to events, breakups, and infatuations, but the way we do that—the art of it—is in putting them into prescribed forms or squeezing them into new forms that perfectly fit some emerging context. That's part of the creative process, and we do it instinctively; we internalize it, like birds do. And it's a joy to sing, like the birds do.

THE BIGGEST ROOM OF ALL

Bernie Krause, a pioneering electronic musician who now focuses mostly on bio-acoustics, has revealed how the calls of insects, birds, and mammals evolved to fit unique spots in the audio spectrum. He has made recordings all over the world, in many different natural environments, and in each case an acoustic analysis of the recordings reveals species keeping to their own part of the audio spectrum; insects take the highest pitches, birds a little lower, and mammals below that, for example.[W]

BORNEO, CAMP LEAKY

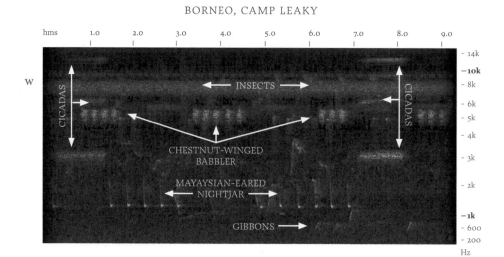

So not only have the calls of songbirds evolved to work best in the acoustic environment where those birds live, they also have evolved to stay out of the way of the other critters that live there. Krause rightly refers to this spectrum of calls as an orchestra—where each animal/instrument plays a part in its own range, and together they make one giant composition. These symphonies change depending on the time of day and season, but everyone always stays in their place.

Sadly, Krause's recordings revealed another truth: even if a landscape looks identical to the way it did a decade ago, acoustic analysis often reveals that a critter that once filled a specific part of the audio spectrum might now be missing. It's as if a color in the visible spectrum has been erased from the landscape. Most of the time, no surprise, this is due to the intrusion or intervention of humans—traffic, farms, houses, global warming. What's interesting is that it's the missing sound—not some visual evidence—that makes this tragic change clear. Acoustic analysis is the canary in the coal mine.

ARCHITECTURE AS INSTRUMENTS

I've staged, several times, an interactive installation called *Playing the Building*, in which mechanical devices cause the infrastructure of empty buildings to emit sounds—all triggered by playing a keyboard, which visitors are invited to do. But I was far from the first to imagine that buildings and natural enclosures could be viewed as instruments.

Acoustician Steven Waller suggests that rock paintings in the southwestern US are often found in places where unusual echoes and reverberations occur. And, Waller suggests, the prevalence of echoes in these sites isn't a coincidence; sound was the driver for nominating a sacred space. He goes further and proposes that the images depicted often seem to correlate with the kinds of echoes that occur. So in places where percussive echoes can sound like hoof beats, we find petroglyphs of horses, while at other sites that favor longer echoes (as if the rocks are "speaking") we tend to find images of spirits and mythological beings.

The sites Waller refers to are all naturally occurring, but archeologists are also finding that these and similar effects were intentionally created by many people.

A series of articles published in *National Geographic* proposes that there are some interesting connections between pre-Columbian architecture, music, and sound.

One notable site is the Mayan Temple of Kukulcan, which is part of the Chichen Itza complex.[X]

Guides are fond of demonstrating for tourists how a handclap at the base of that temple produces an echo that sounds like the "chir-roop" call of the sacred Quetzal bird, whose feathers were more valuable to the Mayans than gold. The bird was considered a messenger of the gods.[Y]

Two sets of echoes come into play to produce that "chir-roop" sound. The "chir" comes from the nearest set of steps, and the lower-pitched "roop" sound is produced by a more distant and higher set of steps.

David Lubman, an acoustic engineer, made recordings of the echoes and compared them to recordings of the bird found in Cornell's ornithology lab. "They matched perfectly," he said. He then worked with the head of the Mexican Institute of Acoustics, Sergio Beristain, who checked out another pyramid near Mexico City. Sure enough, it produced similar chirping effects—sometimes with pitch changes that span as much as half an octave. This really is a building singing.[7]

Scientists have proposed that other pre-Columbian sites have acoustic properties as well. Archeologist Francisca Zalaquett believes that Mayan public squares in the ancient city of Palenque were designed so that someone speaking or singing from a particular spot could be heard way across the square. The stucco coatings of the temples surrounding the square combine with their arrangement and architecture to help "broadcast" the sound of a voice (or of instruments typical at the time) for a length equal to that of a football field.

In Peru, at a sacred site named Chavín de Huántar that was established as early

as 1200 BCE, there is an underground maze,[Z] the acoustics of which were designed to disorient the visitor as much as the winding passages do.[AA]

Archeologist John Rick of Stanford University thinks the various kinds of rock used in these tunnels, along with the multiple acoustic reflections from the bending passageways, can make one's voice sound as if it's coming from "every direction at once." He believes that this labyrinth was used for special rituals, and, like a stage in a contemporary theater, the otherworldly acoustics would have helped set the scene.[8] (That plus a dose of the local psychedelic, San Pedro cactus, which priests and initiates are thought to have indulged in.)

It seems the effect of architecture on music and sound can be reciprocal. Just as acoustics in a space determine the evolution of music, acoustic properties—particularly those that affect the human voice—can guide the structure and form of buildings. We've all heard of concert halls that were designed so that a person singing or speaking from center stage could be heard, unamplified, all the way in the back. Carnegie Hall, for example, is so focused on that goal that it isn't particularly accommodating to other kinds of sounds—percussive sounds especially. But for the voice, and for instruments that imitate the human voice, such an environment offers the kind of sacred space that humans have found attractive for thousands of years.

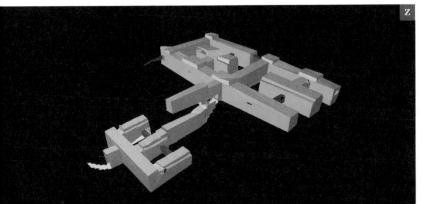

CHAPTER TWO

My Life in Performance

The process of writing music doesn't follow a strict path. For some composers, music is created via notation, the written system of markings that some percentage of musicians share as a common language. Even if an instrument (traditionally a piano) is used as an aid in composition, this kind of music emerges as a written entity. Changes in the score might be made at a later date by performing musicians or by the composer, but the writing is largely done without input from actual players. More recently, music began to be created mechanically or digitally, by an accretion and layering of sounds, samples, notes, and bits dragged and thrown together either physically or in the virtual world of a computer.

Though much of my own music may initially have been composed in isolation, it only approached its final shape as a result of being performed live. As with jazz and folk musicians, everything was expected to be thrown into the crucible of a gig to see if it sank, floated, or maybe even flew. In junior high school I played in bands with friends, covering popular songs, but at some point, maybe after a rival's friend pulled the plug on us at a battle of the bands, I contemplated playing solo.

After some time rethinking things and learning more songs written by others in my bedroom, I began to frequent the coffeehouse at the local university and realized that the folk scene represented there was insular and needed refreshing.

Well, at least that's how it looked to me. This was the late sixties, and I was still in high school, but anyone could see and hear that the purism of folk was being blown away by the need of rock, soul, and pop to absorb everything in their path. The folk scene was low energy too, as if the confessional mode and folk's inherent sincerity was somehow enervating in and of itself. That couldn't be good!

I decided to perform rock songs by my favorites at the time—the Who, Crosby, Stills & Nash, and the Kinks—on acoustic guitar, believing that some of those songs were written with as much integrity as the folkier stuff people in the café more often heard, and that they might therefore find a receptive audience. I seem to recall that it worked; they had somehow never heard these songs! All I'd done was move the songs to a new context. Because I performed them more energetically than the standard folk artist might present his own material, people listened, or maybe they were just stunned at the audacity of a precocious teenager. I played Chuck Berry and Eddie Cochran on ukulele, shifting the context of those songs even further afield. I might have even risked scratching some dirges on a violin I'd inherited. It was an oddball mishmash, but it wasn't boring.

I was incredibly shy at the time and remained so for many years, so one might ask (and people did) what in the world a withdrawn introvert was doing making a spectacle of himself onstage. (I didn't ask myself such questions at the time.) In retrospect, I guess that like many others, I decided that making my art in public (even if that meant playing people's songs at that point) was a way of reaching out and communicating when ordinary chitchat was not comfortable for me. It seemed not only a way to "speak" in another language, but also a means of entry into conversation— other musicians and even girls (!) would talk to someone who had just been onstage.

Performing must have seemed like my only option. There was also the remote possibility that I would briefly be the hero and reap some social and personal rewards in other areas beyond mere communication, though I doubt I would have admitted that to myself. Poor Susan Boyle; I can identify. Despite all this, Desperate Dave did not have ambitions to be a professional musician—that seemed wholly unrealistic.

Years later I diagnosed myself as having a very mild (I think) form of Asperger's syndrome. Leaping up in public to do something wildly expressive and then quickly retreating back into my shell seemed, well, sort of normal to me. Maybe *normal* is the wrong word, but it worked. A study in the *British Journal of Psychiatry* in 1994 by Felix Post claimed that 69 percent of the creative individuals he'd studied had mental disorders.[1] That's a lot of nutters! This, of course, plays right into the myth of the fucked-up artist driven by demons, and I would hope very much that the converse of that myth isn't true—that one does not *have* to be nuts to be creative. Maybe some problem of some sort can at least get the ball in play. But I have come to believe that you can escape your demons and still tap the well.

When I was at art school in the early seventies, I began to perform with a classmate, Mark Kehoe, who played accordion. I dropped the acoustic guitar and focused on the ukulele and my hand-me-down violin, which now had decals of bathing beauties stuck on it. We played at bars and art openings, and together we traveled cross-country and ended up playing on Telegraph Avenue in Berkeley. Busking, as it's called in Britain. By this point we had a look, too—a variation on Old World immigrant, I guess is how you would describe it. Mark adopted a more Eastern European look, and I gravitated to old suits and fedoras. I had an unkempt beard at the time, and once a young black kid asked me if I was one of those people who didn't ride in cars.

We played mainly standards. I would sing "Pennies from Heaven" or "The Glory of Love" as well as our own arrangements of more contemporary fare, like "96 Tears." Sometimes Mark would play an instrumental and I'd strike ridiculous poses—bent over standing on one leg and not moving, for example. Something that absolutely anyone would be able to do, but that I—or my "stage" persona— seemed to think was show-worthy. We realized that in a short amount of time we could amass enough cash to cover a meal and gas for an old car I'd picked up in Albuquerque. One might say that the reviews of a street performance were instant—people either stopped, watched, and maybe gave money, or they moved on. I think I also realized then that it was possible to mix ironic humor with sincerity in performance. Seeming opposites could coexist. Keeping these two in balance was a bit of a tightrope act, but it could be done.

I'd seen only a few live pop-music shows by this point. At the time I still didn't see myself making a career in music, but even so, the varied performing styles in the shows I had seen must have made a strong impression. In high school around

Baltimore, one could attend what were called Teen Centers, which were school gymnasiums where local bands would be brought in to play on weekends. One act was a choreographed Motown-style revue, and at one point they donned gloves that glowed in the dark when they switched to UV lights. It was a spectacular effect, though a little corny. Another act did a Sgt. Pepper—type revue, and to my young ears they sounded just like the records. Their technical expertise was amazing, but it wasn't original, and so it wasn't all that inspiring. Being a cover band, even a really good one, was limiting.

It wasn't only purist folk acts at the university coffeehouse. There were also rock bands, some of which had virtuosic musicians. Most would jam endlessly and aimlessly on a blues song, but one DC-based band, Grin, featured a guitarist named Nils Lofgren whose solos blew the others away. These displays of technique and imagination were humbling. My own guitar playing was so rudimentary that it was hard to imagine we were playing the same instrument. I figured these "real" bands were so far beyond my own abilities that any aspirations I had in that regard were hopeless.

I caught one big outdoor rock festival back then—in Bath, a town a few hours east of London. Exhausted after hours of listening to music, I fell asleep on the damp ground. In the middle of the night I woke up and realized that Led Zeppelin was playing. I think they were the biggest act on the bill, but I went back to sleep. In the early morning I was awake again and caught Dr. John, who closed the festival. He was in full *Night Tripper* mode, and I loved that record, so I was excited to see him. He came out in carnival drag, playing his funky voodoo jive, and the UK audience pelted him with beer cans. I was confused. Here was the most original act of the whole festival, dumped into the worst slot, and he was completely unappreciated by this crowd. It was depressing. Maybe the costumes and headdresses made it seem like too much of a "show" for this bunch, who valued what they imagined as blues-guitar authenticity? But authentic blues played by white English guys? It made no sense. I couldn't figure it out, but I could see that innovation wasn't always appreciated and that audiences could be nasty.

Later, when I was in art school, I caught James Brown at the Providence Civic Center. It was the best show I'd ever seen; it was so tight and choreographed that it seemed to be from another planet, a planet where everyone was incredible. He had sexy go-go dancers who just danced the whole show, and though it was exciting as hell, this too put any thoughts of being a professional musician out of my head—these folks were in the stratosphere, and we were just amateurs. That didn't take any of the enjoyment out of the amateur experience; I'm just saying I didn't have some transformative moment after seeing these acts when I immediately knew that was what I wanted to do. No way.

I was musically curious, and sometimes I would check out performers whose music I was only slightly aware of. I saw Rahsaan Roland Kirk, the jazz saxophonist, at the Famous Ballroom in Baltimore, a downtown venue with glitter cutouts of rocket ships on the walls. I realized there that jazz wasn't always the staid, almost classical and reserved style I'd presumed—it was a show too. It was about musicianship, sure, but it was also about entertainment. Kirk sometimes played two or three horns at once, which seemed like the musical equivalent of playing the guitar with your teeth or behind your back or even smashing it—a stage gimmick. But it got everyone's attention. At one point he took audience interaction to new "heights": he gave out bumps of cocaine on a little spoon to folks up front!

After having played on the streets of Berkeley, back on the East Coast Mark and I opened for a wonderful local band called the Fabulous Motels at the art-school auditorium. I shaved off my scraggly beard onstage while Mark played accordion and his girlfriend held up cue cards written in Russian. I didn't have a mirror and couldn't manage the razor very well, so there was a fair amount of blood. Needless to say, that kept the audience's attention, though the bloodletting drove some of them away. In retrospect, it seems I was saying goodbye to the old immigrant guy in the dark suit. I was ready to embrace rock and roll again.

A brief flash forward—when I first moved to New York, I caught Sun Ra and his Arkestra at the 5 Spot, a jazz venue that used to be at St. Mark's Place and Third Avenue. He moved from instrument to instrument. At one point there was a bizarre solo on a Moog synthesizer, an instrument not often associated with jazz. Here was electronic noise suddenly reimagined as entertainment! As if to prove to skeptics that he and the band really could play, that they really had chops no matter how far out they sometimes got, they would occasionally do a traditional big-band tune. Then it would be back to outer space. There was a slide show projected on the wall behind the band, commemorating their visit to the pyramids in Egypt, and much of the time Sun Ra was wearing spectacles that had no glass in them. They were "glasses" made of bent wire that looped into crazy squiggles in front of his eyes. In its own cosmic way, this was all show business too.

In 1973 my friend Chris Frantz, who was about to graduate from the painting department of the Rhode Island School of Design, suggested that we put together a band. We did, and he proposed we call ourselves the Artistics. Being more social and gregarious than I was, Chris pulled in some other musicians. We began by doing cover songs at loft parties in Providence. We must have done a Velvets or Lou Reed song or two, and some garage-rock songs as well—"96 Tears," no doubt—but interestingly, at Chris's suggestion, we also did an Al Green cover, "Love and Happiness."

I began to write original material around this time, now that I had a band that I hoped would be willing to perform my compositions. I still had no ambitions to become a pop star; writing was purely and simply a creative outlet for me. (My other artistic medium at the time was questionnaires that I'd mail or pass out. Not many came back completed.) The song "Psycho Killer" began in my room as an acoustic ballad, and I asked Chris and his girlfriend Tina for help on it. For some reason I wanted the middle eight section to be in French, and Tina's mom was French, so she had some skills there. I imagined that this serial killer fancied himself as a grand and visionary sophisticate in the model of either Napoleon or some Romantic lunatic. "Warning Sign" was another song written then; I remember the live version being painfully loud. Another guitar player in that band, David Anderson, was probably even less socially adept than I was, and he was a great and somewhat unconventional performer. Chris joked that we should have called the band the Autistics.

Glam rock was the new thing. Bowie made a big impression on me, and at one point I dyed my hair blonde and sewed myself some leather trousers. No doubt this made for a striking image at the time in little Providence, Rhode Island. What might be okay as a stage getup was maybe stretching things as street wear. I was flailing about to see who I was, switching from an Amish look to a crazy androgynous rock and roller—and I wasn't afraid in the least to do so in public.[A]

There were also some discos in Providence, and I remember hearing the O'Jays and the Three Degrees and other Philadelphia acts that were staples on the dance floor. I became aware that the DJs were finding ways to extend the songs longer than what appeared on the records. Somehow, to us, this club music didn't seem antithetical to the rock we were playing and listening to. Dancing was fun, too.

In the mid-seventies I was offered room and board in New York by a painter, Jamie Dalglish, who let me sleep on his loft floor in return for help renovating the place. This was on Bond Street, almost right across from CBGB, where Patti Smith would read occasionally while Lenny Kaye accompanied her on guitar. Television and the Ramones had started playing there as well, and we took advantage of our perfect location to go see these bands as often as we could afford. When Chris and Tina moved to New York, staying at her brother's place in Long Island City, we'd all go there regularly. Soon Chris again took the initiative and suggested we form another band. This time, perhaps inspired by the acts playing at CB's or perhaps by the fact that we already had some original material (that handful of songs I'd written for the Artistics), he suggested we try something with a little more integrity and seriousness. I agreed to give it a try, and if it wasn't well received, well, we all still had ambitions to be fine artists, or at least I did. I began to write songs based on riffs and fragments, which I would cobble together, my guitar plugged into an old Webcor reel-to-reel tape recorder that had a mic input. I filled notebooks with lyrics.

Talking Heads, the name we settled on, started off as a live band. This might sound obvious, but when you think of all the records and musicians that were out there then (and there are more now) who made their records before figuring out how to play their songs live, or how to hold an audience's attention, it's significant.

We all remembered stories of naïve and ambitious acts, singers mostly, plucked out of obscurity and handed material—and then, if the song became a hit, they'd be assigned a band to do the inevitable promotional tour. They'd be styled and choreographed and, in most cases, they'd crash and burn before long. Some great stuff was created this way, and there were lots of pretty phony manufactured stars as well, but it seemed to be a bit of a crapshoot whether any of these acts could actually get an audience to listen. They hadn't learned the ropes of live performance.

These poor souls thrust into the limelight had to compete with the Beatles, Dylan, Marvin Gaye, and Stevie Wonder, who all seemed completely comfortable performing and had taken charge of their own creative destinies (or at least it seemed that way at the time). In a sense, these extremely talented artists made it harder on those whose middling talents needed a little help—whether that meant some coaching on how to sing as if you mean it, how to engage an audience in your performance, or on how to dress and move. Suddenly there was a prejudice against acts that weren't able to hold all the creative reins and do everything by themselves. This prejudice now seems unfair. The highly coached acts—or, to be kind, the more collaboratively put-together acts—were not all bad. Some were the result of teamwork that produced things that were beyond any one artist's or band's vision or abilities, but many of them were underappreciated at the time, and only later were they seen as hip innovators: Nancy Sinatra, the Shangri-Las, the Jackson 5, KC and the Sunshine Band. The fact that some of them weren't great live performers made it doubly hard for them. At that time we couldn't accept that making a great record was maybe all we should expect. As Lou Reed once said, people want to "view the body."

More recently, composers, DJs, and pop, rock, and hip-hop artists have created their music on computers and not, as was often the case in the past, by playing with other musicians. Though this allows them to be more self-empowered—they don't need a band, record-company funding, or even a recording studio—these artists are often (though not always) similarly lost when it comes to, well, showmanship. Some should never get near a stage, as their talents end with the laptop or with rhymes, but others eventually find their way. Expecting them to be good at both things sometimes seems unfair. I've seen too many creative souls who were suddenly expected to go onstage desperately imitating moves, clothing styles, and bits of stage business that they'd obviously seen elsewhere. We've all spent time imagining ourselves inhabiting the bodies of our childhood heroes, like avatars in a way, and it's thrilling, but at some point it's time to put those urges to rest. After all, those bodies are already being used by their original owners.

After auditioning at CBGB one afternoon for Hilly Kristal, the club's owner, and a few others, Talking Heads got offered a slot opening for the Ramones. As twitchy and Aspergery a stage presence as I was in those days, I had a sense from my time busking in Berkeley and elsewhere that I could hold an audience's attention. I wouldn't call what we did then entertainment, exactly, but it was riveting in its own disturbing way. Not quite like looking at an accident, as one writer said, but not that far off either. My stage presence wasn't fake, as weird as it looks to me in retrospect, but it wasn't altogether unconsciously oddball either. Occasionally I'd cross over into something affected, but most of the time the poor soul up there was just doing what he thought was right, given the skills and techniques available to him.

Once we began playing at CBGB, we also got gigs at other venues in Lower Manhattan—Mothers, Max's Kansas City, and eventually the Mudd Club. We played somewhere almost every week but held on to our day jobs. Mine was being a movie theater usher on 34th Street, which was perfect, as the first show wasn't until 11 or 12. We didn't always get much sleep, but the band got pretty tight.

Looking at early video footage of our three-piece combo at CBGB, I now sense that it was less a band than an outline for a band. It was a sketch, just the bare-bones musical elements needed to lay out a song. Nothing more. There was no real pleasure or pleasantness to these arrangements. This wasn't music to seduce the ear, but it wasn't intentionally aggressive or abrasive like punk rock, either. It was like looking at a framework, an architectural drawing, and being asked to imagine where the walls and sink might go.

This was all intentional. The range of preexisting performative models from which to draw on was overwhelming—and artistically invalid, as I've argued, because those tropes were already taken. So the only sensible course was to avoid all of it, to strip everything back and see what was left. Some others in that scene had similar ideas. The Ramones didn't allow guitar solos, for example, but we took reductionism pretty damn far. It was a performance style defined by negatives—no show-offy solos (I remembered Nils Lofgren, and knew it was hopeless for me to go there, though I did love Tom Verlaine's solos with Television), no rock moves or poses, no pomp or drama, no rock hair, no rock lights (our instructions to club lighting people were "Turn them all on at the beginning and turn them off at the end"), no rehearsed stage patter (I announced the song titles and said "Thank you" and nothing more), and no singing like a black man. The lyrics too were stripped bare. I told myself I would use no clichéd rock phrases, no "Ohh, baby"s or words that I wouldn't use in daily speech, except ironically, or as a reference to another song.

It was mathematics; when you subtract all that unwanted stuff from something, art or music, what do you have left? Who knows? With the objectionable bits removed, does it then become more "real"? More honest? I don't think so anymore. I eventually realized that the simple act of getting on stage is in itself artificial, but the dogma provided a place to start. We could at least pretend we had jettisoned our baggage (or other people's baggage, as we imagined it) and would therefore be forced to come up with something new. It wasn't entirely crazy.

Clothing is part of performance too, but how were we supposed to start from scratch sartorially? Of course, back then the fact that we were (sometimes) wearing polo shirts both set us apart and branded us as preppies.[B]

In the nineties, preppy was adopted as a hip-hop look, but back then it smacked of WASP elitism and privilege, which wasn't very rock and roll. That wasn't my background, but I was fascinated by the fact that the old-guard movers and shakers of the United States had an actual look (with approved brands!). And despite their wealth, the clothing choices made by ye olde masters of the universe weren't super flattering! They could afford to pay for flattering clothes, but they opted for house dresses and schlubby suits. What's the story here?!

After leaving funky Baltimore (a city with an eccentric character that had also come to be defined by race riots and white flight) for art school in little Providence, Rhode Island, I met folks with histories way different from mine, and I found it strange and wonderful. Trying to figure all that out was at least as informative as what I was learning in my classes. Some of these folks had uniforms of a sort: not military- or UPS-style uniforms, but they adhered fairly rigorously to clothing regimens that were way different from anything I was familiar with. I realized that there were "shows" going on all the time.

The WASP style was often portrayed on TV and in movies as a sort of

archetypical American look, and some of my new friends seemed to subscribe to it. I decided I'd try it too. I'd tried other looks previously, like Glam Dude and Amish Geezer, so why not this one?

I didn't stay with it consistently. At one point I decided my look would be, like our musical dogma, stripped down, in the sense that I would attempt to have no look at all. In my forays outside of bohemia and away from the winos and addicts that littered the Bowery at that time, I realized that most New York men wore suits, and that this was a kind of uniform that intentionally eliminated (or was at least intended to eliminate) the possibility of clothing as a statement. As with a school uniform, it was assumed that if everyone looked more or less the same, the focus would be on one's actions and person and not on the outward trappings. The intention, I guess, was democratic and meritorious, though subtle class signals were there.

So in an attempt to look like Mr. Man on the Street, I got a cheap polyester suit^C—gray with subtle checks, from one of those downtown discount outlets— and I wore that onstage a few times. But it got sweaty under the stage lights, and when I threw it in the washer and dryer at Tina's brother's place it shrank down and became unwearable. Before that I used to hang out at CBGB in a white plastic raincoat and sunglasses. I looked like a flasher!

The preppy look was at least more practical in a packed sweaty club than plastic or polyester, so I stuck with it for a while. I was aware that our sartorial choice was not without liabilities. We were accused of being dilettantes, and of not being "serious" (read: authentic or pure). My background wasn't upper-class, so this caught me a bit by surprise, and I felt such accusations were a distraction from the music we were making—which was indeed serious, at least in its attempt to rethink what pop music could be. I soon realized that when it comes to clothing it is next to impossible

c

to find something completely neutral. Every outfit carries cultural baggage of some kind. It took me a while to get a handle on this aspect of performance.

After a couple of years we felt ready to flesh out our sound, to add a little color to our black-and-white drawing. A mutual friend tipped us that a musician named Jerry Harrison was available. We loved the Modern Lovers demo record that had recently come out and that he'd played on, so we invited Jerry to sit in. He had some trepidation, having been burned by his experience with that band (their lead singer, Jonathan Richman, dumped the band and went acoustic folkie just as they were closing in on the brass ring), so at first Jerry played with us on just a few songs during some out-of-town shows. Eventually he took the plunge. As a four-piece, we suddenly sounded like a real band. The music was still spartan, sparse, and squeaky-clean, but now there was a roundness to the sound that was more physically and sonically moving—even slightly sensuous at times, God forbid.

There were other changes. T-shirts and skinny black jeans soon became the uniform of choice, at least for Jerry and me.[D]

At that time one couldn't buy skinny black jeans in the United States—imagine! But when we played in Paris after our first record came out we went shopping for le jeans, and, finding them easily, we stocked up. The French obviously appreciated what they viewed as the proto–American Rebel look more than Americans did. But what's more American Everyman than jeans and T-shirts? It was a sexier Everyman than the polyester-suit guy, and jeans and T-shirts are easy to wash and care for on the road.

But make no mistake—these weren't ordinary blue jeans. These were skinny straight-leg black jeans, referencing an earlier generation (much, much earlier) of rebels and festering youth. These outfits and their silhouettes evoked greasers and rockabilly performers like Eddie Cochran, but also the Beatles and the Stones—before they had a wardrobe budget. Symbolically, we were getting back to basics.[E]

Maybe the skinny, dark, stick-figure look alluded to other eras as well, like the tortured emaciated self-portraits of Egon Schiele and stylized bohemian extremists such as Antonin Artaud. The conceptual artist Joseph Kosuth wore only black in those days, as did a girlfriend I briefly dated. It was a uniform that signified that

one was a kind of downtown aesthete; not necessarily nihilistic, but a monk in the bohemian order.

The retro suits and skinny black ties that became associated with the downtown music scene—those I just couldn't figure out. What was that supposed to reference? Was there a noir movie I missed where the guys dressed like this? I'd tried suits, and I wasn't going back there.

Jerry played keyboards and guitar, and he sang too, so we learned that with this arsenal we could vary the textures on each song more than we had before. Texture would became part of the musical content—something that wasn't possible with the stripped-down three-piece band. Sometimes Jerry would play electric piano and sometimes a guitar part, often something contrapuntal to mine. Sometimes one of us would play slide guitar while the other played chords. Previously we'd desperately attempted to vary the texture from song to song by having Chris leave his drums and play vibes or having me switch to acoustic guitar, but before Jerry, our choices were limited. By the time we recorded our first record, in 1976, he had just barely learned our repertoire, but already some flesh was appearing on our bones.

We finally sounded like a band more than like a sketch of a band, and we were amazingly tight. When we toured Europe and the UK, the press commented on our Stax-Volt influences—and they were right. We were half art band and half funky groove band, something that the US press didn't really pick up on until we mutated into a full-on art-funk revue a few years later. But it was all there, right from the beginning, though the proportions were completely different. Chris and Tina were a great rhythm section, and though Chris didn't play fancy, he played solid. That gave us a firm foundation for all the angular shit that I was throwing around.

What does *being tight* mean? It's hard to define now, in an age where instrumental performances and even vocals can be digitally quantified and made to perfectly fit the beat. I realize now that it doesn't actually mean that everyone plays exactly to the beat; it means that everyone plays together. Sometimes a band that has played together a lot will evolve to where they play some parts ahead of the beat and some slightly behind, and singers do the same thing. A good singer will often use the "grid" of the rhythm as something to play with—never landing exactly on a beat, but pushing and pulling around and against it in ways that we read, when it's well done, as being emotional. It turns out that not being perfectly aligned with a grid is okay;

in fact, sometimes it feels better than a perfectly metric fixed-up version. When Willie Nelson or George Jones sings way off the beat, it somehow increases the sense that they're telling you the story, conveying it to you, one person to another. The lurches and hesitations are internalized through performance, and after a while everyone knows when they'll happen. The performers don't have to think about them, and at some point that becomes part of the band's sound. Those agreed-upon imperfections are what give a performance character, and eventually the listener recognizes that it's the very thing that makes a band or singer distinctive.

The musician and neuroscientist Daniel Levitin once demonstrated an experiment he had devised at his research lab in Montreal. He had a classical pianist play a Chopin piece on a Diskclavier, a sort of electronic player piano. The piano memorized the pianist's keystrokes and could play them back. Levitin then dialed back the expressiveness incrementally until every note hit exactly on a beat. No surprise, this came across as drained of emotion, though it was technically more accurate. Alternatively, the expressiveness could be ramped up, and playing became more florid and even less on the grid. This too was unemotional; it veered toward chaos.

Musicians sort of knew this already—that the emotional center is not the technical center, that funky grooves are not square, and what sounds like a simple beat can either be sensuous or simply a metronomic timekeeper, depending on the player.

Throughout the three-piece and four-piece periods, Talking Heads songs, and even the shows, were still mostly about self-examination, angst, and bafflement at the world we found ourselves in. Psychological stuff. Inward-looking clumps of words combined with my slightly removed "anthropologist from Mars" view of human relationships. The groove was always there, as a kind of physical body-oriented antidote to this nervous angsty flailing, but the groove never took over. It served as a sonic and psychological safety net, a link to the body. It said that no matter how alienated the subject or the singer might appear, the groove and its connection to the body would provide solace and grounding. But the edgy, uncomfortable stuff was still the foreground.

While we were on tour, we saw our contemporaries performing. We saw the Clash in a school auditorium in England. It was hard to make out what was going on musically, but it was obvious that the music that was emerging then was viewed as more of a coherent movement there, with the anthemic rabble-rousing aspect bringing that point home. Any rabble-rousing in our own music was buried pretty deep. I still thought the most subversive thing was to look totally normal. To look like a rebel was to pigeonhole yourself in advance as someone who spoke only to other rebels. I never completely achieved that normal look, but it was a guiding principle. So, although some of us might have alluded to the James Deans of the world with our attire, we drew the line at leather jackets and safety pins. Within a couple of years, I'd be wearing oxfords and regular suit jackets in another weird attempt to fit in.

While in London I visited the Virgin Records office, which was then just off Portobello Road, and they let me watch a bunch of Sex Pistols appearances on video. I thought the band was hilarious—not a joke, but definitely a species of comedy. It was almost a parody of a rock and roll band. They couldn't play; they could barely even stand up. Not everyone understood how I could like something and laugh at it at the same time, but don't we love our great comedians?

By the time our second record came out in 1978, we were playing larger venues: small theaters rather than the familiar grotty clubs. We usually headlined, with one act playing before us. We traveled by van. Some other bands took the traditional career path of opening for more established acts, which allowed the emerging bands to play at bigger venues, but that sounded depressing and debilitating to me. The audiences weren't there to see you, and they'd ignore you no matter how good or innovative you were. Remember Dr. John!

Hilly from CBGB bought an abandoned theater on Second Avenue, and we were the first pop act to play there—on New Year's Eve, I think it was. For the occasion I decided to be festive, so I dressed up in primary colors: jeans and T-shirt, naturally, bright red and yellow. There was so much dust in the theater (they hadn't cleaned it properly) that we saw it rise like a cloud as the audience got excited, and after a while we could barely sing. We were coughing for days afterward. The fashion gambit didn't get much response, either.

When our third album came out the next year, we were still a four-piece band, but now there were more overdubs and wiggly treatments from our new friend Brian Eno, who had produced our previous record. We were still touring constantly, and we bought some of the latest gear for our live performances. There were guitar-effect pedals and echo units, and Jerry got a Yamaha portable mini-grand piano, an organ, and a Prophet-5 synthesizer. We could reproduce some of the more far-out studio sounds and arrangements we'd worked on, if only just, but we knew it was equally important to maintain our tight rhythmic core. We were still a live performing band and not simply a group that faithfully reproduced recordings. We knew that the groove was fun and essential for us, and it visibly moved our audiences. With the added instruments and effects, we could really begin to vary the textures from one song to the next. We made sure no song sounded exactly like another one, at least not to us. I didn't dance onstage. I twitched a bit, mainly from the waist down. It wasn't possible to really dance too wildly, even if I wanted to, as I had to stay close to the vocal mic and stomp on my guitar pedals every so often. I also sensed that we were pushing up against the edge as far as representing what we were doing in the studio; the textures, layers, effects, and palimpsest of sounds and rhythms—all of that we were just barely able to reproduce live with four people. It sounded great, and some of my more off-putting (to some) vocal mannerisms were even softening, or so it seemed to me. As the tour went on, night after night of performing, I was on the verge of actually singing.

After the band recorded our next record, *Remain in Light,* we were faced with a dilemma: this was not a record that a four-piece band would remotely be able to reproduce live. Even if one were to decide that a faithful reproduction wasn't a priority, the feeling of that record, and of some that were to follow, was about the meshing of a multitude of parts—a more African approach to music making than we'd taken previously. Even though the music didn't always sound particularly African, it shared that ecstatic communal feeling. The combination of groove and a structure in which no one part dominated or carried the melody by itself generated a very different sensation, and that also needed to be reproduced and evoked onstage. Getting that rhythmic texture right was as important to this material as any other element in the songs—possibly more so.

Although the public consistently thought we'd recorded that album with what soon emerged as our expanded live-band lineup, we didn't. During the recording sessions, only Adrian Belew and a couple of percussionists were added to the core band. The magic of multitracking meant we could add parts ourselves; Jerry could play a guitar part and then add a keyboard track later. We built up twenty-four tracks of knotty interwoven parts, and by switching groups of them on and off, we could create sections that might work in place of conventional verses and choruses.

Brian Eno and I had just finished collaborating on our own record, called *My Life in the Bush of Ghosts.* It was created using the same technique we would soon use on *Remain in Light,* though in this case neither of us sang or wrote the lyrics, which all came from found sources. With its "sampled" vocals, we couldn't play it live back then. However, that experience gave us the confidence to argue that a pop record could indeed be made in that way.

But live performance was another story. In addition to Adrian, we added Steve Scales on percussion, Bernie Worrell on keyboards, Busta Jones on second bass, and Dolette MacDonald on vocals. Initial rehearsals were chaotic. I remember Jerry being especially adept at determining who would play what. Of course, what came out in the end did not sound exactly like it did on the record. It became more extended, funkier, its joy in the groove more apparent.

Our first show with this enlarged band was at the Heatwave Festival outside Toronto. We were terrified. We were going to perform almost all new, unheard material with a completely new sound, though I think to be safe we started the set with some popular favorites played by the old four-piece band. The festival crowd was with us. Audiences love it when a performer walks the tightrope in front of them; like sports fans, they feel like their support is what keeps the team winning. It had the desired effect. We were nervous, but ecstatic too, and the audience sensed that. In the end we might have been a little sloppy, but it worked. Backstage afterward we all jumped for joy. Someone told me it reminded them of Miles's *On the Corner,* which I took as an extreme compliment. It was a totally new kind of performing for me.

I knew the music we'd just recorded was less angsty than the stuff we'd done previously. It was about surrender, ecstasy, and transcendence, and the live performance tended to really bring those qualities to the forefront. It wasn't just an intellectual conceit: I could feel lifted and transported onstage. I think audiences sometimes felt this too.

We'd crossed a line somewhere. With a smaller group there is tight musical and personal interaction, and the audience can still distinguish among the various personalities and individuals onstage. When a group gets too big, that isn't possible anymore, or at least it wasn't given the way we decided to configure things.

Though I was still up front as the singer, there wasn't the visible hierarchy of players that one often sees in large bands. Everyone was both musically and visually part of the whole. The band became a more abstract entity, a community. And while individual band members might shine and take virtuosic turns, their identities became submerged within the group. It might seem paradoxical, but the more integral everyone was, the more everyone gave up some individuality and surrendered to the music. It was a living, breathing model of a more ideal society, an ephemeral utopia that everyone, even the audience, felt was being manifested in front of them, if only for a brief period.

As I experienced it, this was not just a musical transformation, but also a psychic one. The nature of the music helped, but partly it was the very size of the band that allowed me, even as lead singer, to lose myself and experience a kind of ecstatic release. You can sometimes feel transported with a smaller group, but with a large band it is often the norm. It was joyous and at times powerfully spiritual, without being corny or religious in any kind of traditional or dogmatic way. You can imagine how seductive this could be. Its kinship with other more prescribed forms was obvious—the gospel church, ecstatic trance in many parts of the world, and of course other kinds of pop music that derived from similar sources.

Interesting also that we were bringing together classic funk musicians (like Bernie) and white art-rock kids like ourselves. We used our own arty taste to introduce weirdly mutated aspects of black American music to rock audiences—a curious combo. American pop music was fairly segregated at the time, as it often has been. Rock audiences were by and large white, and funk, Latin, and R&B audiences were not. There was little mixing of the two in clubs or onstage. Disco, which had arisen in gay clubs but was also an R&B form, was hated by rock audiences. When we performed in Lubbock, Texas, the club strung a banner across the stage that said THIS AIN'T NO DISCO, inappropriately quoting a lyric from "Life During Wartime" and repurposing it as an anti-disco (and by implication anti-gay and anti-black) anthem.

Radio in the United States had more or less the same reaction. Despite the heavy play that the "Once in a Lifetime" video got on MTV, regular rock radio wouldn't play it, or much else from that album. They said it was too funky; not really rock. And the R&B stations wouldn't play the song either. Needless to say, the song got heard; the racism of US radio didn't hold it back all that much. Interesting how times have changed, and how they haven't. There are indeed media outlets whose audiences are interested in music regardless of the race of the composer, but by and large the world of music in the United States is only slightly less segregated than other institutions. A lot of businesses might not be overtly racist, but by playing to their perceived demographic—which is a natural business decision—they reinforce existing divisions. Change does happen, but sometimes it's frustratingly slow.

Needless to say, white folks like to dance too. Maybe our shows, with some of us grooving onstage, made actual dancing as opposed to thrashing about sort of okay. I got the sense that what was new was not just having black and white folks together on stage—there was nothing new about that—but the way in which we did it. Our shows presented everyone as being part of the band. Everyone played together; that was what was new.

My own contorting onstage was spontaneous. I obviously had to be at the mic when I was singing, but otherwise the groove took me, and I let it do what it wanted. I had no interest in or ability to learn smooth dance moves, though we all watched *Soul Train*. Besides, a white nerdy guy trying to be smooth and black is a terrible thing to behold. I let my body discover, little by little, its own grammar of movement—often jerky, spastic, and strangely formal.

The tour eventually took us to Japan, where I went to see the traditional theater forms: Kabuki, Noh, and Bunraku. These were, compared to Western theater, highly stylized; *presentational* is the word that is sometimes used, as opposed to the pseudo-naturalistic theater we in the West are more used to.[F]

Everyone wore massive, elaborate costumes and moved in ways that were unlike the ways people move in real life. They may have been playing the parts of noblemen, geishas, or samurai, but their faces were painted and they spoke in voices that were far from natural. In Bunraku, the puppet theater, often a whole group of assistants would be onstage operating the almost-life-size puppet. We weren't supposed to "see" them, but they were right there, albeit dressed in black.[G] The text, the voices, would come from a group of guys seated off to the side. The character had in effect been so fragmented that the words they spoke didn't come from close to or even behind that puppet, but from other performers on an entirely different part of the stage. It was as if the various parts of an actor's performance had been deconstructed, split into countless constituent parts and functions. You had to reassemble the character in your head.

Was any of this applicable to a pop-music performance? I didn't know, but over dinner in Tokyo one night the fashion designer Jurgen Lehl offered the old adage that "everything onstage needs to be bigger." Inspired, I doodled an idea for a stage outfit. A business suit (again!), but bigger, and stylized in the manner of a Noh costume. This wasn't exactly what he meant; he meant gesture, expression, voice. But I applied it to clothing as well.[H]

F

G

On a break from the tour, I went south to Bali, a place the choreographer Toni Basil, whom Eno and I had met during the *Bush of Ghosts* sessions, had recommended as being transporting and all about performance. I rented a small motorcycle and headed up into the hills, away from the beach resorts. I soon discovered that if one saw offerings of flowers and fruit being brought to a village temple compound in the afternoon, one could be pretty certain that some sort of ritual performance would follow there at night.

Sure enough, night after night I would catch dances accompanied by gamelan orchestras and shadow-puppet excerpts from the Hindu Ramayana—epic and sometimes ritual performances that blended religious and theatrical elements. (A gamelan is a small orchestra made up mainly of tuned metallic gongs and xylophone-like instruments—the interplay between the parts

H

is beautiful and intricate.) In these latter events some participants would often fall into a trance, but even in trance there were prescribed procedures. It wasn't all thrashing chaos, as a Westerner might expect, but a deeper kind of dance.[1]

As in Japanese theater, the performers often wore masks and extreme makeup; their movements, too, were stylized and "unnatural." It began to sink in that this kind of "presentational" theater had more in common with certain kinds of pop-music performance than traditional Western theater did.

I was struck by other seemingly peripheral aspects of these performances. The audiences, mostly local villagers of all ages, weren't paying attention half the time. People would wander in and out, go get a snack from a cart or leave to smoke a bidi cigarette, and then return to watch some more. This was more like the behavior of audiences in music clubs than in Western theaters, where they were expected to sit quietly and only leave or converse once the show was over.

These Balinese "shows" were completely integrated into people's daily lives, or so it seemed to me. There was no attempt to formally separate the ritual and the show from the audience. Everything seemed to flow into everything else. The food, the music, and the dance were all just another part of daily activity. I remembered a story about John Cage, who, when in Japan, asked someone what their religion was. The reply was that they didn't have a strict religion—they danced. Japanese do, of course, have Buddhist and Shinto rituals for weddings, funerals, and marriages, but a weekly thing like going to church or temple doesn't exist. The "religion" is so

integrated into the culture that it appears in daily gesture and routines, unsegregated from ordinary life. I was beginning to see that theatricality wasn't necessarily a bad thing. It was part of life in much of the world, and not necessarily phony either.

I guess I was primed to receive this new way of looking at performance, but I quickly absorbed that it was all right to make a show that didn't pretend to be "natural." The Western emphasis on pseudo-naturalism and the cult of spontaneity as a kind of authenticity was only one way of doing things onstage. I decided that maybe it was okay to wear costumes and put on a show. It didn't imply insincerity at all; in fact, this kind of practiced performance was all around, if one only looked at it. The services in a gospel church are funky and energetic, but they are prescribed and happen in almost identical sequences over and over. That doesn't make them any less real or less powerful. In the world of the ecstatic church, religion bleeds into performance, and there are obvious musical parallels with what we were doing.

In Los Angeles I collaborated with Toni to make a music video for a couple of the songs from *Remain in Light*. For "Once in a Lifetime," I worked out an elaborate dance routine that borrowed from Japanese street dance, gospel trance, and some of my own improvisations. Toni had worked with untrained dancers before, so she knew how to get me to make my improvised moves, edit them, select the best ones, refine them further, and begin to order them into a sequence. It took weeks to get the moves tight. It was all going to be filmed in one master shot, so I had to be able to perform the whole thing from top to bottom without stopping on multiple takes. It was a song-and-dance routine, as she described it, though nothing like what one normally thinks of when one hears that phrase.

We added little film snippets during the editing that revealed the source material for some of the moves: a few seconds of a kid dancing in Yoyogi Park in Tokyo (dancing there is now forbidden!) and a few frames from an anthropological film about African dance, with the dancers crouching near the ground. I wanted to show my sources, not claim I invented everything, though my jerky improv versions weren't much like the originals in any case.

Talking Heads recorded another record, *Speaking in Tongues*, that was made using a very similar process to *Remain in Light*, though this time without Eno's involvement. In thinking of what kind of performance and tour would follow, I decided to apply my insights from Japan, Bali, and the gospel church. This show would be mapped out from beginning to end.

In retrospect, the earlier tour with a big band had been a work in progress. My movements during rehearsals gradually became more formal as I realized which improvisations worked in which sections of which songs. It was a kind of organic choreography, like what I'd done on the video, but now involving more people and for a whole show. I storyboarded the whole thing, sometimes not knowing which song would go with which staging idea. The songs got assigned to the staging and lighting ideas later, as did details of the movements.[J]

We decided that we'd all wear neutral gray outfits this time. I had realized that people onstage can either stick out (if they wear white or sparkly outfits) or disappear (if they wear dark colors). With music shows, there is inevitably so much gear onstage—guitars, drums, keyboards, amps—that sometimes the gear ends up being lit as much as the performers. To mitigate this a little bit, I had all the metal hardware (cymbal stands and keyboard racks) painted matte black so that it wouldn't outshine the musicians. We hid the guitar amps under the risers that the backing band played on, so those were invisible too. Wearing gray suits seemed to be the best of both worlds, and by planning it in advance, we knew there would at least be consistent lighting from night to night. Typically a musician or singer might decide to wear their white or black shirt on a given night, and they'd end up either glowing brighter than everyone else or be rendered invisible. We avoided that problem.

On all of our previous tours we'd maintained the lighting dogma left over from CBGB: white light, on at the top of the show and off at the end. But I felt it was time to break away from that a little bit. I still confined the lighting to white, though now white in all its possibilities, permutations, and combinations. There were no colored gels as such, but we did use fluorescent bulbs, movie lights, shadows, handheld lights, work lights, household lamps, and floor lights—all of which had particular qualities of their own, but were still what we might consider *white*. I brought in a lighting designer, Beverly Emmons, whose work I'd seen in a piece by the director Robert Wilson. I showed her the storyboards and explained the concept, and she knew exactly how to achieve the desired effects, which lighting instruments to use, and how to rig them.

I had become excited by the downtown New York theater scene. Robert Wilson, Mabou Mines, and the Wooster Group in particular were all experimenting with new ways of putting things onstage and presenting them, experiments that to my eyes were close to the Asian theater forms and rituals that had recently inspired me.[K]

What they were all doing was as exciting for me as when I'd first heard pop music as an adolescent, or when the anything-goes attitude of the punk and post-punk scene flourished. I invited JoAnne Akalaitis, one of the directors involved with Mabou Mines, to look at our early rehearsals and give me some notes. There

was no staging or lighting yet, but I was curious whether a more theatrical eye might see something I was missing, or suggest a better way to do something.

To further complicate matters, I decided to make the show completely transparent. I would show how everything was done and how it had been put together. The audience would see each piece of stage gear being put into place and then see, as soon as possible afterward, what that instrument (or type of lighting) did. It seemed like such an obvious idea that I was shocked that I didn't know of a show (well, a music show) that had done it before.

Following this concept to its natural conclusion meant starting with a bare stage. The idea was that you'd stare at the emptiness and imagine what might be possible. A single work light would be hanging from the fly space, as it typically does during rehearsals or when a crew is moving stuff in and out. No glamour and no "show"—although, of course, this was all part of the show.

The idea was that we'd make even more visible what had evolved on the previous tour, in which we'd often start a set with a few songs performed with just the four-piece band, and then gradually other musicians would take their places on preset keyboard and percussion risers. In this case, though, we'd take the concept further, with each player and the instruments themselves appearing on an empty stage, one after another. So, ideally, when they walked on and began to play or sing, you'd hear what each musician or singer was bringing to the party—added groove elements, keyboard textures, vocal harmonies. This was done by having their gear on rolling platforms that were hidden in the wings. The platforms would be pushed out by stagehands, and then the musician would jump into position and remain part of the group until the end of the show.

Stage and lighting elements would also be carried out by the stagehands: footlights, lights on stands like they use in movies, slide projectors on scaffolding. Sometimes these lighting instruments would be used right after their appearance, so you'd immediately see what they did, what effect they had. When everything was finally in place you'd get to see all the elements you'd been introduced to used in conjunction with each other. The magician would show how the trick was done and then do the trick, and my belief was that this transparency wouldn't lessen the magic.

Well, that was the idea. A lot of it came from the Asian theater and ritual I'd seen. The operators manipulating the Bunraku puppets in plain sight, assistants coming onstage to help a Kabuki actor with a costume transformation, the fact that in Bali one could see the preparation for a scene or ritual, but none of that mattered, none of the force or impact was lost, despite all the spoilers.

There is another way in which pop-music shows resemble both Western and Eastern classical theater: the audience knows the story already. In classical theater, the director's interpretation holds a mirror up to the oft-told tale in a way that allows us to see it in a new light. Well, same with pop concerts. The audience loves to hear songs they've heard before, and though they are most familiar with the recorded versions, they appreciate hearing what they already know in a new context. They don't want an immaculate reproduction of the record, they want it skewed in some way. They want to see something familiar from a new angle.

As a performing artist, this can be frustrating. We don't want to be stuck playing our hits forever, but playing only new, unfamiliar stuff can alienate a crowd—I know, I've done it. This situation seems unfair. You would never go to a movie longing to spend half the evening watching familiar scenes featuring the actors replayed, with only a few new ones interspersed. And you'd grow tired of a visual artist or a writer who merely replicated work they've done before with little variation. But sometimes that is indeed exactly what people want. In art museums a mixture of the known, familiar, and new is expected, as it is in classical concerts. But even within these confines there's a lot of wiggle room in a pop concert. It's not a rote exercise, or it doesn't have to be.

While we were performing the shows in Los Angeles that would eventually become the *Stop Making Sense* film, I invited the late William Chow,[L] a great Beijing Opera actor, to see what we were doing. I'd seen him perform not too long before, and was curious what he would make of this stuff. He'd never been to a Western pop show before, though I suspect he'd seen things on TV. The next day we met for lunch after the show.

William was forthright, blunt maybe; he had no fear that his outsider perspective might not be relevant. He told me in great detail what I was "doing wrong" and what I could improve. Surprisingly, to me anyway, his observations were like the adages one might have heard from a vaudevillian, a burlesque dancer, or a stand-up comedian: certain stage rules appear to be universal. Some of his comments were about how to make an entrance or how to direct an audience's attention. One adage was along the lines of needing to let the audience know you're going to do something special before you do it. You tip them off and draw their attention to you (and you have to know how to do that in a way that isn't obvious) or toward whoever is going to do the special thing. It seems counterintuitive in some ways; where's the surprise if you let the audience in on what's about to happen? Well, odds are, if you don't alert them, half the audience will miss it. They'll blink or be looking elsewhere. Being caught by surprise is, it seems, not good. I've made this mistake plenty of times. It doesn't just apply to stage stuff or to a dramatic vocal moment in performance, either. One can see the application of this rule in film and almost everywhere else. Stand-up comedians probably have lots of similar rules about getting an audience ready for the punch line.

A similar adage was "Tell the audience what you're going to do, and then do it." "Telling" doesn't mean going to the mic and saying, "Adrian's going to do an amazing guitar solo now." It's more subtle than that. The directors and editors of horror movies have taught us many such rules, like the sacrificial victim and the ominous music (which sometimes leads to nothing the first time, increasing the shock when something actually happens later). And then while we sit there in the theater anticipating what will happen, the director can play with those expectations, acknowledging that he or she knows that we know. There are two conversations going on at the same time: the story and a conversation about how the story is being told. The same thing can happen onstage.

The dancing that had emerged organically in the previous tour began to get increasingly codified. It still emerged out of movement that was improvised in rehearsals, but now I was more confident that if a singer, player, or performer did something spontaneously that worked perfectly for us, it could be repeated without any risk of losing its power and soul. I had confidence that this bottom-up approach to making a show would work. Every performer does this. If something new works one night, well, leave it in. It could be a lighting cue, removing one's jacket, a vocal embellishment, or smashing a guitar. Anything can eventually grow stale, and one has to be diligent, but when a move or gesture or sound is right, it adds to the emotion and intensity, and each time it's as real as it was the first time.

Not everyone liked this new approach. The fact that some of the performers had to hit their marks, or at least come close, didn't seem very rock and roll to them. But, going back to William Chow's admonishments, if you're going to do something wild and spontaneous, at least "tell" the audience ahead of time and do it in the light, or your inspired moment is wasted.

But where does the music fit into all this? Isn't music the "content" that should be guiding all this stage business? Well, it seems the juxtaposition of music and image guides our minds and hearts so that, in the end, which came first doesn't matter as much as one might think. A lighting or staging idea (using household fixtures—a floor lamp, for instance) is paired with a song ("This Must Be the Place") and one automatically assumes there's a connection. Paired with another lighting effect, the song might have seemed equally suited—but maybe more ominous or even threatening (though that might have worked, too). We sometimes think we discern cause and effect simply because things are taking place at the same moment in time, and this extends beyond the stage. We read into things, find emotional links between what we see and hear, and to me, these connections are no less true and honest for not being conceived and developed ahead of time.

This show was the most ambitious thing I'd done. Although the idea was simple, the fact that every piece of gear had to come onstage for tech check in the afternoon and then be removed again before the show was a lot of work for the crew. But the show was a success; the transparency and conceptual nature of its structure took away nothing from the emotional impact. It was tremendously gratifying.

I didn't perform for a while after that. It was hard to top that experience. I directed a feature film, married, and had a child, and I wanted to be around for as much of my daughter's early years as I could. I continued to make records and launch other creative endeavors, but I didn't perform.

In 1989 I made a record, *Rei Momo*, with a lot of Latin musicians. The joy of following the record with a tour accompanied by a large Latin band, playing salsa, samba, merengue, cumbias, and other grooves, was too much to resist. There was a lot to handle musically on that outing, so the stage business wouldn't be as elaborate as on the tour that was filmed for *Stop Making Sense*, though I did bring in movie-production designer Barbara Ling, who suggested a tiered set of risers with translucent fiberglass facing that would light up from within. (We used the same material for the stage set of my film *True Stories*.) The semicircular layer-cake design of the riser was based on a picture on an old Tito Rodriguez album cover, though I don't think his risers lit up.

The band wore all white this time, and the fact that there were so many of them meant that their outfits would allow them to pop out from the background. The outfits also alluded to the African-based religions of Candomblé and Santería, whose adherents wear white during ceremonies. There was more than one Santero in the group, so the reference wasn't for naught.[M]

I had referenced religious trance and ritual in earlier performances and recordings, and I never lost interest in that facet of music. I made a documentary in Brazil, *Ile Aiye (The House of Life)*, in Salvador, Bahia, partly to indulge my continued interest in these religious traditions. Santería, the Afro-Cuban branch of West

African religious practice, and Voudoun, the Haitian manifestation, are both very present in New York music and culture. But it was the Brazilian branch, Candomblé, that seemed the least repressed by either secular or church authorities in recent decades, and therefore the most open, so when I was given the opportunity to do a film, that's where I chose to go.

As with gospel music, religion seems to be at the root of much Brazilian pop music and creativity, and as with the Asian ritual and theatrical forms, costumes and trance and dance are completely formalized but incredibly moving. And similar to what I felt in Bali, the practice is completely integrated into people's lives. It's not just something one does on Sunday mornings or Saturday nights. There are evening ceremonies, to be sure, but their influence is deeply felt in everyday life, and that affected my thinking as I prepared for the next round of performances.

I may well be idealizing some of what I saw and witnessed, taking aspects of what I perceived and adapting them to solve and deal with my own issues and creative bottlenecks. Somehow I have a feeling that might be okay.

Rather than having a discrete opening act, I brought Margareth Menezes on board: a Brazilian singer from—surprise!—Salvador, Bahia, who would sing some of her own material with my band and also sing harmonies on my tunes. Some of her songs had Yoruba lyrics and made explicit references to the gods and goddesses of Candomblé, so it was all one big happy family. Margareth was great—too good, in fact. She stole the show on some nights. Live and learn.

I bucked the tide on that tour. We did mostly new material rather than interspersing it with a lot of popular favorites, and I think I paid the price. While the shows were exciting, and even North Americans danced to our music, much of my audience soon abandoned me, assuming I'd "gone native." Another lesson learned from performing live. At one point we got booked at a European outdoor music festival, and my Latin band was sandwiched between Pearl Jam and Soundgarden. Great bands, but I couldn't have felt more out of place.

I followed this with a tour that mixed a band made up of funk musicians like George Porter, Jr. (bass player for the Meters) with some of the Latin musicians from *Rei Momo*. Now we could do some of the Talking Heads songs as well, even some that Talking Heads themselves couldn't have played live. I intended to make explicit the link between Latin grooves and New Orleans funk, or so I hoped. I had begun to do some short acoustic sets with a drum machine. I'd start the show like that, alone onstage, revealing the big band upstage with a sudden curtain drop.

After that, I decided to strip things down again. I recorded and toured with a four-piece band that emphasized grooves. There was a drummer, Todd Turkisher, a bass player, Paul Socolow, and a percussionist, Mauro Refosco—but no keyboard or second guitar such as one would see or hear in a typical rock band. I had written more personal songs, which were better suited to a smaller ensemble. There was little dancing, and I seem to recall I wore black again. The last few records had been recorded before their songs had been played live, so this time I wanted to go back to where I'd started. We played small, out-of-the-way clubs (and some not so out of the way) to break in the material. The idea was to hone the band into a tight live unit and then essentially record live in the studio. It worked, but only sort of. I could hear discrepancies and musical problems in the studio that I had missed in the heat and passion of live performance, so some further tweaking was still required.

Around this time I'd discovered standards. I never lost the enjoyment I had in high school of playing other people's songs in my bedroom, and gradually, going through songbook after songbook I picked up, I was adding more chords and an appreciation for melody to what I knew. Willie Nelson's *Stardust* was an inspiration, as were Philadelphia soul songs, bossa novas, and songs by my favorite Brazilian and Latin singers and songwriters. But I didn't play any of them in public. They felt delicious on the tongue, but I didn't get them all right. I didn't grow up on those songs, but I began to feel an appreciation for a beautiful melody and harmonies—harmonies in the chord voicings and not just in what a second singer might sing. Beauty was a revelation, and these songs were unashamed to be beautiful, which was a difficult thing to accept in the world of downtown musicians and artists. Anything that sounds or looks beautiful would seem to that crowd to be merely pretty, shallow, and therefore deeply suspect—morally suspect, even, I found out. Noise, for them, is deep; beauty shallow.

Well, for a while I'd suspected that wasn't a point of view shared by the wider world. Around 1988, when I began to compile some of my favorite tracks by Brazilian composers (pop musicians are referred to as composers in Brazil), I realized that although many of their songs were rich, harmonically complex, and, yes, beautiful, they definitely weren't shallow. Some of these composers and singers were forced into prison and exile for their "merely pretty" songs, so I began to realize that depth, radical visions, and beauty were not mutually exclusive. Sure, bossa novas had become a staple of every bad piano bar, but the songs themselves are innovative and radical in their way. Later, younger generations of composers there absorbed influences from North America and Europop, but they didn't feel the need to go ugly to be serious. With my new appreciation for song craft, I wanted to have songs of my own that made me feel that way. I was no longer content to just sing other people's songs in the shower.

Inspired by these standards I'd been listening to and by a couple of Caetano Veloso's records, I wrote songs that emptied out the middle of the sonic spectrum of the usual pop-band instrumentation. I let the orchestrations (strings and occasional winds) do the harmonic work that guitars and keyboards often do, and once again there were drums and plenty of percussion, so the grooves were strong and thus avoided the tendencies one might associate with a nice melody and traditional balladry. Since both guitars and keyboards are close to the same range as the human voice, limiting their use meant the singing had a clearing in which to live, and I was increasingly enjoying singing in there.

In the early days, I might have gotten onstage and begun to sing as a desperate attempt to communicate, but I now found that singing was both a physical and emotional joy. It was sensuous, a pure pleasure, which didn't take anything away from the emotions being expressed—even if they were melancholic. Music can do that; you can enjoy singing about something sad. Audiences, likewise, can dance to a tragic story. It happens all the time. My vocal technique had somehow expanded, or maybe just moved into another place, and I realized that though I could still do the desperate yelp, I wasn't inclined to write like that anymore. My body, and the physical and emotional enjoyment I was getting from singing, was in effect telling me what to write.

I gathered a group that helped me express this: a rhythm section and a six-piece string section. We toured, and it worked. We could play arias from operas, Talking Heads songs, covers of other people's songs, and even an extended house track. There wasn't much showbiz, but the group sounded gorgeous, which was the goal anyway.

To some extent, I let the tour finances dictate what that performance would be. I knew the size of the venues I'd be playing, and from that I could figure out how much income there would be. Carrying all these musicians along at that point in my career (I wasn't filling halls as big as the *Stop Making Sense* tour did) was a financial consideration, but I was happy to be restricted in that way. I didn't give up on the visuals completely, though. I wanted us to wear outfits that would unify us onstage, have us appear like a slightly less ragtag bunch, but the budget was limited. First I had jumpsuits made for everyone, modeled on one that I had purchased in a store. The copies didn't turn out to be as flattering to everyone else as I'd hoped; they looked like pajamas.

A fashion mutiny understandably began building steam. We switched to Dickies—workwear with matching tops and bottoms, brown or blue or gray. Those looked somewhat like the originally envisioned jumpsuits, but now there was an everyday workwear angle. Some of the outfits got tailored a bit (the shirts got darts so they accentuated the female string players' figures, for example), but mostly they were right out of the box. I often looked like a UPS man, but I thought that in its own way it was quite elegant.[N]

The audiences sat and listened quietly at times, but they were usually up and dancing by the end. Best of both worlds. I had loosened up onstage by then, and I began to talk to the audience beyond reciting the names of the songs and saying a quick "Thank you very much" afterward. Often—and this never failed to surprise us—audiences at these shows would stop the show in the middle and engage in a lengthy round of applause. Standing ovations, many times. Sometimes this was after a song or two that might have been somewhat familiar and that really showed what this ensemble could do, but I sensed the audience wasn't just clapping for specific songs. They realized that they were happy, that they were really, really enjoying what they were seeing and hearing, and they wanted to let us know. I sometimes think the audience was in a funny way also applauding for themselves. Some of them might also have been a little bit nostalgic, applauding

our joint legacies as performers and audience. One forgets that part of one's performance is one's history—or sometimes the lack of it. You're playing against what an audience knows, what they expect. This seems to be true of all performers; there's baggage that gets carried into the venue that we can't see. The audience wasn't all aging Talking Heads fans either. There was a healthy percentage of younger folks as well, which was great to see. Maybe keeping the ticket prices affordable helped.

In 2008, I did a tour that in some ways harked back to the *Stop Making Sense* extravaganza. I had collaborated on a record with Brian Eno that was more electronic folk/gospel in tone than the fierce funky workouts of *Remain in Light*. I realized that in order to perform this music, I'd need an ensemble similar to that touring band from more than twenty years before—multiple singers, keyboards, bass, drums, and percussion. Conveniently, with this band I could also do some of the songs we'd both been involved in, with Talking Heads and on other projects.

Once again, I had to think about what sort of a show this could be given the financial means available to me. I wanted to do something visual and theatrical again, since there wouldn't be lush strings to wash over the audience anymore. Just standing there and playing wouldn't be enough with this outfit—but what else was feasible? Lots of acts now use elaborate video screens and similar techniques to "make it bigger" onstage. I'd seen a few of these shows. I saw a Super Furry Animals show during which the video was totally in sync with the songs throughout the whole night. Very impressive. I'd seen pictures of U2 and other acts' arena shows; those bands had massive screens and all the latest technology. They hired teams of creative types to make the videos. I couldn't compete with any of that. It costs a fortune, and their results were probably better or at least as good as anything I could pull together. And in any case, they'd already done it.

Then I saw a Sufjan Stevens show at BAM (a piece about the BQE, the Brooklyn-Queens Expressway) during which he brought out dancers who did simple repetitive movements with Hula-Hoops or other such silliness.° It was charming and effective, moving even, something obviously low-tech that almost anyone could do. I thought to myself, "I've never had dancers onstage. Why not?"

I thought I would go a little further with the idea than Sufjan, who had a million other things going on during that show, like films and costume changes. I worked with my manager on a budget. I had learned over the years that we could predict, based on the size of proposed performance venues, how much we might make on a tour, so we could predict if singers, dancers, choreographers, and the cost of carting all of them around along with the band was feasible. In this case, it was. Money and budgets are as much a determining factor in music and performance as anything else, but that's for another chapter.

For the dance elements, I decided to approach "downtown" choreographers rather than the ones who typically do music videos, R&B shows, or Broadway musicals. The dance vocabulary of those shows is emphatic, energetic, and exciting, but everyone has seen that stuff before, so why bother? I thought I'd spread the creative risk to increase my odds, so I approached four choreographers—Noémie Lafrance, Annie-B Parson, and the team of Sonya Robbins and Layla Childs—rather than seeing if just one could do the whole show. This way, if one person's contribution didn't work out for some reason, there were still others who could carry the load. (Luckily, that didn't happen.) Likewise, I suggested that each choreographer initially pick just two songs to work on. (They ended up doing quite a bit more than just six songs.) I provided a proposed set list, and left the choice of what to work on to them. All of the choreographers had worked with untrained dancers before, and often incorporated vernacular movement into their work—moves that weren't based on ballet or typical modern-dance stuff. That was important for me, too; I didn't want worlds in collision. I see dance as something anyone can do, though I knew that inevitably the dancers would have some special skills, as we all do.

Noémie Lafrance had recently done a video with Feist that was widely seen. It used mostly untrained dancers, and though I didn't necessarily require my performers to have no formal dance training, I knew that I didn't want them to obviously look like dancers. I wanted them to blend in with the rest of us. Noémie had also done a lot of site-specific work in swimming pools and stairwells, so I knew she was interested in getting dance into new venues—like a pop-music concert. Annie-B Parson I've known forever. I'm a fan of her company, Big Dance Theater, and she's worked with musicians like Cynthia Hopkins, so she seemed perfect, too. Sonya Robbins and Layla Childs are a performing/choreography duo whose work I saw in a video at an art gallery. In that piece they wore matching primary-colored off-the-rack outfits and did mostly pedestrian moves in unison. Sometimes they rolled down a gully and sometimes they clambered on rocks. It was often funny and beautiful. I didn't know if they'd ever choreographed a "show" like this before, so they were the wild card.

I could afford three dancers and three singers in addition to the band, some of whom I'd worked with on two previous tours: Graham Hawthorne on drums, Mauro Refosco on percussion, and Paul Frazier on bass. Mark De Gli Antoni joined on keyboards. (He was new, though we'd once played together when he was in the band Soul Coughing.) The singers were easy: folks I had crossed paths with or worked with before. They were told that they'd be expected to "do some movement." I used that phrase rather than "dance" because I didn't want to give them the fearsome idea that they'd be expected to do Broadway jazz dance. To find appropriate dancers, the choreographers sent out word to dancers and performers they knew personally. We didn't go the route of taking out an ad, as we'd have been flooded with inappropriate people. Even so, at the beginning of the dance audition there were fifty dancers in the room.

We had two days to whittle them down to three. Cruel, but, well, fun too. We decided that the dancers would be asked to do three types of things: exercises in which they made up their own movement, short routines that they would be asked to memorize, and bits where they would receive notes and suggestions for how to improve what they'd just done. Noémie began with an exercise I've never forgotten. It consisted of four simple rules:

1. Improvise moving to the music and come up with an eight-count phrase.
   (In dance, a *phrase* is a short series of moves that can be repeated.)
2. When you find a phrase you like, loop (repeat) it.
3. When you see someone else with a stronger phrase, copy it.
4. When everyone is doing the same phrase the exercise is over.

It was like watching evolution on fast-forward, or an emergent life form coming into being. At first the room was chaos, writhing bodies everywhere. Then one could see that folks had chosen their phrases, and almost immediately one could see a pocket of dancers who had all adopted the same phrase. The copying had begun already, albeit just in one area. This pocket of copying began to expand, to go viral, while yet another one now emerged on the other side of the room. One clump grew faster than the other, and within four minutes the whole room was filled with dancers moving in perfect unison. Unbelievable! It only took four minutes for this evolutionary process to kick in, and for the "strongest" (unfortunate word, maybe) to dominate. It was one of the most amazing dance performances I've ever seen. Too bad it was over so quickly, and that one did have to know the rules that had been laid out to appreciate how such a simple algorithm could generate unity out of chaos.

After this vigorous athletic experiment, the dancers rested while we compared notes. I noticed a weird and quite loud windlike sound, rushing and pulsing. I didn't know what it was; it seemed to be coming from everywhere and nowhere. It was like no sound I'd ever heard before. I realized it was the sound of fifty people catching their breath, breathing in and out, in an enclosed room. It then gradually faded away. For me that was part of the piece, too.

Having learned from the *Rei Momo* tour, I decided to go back to the white outfits. That way the dancers' movements would pop against the musicians, risers, and bits of gear. But as with the big Latin tour, I sensed that there was a spiritual aspect to the new songs we were playing, as well as many of the older ones, so white also hinted at associations with gospel, temples, and mosques.[P]

We rehearsed for a month. For the first three weeks the band and singers learned the music in one room, while the dancers and choreographers worked in another room two floors below. I'd pop back and forth. In the fourth week we brought the dancers and musicians together. We then did what is called an out-of-town run: a series of shows in smaller towns to get the bugs out, where no one in the press would see what we were up to. Our first show was in Easton, Pennsylvania, in a lovely old restored theater in a little once-industrial town. There were some rough patches, but the big surprise was that the audience—hardly a contemporary-dance crowd—loved it. Well, they didn't go nuts, but they didn't balk at the dance stuff. It was going to be okay.

And it got better. I realized that the dancers, and the singers who sometimes joined them, raised the energy level of the whole show. I joined them when I could, and to do so felt ecstatic, but my interaction was limited by my singing and guitar-playing duties. Even so, they all became part of the whole, not a separate part tacked on. Over the course of the tour we took this idea further: some of the danc-ers would sing, some would play guitar, and eventually we added bits that blurred the boundaries between dancers, singers, and musicians. A little bit of an ideal world in microcosm.

The out-of-town tryout part was kind of a bust. That aspect of putting a per-formance together has been forever altered by cell-phone cameras and YouTube. Barely minutes after our shows were over, someone would announce that some of the numbers were appearing online. In the past, performers would at least try to limit amateur photographers and especially video cameras, but now that idea seemed simply ridiculous—hopeless. We realized there was a silver lining: they liked our show and their postings were functioning as free advertising. The thing we were supposed to be fighting against was actually something we should be encouraging. They were getting the word out, and it wasn't costing me anything. I began to announce at the beginning of the shows that photography was welcome, but I suggested to please only post shots and videos where we look good.

I talked with the dancers and choreographers as the show began to jell, and we all agreed that contemporary dance, a rarefied world where the audiences are usu-ally very small, was indeed, as this show proved, accessible to some part of the general public. It wasn't the movement or choreography itself that was keeping the audiences small for this stuff, but the context. The exact same choreography in a dance venue, without a live pop band? This audience in Easton, Pennsylvania, would never go see it in a million years. But here, in this context, they seemed to like it. The way one sees things, and the expectations one brings to a performance, or any art form, really, is completely determined by the venue. Poetry is a tough sell, but with a beat it's rap, which is wildly successful. Okay, it's not exactly the same, but you get the idea. I once saw a theater piece that had a lot of music in it; it sort of failed as a theater piece, but I told the producer, "If you position it as an imaginatively staged concert, it's incredibly successful."

It's not as if one can shift music, visual art, dance, or spoken word like pieces in a Tetris game until each art form plops into its perfect place, but it does give one the idea that some juggling of contexts might not hurt either.

I also realized that there were lots of unacknowledged theater forms going on all around. Our lives are filled with performances that have been so woven into our

daily routine that the artificial and performative aspect has slipped into invisibility. PowerPoint presentations are a kind of theater, a kind of augmented stand-up. Too often it's a boring and tedious genre, and audiences are subjected to the bad as well as the good. Failing to acknowledge that these are performances is to assume that anyone could and should be able to do it. You wouldn't expect anyone who can simply sing to get up on stage, so why expect everyone with a laptop to be competent in this new theatrical form? Performers try harder.

In political speeches—and I don't think there'll be any argument that they are in fact performances—the hair, the clothes, and the gestures are all carefully thought out. Bush II had a team that did nothing but sort out the backgrounds behind the places where he would appear, the MISSION ACCOMPLISHED banner being their most well-known bit of stagecraft. Same goes for public announcements of all kinds: it's all showbiz, and that's not a criticism. My favorite term for a certain new kind of performance is "security theater." In this genre, we watch as ritualized inspections and pat-downs create the illusion of security. It's a form that has become common since 9/11, and even the government agencies that participate in this activity acknowledge, off the record, that it is indeed a species of theater.

Performance is ephemeral. Some of my own shows have been filmed or have appeared on TV and as a result they have found audiences that never saw the original performances, which is great, but most of the time you simply have to be there. That's part of the excitement; it's happening in front of you, and in a couple of hours it won't be there anymore. You can't press a button and experience it again. In a hundred years it will be a faint memory, if that.

There's something special about the communal nature of an audience at a live performance, the shared experience with other bodies in a room going through the same thing at the same time, that isn't analogous to music heard through headphones. Often the very fact of a massive assembly of fans defines the experience as much as whatever it is they have come to see. It's a social event, an affirmation of a community, and it's also, in some small way, the surrender of the isolated individual to the feeling of belonging to a larger tribe. Many musicians make music influenced by this social aspect of performance; what we write is, in part, based on what the live experience of it might be. And the performing experience for the folks onstage is absolutely as moving as it is for the audience, so we're writing in the anxious hope of generating a moment for ourselves as much as for the listener—it's a two-way street. I love singing the songs I've written, especially in more recent performances, and part of the reason I decide to go out and play them live is to have that experience again. Evolutionary biologist Richard Prum proposes that birds don't just sing to attract mates and to define their territory; they sometimes sing for the sheer joy of it. Like them, I have that pleasurable experience, and I seek out opportunities for it. I don't want to have it happen only once, in the recording studio, and then have that moment get packed away as a memory. I want to relive it, as one can onstage, over and over. It's kind of glorious and surprising that the catharsis happens reliably, repeatedly, but it does.

There's an obvious narcissistic pleasure in being onstage, the center of attention. (Though some of us sing even when there's no one there.) In musical performances one can sense that the person onstage is having a good time even if they're singing a song about breaking up or being in a bad way. For an actor this would be anathema, it would destroy the illusion, but with singing one can have it both ways. As a singer, you can be transparent and reveal yourself onstage, in that moment, and at the same time be the person whose story is being told in the song. Not too many other kinds of performance allow that.

CHAPTER THREE

Technology Shapes Music

Part One: Analog

T he first sound recording was made in 1878. Since then, music has been amplified, broadcast, broken down into bits, miked and recorded, and the technologies behind those innovations have changed the nature of what gets created. Just as photography changed the way we see, recording technology changed the way we hear. Before recorded music became ubiquitous, music was, for most people, something we *did*. Many people had pianos in their homes, sang at religious services, or experienced music as part of a live audience. All those experiences were ephemeral—nothing lingered, nothing remained except for your memory (or your friends' memories) of what you heard and felt. Your recollection could very well have been faulty, or it could have been influenced by extra-musical factors. A friend could have told you the orchestra or ensemble sucked, and under social pressure you might have been tempted to revise your memory of the experience. A host of factors contribute to making the experience of live music a far from objective phenomenon. You couldn't hold it in your hand. Truth be told, you still can't.

As Walter Murch, the sound editor and film director, said, "Music was the main poetic metaphor for *that which could not be preserved.*"[1] Some say that this evanescence helps focus our attention. They claim that we listen more closely when we know we only have one chance, one fleeting opportunity to grasp something, and as a result our enjoyment is deepened. Imagine, as composer Milton Babbitt did, that you could experience a book only by going to a reading, or by reading the text off a screen that displayed it only briefly before disappearing. I suspect that if that were the way we received literature, then writers (and readers) would work harder to hold our attention. They would avoid getting too complicated, and they would strive mightily to create a memorable experience. Music did not get more compositionally sophisticated when it started being recorded, but I would argue that it did get texturally more complex. Perhaps written literature changed, too, as it became widespread—maybe it too evolved to be more textural (more about mood, technical virtuosity, and intellectual complexity than merely about telling a story).

Recording is far from an objective acoustic mirror, but it pretends to be like magic—a perfectly faithful and unbiased representation of the sonic act that occurred out there in the world. It claims to capture exactly what we hear—though our hearing isn't faithful or objective either. A recording is also repeatable. So, to its promoters, it is a mirror that shows you how you looked at a particular moment, over and over, again and again. Creepy. However, such claims are not only based on faulty assumptions, they are also untrue.

The first Edison cylinder recorders weren't very reliable, and the recording quality wasn't very good. Edison never suggested that they be used to record music. Rather, they were thought of as dictation machines, something that could, for example, preserve the great speeches of the day. The *New York Times* predicted that we might collect speeches: "Whether a man has or has not a wine cellar he will certainly, if he wishes to be regarded as a man of taste, have a well-stocked oratorical cellar."[2] *Please, try this fine Bernard Shaw or a rare Kaiser Wilhelm II.*

These machines were entirely mechanical. There was no electrical power involved in either the recording or the playback, so they weren't very loud compared to what we know today. To impress sound onto the wax, the voice or instrument being recorded would get as close as possible to the wide end of the horn—a large cone that funneled the sound toward the diaphragm and then to the inscribing needle. The sound waves would be concentrated and the vibrating diaphragm would move the needle, which incised a groove into a rotating wax cylinder. Playback simply reversed the process. It's amazing that it worked at all. As Murch points out, the ancient Greeks or Romans could have invented such a device; the technology wasn't beyond them. For all we know, someone at that time actually may have invented something similar and then abandoned it. Odd how technology and inventions come into being and fail to flourish for all sorts of reasons that have nothing to do with the skill, materials, or technology available at the time. Technological progress, if one can call it that, is full of dead ends and cul-de-sacs—roads not taken that could have led to who knows what alternate history. Or maybe the meandering paths, with their secret trajectories, would eventually and inevitably converge, and we'd all end up exactly where we are.

The wax cylinders that contained the recordings couldn't be easily mass-produced, so making lots of "copies" of these early recordings was an insane process. To "mass-produce" these items, one had to set up an array of these recorders as close as possible to the singer, band, or player—in other words, you could only produce the same number of recordings as you had recording devices and cylinders running. To make the next batch, you'd load up more blank cylinders and the band would have to play the same tune again, and so on. There needed to be a new performance for every batch of recordings. Not exactly a promising business model.

Edison set this apparatus aside for over a decade, but he eventually went back to tinkering with it, possibly due to pressure from the Victor Talking Machine Company, which had come out with recordings on discs. Soon he felt he'd made a breakthrough. In 1915, when Edison demonstrated his new version of an apparatus that recorded onto discs, he was convinced that now, finally, playback was a completely accurate reproduction of the speaker or singer being captured. The recording angel, the acoustic mirror, had arrived. Well, hearing those recordings, we might now think that he was somewhat deluded about how good his gizmo was, but he certainly seemed to believe in it, and he managed to convince others too. Edison was a brilliant inventor, a great engineer, but also a huckster and sometimes a ruthless businessman. (He didn't even really "invent" the electric light bulb—Joseph Swan in England had made them previously, though Edison did establish that tungsten would be the great long-lasting filament for that device.) And he usually managed to market and promote the hell out of his products, which certainly counts for something.

These new Diamond Disc Phonographs were promoted via what Edison referred to as Tone Tests. There is a promo film he made called *The Voice of the Violin* (oddly, for something promoting a sound recorder, it was a silent film) that helped publicize the Tone Tests. Edison was marketing and selling the Edison "sound" more than any specific artist. Initially he didn't even put the names of the artists on the discs, but there was always a sizable picture of Edison himself. He also held Mood Change Parties (!) in which the (naturally positive) emotional impact and power of recorded music was demonstrated. (No NIN or Insane Clown Posse played at those parties, I guess.) Lastly, the Diamond Disc used proprietary technology; the Edison discs couldn't be played on the Victor machines, and vice versa. We haven't learned much in that respect, it seems—Kindles, iPads, Pro Tools, MS Office software—the list of proprietary insanity is endless. It's a small comfort that such nonsense isn't new.

The Tone Tests themselves were public demonstrations in which a famous singer would appear onstage along with a Diamond Disc player playing a recording of that same singer singing the same song. The stage would be dark. What the audience heard would alternate between the sound of the disc and the live singer, and the audience had to guess which they were hearing. It worked—the public could not tell the difference. Or so we're told. The Tone Tests toured the country, like a traveling show or an early infomercial, and audiences were amazed and captivated.

We might wonder how this could be possible. Who remembers "Is it real or is it Memorex?" These early recorders had a very limited dynamic and frequency range; how could anyone really be fooled? Well, for starters, there was apparently a little stage trickery involved. The singers were instructed to try to sound like the recordings, to sing in a slightly pinched manner and with a limited range of volume. It took some practice before they could master it. (You have to wonder how audiences fell for this.)

Sociologist H. Stith Bennett suggests that over time we developed what he calls "recording consciousness," which means we internalize how the world sounds based on how recordings sound.[3] He claims that the parts of our brain that deal with hearing act as a filter and, based

EDISON
DIAMOND POINTS
for MAY 1916

Vol. 1   No. 6

ALBERT SPALDING—Master of Melody

on having heard lots of recorded sound, we simply don't hear things that don't fit that sonic template. In Bennett's view, the recording becomes the ur-text, replacing the musical score. He implies that this development might have led us to listen to music more closely. By extension, one might infer that all sorts of media, not just recordings, shape how we see and hear the real world; there is little doubt that our brains can and often do narrow the scope of what we perceive to the extent that things that happen right before our eyes sometimes don't register. In a famous experiment conducted by Christopher Chabris and Daniel Simons, participants were asked to count the number of passes made by a group of basketball players in a film. Halfway through the film, a guy in a full gorilla suit runs through the middle of the action, thumping his chest. When asked afterward if they saw or heard anything unusual, more than half didn't see the gorilla.

The gorilla deniers weren't lying; the gorilla simply never appeared to them. Things might impinge on our senses but still fail to register in the brain. Our internal filters are far more powerful than we might like to think. Sir Arthur Conan Doyle was convinced that what are to us obviously faked photos of fairies were in fact real fairies captured on film. He believed that the photo shown below was real until the end of his life.[B]

So the mind's eye (and ear) is a truly variable thing. What one person hears and sees is not necessarily what another perceives. Our own sensory organs, and thus even our interpretations of data and our readings of measurements on instruments, are wildly subjective.

Edison was convinced that his devices made what he referred to as "re-creations" of the actual performances, not mere recordings of them. Is there a difference? Edison thought there was. He felt that the mechanical nature of the recordings— sorry, re-creations—was truer in some sense than the Victor versions that used microphones and amplification, which he claimed inevitably "colored" the sound. Edison insisted that his recordings, in which the sound did not go through wires, were uncolored, and therefore truer. I'd offer that

they're both correct; both technologies color the sound, but in different ways. "Neutral" technology does not exist.

The trickery involved in the Tone Test performances was, it seems to me, an early example of the soon-to-be-common phenomenon of live music trying to imitate the sound of recordings. A sort of extension of Bennett's recording-consciousness idea mentioned above. As a creative process it seems somewhat backward and counterproductive, especially with the Edison version in which the pinched singing was encouraged, but we've now grown so accustomed to the sound of recordings that we do in fact expect a live show to sound pretty much like a record—whether it be an orchestra or a pop band—and that expectation makes no more sense now than it did then. It's not just that we expect to hear the same singer and arrangements that exist on our records, we expect everything to go through the same technological sonic filters—the pinched vocals of the Edison machines, the massive sub-bass of hip-hop recordings, or the perfect pitch of singers whose voices were corrected electronically in the recording process.

Here, then, is the philosophical parting of the ways in a nutshell. Should a recording endeavor to render reality as faithfully as possible, with no additions, coloration, or interference? Or do the inherent sonic biases and innate qualities of recording comprise an art unto itself? Of course I don't believe the Edison discs would fool anyone today, but the differing aspirations and ideals regarding recording still hold. This debate has not confined itself to sound recording. Film and other media are sometimes discussed with regard to their "accuracy," their ability to capture and reproduce what is true. The idea that somewhere out there exists one absolute truth implies a suspension of belief, which is an ideal for some, while for others admitting artificiality is more honest. Flashing back to the previous chapter, this reminds me of the difference between Eastern theater (more artificial and presentational) and Western (with its effort to be naturalistic).

We no longer expect that contemporary records are meant to capture a specific live performance—even a performance that may have happened in the artificial atmosphere of a recording studio. We may treasure jazz and other recordings from fifty years ago that captured a live performance, often in the studio, but now a "concert album" or an album of an artist playing live in the studio tends to be the exception. And yet—somewhat oddly, it seems to me—many recordings that are largely made up of obviously artificially generated sounds use those sounds in ways that mimic the way a "real" band might employ "real" instruments. Low electronic thuds imitate the effect of an acoustic kick drum, though now they appear to be coming from a virtual drum that sounds larger and tighter than anything physically possible, and synthesizers often play lines that oddly mimic, in range and texture, what a horn player might have done. They are not mimicking real instruments, but rather what real instruments do. One would assume, then, that the sonic tasks that "real" instruments once accomplished are still needs that have to be met. A sonic scaffolding has been maintained, despite the fact that the materials it is made of have been radically changed. Only the most experimental composers have made music that consists entirely of rumbles or high-pitched whines—music that doesn't recall or reference acoustic instruments in any way.

The "performances" captured on early wax discs were different both from what and how those same live bands were used to playing, as well as being different from what we think of as typical recording-studio practice today. For starters, there was one mic (or horn) available to record the whole band and singer, so rather than the band being arranged as they might have been on a bandstand or stage, they were arranged around the horn, positioned according to who most needed to be heard and who was loudest. The singer, for example, might be right in front of the recording horn, and then when a sax solo came up someone would yank the singer away from the horn and a hired shover would push the sax player into position. This jerky choreography would be reversed when the sax solo was over. And that's just one solo. A recording session might involve a whole little dance devised so that all the key parts were heard at the right times. Louis Armstrong, for example, had a loud and piercing trumpet tone, so he was sometimes positioned farther away from the recording horn than anyone else, by about fifteen feet. The main guy in the band was stuck in the back!

Drums and upright basses posed a big problem for these recording devices. The intermittent low frequencies that they produce made wider or deeper grooves (in the case of the Edison machines), which make the needles jump and skip during playback. So those instruments were also shoved to the rear, and in most cases were intentionally rendered almost inaudible. Blankets were thrown over drums, especially the kick and snare. Drummers were sometimes required to play bells, wood blocks, and the sides of their drums instead of the snares and kick drums—those thinner sounds didn't make the needles jump, but could still be heard. The double bass was often swapped with a tuba because its low end was less punchy. So early recording technology was limiting not only in terms of what frequencies one heard, but also in terms of which instruments were actually recorded. The music was already being edited and shaped to fit the new medium.

Recordings resulted in a skewed, inaccurate impression of music that wasn't already well-known. It would be more accurate to say that early jazz recordings were versions of that music. Musicians in other towns, hearing what these drummers and bass/tuba players were doing on the recordings, sometimes assumed that that was how the music was supposed to be played, and they began to copy those adaptations that had initially been made solely to accommodate the limitations of the technology. How could they know differently? Now we don't and can never know what those bands really sounded like—their true sound may have been "unrecordable." Our understanding of certain kinds of music, based on recordings anyway, is completely inaccurate.

Edison, meanwhile, continued to maintain that his recorders were capturing unadorned reality. In fact, he was quoted as saying that the recorders know more than you do, implying (accurately) that our ears and brains skew sound in various ways. He maintained, of course, that his recordings presented sound as it truly is.

We all know how weird it is to hear your own recorded voice—the discomforting aspect of this phenomena is often attributed to the fact that we hear ourselves, our voices, though the vibrations in our skulls as well as through our ears, and recordings can't capture these skull vibrations and osseous transmissions. The aspect of our voices that gets recorded is only a part of what we hear. But then there is also the inherent bias and sonic coloration added by microphones and the electronics that are involved in capturing our voices. No microphone is exactly like the human ear, but that isn't mentioned much. The sonic reality we experience via our senses is probably way different from what we hear in an "objective" recording. But, as mentioned above, our brains tend to make these disparate versions converge.

I have heard that Edison recorders aren't as shockingly biased as one might think, that in fact to hear one's own voice played back through an Edison machine is actually less strange than if one were to hear a recording made by a microphone. So there may be a grain of truth to Edison's claim, at least as far as the voice goes. He implied that it was like looking in a mirror. But now I begin to wonder, do mirrors even really reflect us, or are they skewed and biased? Is the face we see while shaving or putting on makeup really us, or is it our "mirror self," a self that—like audio recordings—we have come to be familiar with, but is in some ways equally inaccurate?

A Berlin-based company called Neumann recently came out with a device in which two microphones were placed inside the "ears" of a kind of mannequin head to better simulate the way our ears heard the world. *Binaural recording*, it was called. You had to listen to the recordings through headphones to get the effect. (I heard some of these recordings, and I didn't buy it.) The elusive quest for "capturing" reality never dies.

Phonographs (also known as gramophones) became increasingly popular in the early twentieth century. The early versions (after the ones that were only good enough to record talking) allowed owners to record their own musical performances. Some companies added interactive features to these machines. Here is an ad from a 1916 issue of *Vanity Fair* for something called the Graduola:

> To my friends and associates and indeed to myself, I've appeared until recently, simply a plain, middle-aged, unemotional businessman. And now I find that I'm a musician. How did I find this out? I'll tell you! Last Tuesday night, my wife and I were at the Joneses'.
>
> Jones had a new purchase—a phonograph. Personally, I'm prejudiced against musical machines. But this phonograph was different. With the first notes I sat upright in my chair. It was *beautiful*. "Come over here and sing this yourself!" said Jones. I went to see what the slender tube terminating in a handle [the Graduola] could be. It looked interesting. "Hold this in your hands!" said Jones. "Move the handle in to make the music louder; draw it out to make it softer." Then he started the record again. At first I hardly dared to move the little device in my hands. Presently, however, I

C

gained confidence. As the notes swelled forth and softly died away in answer to my will, I became bolder. I began to feel the music. It was wonderful! I . . . fairly trembled with the depth of emotion. The fact that I was—must be—a natural musician dawned upon me. And with it came a glimpse of the glorious possibilities opened to me by this great new phonograph.[4]

Great ad copy! The record player as orgasmatron!

Soon there was a flurry of recordings of school and parlor performers, sung greetings, holiday wishes, and all sorts of amateur performances. The early phonographs were like YouTube—everyone was swapping homemade audio recordings. Composers were even recording their playing and then playing along with themselves. Soon enough that function was taken away. I would be inclined to believe that this anti-participatory, non-egalitarian move by the manufacturers might have been urged by the newly emerging recording companies, who would have claimed that they weren't being evil but simply wanted to market "quality" recordings that would elevate the musical taste of their customers and the nation as a whole. Victor and Edison had "signed" a number of artists, and naturally they wanted you to buy their recordings, not make your own. The battle between amateurs and "professionals" isn't new; it has been fought (and often lost) many times over.

John Philip Sousa, the march king, was opposed to recorded music. He saw the new music machines as a substitute for human beings. In a 1906 essay entitled "The Menace of Mechanical Music," he wrote, "I foresee a marked deterioration in American music and musical taste... in this twentieth century come these talking and playing machines that offer to reduce the expression of music to a mathematical system of megaphones, wheels, cogs, discs, cylinders and all manner of revolving things."[5] God save us from revolving things!

He's not totally crazy, though. Despite his Luddite ravings, I tend to agree that any tendency to turn the public into passive consumers rather than potentially active creators is to be viewed with suspicion. However, the public tends to surprise us by finding ways to create using whatever means are available to them. Some creative urges seem truly innate and will find a means of expression, a way out, no matter if traditional means are denied to us.

Sousa and many others also deplored that music was becoming less public. It was moving off the bandstand (where Sousa was king) and into the living room. Experiencing music used to *always* be something you did with a group of other people, but now you could experience it (or a re-creation of it, as Edison would have it) alone. Shades of the Walkman and the iPod! To some, this was horrific. It was like drinking alone, they said; it was antisocial and psychologically dangerous. It was described as self-stimulation!

In his book *Capturing Sound: How Technology Has Changed Music*, Mark Katz quotes Orlo Williams, who wrote in 1923, "You would look twice to see whether some other person were not hidden in some corner of the room, and if you found no such one would painfully blush, as if you had discovered your friend sniffing cocaine, emptying a bottle of whisky, or plaiting straws in his hair." Williams noted that we think people should not do things "to themselves."[6] It was as if the individual had selfishly decided to have a strong emotional experience, maybe even over and over again, whenever they felt like it, just by putting on a record, stimulated by a machine—there was something wrong with it!

One might think that these same worrywarts would also disdain recordings on the basis that they sacrifice the visual elements inherent to performance—the costumes and sets of grand opera, the hubbub and smells of a music hall, or the stately atmosphere at the symphony—but that was not always the case. The twentieth-century philosopher Theodor Adorno, who wrote great quantities of music criticism (and tended to dislike popular music), thought that removing music from the accompanying visual spectacle was sometimes a good thing. You could, in his view, appreciate the music more objectively, without the often tacky trappings of performance. Jascha Heifetz, the classical violinist, was a notoriously unexpressive presence on-stage; he was described as being stiff, immobile, cold. But by listening with one's eyes closed, or to a recording, one could discern the deep feeling in what might have previously seemed a soulless performance. Of course, the sound itself didn't change, but our perception of it did—by *not* seeing, we could hear in a different way.

With the ascendance of radio in the twenties, people had another way to experience music. With radio, one definitely needed a microphone to capture the music, and the sound went through a whole lot of other electrical transmutations before the listener heard it. That said, mostly people really liked what they heard on the radio; the music was louder than on the Edison players, for starters, and there was more low end. People liked it so much that they demanded that live acts should "sound more like the radio."

What has happened is to some extent what Sousa feared: we now think of the sound of recordings when we think of a song or piece of music, and the live performance of that same piece is now considered an interpretation of the recorded version. What was originally a simulation of a performance—the recording—has supplanted performances, and performances are now considered the simulation. It seemed to some that the animating principle of music was being replaced by a more perfect, but slightly less soulful, machine.

Katz details how recording technology changed music over the century of its existence. He cites examples of how instrument playing and singing changed as recordings and radio broadcasts became more ubiquitous. Vibrato, the slight wavering in pitch, is often employed by contemporary string players, and it is a good example of the effect of recordings, because it's something we take for granted as always having been there. We tend to think, "That's how violin players play. That's the nature of how one plays that instrument." It wasn't, and it's not. Katz contends that before the advent of recording, vibrato added to a note was considered kitschy, tacky, and was universally frowned upon, unless one absolutely had to use it when playing in the uppermost registers. Vibrato as a technique, whether employed in a vocal performance or with a violin, helps mask pitch discrepancies, which might explain why it was considered "cheating." As recording became more commonplace in the early part of the twentieth century, it was found that by using a bit more vibrato, not only could the volume of the instrument be increased (very important when there was only one mic or a single huge horn to capture an orchestra or ensemble), but the pitch—now painfully and permanently apparent—could be smudged by adding the wobble. The perceptibly imprecise pitch of a string instrument with no frets could be compensated for with this little wobble. The mind of the listener "wants" to hear the correct pitch, so the brain "hears" the right pitch among the myriad vaguenesses of pitch created by players using vibrato. The mind fills in the blanks, as it does with the visual gaps between movie and video frames, in which a series of stills creates the impression of seamless movement. Soon enough, conventional wisdom reversed itself, and now people find listening to classical string playing without vibrato to be painful and weird.

I suspect that the exact same thing happened with opera singers. I have some recordings made at the very beginning of the recording era, and their use of vibrato is much, much less frequent than what is common nowadays. Their singing is somewhat closer to what we might call pop singing today. Well, not exactly, but I find it more accessible and less off-putting than the fuzzy, wobbly pitching typical of contemporary opera singers, who sometimes exaggerate the vibrato so much you hardly know what note they're supposed to be hitting unless you know the song already. (Further proof that the mind of the listener "hears" the melody it wants to hear.) Again, it's assumed now that wobbly is how opera is supposed to be sung, but it's not. It's a relatively recent—and in my opinion, ugly—development forced upon music by recording technology.

Other changes in classical music were not quite as noticeable. Tempos became somewhat more precise with recording technology. Without the "distraction" of visual elements in a performance, unsteady tempos and rhythms can sound pretty damn sloppy and are rudely apparent, so players eventually learned to play to a consistent interior metronome. Well, they tried to, anyway.

This is an issue with pop and rock bands, too. My former bandmate Jerry Harrison has produced a number of first albums by rock bands, and he has observed more than once that the biggest and often primary hurdle is getting the band to play in time. This makes it sound like emerging bands are sloppy amateurs, which is not exactly true. They may sound perfectly fine in a club, or even in a concert hall, where all the other elements—the visuals, the audience, the beer—conspire to help one ignore the lurching and shaking. According to Jerry, the inaccuracies become all too obvious in the studio and make for a slightly seasick listening experience. He had to become very good at finding workarounds or devising rhythmic training wheels for bands who were new to recording.

One wonders if the visual element of performing in the pre-recording era inevitably allowed for more error, and if it made listeners more forgiving. If you can see someone performing, you're slightly less critical of missteps in timing and pitch. The sound in live venues is also never as good as it is on a record (well, hardly ever), but we mentally fix the acoustic faults of these rooms—maybe with help from those visual cues—and sometimes we find that a live experience is more moving than a recording, contrary to Adorno's theory. In many concert halls we simply don't "hear" the slightly exaggerated echo in the low frequencies, for example. Our brains make it more pleasing, more like what we believe it should be—like the pitch of a violin played with vibrato. (Well, we do this up to a point; the sound in some rooms is beyond saving.) Somehow it's harder to do that mental repair work with a recording.

Hearing a recording of a live performance one has witnessed and enjoyed can prove disappointing. An experience that was auditory, visual, and social has now been reduced to something coming out of stereo speakers or headphones. In performance, sound comes from an infinite number of points—even if the performer is in front of you, the sound is bouncing off walls and ceilings, and that's part of the experience. It might not make the performance "better" in a technical sense, but it is absolutely more enveloping. Various people have attempted to bridge these irreconcilable differences, and some odd hybrids, as well as wonderful developments, have resulted.

In his book *Perfecting Sound Forever,* Greg Milner argues that the conductor Leopold Stokowski was a visionary who changed the way orchestral music sounded over the radio and on recordings. He loved the idea of amplifying classical music; he felt it made it bigger.[7] His stated ambition was ultimately to use technology to get the compositions to sound *better* than what the composer had originally conceived. There's a little hubris involved there, but I don't think too many composers complained. Rather than having pushers and shovers, as the early recording studios had, Stokowski conscripted studio technicians to move the mics around during the recordings of orchestras. Anticipating a countermelody from the French horns, for example, he'd signal a mic to be wheeled into position in time for their "solo." He realized—as film-sound recorders and mixers do—that we hear with all our senses in a live situation, and to just stick a mic up and expect it to capture what we have experienced, well, that wasn't going to happen. Recreating the subjective "experience" meant one had to do more than that.

In a live situation, the ear can psychoacoustically zoom in on a sound or isolate a section of players and pick out a phrase or melody—the way we can pick out a conversation at a noisy dinner table if we can see the person talking. Stokowski recognized this phenomenon and made adjustments to help bridge that perceptual gap. All of his innovations aimed to get the *experience* on disc, and possibly even surpass it, by, for example, exaggerating dynamics and shifting perspectives.

Sometimes he went the other way: rather than exaggerating, he would attempt to mask some aspect of the original. At one point he proposed that a big problem inherent in opera performances could now be solved. He pointed out that "the lady who plays the part live may sing like a nightingale but she looks like an elephant." Stokowski suggested that svelte actresses learn to lip-synch to pre-recorded vocals so that the opera visuals could finally match the composer's intention. I saw this done once for a filmed version of Wagner's *Parsifal* directed by Hans-Jürgen Syberberg. He had great actresses and actors playing the parts, lip-synching to great singers. I thought it worked, but this approach never caught on.

FROZEN ARCHITECTURE

Recordings freeze music and allow it to be studied. Young jazz players used to listen to Louis Armstrong's recorded solos over and over until they figured out what he was doing. Later, amateur guitarists would use recordings to break down Hendrix and Clapton solos in the same way. Tenor saxophonist Bud Freeman found that listening to other players in clubs was too distracting—he preferred records. With a recording you could stop time by stopping the record, or you could make time repeat by playing part of a song over and over again. The ineffable was coming under human control.

But learning from records has its limitations. Ignacio Varchausky from the Buenos Aires tango orchestra El Arranque says in the documentary *Si Sos Brujo* that he and others tried learning from records how the older orchestras did what they did, but it was difficult, almost impossible. Eventually, El Arranque had to find the surviving players from those ensembles and ask them how it was done. The older players had to physically show the younger players how to replicate the effects they got, and which notes and beats should be emphasized. So, to some extent, music is still an oral (and physical) tradition, handed down from one person to another. Records may do a lot to preserve music and disseminate it, but they can't do what direct transmission does. In that same documentary, Wynton Marsalis says that the learning, the baton passing, happens on the bandstand—one has to play with others, to learn by watching and imitating. For Varchausky, when those older players are gone, the traditions (and techniques) will be lost if their knowledge is not passed on directly. History and culture can't really be preserved by technology alone.[8]

Recordings uproot music from their place of origin. They allow far-flung artists and foreign genres to be heard in other parts of the world, and these artists sometimes find a wider audience than they ever imagined they could have. John Lomax and his son Alan traveled thousands of miles to record the music of the American South. Initially they used a large and bulky disc recorder. This would be like having a mastering lab in the back of your station wagon, but it was as portable as one could get at the time, if you could call something the size of a small refrigerator portable.

In one instance, John and Alan went to a Texas plantation to record the black "residents" who would, they hoped, sing for them. The fact that those men could be "commanded" to sing might have been the primary reason to go there, but their experience did prove to be enlightening in a way that they hadn't expected. They were looking for someone who could sing the song "Stagolee." It seems slightly suspicious to me that these guys already knew what they wanted—how do you find the unexpected if you know what you want? Milner tells the story like this:

A murmur went through the crowd and soon became a unanimous chorus. "Send Blue!" "Blue knows more about Stagolee than ol' Stag himself!" "Blue, white man ain't gonna hurt you! What you scared of? That horn too little for you to fall into it—too little for you to sing at with your big mouth!" The man named Blue stood up. He certainly deserves the name, Alan thought as Blue walked toward him. The man's skin was so dark it looked blue-back. "Can you sing 'Stagolee'?" Alan asked. "Yessuh," Blue replied. "I knows ol' 'Stagolee,' and I'll sing it for you." He paused. "If you allow me to sing another song first." "Well," Alan stammered, "we would like to hear it first, because we don't have very many unused cylinders…" "No, sir," Blue said, picking up and adjusting the recording horn. "I won't sing my song but once. You've gotta catch it the first time I sing it." Alan relented, and switched on the machine. Blue began to sing: *Poor farmer, poor farmer, poor farmer / They get all the farmer makes / His clothes is full of patches, his hat is full of holes / Stoopin' down, pickin' cotton, from off the cotton bolls...* As he sang, he looked at the plantation manager. The crowd's nervous laughter grew to a roar as Blue continued: *Poor farmer, poor farmer, poor farmer / They get all the farmer makes, / At the commissary, his money in their bags / His poor little wife and children, sit at home in rags.* When he was done, Blue received a standing ovation. But he wasn't finished yet. He motioned to Alan to keep the machine running, looked straight at the horn, and delivered a spoken coda. "Now, Mr. President," he said, "you just don't know how bad they're treating us folks down here. I'm singing to you, and I'm talking to you, so I hope you will come down here and do something for us poor folks down here in Texas." As the crowd cheered, Alan adjusted the machine to play back the recording. People shushed each other as Blue's scratchy voice emerged from the horn. "That thing sure talks sense!" someone yelled.[9]

Blue understood the power of recording, that it could travel to places he could not, and be heard by people he would never meet—like the president. The disenfranchised and invisible could be heard with this new machine. Alan Lomax liked the idea that the recorder could be a means by which these invisible people could be given a voice.

The Lomaxes endeavored to facilitate the spread of this music, though whether they really were helping in the way they thought they were might seem debatable now. Daddy Lomax in particular had disturbing ideas about how best to "help" his subjects. Huddie Ledbetter, better known as Leadbelly, was a singer and guitar player the Lomaxes met in a Southern prison. Leadbelly's talent was recognized by many who heard recordings of him, however John Lomax in particular had a thing about what he considered to be "authentic." Leadbelly was an all-around artist who loved to play pop songs as well as rawer, more folky material. Lomax forbade him to play the pop stuff when he took him up to New York to perform for the sophisticated big-city folks. He wanted to present a "raw Negro," an authentic primitive, straight from prison, for New Yorkers to gawk at—and appreciate as well. He even had Leadbelly dress in overalls when he performed, as if he had no other clothes to wear. (Huddie actually preferred suits.) While Lomax wanted to make sure to show how good a player Leadbelly was, he didn't want him to sound too good, too slick. On the Lomax recordings this roughness was a stamp of authenticity. So although these recordings did allow this "hidden" music from Mississippi, Louisiana, and elsewhere to be heard, there was no possibility of objectivity when it was removed from its context. Show business (yes, this "scientific" folklore collecting might be viewed as a fairly peculiar and prescribed form of show business) took over, and simulated authenticity became a common tool of presenters—and sometimes of artists, too—it's shades of Buffalo Bill and Geronimo and later Bob Dylan, taking on the persona of an innocent yet perceptive country boy. In later years, Alan Lomax in particular was dismayed as the recording world came to be dominated by a few large companies. He saw people being robbed of their voices, and the musical landscape flattened. He was right. Inevitably, recorded music was a branch of proto-globalization—a process that could uncover hidden gems while at the same time flattening them out.

HOW LONG IS A SONG?

Katz asserts that the limited running time of 78s (and later of 45s) changed writing styles. Recording discs were limited to fewer than four minutes (more like 3½ minutes for 45s) a side, which prodded songwriters to shorten their compositions. A three-to-four-minute song seems a natural length to me—it often seems almost inevitable. I can hardly conceive a time when it might have been otherwise. But maybe, as some suggest, we have all internalized this arbitrary aspect of recorded music and now find the exceptions strange and unusual. I remind myself that even folk and blues songs, some of them centuries old, don't stretch on endlessly, and most don't have too many verses—that's how I justify the omnipresent 3½ minute song to myself. Then I realize that some ballads were much, much longer. Epic verse, whether European, Asian, or African, was often delivered in a kind of chant, and a single piece could go on for hours. While shorter forms, like Shakespeare's sonnets, might be closer to what we now view as songs, 3½ minutes is not a universal song length.

Perhaps this is a case where the technology and the circumstances of its wide acceptance conveniently happened to fit a preexisting form like a glove, and that would explain why the technology became so popular. Everyone instinctively knew exactly what to do with it and how to make it part of their lives. Katz says that Adorno didn't like this time-limiting aspect of recording technology; the grumpy Adorno called it *atomized listening*. Adorno suggests that our musical attention spans became shorter as a response to the limited length of recordings. A kind of ADD form of listening was ushered in, and we have come to expect everything musical to be broken down—atomized—into three-to-four-minute chunks. Even longer pieces now had to advance in bite-size steps, Adorno claims, because a piece that develops slowly risked losing our interest.

I can't disagree with that assessment, but I also sense a counter-tendency afoot, an acceptance of musical works that are exactly the opposite: long and textured, rather than melodic; enveloping and atmospheric as opposed to episodic and hierarchical. I'll get to those new developments in a later chapter.

IMPROVISATION BECOMES COMPOSITION

Recording technology had a huge influence on both jazz and classical players. While performing, jazzers would stretch out a tune or theme as long as they or their audience felt like, or, more practically, as long as the dancers were encouraging them. Soloing for thirty-two choruses was not unheard of (basically, jamming on a song thirty-two times in a row), but that would be way too long on a record, so they edited themselves. The recorded versions of their compositions became more concise, and what was previously largely improvised music began to become more "composed." The "tightened" versions of their solos were soon what they played more often. Sections that used to sound different every time now always sounded pretty much the same. I'd argue that for some jazz musicians this was not a bad thing—forced brevity became a restriction that encouraged rigor, focus, creative editing, and structuring. In recording, the dynamic differences between loud and soft sections also needed to be minimized. Such restrictions had the side effect of once again splitting musical creation in two; what worked best for a live performance and what worked best for recordings was not always the same thing.

Music was getting smoothed out, not always for the worse, I'd say, and there would be periodic reactions against this tendency. It's no wonder that many came to believe that roughness and inaccuracy were positive values; they came to represent authenticity and a resistance to the commercial steamroller of smoothness.

Though classical pieces still tended to be longer than what recordings could accommodate at the time, even those composers began to adjust to the new technology: they would write transitions that corresponded to the moment one was supposed to flip over the 78. Stravinsky's "Serenade for Piano" had four movements, which he wrote so that they would each fit onto one side of a record. Decrescendos (a sort of fade out) were incorporated into the music that would occur at the end of one side, and then a crescendo would ramp up on the flip side, so that there would be a smooth transition after you turned the record over. Some composers were criticized for writing graceless transitions, when actually they were merely guilty of not compromising their creativity to better fit the new medium. Ellington began to write "suites" whose sections cleverly accommodated the length of a three- or four-minute recording. This didn't work for everyone. Jazz teacher and author of Remembering Bix Ralph Berton describes how jazz cornetist and composer Bix Beiderbecke hated making records: "For a musician with a lot to say it was like telling Dostoevsky to do the *Brothers Karamazov* as a short story."[10]

THE NEW WORLD

Records were fairly cheap for much of the twentieth century—cheaper than a concert ticket. And as they became more widely available, people in small towns, farmers, and kids in school could now hear giant orchestras, the most famous singers of the day, or music from their distant homeland—even if they'd never have the opportunity to hear any of those things live. Not only could recordings bring distant musical cultures in touch with one another, they also had the effect of disseminating the work and performances of singers, orchestras, and performers *within* a culture. As I suspect has happened to all of us at some point, hearing a new and strange piece of music for the first time often opens a door that you didn't even know was there. I remember as a tween hearing "Mr. Tambourine Man" by the Byrds and, as would happen again and again over the years, it was as if a previously hidden part of the world had been suddenly revealed. This music not only sounded different, it was *socially* different. It implied that there was a whole world of people out there who lived different lives and had different values from the people I knew in Arbutus, Maryland. The world was suddenly a bigger, more mysterious, and more exciting place—all because I'd stumbled onto some recording.

Music tells us things—social things, psychological things, physical things about how we feel and perceive our bodies—in a way that other art forms can't. It's sometimes in the words, but just as often the content comes from a combination of sounds, rhythms, and vocal textures that communicate, as has been said by others, in ways that bypass the reasoning centers of the brain and go straight to our emotions. Music, and I'm not even talking about the lyrics here, tells us how other people view the world—people we have never met, sometimes people who are no longer alive—and it tells it in a non-descriptive way. Music *embodies* the way those people think and feel: we enter into new worlds—their worlds— and though our perception of those worlds might not be 100 percent accurate, encountering them can be completely transformative.

This process of unexpected inspiration flows in multiple directions—out from a musical source to a composer, and then sometimes back to that source again. The European composer Darius Milhaud treasured his collection of "black jazz" recordings. No one would confuse the music Milhaud wrote with that of the jazz players he was listening to, but I'm guessing that the music unlocked something in him that allowed a new direction to be realized in his own work. I wouldn't be surprised at all if Milhaud's compositions found their way to the ears of later jazz composers, effectively making a complete loop. Early British rockers were all inspired by recordings of (mostly black) American musicians and singers. Many of those American singers would never have been able to perform in Liverpool or Manchester (though a few did tour the UK), but their recordings went where they could not. To some extent, those British musicians did initially mimic their American idols; some of them tried to sing like black men from the South or from Chicago. If US radio and concerts hadn't been as segregated as they were (and still are, to a large extent), there would have been no space for these Brits to squeeze through. To their credit, they eventually abandoned the mimicry and found their own voices, and many paid tribute to the musicians who influenced them, which brought them attention that they'd never had before. Another loop of influence and inspiration occurred when African musicians imitated the imported Cuban recordings they heard—which were themselves a mutation of African music. The African guitar-based rhumba that resulted was something new and wonderful, and most folks hearing it wouldn't think it was a poor imitation of Cuban music at all. When I heard some of those African bands, I had no idea that Cuban music had been their inspiration. What they were doing sounded completely original to me, and I was naturally inspired, just as they had been. The process never stops. Contemporary European DJs were blown away when they heard Detroit techno. This process of influence and inspiration wasn't the result of corporate marketing or promotion, it was musicians themselves who usually stumbled upon what were often obscure recordings that opened their ears.

Recordings aren't time sensitive. You can hear the music you want whether it's morning, noon, or the middle of the night. You can "get into" clubs virtually, "sit" in concert halls you can't afford to visit, go to places that are too far away, or hear people sing about things you don't understand, about lives that are alien, sad, or wonderful. Recorded music can be ripped free from its context, for better and worse. It becomes its own context.

The jazz soloing that had evolved in response to those dancers in juke joints could now be heard rattling the teacups in distant living rooms and parlors. It was as if, as the result of watching television, we eventually came to expect ordinary conversation to be as witty and snappy as sitcom banter. As if that reality supplanted our lived reality. Had recordings done the same thing to music? Everyone knows sitcom dialogue isn't how people talk, don't they? Don't people know that recordings aren't "real" either?

TECHNO UTOPIANISM PART 1

In 1927, *The Jazz Singer*, the film in which Al Jolson sang in sync with the picture for some scenes, changed the idea of sound in movies. All the studios wanted sound now. In 1926, AT&T created a new division, Electrical Research Products Inc. (ERPI), to soundify theaters, not just in North America but around the world.

An essay by Emily Thompson called "Wiring the World" tells the story of this relatively short-lived organization. Thompson says that the technicians and engineers of ERPI saw their goal as more than just a technical accomplishment; they attached an ideological, cultural, and even moral aspect to their mission. To prepare themselves, the ERPI team was first given "aural training," which meant some lessons in theater acoustics, sound reinforcement, and learning how to keep the sound of streetcars and subways out of the theaters. ERPI's newsletter, *The Erpigram*, painted a vivid picture: "Each man has been equipped with a large fibre knapsack in which to carry his equipment... the kit also contained a cap pistol to 'hunt out reverberation, and his echoes, and banish him from the theater.'"[11]

I prefer to imagine this aural training as something more esoteric, an intensive course in listening, learning to hear, and practicing focusing one's ears. I can picture a group of uniformed men, heads slightly forward, brows furrowed, listening intently, communicating with each other through hand signals in perfect silence. The skills they were developing were, in my version, almost mystical, in that they might have been training themselves to be able to hear things the rest of us would miss or to become aware of sounds that we would hear only subconsciously. Like some acoustic Sherlock Holmes, they could survey a room with their ears and be able to tell you things about it, even what was going on outside of it—things that ordinary mortals without their special powers would miss. But, as with Holmes's explanations, it would all seem obvious once it was revealed to us by the ERPI master. While the listening training may have been important, in truth much of what they were assigned to do was pretty prosaic: wiring and hanging drapes to muffle echoes and help with soundproofing.

Thompson writes about an ERPI team in Canton, Ohio, who heard a roaring sound coming from somewhere near the screen, and of course they had to track it down, find its source, and eliminate the offending noise. After "considerable time spent tracking the noise through the circuit," they looked behind the screen to find six caged lions belonging to the circus.

ERPI was more than a little evangelical. Much like our present-day techno-utopians, they believed that there would be all kinds of profound repercussions and knock-on effects (many of them completely unrelated to sound) around the world as theaters were converted to sound. In the early days of cinema, America was the primary source of films, so it was imagined that along with movies, American values—democracy, capitalism, free speech, and all the rest—would go along for the ride. Talkies would bring "civilization" to the rest of the world! ("Civilization" being defined rather parochially, as it often is. One hears the same claims today being made for Facebook and all the other new technologies—that they will "bring democracy to the world." Hell, they haven't brought democracy to the USA!) Interesting that "mere" film-sound technology was presumed to carry so much of this baggage.

The Erpigram published a poem expressing ERPI's hopes and aspirations:

The Chinaman rejects his jos
The Jap his hari kiri
Mahomet's stocks are wearing thin
For ERPI is established in
The Lands of Rice and Curry!
Quite soon among the Eskimos
The fetish will be known
While mid-equator cannibals
Leave their cooking pots and Anabelles
To hear the white sheet groan!
Where nations lack a common bond
And hate grows like a cancer
Who'll banish ignorance and strife And give the world new lease on life?
Why ERPI—is the answer![12]

Thompson writes, "The [evangelical] language became military, and a little sexual—the engineers were referred to as the American Expeditionary Force...and as shock troops... also as American Experts... The headline as a theater in Cairo was being equipped for sound was 'Africa Falls Under ERPI's Advance.'"[13]

This techno-crusade assumed that influence would essentially flow one way, from the United States to all the other nations of the world, which would naturally become willing and happy consumers of superior American products. And that's precisely what happened at first, because few countries had native film industries, and none of those had sound technology. In India they were treated to *Melody of*

Love and in Fiji to *Abie's Irish Rose;* folks in Shanghai got *Rio Rita* and *Hollywood Revue.* Only the very best in American culture.

This state of affairs didn't last long. The French, unsurprisingly, took offense at English blasting out of their cinemas, and they destroyed a theater. Aspiring Indian filmmakers quickly learned how to use sound technology and began making their own movies. Before long, India was the largest movie-producing country in the world. Movie studios equipped for sound also opened in Germany and Brazil, where a factory producing lightweight musicals churned out films for decades. As with most missionary initiatives, the final result was not exactly what had been intended. Instead of global hegemony and standardization, sound in films allowed hundreds of cultures to find their own cinematic voices. In fact, some argue that it was the homegrown Indian cinema that forced that country's citizens to learn a common language, which may have helped Indians find national identity as much as the efforts of Gandhi did. And that common language eventually enabled the unity that led to the ouster of the British Empire.

BEYOND PERFORMANCE: TAPE RECORDING

Milner tells the curious history of the advent of recording tape—the next medium on which sound would be captured. The sequence of events that led to the adoption of tape is so accidental and convoluted that its invention and adoption were far from inevitable.

Just before World War II, Jack Mullin, an engineer from California, tried record-ing onto various mediums other than discs, but with limited fidelity or success. When he was stationed overseas during the war, he sometimes heard broadcasts of radio programs featuring German symphonies. Nothing unusual about that: lots of radio stations had their own orchestras that played live in large studios or theaters, and those performances were primarily broadcast live. The odd thing was, these "performances" were happening in the wee hours of the morning, and Mullin heard them when he was working late. So unless Hitler was commanding orchestras to perform in the middle of the night, Mullin's only conclusion was that the Germans somehow had developed machines that could record orchestras with such fidelity that on playback they sounded live.

Through a happy accident, Mullin ended up in Germany right after the end of the war, and someone said that those radio transmissions had come from a town near where they were stationed. Mullin went to look, and sure enough, there were a couple of tape machines that had been modified in such a way that their fidelity vastly improved on what any other existing technology could achieve. Germany's technical innovations, like its rocket technology, were now free for the taking, so Mullin dismantled one of the machines and had the parts sent to his mother's house in Mill Valley.

When he got back to California, he reassembled the machine, and in the process figured out what the Germans had done. Among other things, they had added a "bias tone" to the recordings—a frequency you can't hear but that somehow makes all the audible frequencies "stick" better. Mullin eventually put these machines to work, and he discovered that in addition to being a good recording medium, tape also opened up some unexpected possibilities.[D] If a radio announcer flubbed a line, Mullin could edit out the mistake by splicing the tape. You couldn't do anything like that on disc! If a comedian didn't get the same laughs he got on his run-through, then, assuming the run-through had been recorded, the laughter from that performance could be spliced into the "real" performance. The birth of the laugh track! Furthermore, laughs could be reused. "Canned" laughter could be added to any recorded program if the live audience didn't yuk it up sufficiently.

The use of editing and splicing meant that a "recording" no longer necessarily represented a single performance, or at least it didn't have to. The beginning of a song, for example, could be from one "take" and the end from a take done hours later. The broadcast version could even be the result of performances that had been done in many different places spliced together. The elements of a "performance" no longer had to be rooted in contiguous time or space.

After seeing a presentation by Mullin of his tape recording device, Alexander Poniatoff formed a company, Ampex, to make more tape machines based on Mullin's design. The banks, however, wouldn't give Ampex the loans it needed in order to get things up and running—constructing the early machines required considerable capital—so it looked bad for the future of tape recording.

Around this time, Bing Crosby, the singer who had mastered an innovative use of microphones, was getting tired of having to do his very successful radio show live every day. Bing wanted to spend more time playing golf, but because his shows had to be done live, his time on the links was limited. Crosby realized that by using these new machines to record his shows, he could conceivably tape a couple of shows in one day and then play golf while the shows were being broadcast. No one would know the shows weren't live. He asked ABC radio if they would agree to the plan, but when they saw Poniatoff's "factory"—which was a complete shambles, with parts scattered all over—they said no way. So Crosby wrote a personal check to Ampex that guaranteed the machines would start getting built. They did, and after Crosby's initial order, ABC soon ordered twenty more. The era of tape recording, and all the possibilities that went with it, was under way.

GLENN GOULD'S PROPHECY

Some years later, after the tricks and techniques that tape recording made possible began to be more widely used, the Canadian pianist Glenn Gould wrote a manifesto, *The Prospects of Recording*, that expressed his perspective on recorded music and performance. Like Crosby, he was annoyed by the restraints and limitations of having to perform live, and he eventually retired from the stage completely—though not to play golf. Gould's manifesto was both prescient and way off base.

For example, Gould predicted that live concerts would be more or less a thing of the past by the end of the twentieth century. This didn't happen, but the fact that we often think of recordings as a more definitive version of a piece of music than a live performance indicates that Gould wasn't necessarily completely wrong. To the great dismay of some classical listeners, Gould embraced tape technology. He began to create "perfect" performances by editing takes together, and as a result his dissatisfaction with live performance—his own especially—increased. He felt that there was an unfortunate temptation for live performers to woo the audience, to pander to their desires, and one presumes this expression of disdain meant that he believed the music suffered as a result. I can see his point. I've been to performances, usually of pop music, where the desire of the performer to please the audience becomes such an integral part of the show, and eventually so annoying, that I can't hear the music anymore.

On the flip side, I've been to performances where the performer attempts to go into a trance and ends up ignoring the audience completely, possibly in order to give a deeper and more perfect rendition of a song or piece of music. When that happens I feel I may as well go home and put on a recording of the same music, which usually sounds better anyway. In that sense I agree with Gould—if the goal of your performance is perfection, then maybe that's better achieved in the studio, with the help of tape editing and splicing.

Gould wasn't alone. He writes about fellow classical artist Robert Craft, who "seems to feel that his audience—sitting at home, close up to the speaker—is prepared to allow him to dissect his music and to present it to them from a strongly biased conceptual viewpoint, which the private and concentrated circumstances of their listening make feasible."[14] He seems to be implying that Craft, too, realized that many music fans now got their music from the record player or the stereo console, and thus changed the way his recordings were produced and the way the music on them was arranged, so that a listener in a living room would have a more perfect experience.

There were and are dissenters to these new uses of tape. The shit really hit the fan when someone was brought in to sing a high note on an opera recording that the principal singer missed or couldn't reach. It was considered blasphemy, and this was way before Milli Vanilli got "busted" for not singing on "their own" records. I would agree that there's deception at work when the "singer" isn't actually doing the singing and we aren't informed of that fact, and it's not part of the conceptual framework. When I'm on the road performing, the band and crew are often outspokenly critical of other touring acts whose backing singers (or even lead singers) are on "tape," or those who have hidden extra "bandmembers" in the basements of the venues. That said, a playback show can have an integrity all its own. There are no hard and fast rules as far as I'm concerned.

Gould foresaw much of what we do today that was facilitated by tape recording as creation and as a way of composing. After he retired from the stage, he branched out from making classical records and did some innovative radio programs for the CBC, one of which, *The Idea of North*, is partly a multilayered audio collage of voices and sounds that could only have been created using tape and its editing possibilities. It's a wonderful piece. Milton Babbitt, the electronic-music composer, carried this idea to its logical conclusion:

> I can't believe that people really prefer to go to the concert hall under intellectually trying, socially trying, physically trying conditions, unable to repeat [replay] something they have missed, when they can sit home under the most comfortable and stimulating circumstances and hear it as they want to hear it.[15]

INSTRUMENT TECHNOLOGY AND ITS INFLUENCE ON MUSIC

Leo Theremin invented his eponymous electronic instrument in 1920. 1920! The theremin wasn't widely heard until it was featured in a number of movies, such as *Spellbound* in 1945 and *The Day the Earth Stood Still* in 1951, and eventually in the Beach Boys song "Good Vibrations." The instrument is notoriously difficult to play, as the player doesn't actually touch it (you control volume and pitch by proximity of a body part—usually your hands), and maybe this was why the theremin didn't catch on like he thought it deserved to. Though Theremin was Russian, one could say that this instrument, and some other electronic instruments and samplers that followed, had no national or cultural provenance. They didn't emerge out of an ongoing musical tradition, and they weren't better suited to play music of one tradition over another. Organs, for example, emerged from liturgical music, and as with most Western instruments, they play Western scales and tuning easily, and anything else with great difficulty. You press a key on these instruments and you're automatically in the world of Western music—no variations of pitch or bending of notes is possible. The theremin offered up less culturally specific options. You could play pitches in between standard Western pitches and you could bend notes and slide up and down. But the difficulty in mastering the instrument kept a large number of musicians from utilizing those capabilities. The adoption of instruments with no cultural baggage would have to wait.

In the thirties, a number of inventors independently developed a way to electrically amplify guitars. (Theoretically their process could be applied to any instrument with steel strings—a piano, for example—but these guys were guitar players, and their tweaks, innovations, and prototypes could be conveniently made in their home workshops.) Unamplified guitars and some other instruments were getting drowned out in bands of the day. Horns and pianos are much louder acoustically, and though placing a mic in front of the guitar player works to remedy this, there was the risk of feedback—the howling sound of the amplified guitar "feeding back" into its microphone. Some early electric guitars were basically microphones shoved into the sound hole of the guitar or clipped over the bridge, and they did sound louder, but they didn't solve the feedback problem. Transducer-type pickups, which respond to physical vibrations, worked a little better. Rickenbacker made a guitar in 1931 out of solid aluminum (it must have been incredibly heavy) that was nicknamed "the frying pan."

In 1935, Rickenbacker made another one out of Bakelite—a kind of plastic more often used for telephones and Kalashnikov rifles. The first commercial recordings of these instruments were of Hawaiian music. Later, a new instrument called the lap steel (essentially a guitar neck that you lay across your lap and play with a metal slide) was adopted by Western swing bands. Jazz musicians and virtuosos like Charlie Christian picked up the electric guitar, and one could argue that without this technology Christian's playing would never have been heard. Blues musicians found that the increased volume of the electric guitars worked great—they could now be heard in noisy clubs.

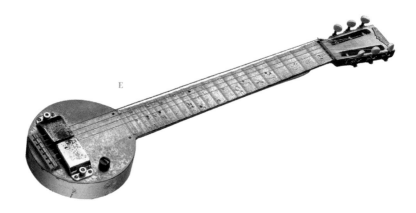

E

Guitar pickups were mostly magnetic at first. A pickup developed in 1940 sensed the vibration of each of the steel strings individually, and a small amplifier boosted the level of that signal so that the guitar player could finally compete with the rest of the band. Guitar makers assumed that since the pickup was only sensing vibrating metal strings and not "hearing" the acoustic sound of the guitar, one could eliminate the problematic resonant chamber of the acoustic guitar that gave much of the quality to its unamplified sound. Les Paul's early guitar was nicknamed "the log," because that's pretty much what it looked like—the resonant chamber of a typical guitar had been eliminated entirely.

I first heard "Purple Haze" over a transistor radio when I was kid, and I remember telling my dad that something new had happened. I excitedly explained to him that electronic music (the weird sounds of Stockhausen and Xenakis that I was vaguely aware of, to say nothing of the theremin) was, via the amplified guitar in Hendrix's hands, now being melded and shaped by an acoustic instrument. The sounds Hendrix (and others I didn't yet know about) were getting were nothing like what an acoustic instrument sounded like. That unwritten law of staying true to the sound of a traditional instrument had been violently broken, and the amplifier and signal-processing devices (pedals mostly) had become an integral part of the sound of the instrument. As with Theremin and his instrument, the electric guitars were breaking free of history. Their available range of sounds wasn't constrained by any specific cultural trajectory. It seemed that music would be liberated from the past.

The electric guitar still privileged Western scales, unless you used a slide (as with those Hawaiian records). The frets that determined the notes were still, like a piano, set to play recognizable scales and pitches, but the sounds you could get from an amplified instrument were almost limitless. Piano-like plunks, percussive scratchy chords, saxophone-like rasps, and gamelan-like bell tones. No other instrument could do all this—certainly not to the same extent—and as a result texture and tonal quality increasingly became part of composition. The same parts played on another instrument might be the same song, as far as traditional copyright or a written score is concerned, but at some point we began to associate songs with the specific guitar sounds used in the most well-known recordings. This wide sonic palette is almost impossible to pin down in conventional notation, and it still isn't considered as much a part of composition as the melody that the singer sings or the choice of chords that accompanies that melody. That definition of a song, of composition, still derives from an acoustic era, and mostly evokes a songwriter or composer sitting at a piano coming up with a top-line tune and some interesting chords to harmonize with it. Naturally, the *sound* of the piano or the voice isn't really considered a factor in what is written—at least not in this traditional view. Some of Tom Waits's songs, for example, would sound pretty corny sung "straight," without his trademark growly vocals. The sound of his voice is what makes them work. Jangly or wah-wah guitars became as much a part of a song as the lyric or top-line vocal melody.

The synthesizers that emerged in the seventies and early eighties were, like the theremin, unhooked from the provenance of musical culture and tradition. The blips and gurgles they produced weren't an extension of any existing tradition, so, despite the fact that they were sometimes used to imitate existing instruments, they could be incredibly liberating tools. The Minimoog, invented by Bob Moog in 1970, was the first really affordable and portable synthesizer. Earlier versions of these instruments were massive and massively complicated affairs that took days to program. Moog's innovation eventually made something esoteric familiar. An early pioneer in this technology, Bernie Krause, said that the Chinese, then quite doctrinaire in their version of communism, felt that this instrument, untethered as it was from history and traditional culture, was perfect for their New Society. They brought Krause over to teach them how to operate this revolutionary instrument, but the Minimoog was never embraced by the masses, and revolutionary operas continued to be based on older musical models.

PLAYING WITH YOURSELF

Les Paul, the same guy who built one of the first electric guitars, can also lay claim to having invented multitrack recording. Multitracking involves recording a performance and then rewinding the take to the beginning in order to add more music to it. You can add your wife singing, as Paul did with his wife, the singer Mary Ford. Or you can "play with yourself," as Paul also did—recording and playing the drums first and then adding more than one guitar part, creating a virtual one-man band. You can also vary the speed of the recorder to create odd effects—impossibly fast runs, for example. In 1947, Paul and Mary recorded a song called "Lover," which was the first commercial single to have been recorded in multitrack. Les Paul's multitrack was closer to what we now call a sound-on-sound recorder. In his early version of this technology, you could add to a previously recorded track, but then those two performances would be forever joined. If you made a mistake, you had to start over from the beginning. A bit like painting with watercolors, or cooking.

My dad modified a small Norelco reel-to-reel recorder when I was in high school so that it could do this. I recorded layer upon layer of guitar feedback, eventually ending up with a howling, screeching virtual guitar ensemble. A friend and I then tried to do something a bit more accessible, recording a version of the Turtles song "Happy Together" using potato-chip cans for drums and singing harmonies with ourselves. It was endless fun, but annoying and frustrating as well—a single mistake meant starting from scratch.

With sound-on-sound machines, the "tracks" you recorded first were effectively being copied over every time you added another layer, so they diminished in quality, sounding more muffled the more new parts you added. You would therefore often record the tracks you knew would be in the forefront last, as those needed to be clearest and most hi-fi—usually that would be the vocal.

Many bands, including the Beatles, used a variation of this technique. Although they had a true multitrack recorder at their disposal, it only had four separate tracks. If they wanted to add a fifth track, they had to record the four existing tracks onto two tracks of a second four-track machine, effectively giving them two new tracks on that second machine to record on. However, by doing this, all the previous recordings on the original four-track machine had now gone through an extra generation of recording, and the balance between those tracks was now set in stone, just like with Les Paul's technique. Mostly this was unnoticeable, but if it happened repeatedly, the dulling effect began to show.

With the introduction of long-playing records (LPs) in 1948, record companies encouraged artists to record music specifically for this new medium, as the new discs could be sold for more money and generate more profit per unit than mere 45s (or 78s, which were being discontinued). Some artists took to the idea, and they began to stretch out a little to fit the new format. Thematic LPs emerged. (Frank Sinatra was an early adopter of this format, with his collections of low-key songs designed for late nights in bachelor pads.) LPs containing thematically linked songs—typically from Broadway musicals like *Oklahoma* or *The Sound of Music*—were hugely popular. By the end of the sixties, extended jams made their way to discs, as did compositions by Miles Davis and various rock bands, which often took up an entire side of an album.

LPs had their own technical limitations. They hold about twenty to twenty-four minutes of music on a side, and the louder the music (especially the lower pitches), the deeper and wider the grooves that get etched into the master disc. That meant these low or loud passages ended up using more physical space on the disc, and therefore there would be less total time available on the LP for the music. Big-bottomed music had to be either quieter or shorter to fit on discs. You could have plenty of low end on your record, but then the overall volume level would often have to be adjusted lower, and though folks could always hit the volume knob on their home player to compensate and make that record as loud as any other, low volume on radio and jukeboxes created a real disadvantage.

With classical music, the size and depth of the grooves would vary over the length of one LP. In the quiet passages, the grooves could be very skinny and tightly spaced, and more time and music could therefore be squeezed into a given space, which might then be offset by the wider grooves necessitated by louder, lower-pitched movements. Technicians called mastering engineers became adept at figuring out how best to squeeze the greatest amount of music onto a disc while maintaining the maximum possible volume and dynamic range. Cutting lathes, the machines that etched the grooves, automatically adjusted the groove size according to the sound being recorded, but the mastering engineers were the ones who decided how much could fit on a side and whether to lower the volume of the whole side or subtly alter the music a bit by selectively decreasing the volume of the lower pitches.

There are actually people out there who can identify classical recordings just by looking at the grooves on the LP. They can hold up a piece of vinyl and see that there is, for example, a quiet passage occurring about three minutes into the record, a loud crescendo at minute fifteen, and a medium-volume passage at the side ending at around twenty-two minutes—and from that they can guess what recording it is. Such a feat wouldn't be so easy with pop music, which tends to be recorded (and composed) at a more constant volume. In live performance, pop music needs to be heard over a boisterous and often drunken audience, and quiet passages can get lost. With the advent of radio it quickly became apparent that extremely loud and extremely quiet passages were abrasive and distorted on the one hand or would get lost on the other, so a kind of standardized consistency of volume came to be favored. Volume became a make-or-break quality for records. Records that *sounded* louder jumped out of the radio or jukebox speakers and caught the attention of listeners, at least for a moment, but that was enough to stop the listener from turning the radio dial. I emphasized "sounded" because the sounds couldn't actually *be* louder than those of their competition. Radio stations had legal power, and therefore volume limitations; they couldn't actually play some songs louder than others. But there are psychoacoustic tricks that both musicians and record producers began to employ that could fool the ear into *thinking* a song was louder than the one that had preceded it. The use of compressors, limiters, and other devices to create apparent volume became more and more popular. On radio, these devices could—when applied to the entire broadcast output—make one radio station sound louder, and possibly more exciting, than its neighbor.

Other tricks for increasing apparent volume were musical. By skillfully adjusting the arrangement of the instruments in a recording, one can achieve some of the same effects as a compressor, but without the sometimes annoying, artificial, and intrusive (if it is audible) "squashing" effect. If fewer instruments are played along with the singer while he or she is singing, then the vocal can be heard clearly without having to be louder than everything else. Spreading instruments and arrangements over the pitch spectrum helps too. Instruments that play in the same pitch range compete with one another to be heard, so it is generally better to assign different frequency levels to each part if you want them to stand out. If everyone plays parts in the low end of their pitch range there's a good chance everything will end up fairly muddled and indistinct, but if they spread the wealth, then the individual parts will appear more distinct and the whole thing will appear to be louder.

CASSETTES

In 1963 a Dutch company called Philips developed the cassette tape. Tapes were originally used only in dictation machines because the quality of the recordings was not very high. But by 1970 that changed, and they began to be used for music. These little things were portable, you could play them in cars, and they didn't scratch or wear out as quickly as the more fragile LPs. Philips also decided to license the format royalty-free, and as a result other companies adopted it without having to give a piece of their income to Philips. By the mid-seventies these pocket-size plastic things were everywhere. Cassettes could hold a little more music than LPs, but more importantly, the machines that played them could sometimes record as well. The general public was now back in the recording business, just like it had been in the early days. (Home-style reel-to-reel recorders had been available previously, but they were bulky and expensive.) People began to make tapes of themselves singing for Grandma, they copied their favorite songs from their LP collections, they recorded radio programs and music that they played or composed themselves. With two machines (or the soon not-uncommon double-deck cassette machine), you could copy cassettes, one at a time, and give the duplicates to friends.

Record companies tried to discourage "home taping," as they called it. They worried that people would record hit singles off the radio and never have to buy their 45s again. They mounted a huge (and fairly ineffectual) propaganda campaign that mainly served to alienate the consumer and music fan from the companies that sold pre-recorded music. "Home Taping Is Killing Music" was their slogan. I myself occasionally bought pre-recorded audiocassettes, but mostly I still bought LPs. Like many of my friends, I'd make mixtapes that consisted of my favorite songs in various genres, for myself and others. Rather than lending out precious, fragile, and bulky LPs, we'd exchange cassettes of our favorite songs, each tape focusing on a specific genre, theme, artist, or mood. There was a lot of nerdy musical categorizing going on. Pocket-size audio wonder cabinets. I found out about a lot of artists and whole styles of music through the cassettes given to me by my friends, and I ended up buying more LPs as a result.

The mixtapes we made for ourselves were musical mirrors. The sadness, anger, or frustration you might be feeling at a given time could be encapsulated in the song selection. You made mixtapes that corresponded to emotional states, and they'd be available to pop into the deck when each feeling needed reinforcing or soothing. The mixtape was your friend, your psychiatrist, and your solace.

Mixtapes were a form of potlatch—the Native American custom by which a gift given requires that a reciprocal gift be received in the future. I'd make you a mixtape of my favorite songs—presumably ones you would like and might not already have or know about—and you'd be expected to make a similar tape for me of songs you think I'd like. The reciprocal giving wasn't super time-sensitive, but you couldn't forget. The gift of a mixtape was very personal. Often they were made for exactly one person, no one else. A radio program with one listener. Each song, carefully chosen, with love and humor, as if to say, "This is who I am, and by this tape you will know me better." The song choice and sequence allowed the giver to say what one might be too shy to say outright. The songs contained on a mixtape from a lover were scrutinized carefully for clues and metaphors that might reveal the nuances and deeper meanings secreted in the emotional cargo. Other people's music—ordered and collected in infinitely imaginative ways—became a new form of expression.

Record companies wanted to take all that away from us. I taped songs off the radio, just as the record companies feared I would. I carried a boombox on my first trip to Brazil, and every time something amazing came on the radio I taped it. Later I'd ask who those singers or bands were, and then I'd begin a search and eventually buy their LPs. I even licensed some of them for release on a record label I had for a while. If I hadn't been able to tape those radio programs, I never would have found out who those artists were. I also recorded other kinds of radio programs on cassettes: gospel music, preachers, exorcists, radio talk-show hosts, and radio dramas. The piles of cassettes got a little out of control, but they were a constant source of inspiration and they became tools in my own music-making process.

Boomboxes had built-in mics, and, maybe more significantly, they had built-in compressors. A compressor is a bit of circuitry that squashes the sound and effectively acts as an automatic volume control, so that louder sounds are pushed down and quieter ones are brought up. For example, if you recorded one big piano chord on your boombox, the attack—the loud initial hit—would be smacked down, and, as the "tail" of the chord lingered, decayed, and got softer on playback, you would hear the circuitry trying to make it louder. Almost as if someone were working a volume knob in a frantic attempt to maintain a constant sound level. It's a fairly unnatural effect when overused, but it's also pretty cool, and can sometimes make amateur recordings sound weirdly exciting. For a while I used boomboxes as compositional tools—recording band rehearsals and improvisations, which I would later listen to and make note of the best parts, imagining how the good bits could be stitched together. The built-in compression had a huge influence on these decisions: by favoring some passages and making others sound terrible, it made invisible creative decisions.

Whole genres of music thrived as a result of cassettes. Punk bands that couldn't get a record deal resorted to churning out copies of homemade tapes and selling them at shows or by mail order. These second- and third-generation copies lost some quality—the high frequencies would inevitably be reduced, and some dynamics would disappear as well, but no one seemed to care too much. This technology favored music that has been described as either "ethereal, ambient or noisy."[16] I remember getting self-copied cassettes of Daniel Johnston's songs that must have been copied multiple times. The audio quality sucked, and it seemed like he had "overdubbed" vocals or instrumental parts on some songs while creating the recordings—all on cassette. It was an era of murky music. Quality was sliding down a slippery slope, but the freedom and empowerment that was enabled by the technology made up for it.

Cassettes had different, though related effects in other parts of the world. In India, the Gramophone Company virtually had a monopoly on the LP market. It recorded only specific styles of music (mainly *ghazals*—love songs—and some film songs), and they only worked with a handful or artists: Asha Bhosle, Lata Mangeshkar, and a few others. Their stranglehold on recorded music lasted until 1980, when the Indian government decided to allow cassettes to be imported. The effect was rapid and profound: smaller labels blossomed and other kinds of music and artists began to be heard. Soon 95 percent of all commercial recordings in India were being released on cassettes.

This wholesale adoption of cassettes was the pattern in a lot of other countries as well. I have "commercial" cassettes that I treasure from Bali, Sudan, Ethiopia, and elsewhere. Sadly, the quality is often atrocious; the copying machines could have been misaligned, or the copies might have been made hastily by the store or kiosk owner. But a lot of music got disseminated that never would have been heard without the cheap and reproducible cassette.

Another side effect of the cassette deluge was that many musical forms that had been edited and shortened for disc recording could now return to something resembling their original form. Indian ragas last at least an hour, and though the side of a cassette tape is rarely that long, they can easily be quite a bit longer than the twenty-one minutes of the standard LP. Rai songs, the Algerian pop format, can go as long as the performer and audience feel like (or can afford), so cutting them down to the three-to-four-minute songs that were suitable for disc and Western audiences killed the party before it could get started.

Wider and more ecumenical dissemination of cassettes wasn't always for the better. In Java, cassette recordings of local gamelan ensembles circulated widely. Before the advent of cassettes, every village had its own unique gamelan ensemble with its own instruments, each with their own idiosyncrasies. There were variations in the playing and arrangements as well. But as cassettes of popular ensembles circulated, the styles became more homogenized. Similar patterns began to show up everywhere, and even the tuning of the gongs began to conform to those heard on the cassettes.[17]

There is always a trade-off. As music gets disseminated and distinct regional voices find a way to be more widely heard, certain bands and singers (who might be more creative, or possibly have just been marketed by a bigger company) begin to dominate, and peculiar regional styles—what writer Greil Marcus, echoing Harry Smith, called the "old weird America"—eventually end up getting squashed, neglected, abandoned, and often forgotten. This dissemination/homogenization process runs in all directions simultaneously; it's not just top-down repression of individuality and peculiarity. A recording by some previously obscure backwoods or southside singer can find its way into the ear of a wide public, and an Elvis, Luiz Gonzaga, Woody Guthrie, or James Brown can suddenly have a massive audience—what was once a local style suddenly exerts a huge influence. Pop music can be thrown off its axis by some previously unknown and talented rapper from the projects. And then the homogenization process begins again. There's a natural ebb and flow to these things, and it can be tricky to assign a value judgment based on a particular frozen moment in the never-ending cycle of change.

IN THE CLUB

Around 1976, 12" dance and DJ singles emerged. Because the grooves on these oversize singles could be wider, and because they were spinning as fast as a 45, they were louder than LPs that spun at 33RPM. I remember in the late seventies hearing how the low end (the sound of the kick drum and bass) could be brought forward on this format and made louder. Discos had speakers that could accommodate those frequencies, and they became a world of throbbing, pulsing low end—an experience that had to wait for the CD and digital recording to be experienced outside the club environment.

Low frequencies are felt as much as they are heard. We feel that bass in our chest and gut; the music physically moves our bodies. Beyond any audible and neurological apprehension of music, in the disco environment it was pummeling and massaging us physically. These frequencies are sensuous, sexy, and also a little dirty and dangerous.

At the same time that disco sound systems featured big bottoms, they also featured arrays of tweeters—tiny speakers that could project over the heads of the dancers the extreme high frequencies present in a recording. While being massaged by the bass, these speakers were simultaneously filling the air with the sound of high hats flying around like a million needles. I suspect there was a drug connection as well; those high frequencies in particular sounded sparkly fresh if you were on amyl nitrate or cocaine. Naturally enough, the mixers in recording studios began to accommodate that drug-altered hearing as well, and for a while in the eighties, a lot of records had piercing high end in their mixes. Ouch. Some artists worked exclusively in this style, and their music was made primarily to be heard over club speaker systems. You'd hear an amazing song in a club, but it just didn't sound the same at home. Jamaican sound systems did the same thing. The huge sound of the bass and the high-frequency chucks of the guitars and high hats left a gaping sonic hole in the middle of the music—a hole perfectly suited for toasters and MCs to sing and rap over.

DJs in discos gravitated to 12" discs not just for the increased volume and louder low end that the format could accommodate, but also as a medium that could combine those features with what were then called "extended mixes." A club mix of a song would not only be more earthshaking sonically, but it was generally lengthened and would contain breaks—sections where the vocal and often much of the "song" disappeared, leaving only the groove. A DJ could "extend" these breaks even further by playing the same record on two turntables. They could switch from one turntable to the other, making an instrumental break in the song segue into the same section on the other copy, and then do the same in reverse, repeating the process over and over, creating a break that was as long as he, she, the dancers, or an MC wanted. As with early jazz, people beyond the actual musicians, like the dancers, were influencing the music.

Jamaicans were among the first to exploit these possibilities. When the technology moved to Manhattan and the Bronx and was supplemented by some breakdancers and an MC, you had early hip-hop. The beats changed when they got to New York, but the principle was the same: repurpose a medium that was originally created for listening to music, or for DJs to play in clubs, and then use it as a medium to make new music. Music eats its young and gives birth to a new hybrid creature. I doubt there is a single hip-hop artist whose beats still originate from a DJ manipulating vinyl by hand, but the organizing principle hasn't changed much in thirty years.

Rock musicians and their fans didn't initially appreciate these developments. The reasons largely have to do with race and homophobia—many of the most popular dance clubs were black, gay, or both. Part of the disdain might have also stemmed from the idea that this new kind of music wasn't being made by traditional musicians. Drummers and guitar players weren't seen playing in these clubs, even though they were often audibly present on the original records being spun. That complaint could be accurate and justified, though I don't really think most of these grumbling rock fans were that interested in or emotionally sympa-thetic to the employment situation of drummers and guitarists.

The other issue often mentioned was that club music was "manufactured," made my machines, robotic—the implication being that the heart had been taken out of it. It was also claimed that this music wasn't original; it was made by cob-bling together bits of other people's recordings. Like mixtapes. I'd argue that other than race and sex, this latter aspect was the most threatening. To rock purists, this new music messed with the idea of authorship. If music was now accepted as a kind of property, then this hodgepodge version that disregarded ownership and seemed to belong to and originate with so many people (and machines) called into question a whole social and economic framework. With digital technology around the bend, the situation would only get worse—or better, depending on your point of view.

CHAPTER FOUR

Technology Shapes Music

Part Two: Digital

I heard computer scientist Jaron Lanier speak at a symposium recently. After playing some pieces on a *shen*, a Chinese mouth organ, he said that it had a surprising and prodigious heritage. He claimed that this instrument was maybe the first in which the notes to be played were chosen by a mechanism, a mechanism that was a precursor to binary theory and thus to all computers.

That ancient bit of gear found its way to Rome via the Silk Road, and the Empire had a giant version built—as Empires are wont to do. This larger instrument required an assistant to pump the air—it was too big to play by mouth anymore—and, more significantly, a series of levers that selected the notes. This system was the inspiration for what we now know as the keyboard—the series of levers that are used to play the notes of the organ (which is also a large wind instrument) and piano. It was also inspirational to the Frenchman Joseph Marie Jacquard, who in 1801 made a weaving loom in which complicated patterns were guided by punch cards. One could control the design of a fabric by stringing the cards together.

Decades later, Jacquard's loom was inspirational to Charles Babbage, who owned one of Jacquard's self-portraits, in which he used these cards to make an image of himself woven in silk. Babbage designed his Analytical Engine—a computational machine that, were it ever built, would also have been controlled by punch cards. In Babbage's version, the cards no longer controlled threads but made the leap to binary abstraction—making pure calculations. Babbage's young friend Ada Byron (daughter of the poet) was fascinated by the device, and many years later became celebrated as the first computer programmer. So, according to Lanier, our present computer-saturated world owes something of its lineage to a musical instrument. And computer technology, not too long after it came into being, affected music as well.

The technology that allowed sound information (and, soon thereafter, all other information) to be digitized was largely developed by the phone company. Bell Labs, the research division of the Bell Telephone Company, had a mandate to find more efficient and reliable ways of transmitting conversations. Prior to the sixties, all phone lines were analog and the number of conversations that could be handled at one time was limited. The only way to squeeze more calls through the lines was to roll the high and low frequencies off the sound of the voice, and then turn the resulting lo-fi sound into waves that could run in parallel without interfering with one another—much like what happens with terrestrial radio transmissions.

Bell Labs was huge and gave birth to a slew of new inventions. The transistor and semiconductors that form silicon-based integrated circuits (making today's tiny devices possible), the laser, microwave technology, solar panels—the list goes on and on. When you're a monopoly you can afford to spend on R&D, and they had the luxury and foresight to take the long view. Scientists and engineers could work on a project that might not show results for ten years.

In 1962, Bell Labs figured out how to digitize sound—to, in effect, sample a sound wave and slice it into tiny bits that could be broken down into ones and zeros. When they could do this in a way that was not prohibitively expensive and that still left the human voice recognizable, they immediately applied that technology to making their long-distance lines more efficient. More calls could now be made simultaneously, as the voice was now just a stream of ones and zeros that they could squeeze (via encoding and transposing), along with other calls, into their telephone cables. This was especially relevant considering the limitations imposed by long-distance underwater phone cables; you couldn't just go out and lay more lines down if suddenly it seemed more people wanted to talk to France.

A voice is, in the abstract sense, a kind of information, viewed from Bell's perspective. Therefore, much of their research regarding what made a transmission understandable, or how you could squeeze more transmissions in, involved applying the science of information in combination with insights gleaned from the science of psychoacoustics—the study of how the brain perceives sound in all its aspects. So understanding how we perceive sound became integrated with the quest for how to most efficiently transmit information of all kinds. It was even relevant to the meta question "What is information, anyway?"

Psychoacoustics has applications to the sound of ambulances (Why can we never tell where they're coming from?), the speaking voice, and, of course, music. The *psycho*-prefix is there because what and how we hear is not simply mechanical, it's mental (meaning the brain "hears" as much as the ear does—not mental as in insane, or insanely great).

Of course, much of what we hear is partly defined and limited by the mechanics of our ears. We know that we can't hear all the high-pitched sounds that bats emit or the full range of sounds that a dog can hear. There are low-pitched sounds that whales produce that we can't really hear either, though they are strong enough to do us physical harm if we are too close to the source.

But there are things we "hear" that have nothing to do with the physics of the eardrum and the auditory canal. We can, for example, isolate the voice of someone talking to us in a noisy environment. If you were to listen to a recording of a noisy restaurant it would sound like acoustic chaos, but sometimes we manage to make order out of it and carry on a rudimentary conversation. Repetitious sounds, the sound of waves or constant traffic, become somewhat inaudible to us after a while. We have the ability to selectively hear just the stuff we're interested in and make the rest recede into some distant acoustic background. We also have the ability to perceive patterns in sounds. This too has nothing to do with our ears. We can remember pitches, and some people with perfect pitch can accurately determine notes heard out of a musical context. We can tell if the sound of squealing subway brakes and the highest note on a clarinet are the same. We can remember sequences of sounds—a bird's song or a door creak followed by a slam—and the exact timbre of sounds—we sometimes recognize a friend's voice by hearing a single word.

How does this work? Can we simulate that mental process with a mathematical formula or a computer program? As you can imagine, such questions—how little information do we need to recognize someone's voice, for example—were of prime importance to a phone company. If they could understand what exactly makes speech understandable and intelligible, and isolate just that aspect—refine it, control it—then they might increase the efficiency of their phone system by eliminating all the superfluous parts of the transmissions. The goal was to eventually communicate more and more using less, or the same amount, of the mechanical and physical electrical stuff. This possible increase in information flow would make them a lot more money. Psychoacoustics would eventually lead to an increased understanding of information transmission. This arcane science was suddenly hugely useful.

An unforeseen consequence of this phone-related research was the emergence of digital-based audio technology that was eventually used in, among other places, recording studios. In the seventies a new piece of equipment the size of a briefcase appeared in recording studios. It was called a harmonizer, and it could change the pitch of a sound without changing its speed or tempo, as would happen if you changed the pitch by speeding up a tape. It achieved this by slicing up the sound waves into digital slivers, mathematically transposing what were now merely numbers and then reconstructing those as sounds at a higher or lower pitch. The early versions of this machine sounded pretty glitchy, but the effect was cool, even when it didn't work.

Around that same time there appeared other devices called digital delays, which were in effect primitive samplers. The digital samples they created in order to mimic acoustic echoes were usually much less than a second long and they would be used to produce very short delay effects.

More devices followed: machines that could grab and hold longer sound samples with greater resolution, and some that could manipulate those "sounds" (they were really just numbers) more freely. All sorts of weirdness resulted. Bell Labs was involved in manufacturing a sound processor called a vocoder that could isolate certain aspects of talking (or singing) like speech formants (the shape of the sounds that we use to form words). This device could remove these aspects of our talking or singing from the pitch—like isolating just the percussive parts—the T's and B's and the sibilants of S's and F's. This machine could transmit these formant aspects of a voice separate from the rest of a vocalization, and the resulting gibberish, when transmitted, was more or less unintelligible. But the components of intelligent speech were still there. The elements of the sound of speech or singing had been deconstructed and could make sense again when put back together. Wonderful, but what do you do with this technology? One use for it was a sort of cryptology for the voice: the garbled nonsense could be "decoded" at the other end if you knew what had been taken out and where. These machines were also adopted for music production. Below, the German band Kraftwerk's vocoder, made especially for them.[A]

A vocoder was typically used to apply those isolated and separated speech formants to the sound of a pitched instrument. The instrument then appeared to be talking or singing. Often the resulting "voice" was somewhat robotic sounding, an aspect that likely appealed to Kraftwerk. I once used a vocoder like this that I borrowed from Bernie Krause, a musician and early synthesizer pioneer, whom I met when Brian Eno and I did the *Bush of Ghosts* record. The vocoder was beautifully made, but rather complicated, and very expensive.

An early harmonizer (that digital pitch shifter) cost thousands of dollars. A good digital reverberation unit set a studio back maybe ten thousand dollars, and a full-fledged digital sampling device, like the Fairlight or a Synclavier that emerged soon after, cost much, much more. But soon the price of memory and processing dropped, and the technology became more affordable. Inexpensive Akai samplers became the backbone of hip-hop and DJ mixes, replacing the earlier use of vinyl, and sampled or digitally derived drum sounds took the place of live drummers in many recordings. We were off to the races, for better or worse.

With the digitization of sound, digital recording and consumer products like the CD became possible, and entire record albums were soon sliced into these tiny slivers of ones and zeros. Not long after that, the capacity and speed of home computers became sufficient to allow individuals to record, archive, and process music. All of this follows from Bell Labs's desire to improve the efficiency of their phone lines.

Bell Labs eventually became Lucent. I visited their labs in the mid-nineties and they showed me a

A

processor that could squeeze what sounded to the ear to be CD-quality music into a minuscule bandwidth. I believe encoding music as MP3s had already been invented in Germany by that time, so this extremely efficient compressing/encoding trick was not a complete surprise. And it was certainly no surprise that squeezing more sound information into smaller spaces continued to be a priority for a subsidy of a phone company. But like many people, I worried that the quality of music might somehow get sacrificed in this "rezzing down" process.

I was right. Those early, low-bandwidth digital files sounded slightly off, as if something ineffable was missing. It was hard to put your finger on why they sounded wrong, but they did. All the frequencies seemed to be there, but something seemed to have been sucked out in the process. Zombie music. MP3s have improved quite a bit since then, and now I listen to most of the music I own in that format. I believe what Lucent was working on ended up being used for satellite-radio transmission: getting "CD-quality" sound into smaller bandwidth transmissions, so that a satellite could send out lots of channels of sound that seem to be of high quality. Similar processing would be applied to photographs and video signals, which allows us to stream movies without them looking completely grainy or pixelated.

In 1988, I got an advance peek at this technology as it was applied to visual information when the designer Tibor Kalman and I visited a printing studio on Long Island. The studio had a machine that could digitize and then subtly manipulate images (we wanted to "improve" the image that was to be used on a Talking Heads record cover). Like the early computers and recording-studio gear, this machine was incredibly expensive and rare. We had to go to it (it couldn't be brought to the design studio), and we had to book time in advance. A Sytex machine, I think it was called. Impressed as we were, its cost and rarity meant we didn't think much about incorporating its talents into future projects.

After a while, as with sampling, the price of scanning images dropped, and manipulating images using Photoshop became common. There are some film holdouts, and I have no doubt that, as with MP3s, something has been lost with digital images, but, well, for most of us the trade-off seems acceptable—and inevitable. Needless to say, as images become digitized, they enter the river of networked data. Images for us are increasingly sequences of ones and zeros—information, like everything else. The digitization of every form of media enabled the Web to be what it is, much more than a way of transmitting text-based documents. This slicing of content allowed a wide variety of media to flow into that river, and in a way we owe all the pictures, sounds, songs, games, and movies that are part of our Internet experience to the phone company, information science, and psychoacoustics.

CDS

CDs, which made their debut in 1982, were jointly developed by Sony in Japan and Philips in Holland. Previously, digitized movies had been stored on Laser-Discs, which were the size of LPs, and the prospect of encoding an entire record album's worth of sound therefore seemed within reach. If the discs could be made smaller, it could be lucrative. Philips had the laser aspect in development and Sony had the manufacturing prowess, so they agreed to work on this new format together. The arrangement was unusual; usually one company developed a format on its own and then tried to exert control over it so it could start charging others for using it. As a result, a lot of proprietary nonsense that could have burdened the acceptance and dissemination of CDs was avoided.

It was rumored that the length of the CD was determined by the duration of Beethoven's Ninth Symphony, because that was Norio Ohga's favorite piece of music, and he was the president of Sony at that time. Philips had designed a CD with an 11.5 cm diameter, but Ohga insisted that a disc must be able to hold the entire Beethoven recording. The longest recording of the symphony in Polygram's archive was seventy-four minutes, so the CD size was increased to a 12 cm diameter to accommodate the extra data.

Unlike LPs, whose grooves and bouncing needles limited the volume, the low frequencies were practically unlimited with the super-high-end CD technology. The music was no longer mirrored by physical grooves but was now encoded in a series of digital ones and zeroes. Though these discs spun around like LPs, they were technically nothing like the old records. Their extended audio range resulted from the fact that since there was no physical analogue of the sound, the coded messages "told" the CD player what frequencies to play. The ones and zeroes could tell the stereo system to play anything audible to the human ear, at whatever frequency or volume was desired. This sonic range in digital music was really only limited by the playback and sampling mechanisms that allowed sounds outside the human hearing range to be recorded. The expanded and unlimited sound range was now, or would soon be, available to everyone.

Inevitably, this sonic freedom got abused quite a bit. Some records (the writer Greg Milner mentions most Oasis albums and *Californication* by the Red Hot Chili Peppers) were made so artificially loud that though the music seemed amazing on first listen (it was louder, and more consistently louder, than anything else), it rapidly wore on the ears. Milner claims that this "volume war" was spurred by radio DJs and technicians who wanted their stations to seem louder than the stations near them on the radio dial.[1] To achieve this, inventor Mike Dorrough developed a device in the sixties called a "discriminate audio processor," which caught on widely years later when every station was trying to be louder than every other. Milner speculates that musicians and record producers responded to this competition by figuring out how to make their records sound louder, and stay louder, for the whole length of the record.[2] Pretty soon there was ear fatigue all around. The listener never got a break; there was no dynamic range anymore. Milner suggests that even rabid music fans can't listen to these records over and over, or very much at all. The actual enjoyment of them is short-lived, and he proposes that this might have had something to do with pushing consumers away from purchasing recorded music. The technology that was supposed to make music more popular than ever instead made everyone run away from it.

CRAPPY SOUND FOREVER

Early CDs, like the MP3s that followed, didn't sound all that great. Dr. John Diamond treated psychotic patients with music, but by 1989 he sensed that it had all gone wrong. He claims that the natural healing and therapeutic properties of music were lost in the rush to digitize.[3] He believes that certain pieces of music can help soothe and heal, if they are the entirely analog versions, while the digital versions actually have the reverse effect. When his test subjects are played digital recordings, they get agitated and twitchy.

Throughout the history of recorded music, we have tended to value convenience over quality every time. Edison cylinders didn't really sound as good as live performers, but you could carry them around and play them whenever you wanted. LPs, revolving slower, didn't sound as rich as 45s or 78s, but you didn't have to attend to them as much. And cassettes? Are you kidding? We were told that CDs would last forever and sound squeaky clean, but they really don't sound as good as LPs, and the jury is out regarding their durability. The spectrum of sound on analog mediums has an infinite number of gradations, whereas in the digital world everything is sliced into a finite number of slivers. Slivers and bits might fool the ear into believing that they represent a continuous audio spectrum (psychoacoustics at work), but by nature they are still ones and zeros; steps rather than a smooth slope. MP3s? They may be the most convenient medium so far, but I can't help thinking that the psychoacoustic trickery used to develop them—the ability to cause the mind to think and feel that all the musical information is there when in reality a huge percentage has been removed—is a continuation of this trend in which we are seduced by convenience. It's music in pill form, it delivers vitamins, it does the job, but something is missing. We are often offered, and gladly accept, convenient mediums that are "good enough" rather than ones that are actually better.

Where does this road of compromise end, and does it really matter if we lose a little quality along the way? Isn't the quality or accuracy of a recording somewhat irrelevant to music's use and enjoyment? We laugh out loud at antics on fuzzy, grainy, and atrociously low-resolution YouTube postings, and we talk to our loved ones on mobile-phone networks with voice quality that would make Alexander Graham Bell roll over in his grave. Information theory tells us that the amount of bits needed to communicate certain kinds of content—what someone is saying, or the antics of a cat, for example—can really be much lower than we think. If we only need to understand the verbal content of someone on the telephone, then the quality can be surprisingly bad and we'll still know what our friends and family are saying. It doesn't seem to matter that so much is missing. Maybe "good enough" is okay.

Or maybe not. Reacting to this tendency, some musicians have decided to go back to analog recording, and some have perversely gone out of their way to make their recordings sound as lo-fi as possible—as bad as they can get away with. They want to get as far from digital cleanliness as possible. Why would bad quality, fuzziness, and distortion imply that the music is more authentic? The idea is that if one accepts that crisp and clean recordings are inherently soulless, then the opposite, dirty and rough, must therefore be straight from the heart. That might not sound logical, but that's the way we think. It's all part of the recurring belief that conflates new technologies with being inauthentic. Bad—even fake bad, in this way of thinking—means good. It's confusing, because most digital music does not sound "bad." If anything, it sounds conventionally good—clean, spotless, with a full range of frequencies. Though it is actually less rich sounding than previous technologies, it fools the ear into believing that it sounds better. It's this shiny, glossy quality that is considered suspect by many music fans. In response, they overvalue the easily audible drawbacks of a previous era—the hiss, crackle, and distortion. In my opinion, realness and soul lie in the music itself, not in the scratches and pops of old records. So, while the cleanliness and "perfection" of much current music is not a guarantee of a moving musical experience, neither is their opposite.

If, following the lead of the phone company, we find ourselves talking about communication and information transmission when we talk about music, then maybe some of the sonic richness of LPs is indeed superfluous and can be eliminated with no serious loss. Could this work with speech as well? Yes and no. Music has more going on simultaneously than speech, for starters. Looking at a reproduction of a painting is certainly not the same as standing in front of the real thing, but an awful lot of the emotion, intent, ideas, and sensibility can indeed be communicated—even via a cheap reproduction. Similarly, I can be moved to tears by a truly awful recording or a bad copy of a good recording. Would I be moved even more if the quality were higher? I doubt it. So why bother?

There does come a time, however, when the richness of the retinal or aural experience is so diminished that the communication—in this case the enjoyment of the music—becomes unintelligible. But how can we define that? I first heard rock, pop, and soul songs on a crappy-sounding transistor radio, and they changed my life completely. The sound quality was atrocious, but that tinny sound was communicating a wealth of information. Though it was an audio transmission that carried the news, it was the social and cultural message embedded in the music that electrified me as much as the sound did. Those extra-musical components that got carried along with the music didn't demand a high-resolution signal—good enough was good enough. I'm not saying that tinny sound should be considered satisfying or desirable, or that we should never strive for more than "good enough," but it's amazing how *much* lo-fi or lo-res information can communicate. Live concerts don't generally have perfect sound either, but they can move us deeply.

Now I begin to ask myself if the fuzziness and ambiguity inherent in low-quality signals and reproductions might actually be a factor that gives the viewer or listener a way in. I know from writing lyrics that some details—names, places, locations—are desirable; they anchor the piece in the real world. But so are ambiguities. By letting the listener or viewer fill in the blanks, complete the picture (or piece of music), the work becomes personalized and the audience can adapt it to their own lives and situations. They become more involved with the work, and an intimacy and involvement becomes possible that perfection might have kept at bay. Maybe the lo-fi music crowd has a point?

MUSIC SOFTWARE AND SAMPLE-BASED COMPOSITION

Music composition changed a lot with the advent of digital recording. As we've seen, the first digital samples were short and primarily used by the phone company. People used them for gimmicks and special effects, but these early developments did not have a wide musical influence. Soon enough, though, it became possible to grab or sample a whole bar of music, and though the samples were not of super-high quality, it was enough. Looping beats became ubiquitous, and rhythm tracks made of sampled measures (or shorter intervals) now function as the rhythm bed in many songs. You can "hear" the use of Akai, Pro Tools, Logic, and other digital recording and sample-based composition in most pop music written in the last twenty years. If you compare recent recordings to many made in previous eras, you might not know what makes them sound different, but you would certainly be able to hear it.

The software has affected not just the sonic quality but also the composition process. Maybe you can also hear the effects of the ones and zeros that make up digital recording, though that may be less true as time goes by and technology passes the limits of the differentiating aspects of our hearing. What you do hear, though, is a shift in musical structure that computer-aided composition has encouraged. Though software is promoted as being an unbiased tool that helps us do anything we want, all software has inherent biases that make working one way easier than another. With the Microsoft presentation software PowerPoint, for example, you have to simplify your presentations so much that subtle nuances in the subjects being discussed often get edited out. These nuances are not forbidden, they're not blocked, but including them tends to make for a less successful presentation. Likewise, that which is easy to bullet-point and simply visualize works *better*. That doesn't mean it actually *is* better; it means working in certain ways is simply easier than working in others. Music software is no different. Taking another avenue would make music composition somewhat more tedious and complex.

An obvious example is quantizing. Since the mid-nineties, most popular music recorded on computers has had tempos and rhythms that have been quantized. This means that the tempo never varies, not even a little bit, and the rhythmic parts tend toward metronomic perfection. In the past, the tempos of recordings would always vary slightly, imperceptibly speeding up or maybe slowing down just a little, or a drum fill might hesitate in order to signal the beginning of a new section. You'd feel a slight push and pull, a tug and then a release, as ensembles of whatever type responded to each other and lurched, ever so slightly, ahead of and behind an imaginary metronomic beat. No more. Now almost all pop recordings are played to a strict tempo, which makes these compositions fit more easily into the confines of the recording and editing software. An eight-bar section recorded on a "grid" of this type is exactly twice as long as a four-bar section, and every eight-bar section is always exactly the same length. This makes for a nice visual array on the computer screen, and facilitates easy editing, arranging, and repairing as well. Music has come to accommodate software, and I have to admit a lot has been gained as a result. I can sketch out an idea for a song very quickly, for example, and I can cut and paste sections to create an arrangement almost instantly. Severe or "amateurish" unsteadiness or poorly played tempo changes can be avoided. My own playing isn't always rock steady, so I like that those distracting flubs and rhythmic hiccups can be edited out. The software facilitates all of this. But, admittedly, something gets lost in the process. I'm just now learning how to listen, value, and accommodate some of my musical instincts that don't always adhere to the grid. It makes things a little more complicated, as I still use the software, but I sense that the music breathes a little more as a result of me not always bending to what the software makes easiest.[B]

Sometimes, after having begun a songwriting process using computer software, I find that I have to sing or play it apart from that recording to free myself from its straightening tendencies. In singing a song freely, for example, I might find that the note at the high point or at the end of a melodic arc "wants" to hang on just a little bit longer than the grid of measures on the computer might indicate as normal. The result is that a verse might end up being nine measures long, rather than the traditional eight. Alternately, a half measure might feel like a nice emotionally led extension, as well as giving a short, natural-feeling breathing space, so then I'll add that half measure to the grid on the software. In a recent collaboration with Fatboy Slim, I discovered that he often added "extra" measures to accommodate drum fills. It felt natural, like what a band would do. Shifting off the grid is sometimes beneficial in other ways, too. If a listener can predict where a piece of music

B

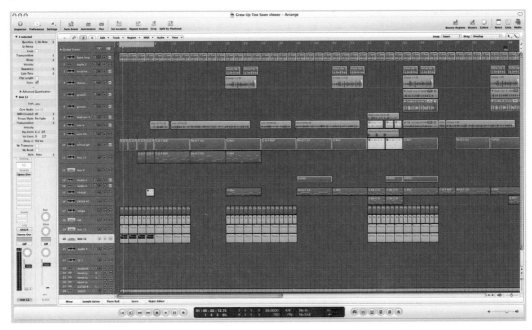

is going, he begins to tune out. Shifting off an established pattern keeps things interesting and engaging for everyone, though it sometimes means you have to avoid the path of least resistance that digital recording software often offers.

Quantizing, composing, and recording on a grid are just some of the effects of software on music. Other effects are created by the use of MIDI, which stands for musical instrument digital interface. MIDI is a software/hardware interface by which notes (usually played on a keyboard) are encoded as a series of instructions rather than recorded as sounds. If you strike a middle A on a keyboard, then the MIDI code remembers when that note was played in the sequence of notes in the composition, how hard or quickly it was struck, and how long it was sustained. What's recorded is this information and these parameters (a bit like a piano roll or the tines on a music box), but not the actual sound—so if that sequence of instructions is played back, it will tell the keyboard instrument to play that note and all the rest exactly when and how you played it previously. This method of "recording" takes up much less computer memory, and it also means the instructional information recorded is independent of the instrument played. Another MIDI-equipped instrument with a completely different sound can be told to play the same note, at the same time. What began as a piano sound might be changed later to synthesizer strings or a marimba. With MIDI recording, you can make arrangement decisions easily and at any time.

The way MIDI remembers how hard or fast you hit a note is by dividing the speed of the note strike into 127 increments. The speed of your hit will be rounded off so that it will fall somewhere in that predetermined range. Naturally, if you strike a key faster, slower, or with more subtlety than the MIDI software and its associated sensors can measure, then your "expression" will not be accurately captured or encoded; it will be assigned the nearest value. As with digital recording, music gets rounded off to the nearest whole number, under the assumption that finer detail would not be discernible to the ear and brain.

There are instruments that can be used to trigger MIDI fairly well: keyboards, some percussion pads, and anything that can be easily turned into switches and triggers. But some instruments elude capture. Guitars aren't easily quantifiable in this way, nor are wind, brass, or most bowed string instruments. So far, the nuances of those instruments have been just too tricky to capture. Using MIDI therefore tends to entice people away from using those instruments and the kinds of expression they are uniquely good at. A lot of MIDI-based recordings tend to use arrays of sounds generated or at least triggered by keyboards, so, for example, it's easiest to play chord inversions that are keyboard friendly. The same chords on guitars tend to have a different order of the same notes. Those keyboard chords, then, in turn, incline composers to vocal melodies and harmonies that fit nicely with those specific versions of the chords, so the whole shape, melody, and arc of the song are being influenced, not just the MIDI parts and instruments. As soon as technology makes one thing easier, it leaves a host of alternatives in the dust.

The uncanny perfection that these recording and compositional technologies make possible can be pleasing. But metronomic accuracy can also be too easy to achieve this way, and the facile perfection is often obvious, ubiquitous, and ultimately boring. Making repetitive tracks used to be laborious and time-consuming, and the slight human variations that inevitably snuck in as a musician vainly attempted to be a machine were subliminally perceptible, if not consciously audible. A James Brown or Serge Gainsbourg track often consisted of a riff played over and over, but it didn't sound like a loop. Somehow you could sense that it had been played over and over, not cloned. Imagine a row of dancers moving in unison—something that has a huge visceral impact. Besides implying hard work, skill, and precision, it also works as a powerful metaphor. Now imagine that same row created by a series of mirror reflections or CGI technology. Not so powerful.

For many years, DJs, mixers, and hip-hop artists constructed tracks from digital samples of riffs and beats taken from existing recordings. Some artists lifted entire hooks and choruses from pop songs and used them like a knowing reference or quote (P. Diddy does this a lot, as does Kanye West), the way you might quote a familiar refrain to a friend or lover to express your feelings. How many times has "put a ring on it" been used in conversation? Song references are like emotional shortcuts and social acronyms.

In much contemporary pop, if you think you're hearing a guitar or piano, most likely you're hearing a sample of those instruments from someone else's record. What you hear in such compositions are lots of musical quotations piled on top of one another. Like a painting by Robert Rauschenberg, Richard Prince, or Kurt Schwitters made of appropriated images, ticket stubs, and bits of newspaper, this music is a species of sonic collage. In some ways it's meta-music; music about other music.

However, many artists found out relatively quickly that when songs were created in this way, they had to share the rights and profits with the original record companies and the original composers of those fragments and hooks. Half of the money from a song often goes to the source of a hook or chorus. A few of my songs have been sampled in this way, and it's flattering and fun to hear someone add a completely new narrative to something you wrote years ago. The singer Crystal Waters sampled a Talking Heads song ("Seen and Not Seen"—whoa, what a weird choice!) in her hit "Gypsy Woman (She's Homeless)," and that wonderful song of hers (which I even covered at one point) bears no relation to the original. As far as I know, she or her producers were not intentionally referencing the original song; they simply found something about it, the way the groove felt or its sonic texture, useful.

Besides the fact that being sampled pays well, I don't feel that it compromises the original. Anyone can tell it's a quote, a sample, right? Well, that depends. Trick Daddy, Cee Lo, and Ludacris used another Talking Heads song, the demo "Sugar on My Tongue," in their hit song "Sugar (Gimme Some)." In that case the reference to the original was obvious, to me at least. They used our chorus hook for their own. But since that was never a popular Talking Heads song (it was a demo included in a boxed set), that "quotation" aspect was probably lost on most listeners. (For those keeping track, I did get paid and credited as a songwriter on that track, not a bad second life for what was originally a demo!) Since the song was already a bit of silly sexual innuendo, those guys taking it one step further was no big deal. But, if someone hypothetically proposed repurposing the hook of a song I'd written as a new song about killing Mexicans, blowing up Arabs, or slashing women, I would say no.

Many artists soon began to find that the ubiquitous use of samples could severely limit the income from "their" songs, which led many of them to eventually stop or curtail their use of sampling technology. Sometimes even what is easiest (grabbing a beat from a drum break on a CD, which only takes minutes) becomes a thing to be avoided. Bands like the Beastie Boys picked up instruments they'd put down years earlier, and hip-hop artists either disguised their samples better, found more obscure ones, or, more often, began to create or buy tracks made from scratch (often on synthesizers and drum machines). Technology, or rather the aspect of technology that enabled the use of copyrighted material, had, thanks to the efforts of rights enforcers and guardians, sent some musicians back to the drawing board. A group of hot young programmers soon emerged whose skills were in constructing, for use by others, these grooves made from scratch. With a relatively inexpensive piece of gear or software, you could make contributions to major songs from your bedroom. In contemporary hip-hop, there is now often no relationship between a composition's backing track and a simulation of a live performance by musicians in the traditional sense. In the early days, there were live DJs using vinyl to loop drum breaks, but now everything—every instrument—is sampled, processed, or in some way shamelessly and boldly artificial.

This music floats free of all worldly reference. Most other pop genres retain some link to simulated live performance, or at least to the instruments used in one, but a song put together with finger snaps, super-compressed or auto-tuned vocals, squiggly synths, and an impossibly fat and unidentifiable bass sound doesn't resemble any existing live band at all. In my opinion, this isn't a bad thing. A new musical avenue has opened up, one that maybe had its roots with Kraftwerk and other electronic acts, but that has now morphed into something very different. It's music that, by design, affects the body. It's very sensuous and physical, even though the sounds themselves don't relate to any music that has ever been physically produced. You can't play air guitar or mimic playing an instrument to a contemporary hip-hop record; even the sounds that signify "drums" don't sound like a drum kit.

These artists therefore have a difficult decision to make when they're expected to perform. Nothing on their record was played by anything that sounds like a "real" instrument, so the performance becomes a kind of karaoke spectacle with most of the sounds pre-recorded—or sometimes artist and band deconstruct the recording in order to "play" its component parts in a way that resembles, visually at least, a traditional band. This sounds like I'm being critical, but actually playing and performing to samples and pre-recorded tracks can free the artist to create something more theatrical. The R. Kelly *Light It Up* tour pushed a traditional R&B concert into the realm of surreal theater. The music in these shows can be viewed as a soundtrack for a spectacle; a gathering; a show of camaraderie, visual bombast, and effects. Grace Jones and Pet Shop Boys did this years ago. They were mainly dance-club bands and visual icons, not live acts, and they were both very arty about it. Now this kind of karaoke spectacle has gone mainstream. Even if the lead vocal is live, the audience often doesn't care whether there is a band or not—the band is often just there to dress the set. I will admit that there is an inevitable excitement ceiling when it comes to these karaoke spectaculars, at least as far as the music goes, since there is never the possibility of the music rising beyond its preexisting programmed level (and I don't mean volume). But if the social and the visual elements are good enough—and using this technology they are freer to become so—then it can be a reasonable trade-off.

Hip-hop artists have also revived the mixtape (or maybe it never went away). Sampled beats and digital recording have allowed mixtape artists to create seamless sequences of songs, dialogue, beats, and assorted weirdness in ways that were never really possible using cassette recorders. Most of these are "released" as CDs, though the name harks back to the cassette era. But I have a feeling that the era of the CD mixtape is also coming to an end. I have digital mixes that are one continuous hour-long piece of music, but now, in a technical sense, there's really no limit. The artificial length that Sony imposed on CDs no longer applies. You could make a downloadable album that's ten hours long, or one that's only ten minutes. Jem Finer recently created a piece of music that runs for a thousand years. Marketing and promotion aren't very cost effective for one song at a time, so temporarily at least we still market and acquire songs in clumps (an hour or less is typical), as we have for decades. But there's no reason that will remain the standard indefinitely.

Looking at the short end of the musical-length spectrum, ringtones haven't yet been recognized as a valid form of stand-alone musical creativity, and they may never be. But shortness shouldn't matter anymore. One could argue that the Mac start-up sound is a musical composition, as is the short, mysterious, ascending five-second bumper that signaled the end of each scene in the TV series *Lost*.

Doorbells, whooshes, email alerts, and car horns are all valid forms of composition. Our musical landscape is indeed broadening, as length doesn't matter anymore: short, long, and in between all coexist.

PRIVATE MUSIC

The iPod, like the Walkman cassette player before it,^c allows us to listen to our music wherever we want. Previously, recording technology had unlinked music from the concert hall, the café, and the saloon, but now music can always be carried with us. Michael Bull, who has written frequently about the impact of the Walkman and the iPod, points out that we often use these devices to "aestheticize urban space."[4] We carry our own soundtrack with us wherever we go, and the world around us is overlaid with our music. Our whole life becomes a movie, and we can alter the score for it over and over again: one minute it's a tragedy and the next it's an action film. Energetic, dreamy, or ominous and dark: everyone has their own private movie going on in their heads, and no two are the same. That said, the twentieth-century philosopher Theodor Adorno, ever the complainer, called this situation "accompanied solitude," a situation where we might be alone, but we have the ability via music to create the illusion that we are not.[5] In his somewhat Marxist way, he viewed music as an opiate, especially popular music. (I've met some serious Wagner fans, and I'd be wary of limiting the accusation that music is an addictive palliative solely to pop.) Adorno saw the jukebox as a machine that drew "suckers" into pubs with the promise of joy and happiness. But, like a drug, instead of bringing real happiness, the music heard on jukeboxes only creates more desire for itself. He might be right, but he might also have been someone who never had a good time in a honky-tonk.

Private listening could be viewed as the height of narcissism—these devices usually exclude everyone else from the experience of enjoying music. In *Brave New World*, Aldous Huxley imagined a drug called soma that blissed everyone out. It was like taking a holiday, and you could regulate the length of the holiday by the dosage. Has technology turned music into a soma-like drug? Is it like a pill you take that is guaranteed to generate a desired emotion—bliss, anger, tranquility?

ACOUSTIC ASSOCIATIONS

Some of us sing to ourselves or even just whistle when we think no one is listening, and often there is music "playing" in our heads. A region of the brain seems to be devoted primarily to sonic memory, and that includes not just ringtones, dog growls, and ambulance sirens, but also snippets of songs, mainly recordings, that we've heard as well. These sonic fragments function as nodes in a network of related memories that stretch beyond their acoustic triggers. Everyone has had a song "transport" them to a vivid memory of an early romance or some other formative experience. Songs are like smells that way; they dredge up worlds, very specific places and moments. Other sounds do this, too: intense rain, the voice of a well-known actor, a knife on a cutting board, a distant train.

Are mobile music devices and the musically cluttered world we inhabit starting to substitute for our interior voices? Do we, little by little, stop singing and whistling because professionals are now singing and playing for us, right into our ears? A slew of musical associations bounce around in our heads, linking to recurring memories and feelings that, after a while, facilitate the creation and reinforcement of specific neural pathways. These pathways help us make sense of those experiences. They make us who we are. Is that space now inhibited by the inundation of the music and sounds of others? Are the voices in our heads, the inaudible chatter that we use to sort out who and where we are, being replaced by the voices of professionals? Well, I haven't stopped singing to myself, so maybe not.

THAT WHICH CANNOT BE PRESERVED

I listen to music only at very specific times. When I go out to hear it live, most obviously. When I'm cooking or doing the dishes I put on music, and sometimes other people are present. When I'm jogging or cycling to and from work down New York's West Side bike path, or if I'm in a rented car on the rare occasions I have to drive somewhere, I listen alone. And when I'm writing and recording music, I listen to what I'm working on. But that's it. That relatively short list defines, to a large extent, where and how I hear music. I find music somewhat intrusive in restaurants or bars. Maybe due to my involvement with it, I feel I have to either listen intently or tune it out. Mostly I tune it out; I often don't even notice if a Talking Heads song is playing in most public places. Sadly, most music then becomes (for me) an annoying sonic layer that just adds to the background noise. It might sound like I'm a picky eater, but I actually do listen to a lot of music.

As music becomes less of a thing—a cylinder, a cassette, a disc—and more ephemeral, perhaps we will start to assign an increasing value to live performances again. After years of hoarding LPs and CDs, I have to admit I'm now getting rid of them. I occasionally pop a CD into a player, but I've pretty much completely converted to listening to MP3s either on my computer or, gulp, my phone! For me, music is becoming dematerialized, a state that is more truthful to its nature, I suspect. Technology has brought us full circle.

I go to at least one live performance a week, sometimes with friends, sometimes alone. There are other people there. Often there is beer, too. After more than a hundred years, we're heading back to where we started. A century of technological innovation and the digitization of music has inadvertently had the effect of emphasizing its social function. Not only do we still give friends copies of music that excites us, but increasingly we have come to value the social aspect of a live performance more than we used to. Music technology in some ways appears to have been on a trajectory in which the end result is that it will destroy and devalue itself. It will succeed completely when it self-destructs. The technology is useful and convenient, but it has, in the end, reduced its own value and increased the value of the things it has never been able to capture or reproduce.

Technology has altered the way music sounds, how it's composed, and how we experience it. It has also flooded the world with music. The world is awash with (mostly) recorded sounds. We used to have to pay for music or make it ourselves; playing, hearing, and experiencing it was exceptional, a rare and special experience. Now hearing it is ubiquitous, and silence is the rarity that we pay for and savor.

CHAPTER FIVE

In the Recording Studio

B y the time I entered the music business, multitrack recording was commonplace; at least sixteen tracks were available to record on, and often there were twenty-four. Recording took place in a special soundproof studio with super-thick doors (often covered with carpeting), lots of wood (often arrayed at odd angles), and the entire place built around a massive console that looked like the deck of the starship *Enterprise*. Obviously, or so it seemed, mastering this control panel would be far beyond the abilities of mere musicians. The recording engineers and producers relegated us to another soundproof room in which we played, and then to plush couches situated in the back of the control room, where we could hear how we sounded. It was all pretty intimidating. As I write this, that era is coming to an end.

When I was in high school, I heard pop records that I knew had been made by overdubbing instruments on top of existing band tracks. The strings on "Sound of Silence" and many other pop tunes were added after the guitars and vocals had been recorded—sometimes, as with that song, without the band's knowledge! Sound effects were added to recordings, quiet instruments could magically compete with loud ones (due to the ability to now control the relative volume of each instrument), and impossible sonic effects could be achieved, like a singer harmonizing with himself. In the realm of experimental music, composers were cutting up tapes on which sounds had previously been recorded, tossing them in the air, and then reassembling them. They were mixing electronic and acoustic instruments and speeding up and slowing down the recordings, creating otherworldly effects. I knew this was how the records I was listening to had been put together, and I wanted to do it too. Not with the idea of being a pop star or having a musical career, but for the sheer excitement of it.

I began to mess with my father's modified tape recorder, recording layer upon layer of guitar feedback and other "experimental" odds and ends. Inspired by John Cage, the Beatles, and others, I cut the tape into short fragments and reassembled it at random—some sections inevitably ending up backward. (That sounded pretty cool to me as well.) Happy accidents were welcome. The possibilities of recording as a medium in its own right were immediately apparent, but my early experiments were pretty unlistenable. Later, in art school, inspired by Philip Glass, Terry Riley, and Steve Reich, I layered multiple staccato guitar parts, played at different speeds, to make a soundtrack for a student film. It was terrifically atmospheric, but it didn't work so well as stand-alone music. That was when I first realized that whether music "works" or not has a lot to do with context.

Years later, with Talking Heads, we recorded demos of some of our songs. These weren't meant for public consumption but to "demonstrate" the songs to others—people in the music business, most likely. Some recordings were made at the home studio of a friend who had an affordable piece of gear, the Tascam prosumer four-track recorder. Tascam and a few other companies made equipment that was almost good enough to make commercial records with, but that was mainly aimed at the "prosumer" (half professional, half regular consumer) market, the aspiring recording engineer and his or her musician friends; other Talking Heads demos were recorded at big professional studios, but not via multitrack—we recorded mostly live to stereo. One was recorded at a studio on Long Island where bubblegum hits had been made. Two others were paid for by record companies, partly so they could hear us over and over without having to visit grotty clubs every time. These recordings sounded tinny and thin and gave no sense of what the band sounded like live. There is an art to capturing the sound of a band, and it seemed at the time that neither we nor the guys who made those recordings possessed that particular skill. Even those professionals in their big studios didn't seem to know how to do it, and we thought those skills came with the job!

This was a real mystery. One could see why musicians and recording engineers would be inclined to get magical and mystical about studios where epochal recordings were made. It was as if glorifying the aura of those places was a way of admitting that skill is not enough, that some invisible mojo was present in the woodwork at Sun Studio or Motown Studio, and it was that ineffable essence that made the records made in those places so good.

When we eventually made our first proper record, *Talking Heads: 77*, it was by and large a miserable experience. Nothing really sounded like it did in our heads, or like we were used to hearing ourselves onstage, although that might say as much about our heads, our expectations, or our sound as we imagined it as it does about how the recordings turned out. Or it could just have been bad mojo. Everybody knows the weird sensation of hearing your own voice played back for the first time. Well, imagine a whole band hearing themselves played back for nearly the first time. It sounded weirdly enervating, jarring at best. Then add to that the experience of working with a producer who we felt didn't "get" what we were about. He had produced some disco hits (we liked that) and had a current one with a disco version of the *Star Wars* theme (we thought this was kind of tacky). We loved and appreciated commercial pop recordings, but we were also the children of the Velvet Underground, the Stooges, Beefheart, and all sorts of other fringe characters. That part of our schizophrenic makeup wasn't, we felt, acknowledged or understood by this guy, so sometimes it was tough staying optimistic about the project from day to day. It was probably tough for the producer and his team, too. Our experience in a real recording studio, making a real record, certainly didn't turn out to be the big exciting and satisfying thing I'd imagined in high school.

In those days, the drummer would be set up in a booth a little larger than a handicapped toilet stall, with a glass window for viewing, and the bass player's amp would be miked up and surrounded by sound-absorbent panels. In this way, the band would be completely sonically deconstructed. We had to wear headphones just to hear each other. The producer would then try mightily to re-create the sound of the live band by feeding the signals from the various mics back into those headphones. Taken apart and put back together by a stranger—no wonder it felt uncomfortable!

To their credit, the producer and his team did try to bring out the accessibility inherent in our somewhat minimalist, stripped-down sound. So while the other singles on the CBGB jukebox were guitar-centric, ours had Stax-Volt-type horns. The record was fairly well received, but I didn't think it captured the band very well.

DECONSTRUCT AND ISOLATE

That phrase sums up the philosophy of a lot of music recording back in the late seventies. The goal was to get as pristine a sound as possible, and even before multitrack recording became ubiquitous, it was typical to try to remove or avoid all ambient sounds—not only the sounds of birds, traffic, and conversations in other rooms, but all of the room ambience as well. Studios were often padded with sound-absorbent materials so that there was almost no reverberation. The sonic character of the space was sucked out, because it wasn't considered to be part of the music. Without this ambience, it was explained, the sound would be more malleable after the recording had been made. You'd keep your options open as long as possible, in other words. Dead, characterless sound was held up as the ideal, and often still is. In this philosophy, the naturally occurring echo and reverb that normally added a little warmth to performances would be removed and then added back in when the recording was being mixed. Sometimes this echo and reverb, the stuff that would be used to re-create the missing ambience, could be treated as an effect, too—one could "overdo" the reverb for a distant spacey sound or add short delays, as was typical of the vocals in early Elvis recordings. But the rest of the time, adding echo and reverb meant trying to artificially re-create something that had been purposefully and expensively eliminated. Seems like kind of a crazy system, but it was all about keeping control throughout as much of the process as possible.

Recording a performance with a band and singer all playing together at the same time in the same room was by this time becoming a rarity. An incredible array of options opened up as a result, but some organic interplay between the musicians disappeared, and the sound of music changed. Some musicians who played well in live situations couldn't adapt to the fashion for each player to be isolated. They couldn't hear their bandmates and, as a result, often didn't play very well. I also hated this situation myself at first, but after many years I began to adapt. I'm not proud that I got used to this arrangement, but I did. I persisted in believing that what the microphone and the tape machine played back was more or less exactly what we had played, despite the fact that often what I heard on tape didn't sound like what I had just heard in the room. I assumed, as Edison claimed, that technology was neutral, though now I know it isn't. My ears were telling me one thing and conventional wisdom another. Which was I to believe? Other musicians and producers blossomed in this world and took advantage of the opportunities that allowed them to construct elaborate simulations of bands and orchestras, but I felt like it wasn't working for me at all.

As pianist Glenn Gould pointed out, recording technology put part of the creative process in the hands of the producer, the tape editor, and the recording engineer:

> It would be impossible for the listener to establish at which point the authority of the performer gave way to that of the producer and the tape editor, just as even the most observant cinema-goer cannot ever be sure whether a particular sequence of shots derives from circumstances occasioned by the actor's performance.[1]

One could argue that these technicians were as responsible for how records came to sound as the composers or performers were. In effect, the authorship of a recording, and of music in general, was being spread around, dispersed. It became harder and harder to know who did what, or whose decisions were affecting the music we were hearing. Though music copyright and publishing still reflect an older, more traditional view of composition, these creative technicians demanded (and often received) an ever-larger piece of the monetary pie. Often they got a larger percentage than the individual performers.

Just as theater is an actor and writer's medium, and cinema is a director's medium, recorded music often came to be a producer's medium, in which they could sometimes out-auteur the artists they were recording.

Earlier I mentioned that this recording philosophy meant idealizing the isolation of each instrument. This made eminent sense for vocals, which would inevitably have to be mixed so that they could be heard clearly above the din of the instruments that were often acoustically louder. However, there were risks in doing this. If there was a lot of drum "leakage"—if the sound of the drummer could be heard on the vocal mic—then every time you made the singer louder to hear a lyric better, the drums would inevitably get louder too. But isolation, which was the solution to this problem, often meant that we later found it hard to play together live. A band would go from being a tight unit to a chaotic mess.

Yet this divide-and-isolate approach still had much to recommend it: mistakes on individual instrumental tracks could be fixed later, effects could be added to one instrument at the mixing and balancing stage without affecting another, and the relative volume of each instrument could be determined in mixing so that, for example, the brass parts could be made quieter during the sung verses.

As we discovered with Talking Heads, simply sticking up a mic and assuming that it would capture the truth of a performance didn't necessarily result in something that *felt* like a band, even though it was, objectively, capturing exactly what you'd played. I have gone out into the world with a good-quality recorder, and it's fascinating to listen to the results of recording common places whose sound you're super familiar with. The true audio chaos of a place is evident in a recording. Though I use the word *true*, and though this might be what enters our ears, it's not what we "hear" when our brains process that sound. As far as our brains are concerned, what is "true" is often wrong.

Sound mixers in movies work much like recording engineers do. They isolate the sound of the actor's voice as much as possible, and then re-create the ambience of the environment later, adding birds, crickets, restaurant chatter, or whatever else is needed. What's fascinating is that even those "natural" sounds are not "true" documents of an environment. For example, the sound of *one* solitary cricket mixed quietly into a scene can evoke a complete outdoor nighttime ambience in the mind of the audience, even though a *true* nighttime ambience would likely include distant traffic, wind, a faraway plane, a couple of barking dogs, and, yes, a whole bunch of crickets. All of this would be, if heard all together, perceived as sonic chaos, and wouldn't convey the tranquil nighttime mood that was intended. Our brains organize the sound we hear in the same way our eyes selectively see. Re-creating what something sounds like, what a sound or sonic environment *feels* like, in a music recording or a film, has become an art that some people are better at than others.

Some musicians and producers ignored this isolate/deconstruct/reconstruct dogma. The Cowboy Junkies made their first record using one mic to record the whole band, and Steve Earle did something similar with a bluegrass band. In 2012, I participated in some recordings on which some brass players were seated next to one another (which meant their playing wasn't isolated) while others were in completely isolated booths. Furthermore, the guitar and vocal tracks had been recorded beforehand in an apartment with no sound isolation at all. Nowadays the dogma isn't adhered to quite as strictly; it's one of a number of approaches one can take, and sometimes many approaches coexist on the same recording.

By the time Talking Heads recorded our second record, *More Songs About Buildings and Food*, we had become friends with Brian Eno. We liked his music, so we asked ourselves, "Why not have him be our producer? At least he gets what we're about, and we're already friends." Friendship, common interests, and sensibilities seemed more important to us, especially based on our previous experience, than whatever technical skills or hit-making track record he might have possessed.

Seeing that we had turned into a pretty tight live band, Eno suggested we play live in the studio, without all of the typical sonic isolation. His semi-blasphemous idea seemed worth a try, despite the risk of it resulting in a muddy recording. Removing all that isolating stuff, or at least most of it, was like being able to breathe again. The result sounded—surprise!—more like us, like the way we were used to hearing ourselves onstage, and so our playing was more inspired (or so we felt). Removing some of the sound-absorbent stuff meant that you could hear the faint sound of guitars in the background of the drum tracks, and maybe an electric piano might be audible in the background of the bass track. There wasn't absolute separation of instruments, but we felt that the comfort factor more than compensated for this technical challenge. Eno even believed that the two mics he placed in the center of the room might be all that was needed to capture the entire band. That proved not to be entirely the case, though the sound of those mics did come in handy as a kind of supplementary ambience.

Eno suggested we try some fairly unconventional vocal-recording approaches also. Sometimes I sang along to all the music after it had been recorded, mic in my hand, often right in the control room with the speakers blasting, like a big live sound system positioned on either side of me. This wasn't a kosher recording technique back then. The sound of the band coming through the speakers behind me could be heard on my vocal tracks, and typically producers would insist that singers go into silent padded booths. That isolation works for some, but it requires a leap of faith, as even the greatest headphone mix doesn't sound as good as singing in front of a live band or blasting speakers. You have to imagine while you're singing in the booth that the not-so-exciting band you're hearing over the headphones is one day going to sound better than it does. I wondered how those professional singers did it. I wasn't going to acquire those skills instantly, so, to his credit, Eno's suggestion was a good workaround. I've heard this is what Bono does, too.

Most of the songs we recorded we had been performing live for a while, though a couple—"Found a Job" and "The Big Country"—were brand-new, written for that record. In subtle ways those songs were shaped in the studio, though I'd initially written them as something I could play solo on my guitar. This process of learning new songs just before recording them would become commonplace for us. It was practical, but it meant that the songs often didn't get as "broken in" before recording as they would have after a series of live performances.

More Songs About Buildings and Food took three weeks to make. I think 77 might have taken two weeks, including mixing. That meant that the recording costs advanced (i.e., loaned) to us by the record company were low enough that, even with modest sales, we were able to pay them back relatively quickly. It also meant that the record company itself would probably make a profit on the record, ensuring (we hoped) a continuing relationship between them and the band.

Did we think about those costs, and did they affect the way we recorded the music? Do music-business finances, especially those dictated by recording technology, in some ways determine what music sounds like? Absolutely. Limited finances acted as a set of creative restrictions, which, for us, was generally a good thing. Decisions about whether an overdubbed part worked or was well played had to be made relatively quickly. Indecision cost time, which we knew was constrained by our budget. The question of whether to rearrange a song or try it in a manner different from how we played it live often never came up—these were non-decisions that saved time and money. Using few outside players, who would have had to be paid, was another cost-saving move. These factors make certain records sound the way they do; they are not purely the result of musically inspired directives. Financial strictures don't determine a melody, the lyrics, or harmony, but they do affect how a record is recorded, and therefore what it ultimately sounds like.

For *Fear of Music*, the next Talking Heads album, we worked with Eno again. We decided to take our comfort level one step further: we recorded all the basic tracks (the four of us playing together, without me singing) in the loft where we rehearsed, which was also where Chris Frantz and Tina Weymouth lived. We hired one of those mobile recording studios that are used to record live concerts and sporting events, and parked it outside on the street, stringing the various cables through the window.[A, B]

I'm not sure why, but it sounded far better than the messy lo-fi sound one would expect from recording outside of the pristine studio environment. We were finally beginning to capture what we sounded like live! Stepping outside of the acoustically isolated recording-studio environment wasn't, it turned out, as catastrophic as it was made to sound. Hmmm. Maybe those rules of recording weren't as true as we'd thought.

This wasn't the only way our recording process had changed. We also recorded some basic tracks for songs that I hadn't written words to yet, and later we altered and supplemented some of the sounds of the instruments well after they had been recorded; some now-familiar arrangements were actually created after the performance. Recording songs that were "incomplete" was risky for me. I wondered, could I really create a song by singing over prerecorded riffs and chord changes? In some cases I did so quite successfully ("Life During Wartime"), but other tracks never got finished ("Dancing for Money"). But succeeding even half the time meant that this was indeed a feasible working method. I knew that in

the future this meant I might be able to write words that responded to and were guided by prerecorded music, instead of getting all bent out of shape trying to get the music to fit—not just melodically, but sonically and texturally—prewritten lyrics. Others do this all the time now. St. Vincent (Annie Clark) went into the studio to do her second record, *Actor*, with no complete "songs" written; she had only musical fragments. You wouldn't know this immediately from listening to her records, but it can be evident when others write their vocal melody over a sample of someone else's song. In those instances, you know that the music existed years before the new song was written. The authorship is dislocated in such cases, both temporally and spatially. There can be no illusion that the music and lyrics were conceived together. Sometimes the writer of the music and the writer of the lyrics never meet.

Eno was the one who encouraged us to mess with the sounds after they were recorded. He'd done a little of that on our previous record, but now the gloves were off. The furthest we went was on the song "Drugs." We had initially recorded a fairly straightforward backing track that seemed a bit conventional, so we began to mute some of the instruments, sometimes just silencing specific notes. This made some parts open up; there were more gaps, more air. I had a recording of koalas that I'd made while we were on tour in Australia (they mainly grunt and snort, in contrast to their cutesy appearance), and that got added in here and there. The grunts worked like indeterminate animal answers and echoes to my singing. More sounds went on—an arc-like melody created using an echo machine, and then a guitar solo at the end that was made by selecting fragments from a number of improvised solos. Finally, I sang the song after jogging in the studio, because for some reason I wanted to sound out of breath. Of course, I was singing the same words and melody as I had been on the earlier, straighter, version of the song, but now to a vastly altered musical track—a fact that also affected how I sang. The song, as it was released, was an arrangement of sounds that one would never have come up with in rehearsal or by sitting writing with a guitar. It could only have been created in a studio. As Eno observed at the time, the recording studio was now a compositional tool.

IMAGINARY FIELD RECORDINGS
(MY LIFE IN THE BUSH OF GHOSTS) 1980

Around this time, Eno and I were listening to a lot of the beautiful recordings released on the French Ocora label.[c] Some of these were typical field recordings, similar to the ones Alan Lomax had collected in the United States: they were often made with one mic and a portable recorder and featured African guys playing rocks, Pygmies singing their intricate hocketing songs, and Muslim calls to prayer. Other Ocora releases were recorded in more controlled situations: in concert halls, churches, temples, and maybe even a few studios. There were Georgian choirs, classical Indian musicians, Iranian traditional music, and North African griots, or praise singers.

Ocora records treated a huge variety of music as if it was the equal of Western classical or art music. The recordings were given respect, thoughtful presentation, and technical attention that was all too rare for non-Western music. I had grown up on Folkways's *Nonesuch* field recordings and the stuff Lomax had done for the Library of Congress, but the production values on the Ocora releases were on a whole

other level. Eno and I realized that music from elsewhere didn't need to sound distant, scratchy, or "primitive." These recordings were as well produced as any contemporary recording in any genre. You were made to feel, for example, that this music wasn't a ghostly remnant from some lost culture, soon to be relegated to the almost forgotten past. It was vital, and it was happening right now. To us there was strange beauty there, deep passion, and the compositions often operated by rules and structures that were radically different from what we were used to. As a result, our limited ideas of what constituted music were exploded forever. These recordings opened up myriad ways that music could be made and organized. There were many musical universes out there, and we had been blinkered by confining ourselves to only one.

By the end of 1979, Talking Heads had just completed what for us was a long world tour for *Fear of Music*. It was the first time we'd received offers to play in many places (the south island of New Zealand comes to mind), and we accepted almost every one of them. After we got back I took some time off to recuperate. I began spending time with Eno and Jon Hassell, who was beginning to develop and elucidate his "fourth world" concept, and we enthusiastically exchanged cassettes and vinyl we had found. Most of the music we were excited about came from outside the English-language pop-music axis. At the time, there was no way to find out about this kind of music except by word of mouth. There was no Internet yet, and there were almost no books about the pop music, not to mention folk or classical music, that was flourishing outside the English- or European-language zones.

I seem to remember one day when Jon played some Milton Nascimento records, which I didn't get at the time—it took years until I did. Brian and I shared a fascination with African pop music, although aside from Fela Kuti we could find little information about any of the artists whose records we'd stumbled across. Pop music in many other countries, we discovered, came in wildly different flavors, and it wasn't yet a suitable subject for ethnomusicologists. The Lebanese-Egyptian singer Farid al-Atrache was a big favorite, as was duduk player Djivan Gasparyan.

I had some cassettes of Balkan brass bands and Ghanaian pop groups. We passed around our records, lugging vinyl from coast to coast, apartment to apartment.

Inspired by these records, Brian, Jon, and I fantasized about making a series of recordings based on an imaginary culture. (Unbeknownst to us, at that moment in Germany, Holger Czukay and his fellow band members in Can, who were students of the composer Karlheinz Stockhausen, were beginning their own "Ethnic Forgeries" series.) For a brief minute, we had the idea that we might be able to create our own "field recordings"—a musical documentation of an imaginary culture. It would be sort of like a Borges or Calvino story, but this would be a mystery in musical form. It appealed to us, I suspect, partly because it would make us more or less invisible as creators. In our vision, we'd release a record with typically detailed liner notes explaining the way music functioned in that culture and how it was produced there—the kind of academic notes common on such records. One might think the sort of dark and wiggly sounds we were known for would not be credible as music that had been found and recorded in some far-off cultural oasis, evidence of a kind of lost world where some branch of the pop-music tree had become isolated from the rest of the world. But then you come across a real group like Konono N°1, a group of Congolese musicians who play amplified mbiras (thumb pianos) that they construct by wrapping wires around a magnetic lodestone, plopping those inside the instruments, and then feeding the wires into a guitar amp, greatly distorted. I once heard one of the best lead-guitar players ever on a cassette that seemed to come from Sudan. The eddies and backwaters of pop music do indeed produce some magical, unexpected meetings, so our imaginary group that played cardboard boxes for percussion and Arabic solos on Minimoogs is not inconceivable.

Needless to say, that whole plan was abandoned, but some of the inspiration behind it lingered. We decided to use our usual instruments in new ways, and whatever materials happened to be lying about would be used for sound production. We'd try to pretend that we didn't necessarily already know how a guitar or piano was meant to be played, and we would reject some approaches if they seemed too informed by our own past experience. On the record we ended up making, *My Life in the Bush of Ghosts*, we sometimes used guitar cases or the above-mentioned cardboard boxes for drums, and pots and pans for percussion. This might have all been a bit silly, but it did serve to shake us out of tried-and-true patterns.[D]

Eno had already begun work on some recordings that incorporated found voices, and he brought these to the table. One of these led to the song "Mea Culpa," which had a foundation consisting of layers of vocal loops of radio call-in-show voices hemming and hawing. We both soon realized that the "found vocal" idea might serve as the thread and theme that would pull the new record together.

I suspect that this idea appealed to us partly because it eliminated any conflict or likelihood of competition between the two of us as singers: neither of us would sing on the record. (This fact proved to be an issue for some folks down the line—how could it be "our" record if we weren't singing on it?) Relying exclusively on found vocals also solved a content problem: the lyrics would clearly not be derived from autobiographical or confessional material. Often, what the vocalists were actually saying didn't matter to us at all. It was the *sound* of their vocals—the passion, rhythm, and phrasing—that conveyed the emotional content. This approach retained some of the "authorless" aspect that had appealed to us when we came up with the fake field-recording concept, but it also turned out to be contentious to those who view songs primarily as vehicles for texts.

Using found elements in creative works certainly wasn't a new idea. Duchamp had nominated stuff from the hardware store as fine art, Kurt Schwitters had made collages out of labels and packages, and Warhol had made "paintings" out of photos clipped from the tabloid press. In the plastic arts, this idea was, if not commonplace, at least acceptable. Bern Porter, James Joyce, JG Ballard, and the collage books of Marshall McLuhan and Quentin Fiore lifted passages from type and advertising copy and repurposed them. John Cage and others had made sonic collages out of multiple records playing simultaneously or multiple radios tuned to different stations, but in pop music the idea was limited to novelty records ("The Flying Saucer" and "Mr. Jaws") or self-conscious avant-garde experiments like the Beatles' "Revolution 9."

While we were in LA, Eno and I hung out a bit with Toni Basil, whom we both admired. Her appearances on *Soul Train* with the dance group the Lockers were unforgettable, and the group she was working with and organizing at that time, the Electric Boogaloos,[E] were creating some of the most amazing and innovative dance we'd ever seen. Their moves put the arty dance world to shame. They were funky and robotic at the same time, a combination that somehow seemed apt. Either the machines had gotten funky, or the funk had been infected by a robot virus; whatever it was, it felt right. Eno described the way the Boogaloos moved as "somadelic"—something that made your body go all wobbly the way LSD did your head.

Toni had an offer to do a TV special featuring these dancers, and for a short while we imagined that *My Life in the Bush of Ghosts* would end up as the score or soundtrack. Our ever-morphing guiding principle had changed from an audio document of an imaginary culture to beats and sounds for funky urban dancers for a Hollywood TV show! That project fell through, but like the imaginary-civilization idea, it became another subtext for our recordings, because it allowed us to imagine that we were making a dance record. Of course, the influence of music on dancers is a recurring theme in this book, and we hoped our project could be a new kind of psychedelic dance music that might, at a stretch, get played in dance clubs, which would have been hugely validating for us. Years later, I was predictably excited when I heard DJ Larry Levan play something off our record at the Paradise Garage, a huge dance club in New York.

This was the very early eighties, and some of the most innovative mixing and arranging in pop music was happening in the dance-music world. The rock scene was becoming increasingly conservative and entrenched, despite all the shouting about freedom, individuality, and self-expression. The influence of dub and what were then called "extended mixes" of songs in the dance-club world were just gaining momentum. The fact that DJs and remixers were using other people's tracks as raw material resonated with our use of found vocals and the way we arranged songs by switching tracks on and off. We were turning the mixing board into a giant instrument. This arranging and composing technique soon became extremely common in hip-hop. No credit to us—it was simply in the air at that time.

Neither Eno nor I saw ourselves as virtuoso musicians, but we aimed to turn our limitations into advantages. We used those cardboard boxes as kick drums, biscuit tins as snare drums, and bass guitars as rhythm instruments. This had the advantage of making everything sound a little "off." A kick drum made out of a guitar case did the job. It made a nice thud in the low range, but it also sounded slightly unfamiliar and fresh. We'd generally play each part that

E

would eventually constitute the bed of the piece over and over, as if we were a human loop. Digital loops and sampling didn't exist yet, but by playing the same part over and over, one could create a rhythmic and hypnotic textural bed that could be manipulated and layered over later. There were wonderful real players involved, too—drummers and bass players were the foundation on some tracks, but by and large it was a DIY affair.

Without samplers, we had to place the found vocals into our music by trial and error. We'd have two tape machines playing simultaneously, one containing our music track and the other the vocal, and if the gods willed, which they often did, there would be serendipity. The resulting "vocal" over our track would feel like the parts had always belonged together, and we'd have a "take." The tape recorders were all "played" manually, and getting the voices to sync with the music tracks in a way that seemed like what a singer would do was very seat-of-the-pants—there was none of the incremental tweaking and time-correcting of tracks that's possible with modern samplers and recording software, so throwing the vocals against the music entailed a kind of performance. We would start and stop the "singer" (which was now the tape with the vocal on it) as if he or she were responding to our music, coming in with a particularly emotional line as the track modulated up to a new key, for example. These "performances" were witnessed only by us and one or two others, but as we'd fly those vocals in, there was a vibrant energy present, as if we were actually singing ourselves.

Sometimes, at night, back in our apartments, we'd record radio sermons on the cassette recorders of our late-seventies boomboxes. The quality of these recordings was sometimes dubious (on "Come with Us" we had to make the background hiss that was due to intermittent radio reception part of the dark ambience of the song), but overall we came to realize that these vocals recorded on cassettes sounded fine—or at least good enough (there's that phrase again). High fidelity, we realized, was a vastly overrated convention that no one had bothered to question. Sometimes the harsh megaphone-like quality of these vocals actually had much more character than a "good" recording. One was subliminally aware that these vocals were "secondhand" or disembodied, and this quality made them feel like transmissions from a desperate planet—ours. At times, the vocals we used came from the records we'd been passing around for the past year. Arabic pop records, field recordings, ethnographic recordings, gospel records—all were being scoured for possible vocal "samples" now that we realized this would be the unifying aspect of this record.

The amazing thing was how easy it was (well, relatively), and how much the vocals felt like they had been performed or "sung" with the "band." Part of this effect was, of course, entirely in the ear of the beholder—a phenomenon we noticed early on. The mind tends to find congruencies and links where none previously existed—not just in music, but in everything. More than just a way of tricking the mind, we also felt that, when successful, this effect also "tricked" the emotions. Some of the tracks generated genuine (to us) emotional reactions. It felt like the "singer" really was responding to the music we had made, and vice versa, in a way that often elicited powerful feelings—uplift, ecstasy, dread, or sexy playfulness. Perhaps it's wrong to say the emotions were being "tricked"; maybe these passionate voices and rhythms triggered emotional responses because our brains have neurological "receptors" awaiting musical and vocal combinations just like these, and we provided the necessary materials for that process to take place. Maybe that's what artists do. A big major chord is a "trick" too.

We gravitated toward passionate "vocalists," and this made it seem to us that the natural cadences and metric of any impassioned vocal—even ones spoken, not sung—might be in some way innately and intrinsically musical. It's easy to hear this musical speech in the sermon of a gospel preacher where the line between singing and speaking is intentionally fuzzy, but it's there in talk-show hosts, political speeches, and, well, maybe in all our vocalizations. Maybe the difference between speech and music isn't all that great. We infer a lot from the tone of someone's voice, so imagine that aspect of speech pushed just a little further. The weird cadences of a Valley girl, for instance, might be viewed as a species of singing. The malls of Sherman Oaks are a setting for a kind of massed choir.

Some people find all this disturbing. In the West, the presumption of a causal link between the author and performer is strong. For instance, it's assumed that I write lyrics (and the accompanying music) for songs because I have something I need to express. And it's assumed that everything one utters or sings (or even plays) emerges from some autobiographical impulse. Even if I choose to sing someone else's song, it's assumed that the song was, when it was written, autobiographical for *them*, and I am both acknowledging that fact and at the same time implying that it's applicable to my own biography. Nonsense! It doesn't matter whether or not something actually happened to the writer—or to the person interpreting the song. On the contrary, it is the music and the lyrics that trigger the emotions within us, rather than the other way around. We don't make music—it makes *us*. Which is maybe the point of this whole book.

Granted, a writer has to draw on some instinctual understanding of a feeling in order to put something with some emotional truth down on paper, but it didn't necessarily have to happen to them. In writing and performing music we are pushing our *own* buttons, and the surprising thing about *My Life in the Bush of Ghosts* is that vocals that we didn't write ourselves—or, in the case of the found vocals, didn't even sing—could still make us feel such a gamut of emotions.

Making music is like constructing a machine whose function is to dredge up emotions in performer and listener alike. Some people find this idea repulsive, because it seems to relegate the artist to the level of trickster, manipulator, and deceiver—a kind of self-justifying onanist. They would prefer to see music as an expression of emotion rather than a generator of it, to believe in the artist as someone with something to say. I'm beginning to think of the artist as someone who is adept at making devices that tap into our shared psychological makeup and that trigger the deeply moving parts we have in common. In that sense, the conventional idea of authorship is questionable. Not that I don't want credit for the songs I've written, but what constitutes authorship is maybe not what we would like it to be. This queasiness about rethinking how music works is also connected with the idea of authenticity: the idea that musicians who appear to be "down-home," or seem to be conveying aspects of their own experience, must therefore be more "real." It can be disillusioning to find out that the archetypical rock and roll persona is an act, and that none of the "country" folk in Nashville really wear cowboy hats (well, except during their public appearances and photo shoots).

This issue was resolved years later by electronic and hip-hop artists, whose music was often either rarely played by them (in the case of hip-hop artists) or who, like Eno and me on this record, remained more or less faceless. Electronic and lounge artists like NASA, Thievery Corporation, David Guetta, and Swedish House Mafia often use a variety of friends and name-brand singers on their tracks and almost never sing on their own records. Now it has become accepted that the author can be the curator, the guiding sensibility, rather than the singer.

After finishing an initial version of *Bush of Ghosts* in 1980, we set about the task of "clearing"—getting permission to use—the found vocals. This is a common practice nowadays, and there are established companies who do nothing but clear samples, but back then, no one that we approached for the rights to their recordings had any idea what the hell we were up to. The record sat on the shelf ready to go while the phone calls and faxes went back and forth. Most of the vocals we hoped to use were cleared, but in a couple of cases we were denied rights and were forced to find alternatives. Sometimes this resulted in newer, better tracks, and sometimes not. In the meantime, we had returned to New York and begun work on the next Talking Heads record, which would become *Remain in Light*.

MODULAR MUSIC (*REMAIN IN LIGHT*)

Eno and I were full of enthusiasm after everything we'd learned and experienced making *Bush of Ghosts,* and we felt confident that a Talking Heads sort of pop record could be made using some of the same recording and composing techniques. The rest of the band agreed that starting with a blank slate would be a creative and revolutionary way to make our next record. We didn't intend to use the found voices or cardboard drums this time, but the process of creating repetitive tracks and then making sections by switching instruments on and off using the mixing board was retained.

We gave ourselves two weeks to build this instrumental scaffolding, but we knew we wouldn't finish the record—the vocals would have to come later. In a nod to a strange ritual of the era, we recorded these initial tracks at a studio in the Bahamas. Maybe a decade earlier, the idea had taken hold that making pop records should be like sequestering oneself to write the Great American Novel. Studios were built in idyllic locations—Sausalito, deep in the Rocky Mountains, in a barn in Woodstock, New York, a French château, St. Martin, Miami Beach, or Nassau—with the idea that a self-contained musical act would hole up there, avoid distractions, and emerge with a polished finished product. There were often beaches nearby, and sometimes meals were communal and catered. (The financial climate for the music business was obviously different then.) Isolation and time to focus has a lot to recommend it, but many bands (my own included) found ways to achieve those things through much less expensive means.

We worked rapidly. One or two people would lay down a track, usually some kind of repetitive groove that would last about four minutes, the presumed length of a song. Maybe it would be a guitar riff and a drum part, or maybe a sequenced arpeggio pattern and an intermittent guitar squeal. Others would then respond to what had been put down, adding their own repetitive parts, filling in the gaps and spaces, for the whole length of the "song." As we'd listen to one part being recorded, we'd all be scheming about what we could add—it was a kind of game. This manner of recording had the added advantage that we weren't trying to replicate the sound of the live band. We hadn't gotten attached to the way these songs and their instruments and arrangements sounded in performance, so in some ways the conflicts we had confronted when we'd first entered a recording studio years previously were bypassed.

After the tracks began to fill up, or when the sound of them playing simultaneously was sufficiently dense, it was time to make sections. While the groove usually remained constant, different combinations of instruments would be switched on and off simultaneously at different given times. One group of instruments that produced a certain texture and groove might eventually be nominated as a "verse" section, and another group—often larger-sounding—would be nominated as the "chorus." Often in these songs there was no real key change. The bass line tended to remain constant, but one could still imply key modulations, illusory chord changes, which were very useful for building excitement while maintaining the trancelike feeling of constant root notes. Up to this point, there was still no top-line melody, nothing that the singer (me) would put words to. That came later.

So far, this was all very much like the process Eno and I had used in the *Bush of Ghosts* sessions. But we weren't going to use found vocals this time, so when these sections had been created, Eno or I would go into the studio and sing to them, improvising a wordless melody. Often it took a few tries before arriving at a suitable melody for a verse and a different one for the chorus. Sometimes even harmonies, also wordless, were added, to give the impression of a rousing chorus.

We then did rough mixes of these "songs"—including these gibberish vocals—for everyone to listen to, while I took them home to write actual words. We agreed to reconvene in New York after I'd finished my lyric-writing assignment. On a previous record, the song "I Zimbra" actually got left as gibberish—or rather, the gibberish early-twentieth-century Dada poet Hugo Ball had written seemed a perfect fit. But now I wanted to find real words to substitute, which was going to be tricky.

How did this recording process affect the music? A lot. For starters, the constant looplike grooves on these tracks and the unchanging bass line that carried through many of the songs meant that tricky structural devices like meter changes or half measures were unlikely to occur. Complex chord changes of the sort one might hear in ordinary pop songs, bossa novas, or standards were very unlikely, too (usually there were no chord changes at all). Such devices are often employed to keep a song interesting, so we had basically abandoned the rules we had previously accepted for determining structure and arrangement. While punk rock was celebrated for needing only three chords, we had now stripped that down to one. This fairly strict self-limitation might seem perverse, as it restricted the kinds of top melodies one might write, and a melody that doesn't change keys has a hard row to hoe—it runs the risk of being overly repetitive and boring. But using only one chord has its advantages, too: more emphasis gets placed on the groove. Even if a given song wasn't particularly aggressive rhythmically, the groove tended to feel insistent, and you noticed it more. This made the tracks feel more trancelike, somewhat transcendent, ecstatic even—more akin to African music or gospel or disco, though the way we played placed us well outside those traditions. Not only were these tracks groove-centered, they were also very much about texture. The changes from one section to another were sometimes driven more by textural variation than by melody or harmony— more like minimal classical music or some traditional forms of music around the world than the rock and pop traditions we came out of.

I'm exaggerating a little here—there were certainly other kinds of pop music in North America that worked this way. Many James Brown songs, Hamilton Bohannon, and some Mississippi blues guys basically groove, twist, and elaborate around one chord. We knew and loved much of that music too. We had, it seemed, taken the long way around to arrive at a place that, structurally at least, we should have been slightly familiar with already. Like that T.S. Eliot quote about arriving where we started and knowing it for the first time, we were essentially reinventing something we already knew, something right there in our own backyard. But of course in the reinvention process we got much of it "wrong," and, for example, the version of funk we ended up with was skewed, herky-jerky, and somewhat robotic. The result was something with that familiar structure, but now made of strange and different parts.

MUSIC WRITES THE WORDS

Significantly, rhythm and texture are the two most difficult aspects of music to express in conventional Western musical notation. These qualities, some of the most resonant and important in contemporary popular music, and in some ways the most "African," were excluded from, or maybe simply outside of, the system by which music was traditionally taught, passed on, notated, discussed, criticized, and—very important—copyrighted. The copyright of a musical composition is based on the top-line melody, the specific harmonies that support it, and, in the case of a song or opera, the lyrics. There is no acknowledgment of groove, sound, texture, or arrangement—all of which are features of the recorded music of our era that we listeners have come to savor and identify as integral to an artist's work. This failure would lead to some conflicts down the road. The drummer on James Brown's tune "Funky Drummer," Clyde Stubblefield, claimed that he was due some percentage of the money received by Brown and his publishers when that song (the drum break especially) was sampled by countless acts in recent years. Legally, Stubblefield's contribution fell outside of what one would traditionally call "composition," but realistically those were his drum breaks that everyone wanted. Determining and attributing these contributions is complex. One could argue that it was Brown who suggested that Stubblefield take his famous break, and similarly, that if it wasn't on a James Brown record, no one would ever have heard it. Stubblefield has suggested that he should be compensated, but the issue has not been resolved.

I felt that the melodies and the lyrics I was going to write for *Remain in Light* had to respond to all these new (for us) musical qualities. One might even say that the recording process, because it privileged trancelike and transcendent music, was about to affect the words that I would gravitate toward. The gently ecstatic nature of the tracks meant that angsty personal lyrics like the ones I'd written previously might not be the best match, so I had to find some new lyrical approach. I filled page after page with phrases that matched the melodic lines of the verses and choruses, hoping that some of them might complement the feelings the music generated.

On the following page is a small sample of some of the phrases I jotted down in this manner for the song that eventually became "Once in a Lifetime."[F] Judging by the fact that on this particular page there are actual stanzas and couplets, I suspect I was pretty far along in the process—earlier pages would have included anything, absolutely anything, that fit the meter and syllabic form, and might not have included any rhymes or been on a trajectory toward a subject. What's with the color coding? I believe that the red texts were the culled favorites. I still often write in very much the same way today, but without the color coding and minuscule handwriting.

I tried not to censor the potential lyrics I wrote down. Sometimes I would sing the melodic fragments over and over, trying random lyric phrases, and I could sense when one syllable was more appropriate than another. I began to notice, for example, that the choice of a hard consonant instead of a soft one implied something, something emotional. A consonant wasn't merely a formal decision, it *felt* different. Vowels, too, had emotional resonances—a soft *ooh* and a pinched nasal *aah* have very different associations. I felt I had to adhere to whatever syllables seemed to fit the existing melody best, so I'd listen to the gibberish vocals respectfully and let those be my guide. If I seemed to instinctively gravitate to an *aah* on the gibberish vocal mix, I'd try to stick to that sound in the lyrics I was writing. More restrictions, but okay.

In keeping with the rapturous nature of some of the tracks, I was also drawing lyrical inspiration from the radio preachers I'd been listening to and that we'd used on the *Bush of Ghosts* record. At that time, American radio was a cauldron of impassioned voices—live preachers, talk-show hosts, and salesmen. The radio was shouting at you, pleading with you, and seducing you. You could also hear great salsa singers, as well as gospel being broadcast straight from the churches. I can only imagine Eno's reaction, coming from a country with four fairly restrained radio stations! I don't listen to the radio much anymore, though. There is still variety on some stations, but it's mostly been homogenized, like so many other parts of our culture.

RIGHT START

2ND HALF OF
DOUBLE CHORUS
2

(3B) INTO THE BLUE AGAIN
AFTER THE MONEY'S GONE
ONCE IN A LIFETIME
WATER FLOWING UNDERGROUND

(1 A) LETTING THE DAYS GO BY
LET THE WATER HOLD ME DOWN
* (LETTING THE DAYS GO BY
WATER FLOWING UNDERGROUND

INTO THE BLUE AGAIN
AFTER THE MONEY'S GONE
* (LETTING THE DAYS GO BY ONCE IN A LIFETIME
WATER FLOWING UNDERGROUND

INTO THE BLUE AGAIN
INTO THE SILENT WATER

LETTING THE DAYS GO BY

INTO THE BLUE AGAIN
INTO THE SILENT WATER
UNDER THE ROCKS & STON
THERE IS WATER UNDERGROUND

LETTING

SUBSTITUTE
FOR * IN LATER
CHORUSES THAT
REPEAT 1 A

(3) TIME TO REMEMBER
INTO THE SILENT WATER
UNDER THE ROCKS AND STONE
THERE IS WATER UNDER GROUND

NOTHING CAN STOP ME NOW
THERE IS WATER UNDERGROUN
LETTING THE HOURS DISSAPEAR
UNDER THE

INTO THE BLUE AGAIN
AFTER THE MONEY'S GONE
ONCE IN A LIFETIME
WATER FLOWING UNDERGROUN

UNDER THE ROCKS AND STONE
THERE IS WATER UNDERGROUN

2ND HALF OF
DOUBLE
CHORUS 1

LETTING THE DAYS GO BY
INTO THE SILENT WATER
NOTHING CAN STOP ME NOW
LETTING th HOURS DISSAPEAR

(TIME ISN'T HOLDING US)
(TIME IS A PONY RIDE)
TIME TO REMEMBER

(To 3B)

LETTING THE DAYS GO BY
LET THE WATER HOLD ME DOW
LETTING THE DAYS GO BY
AND YOUR LOVE IS STILL AROU

AND THE SMOKE IS ALL ABOUT
WATER RUNNING UNDERGROUND

LETTING THE DAYS GO BY
LET THE HOURS DISAPPEAR
SPLITTING IN TWO AGAIN
WAITING FOR ___ AGAIN
WAIT FOR SOMEONE TO EXPLAIN
UNDER THE WATER

INTO THE BLUE AGAIN
AFTER THE MONEY'S GONE
INTO THE SILENT WATER
GIMMIE THE THING AGAIN
AT THE BOTTOM OF THE OCEAN

SAME AS IT EVER WAS

LOOKIN' AT SOMETHING/GOOD
NOTHING CAN STOP ME NOW

GET THE TWISTER BACK
GET THE TWISTER BACK AGAIN

ONCE IN A LIFETIME
HERE IS YOUR MOMENT BOY

GET YOURSELF READY/NOW
THE ___ IS COMIN' BAC
HERE COMES THE ___ AGAIN

AT
LOOK WHERE MY HAND IS /NOW

THE SHORTCUT / HERE
TAKIN' MY CHANCES / NOW

F

I wrote the verses of "Once in a Lifetime" at my home on East Seventh Street in the East Village. I started by taking on the character of a radio preacher I'd heard on one of my cassettes. There was a serious use of anaphora—employing the same phrase to begin each sentence. It's a common device that preachers use, and it brings their speechifying one step closer to poetry and song. One or two fragments that I used—the repetition of the phrase "You may find yourself," for example—were straight lifts from the radio preacher, but from there I'd improvise and change the focus from a Christian message to, well, I wasn't sure at first what I was getting at. The preacher was focusing on the lack of spirituality in material striving; he may have begun by telling the listener that there was nothing wrong with living in a shotgun house, a house in which all the rooms are in a line so straight, you could shoot a shotgun straight through (you see them a lot in New Orleans). So the mention of the beautiful house, the beautiful wife, and the trappings of an ideal life situation would have been a natural segue for me. I'd get myself worked up, pacing back and forth, breathing in sync with the preacher, phrases would come into my head, and I'd jot them down as quickly as possible. I maybe went off topic once or twice.

The lyrics for another song, "The Great Curve," were inspired by Robert Farris Thompson's writings about African spirituality, and the feminine goddesses that survive today in remnants like Mother Nature or Yansan and Oshun in Afro-Atlantic cultures. My lyrics, though they didn't all start out addressing that subject, began to approach and circle around that idea, so I tried to urge them closer, and to reject ones that seemed to go in a different direction. It was tough work—I had to reinvent myself as a lyricist to match those tracks. I wasn't writing about my own anxieties anymore—I had to leave much of that behind. Not every track we recorded became a finished song. There were some really wonderful tracks that I just couldn't find words to fit. But we had ample music, so when we went back into the studio I could sing the words I'd written, get everyone's reaction, and if one set of lyrics worked, we'd record a properly sung vocal and then move on.

We spent maybe two weeks in New York recording vocals and some additional overdubs—Adrian Belew's amazing guitar solos, some trumpets and percussion. It was all fairly exciting. But when the record finally came out in 1980, radio stations balked. I suspect it may have been the videos on MTV that introduced that record to many people. MTV had just launched, and they were starving for content; they'd play pretty much any decent material they were handed. Not too many people had cable TV back then, so MTV had no hesitation about playing the same videos over and over. Hard to believe, but at the time, if you made almost any halfway interesting video you could possibly have it up and running on cable TV almost instantly. For me it was a godsend—a way to reincorporate my art-school roots into the music side of things. The video for "Once in a Lifetime" and the one for "Burning Down the House" were made fairly cheaply, and they both went into pretty heavy rotation. Years later I gave MTV an animated video for a song by a Brazilian singer, Jorge Ben ("Umabarauma"), and even that got played.

Arranging songs by switching tracks on and off like we did for *Remain in Light* (and on the two records that followed) was very much what hip-hop artists were doing at the same time: looping a groove to make an underlying bed and then making sections by nominating other sounds and parts to go in designated places. Samplers didn't really exist yet, so even the hip-hop artists were looping somewhat manually by playing break sections of records over and over and then layering other sounds and vocals on top of the breaks.

I went a bit further texturally with this process on *The Catherine Wheel*, a score I wrote for choreographer Twyla Tharp in 1981. On *The Catherine Wheel*, I worked with some musicians outside my band—ney player Richard Horowitz, Adrian Belew, who came back after touring with us, drummer Yogi Horton, and Bernie Worrell, who added some keyboards. I got to pay back writer and drummer John Miller Chernoff, whose book on African drumming had inspired both Eno and me, when I invited him to play some African drum patterns on a prepared upright piano. The strings inside the piano were muffled so the sound didn't ring out, and the result was pitched thuds. It worked.

TWO RECORDS AT ONCE

We did another record, *Speaking in Tongues*, that continued with this idea of using improvised initial riffs and gibberish vocals as a guide for lyric writing. That record turned out to be the most commercially successful so far.

After completing a tour that was filmed (*Stop Making Sense*), I got it into my head to direct a movie. Talking Heads, as a band, was fairly popular by then, and I figured if the movie had some songs scattered throughout, it would help me get financing. I was right, but it still took a long time to get the funding and production in place, so in the meantime, I wrote some songs that could be used for a new Talking Heads record. I decided to write them ahead of the recording sessions, in what now seemed to us the old-fashioned way—playing a guitar and singing along. Sometimes I wrote the songs by using two boomboxes. I recorded the guitar chords on one machine, then played that back and sang along, recording the result of that live "overdubbing" on a second machine. Other times I used a Tascam, an attaché-sized four-track recorder that used ordinary audiocassettes played at high speed. The quality wasn't great, but as a writing tool and a way to make demos for the band, it was sufficient.

We decided to economize. After rehearsing the new songs, we recorded them relatively quickly and conventionally in New York. We were fairly comfortable in the studio by now; much of the alienation and terror had worn off. When we had finished the overdubs and the singing on that batch of songs, we let Eric Thorngren start mixing them while we went into the adjacent live room and began rehearsing another album's worth of material that I'd written for the movie. These would be recorded with my "guide vocals," but in most cases it would be the actors who would later sing the songs, replacing my voice singing over our tracks.

This was all very workmanlike, and by the time *Little Creatures*, the first of these records, came out, I was already in Texas preparing to shoot the movie, *True Stories*. I took the multitrack tapes of our backing tracks for the movie songs to the Dallas set and added some local Texas flavor—fiddle and pedal steel on some songs, norteño accordion on another, a gospel choir on yet another. The actors from the movie came into a local studio in Dallas and sang as well.

They didn't sing live when they were being filmed—they lip-synched, as I'd been doing in music videos for a few years. Lip-synching was an old Hollywood musical technique that allowed the audio part of performances to be more consistent, as everyone mimes to preexisting recordings. It also enabled the camera and other departments to plan, down to the second, how long or involved each shot might be, since they can time each bit of the audio recording. The camera might plan a dolly shot for a particular lyric, and by using these recordings they'd know how long they had, down to the second. One might sacrifice some spontaneity and happy vocal accidents with this approach—it's not entirely without its downside— but it also meant that all the takes would match, something that's hard to do in a performance unless there are multiple cameras on a shoot. Recently I was involved in a film by the Italian director Paolo Sorrentino, who wanted a performance by my band, which consisted of me, a rhythm section, and six string players. Rather than have us lip-synch, he wanted to film it live, so we'd be performing and recording at the same time as the cameras ran. This approach is more authentic—the sound is actually us playing and singing—but it's possible that artifacts of the documentation of a live performance (the less than pristine sound, for example) might be distracting to the viewing audience. In the screening I saw, the sound mixer had "helped" the reaction of the audience of extras later by adding in the applause and shouting. And it worked! I believed the hype as much as a potential movie audience presumably would. The scene was definitely more exciting; even knowing how all the parts were put together, I'm as easily manipulated as anyone else.

PARIS, AN AFRICAN CITY

After Little Creatures and *True Stories*, Talking Heads wanted to return to the more collaborative writing approach we'd used before—but with some adjustments. Instead of going into the studio with absolutely no songs, as we'd done on *Remain in Light* and some other records, we decided that we'd improvise some grooves and riffs ahead of time and choose the best of them as the foundation for studio recordings. I recorded some of these rehearsal jam-fragments on audio cassettes, and by cueing up specific moments I managed to string together a few sequences that could be used to make a song structure. We'd learn how to play a bit of fragment A, then we'd move on to a bit of riff B, then go back to A, and then on to C. In this way we already had some song framework—the material for what might become verse and chorus sections. Still no words or top-line melodies, though. I'd do those later, as I had before.

Over the years I'd been to a number of Paris clubs to hear music with the late

Jean-François Bizot, who had a magazine called *Actuel* that I admired. We'd see Cuban or African bands or singers, and we'd eat at African restaurants. The African diaspora was turning Paris into a hub that featured some of the best African music in the world—many of the best musicians had moved there, or spent much of their time there. I proposed to Talking Heads that we record in Paris to take advantage of what seemed to me like a special moment and to work with some of those musicians. Not to pretend to be an African band, but to see if something new—a third thing—could emerge. It helped that we already had basic parts and structures to play—a minimal foundation, but one that could be built on.

We worked at Studio Davout, a former movie theater out on the Périphérique. The room was immense, unlike most New York studios, and we were going to use digital recorders, which made us feel that our record was going to sound sparkly fresh. As an ensemble, we were all playing at the same time, and there was enough distance between us that we could hear and see each other but still have some acoustic separation.[G] Our new producer, Steve Lillywhite, enjoyed having some of that comforting isolation between instruments.

The local musicians, among them guitarist Yves N'Djock, percussionist Abdou M'Boup, and keyboard player Wally Badarou, were great. They were professionals, very much in demand locally. They could adapt to styles outside of the traditions they had grown up with, and their response to our music was also entirely one of enthusiastic adaptation and accommodation.

There was a new development in my writing for this record. Though I knew it might present problems when the time came to write the melodies and, even worse, the lyrics, I either bravely or foolishly decided to put together non-repeating sequences based on our instrumental sections. The passages I proposed we play in sequence would be similar to one another in certain ways, but they'd also keep changing and evolving as the song went on. Your typical pop song has a verse section, then a chorus section that is often bigger and might contain the "hook," then back to the verse arrangement, and the whole thing repeats again. There are variations on this structure, but it's fairly pervasive—even opera arias repeat sections this way. But what if each section, rather than being identical, were instead a stepping stone, a variation and elaboration leading to another similar but slightly different section, and there were no clear repetitions? I liked this idea. It proposed a song structure that was more like a conversation or a narrative. As a listener, you'd be on familiar ground and accompanied by familiar faces, but the landscape and settings would keep changing.

One new song, "Cool Water," maintained a repetitive rhythm, but the key changed over and over until the very end, when it settled on a big G major chord. Other songs, such as "The Democratic Circus," also proceeded through a series of similar but distinct sections. By the end, you were somewhere very different from where you'd started, but each step along the way was gradual and logical. Not every song worked like this, but I was curious to see if I could gently break the routine of slipping into familiar song structures without things sounding "difficult." Sometimes the usual verse-chorus verse-chorus-bridge pattern could seem a little predictable—and, as I'd learned, your attention can wander when you know what's coming.

I improvised vocal melodies over the recorded tracks, just like I had in the past. We made rough mixes and then took a break, as before, while I sequestered myself and wrote words to match these "vocals." I remember coming up with the words for the song "(Nothing but) Flowers" while driving around suburban Minneapolis. My wife at the time was working on a theater project there, and the only gear I needed to write lyrics was a cassette player to play the tracks for inspiration, another small one to record my lyric ideas, and a pad of paper to write them down on. I could work anywhere that I wasn't going to be bothered—anywhere no one would hear me singing little fragments over and over, trying different words out.

It wasn't surprising that while driving around the suburbs, not all that far from the Mall of America, I began to imagine a scenario in which the economy had changed and the malls and housing developments had all begun to crumble and devolve to a prior state. The twist was that this scenario allowed me to also frame the song as a nostalgic look at vanishing sprawl, a phenomenon I hadn't thought that I was terribly sentimental about. It was obviously ironic in intent, but it also allowed me to express a love and affection for aspects of my culture that I had previously professed to loathe.

NEW YORK, THE SECRET LATIN CITY

For the Talking Heads record that was eventually titled *Naked,* I brought in Angel Fernandez to arrange Latin horns for "Mr. Jones"; I had also recently recorded a duet called "Loco de Amor" with my idol, the Queen of Latin music, Celia Cruz[H]— a kind of salsa-reggae song for a movie soundtrack. But my love for Latin music hadn't quite been quenched. I was still grooving to those records, particularly the older ones. At home and on the road I played them on a boombox and danced around to them in hotel rooms or rented apartments. I didn't know the right steps, but no one was watching.

I decided in 1988 that I would try to make a pan-Latin record, to dive into that world using a batch of songs I'd written as a foundation. I'd gotten into the habit of visiting Latin clubs and continued to immerse myself in the old records—it was all part of the history of my city, New York, so why not partake of it? Some songs had words and vocal

H

melodies already, and others were instrumental tracks with verse and chorus sections in place. Jon Fausty, who'd recorded so many classic New York salsa records, joined Steve Lillywhite and me, and we decided to ask some experts how best to rhythmically and musically approach and develop my demos. Fausty brought in Milton Cardona and José Mangual Jr., two amazing percussionists from the New York salsa scene, to listen to my musical sketches and recommend appropriate approaches to rhythms and arrangements. I knew I wanted to include grooves drawn from a wide swath of South America—a cumbia rhythm from Colombia and a samba from Brazil, as well as the classic *son montuno* and cha-cha grooves that formed the Afro-Cuban base of New York salsa. I was being pretty ambitious. Latin musicians generally tend to specialize in one or another of these styles; salseros don't usually play sambas, just like blues-rock guitarists don't often play speed metal. But we recruited players from all around the New York metropolitan area, where pretty much every kind of musician from the New World could be found, and in this way we began the advance work.

We organized a series of recording sessions to lay down the rhythmic and harmonic beds for these songs—we wouldn't worry about brass or strings or other arranged parts yet. Usually in the rhythm section there would be three percussionists working side by side, plus Andy González laying down a bass part on an electric upright and Paquito Pastor on piano. We were recording on a digital reel-to-reel recorder, like we had on *Naked*, though in retrospect this might not have been the best idea. The promoters of this new technology advertised a more accurate and pristine sound, but, as with the early generation of CDs, I don't think the technology was up to the job yet. Those recordings have a slightly brittle quality that we might have convinced ourselves was actually crystalline clarity. The excitement of using new technology also inspired everyone to believe that what we were doing was important, of the moment, and top quality, just in case anyone had any doubts.

As usual, I often improvised melodies to tracks that didn't yet have any melodies or words. The horn and string arrangements would be recorded after I had these vocal melodies in place. Fernandez and other arrangers would react to my wordless vocal melodies. Their horns and strings would fill in the gaps around the vocals and leave a musical space for them to be heard.

My singing style was inspired to change again, just as it had when we recorded

Remain in Light. The vaguely melancholy melodies over the syncopated grooves—typical of Latin music—was attractive as an emotionally liberating combination. That the melodies and often the lyrics could be tinged with sadness while the buoyant music acted as a counterweight—a sign of hope and an expression of life going on amid life's calamities. The vocal melodies and lyrics often hinted at the tragic nature of existence, while the rhythms and music said, "Wait—life is wonderful, sexy, sensual, and one must persevere, and maybe even find some joy." When it was time to record the vocals, I began to sing in the studio with as much of that feeling as I could muster, which maybe wasn't all that much, given my background, but it was the beginning of another big change for me. My daughter was born around that time, so perhaps my evolving a more open singing approach might have reflected this big change in my life.

With the help of Fernandez, I put together a live band, a fourteen-piece orchestra, including Brazilian singer Margareth Menezes, for a world tour. Near the end, in the middle of a South American leg, there was a bit of trouble. Some of the percussionists left (pushing everyone to play in myriad styles had its limits), and they were replaced by Oscar Salas, a great Cuban drummer from Miami. He knew all the grooves from the various regions, so it wasn't as crazy a swap as it might have seemed. I realized that by adding a kit drummer, I could possibly make some music that fused the muscle of funk and other styles with the lilt and swing of Latin grooves.

I didn't forget that insight, and for my next record, *Uh-Oh*, I continued working with Salas, and I brought in George Porter, Jr., the incredible bass player from the New Orleans band the Meters, to work with us. Much Latin music has a framework referred to as the *clave* (the key), which sometimes isn't even played or audibly articulated by any one instrument. (What a beautiful concept that is: the most important part is invisible!) The clave divides the measures into a three-beat and a two-beat pattern—for rockers it's like a Bo Diddley beat, or the Buddy Holly song "Not Fade Away." (Rock and roll didn't just come from country and blues mixing; there was Latin flavor in there, too!) All the other parts, even the horns and the vocals, acknowledge the clave pattern and play with awareness of it, even if it isn't always audible.

I heard an undercurrent of clave in the New Orleans funk that the Meters made famous, which is not surprising given that city's waves of immigration from Cuba and Haiti. I thought George might help me find a way to create a hybrid out of Latin grooves and the funk he was accustomed to. By now I was a little more familiar and comfortable with some of those grooves, and I felt I could let things move into uncharted and undefined territory. The rhythms didn't have to be restricted to only one genre. I didn't feel the need to have Milton or José determine how a song would go on this project; I more or less knew when I was writing the songs what the rhythms would be.

I asked the Brazilian musician Tom Zé to do the arrangement for one of these songs, "Something Ain't Right." The groove was based on an ijexa rhythm, which is usually played on cowbells and is often associated with Candomblé, the Afro-Brazilian religion. The groove is featured in a number of songs by artists from Salvador, in Brazil's Bahia region, so I knew Tom would be familiar with it. He did some wonderful horn arrangements, but then he surprised us all by pulling out some Bic pens, minus the ink cartridges, and passing them out to the horn players. Each plastic penholder had a thin little piece of plastic taped to the end, which functioned like a reed on a saxophone or clarinet. He had an arrangement all worked out for these guys to play the pens in one section of the song. It wasn't just noise, either. He had them play a hocket pattern, where each player plays just one note, quickly, and by deciding which players played what, and when, an intricate pattern resulted. It was brilliant. Only Tom Zé would have had the nerve to ask these New York session guys to play Bic pens.

BACK TO THE BEGINNING

In 1993, I wanted to write some songs that were more stripped down, and to foreground their emotional content. I sensed that if the horns and strings and multiple percussionists were stripped away a bit, then what I was singing about might communicate more directly. Maybe I had been getting carried away with the window dressing. This emphasis on a thoroughly personal kind of writing was a big change for me, and it was possibly as much in response to a recent death in the family as it was musical evolution.

I wanted to jettison everything, to start from scratch. I had heard Lucinda Williams and my friend Terry Allen, and I wanted to write songs that seemed to come from the heart as much as theirs did. Writing from experience went against the grain for me, but I wanted to let the lyric content dictate the music a little more. I had the concept, though not the same instrumentation, of traditional jazz combos in mind. Musically I might have been inspired by the recent rise of the improvisation scene around the old Knitting Factory on Houston Street. I liked the idea of a small ensemble that listened to and played off each other and whatever the lead instrumentalist or vocalist was doing. So I wrote the songs, and instead of going straight into a recording studio, I put together a small band and performed them live, in small clubs.

The songs and their arrangements began to jell as they were tested in front of live audiences. The plan was to more or less record the band playing live in the studio relatively soon, as I had an image in my mind of classic small-ensemble jazz recordings, with all the musicians more or less in a circle in the middle of a studio—a re-creation of a club stage or bandstand. A situation in which everyone could hear and see everyone else, very old-school. I hoped that after having done some live shows, the band would know the arrangements and would play each song as if it were second nature, an old friend.

It didn't work out that way. A band member was fired, producers came and went, the whole plan fell to pieces. But the core group—the rhythm section of Todd Turkisher and Paul Socolow—survived. The fairly stripped-down and bared-soul aspect of that *David Byrne* record managed to allow me an escape from the musical cage I'd made for myself. I'd just recorded and toured with two very large, Latin-inspired bands, and as much as I loved that experience, I could tell I was being branded as the rocker who had abandoned the cause. This new record did feel like a fresh start, even though it was born out of death and thwarted plans.

THE STUDIO COMES HOME

By the late nineties, new audio technology had emerged that allowed musicians to make professional-caliber recordings in their home studios. I bought a little mixing board and a couple of DA-88 machines, which used Hi-8 video cassettes to record eight tracks of good-quality digital audio. Other companies came out with other machines. The ADAT devices used super-VHS videocassettes, which were cheaper than the Hi-8 cassettes, so more musicians adopted these for their home studios. They often synched the recorders to MIDI devices too, so as tape rolled, the sampler or other devices could be instructed to play pre-determined notes or drum samples along with the recorded tracks. Cheap Atari computers sometimes entered the picture as well. They had software that allowed you to make visual representations of these MIDI sequences that would then be used to trigger beats (typically), samples, and synthesizers. A whole song arrangement could be created without actually playing anything, and without the need for recording tape. With this gear one could see that the need for an expensive recording studio was beginning to become superfluous.

TECH TALK

These days I work in a home studio, which I've carved out of the larger room you can see on the bottom of this page.[i] Tidy, eh? Embarrassing, actually.[j]

There is no professional sound-absorbent baffling here as there might be in a professional recording studio, but the floors of this former industrial building are concrete, so sound doesn't really escape and bother the neighbors. I put industrial carpet down, and one wall is covered with a kind of sound-absorbent Sheetrock, so I've taken some precautions to prevent sound leaking out. Unwanted sound coming in can be an issue too, but unless a truck backfires outside or an ambulance goes by, I've found that it is perfectly adequate, at least for recording vocals and guitars. There's no space in my room for drums or anything like that, but for

writing, playing one instrument, programming, and singing, it's fine. There's a good tube microphone, another mic for a little old guitar amp, and a nice preamp and compressor to massage the mic signals before they become ones and zeros. That's pretty much all you need to find out where a song wants to go and, I've found, even enough to record real vocals and some guitar parts.

Serial numbers and security codes for software are pinned to the wall, along with a Tammy Wynette poster. The computer is tucked under the desk. It's a mess, but amazingly, this is how we make records now.

Home-studio recordings can now sound as good as the big-name studios', and the lower-pressure (and less expensive) vibe in a home environment is often more conducive to creativity. Home recordings can be used for more than just demos. This idea is somewhat revolutionary as far as recording and composing music goes, and the repercussions of these baby steps will be huge further down the road.

By 1996, I'd written some new songs, which arrived in a wide variety of styles—maybe because I wasn't writing for a specific band anymore. It seemed to me that the songs would best be interpreted by either different musical groups or by a single group pretending to be a variety of groups. For most of this record, I chose the former, deciding to record the material by inviting a lot of musicians and producers I liked to perform and record specific songs. Judicious casting of these collaborators, who would also be creative producers, helped me get the variety I felt the songs were asking for. I worked with Morcheeba at their studio in London, with the Black Cat Orchestra in Seattle, with Devo at their studio in LA, with Joe Galdo in Miami, with Hahn Rowe at my New York apartment, and with Camus Mare Celli and Andres Levin at a brownstone in Brooklyn. I racked up lots of frequent-flyer miles in the process, but most of the time I recorded economically, as each group had their own home-style studio.

The record, *Feelings*, was necessarily done piecemeal, a few songs at a time, rather than in a concentrated burst. This too was new to me. The record evolved incrementally, and I had time to think about where it was going (or where it could go) as bits of each song and eventually the variety of song styles became audible. This more leisurely approach opened up the risk of my becoming indecisive, because I'd now have the option to postpone decisions regarding arrangements or which vocal take was the good one. However, I hoped that by this point in my life I'd internalized a fairly rigorous decision-making process and that I wouldn't leave too many options dangling. Although it was technically possible to pile up tracks and delay making most decisions, I knew that I did have some intuitive sense of where a song wanted to go, so I would make a commitment quickly whenever possible.

Though visiting all these folks where they lived became expensive, one could sense that a whole new era of music making was beginning. With the advent of relatively cheap recording equipment with studio-quality sound, not only would anybody with two turntables and a microphone be making records, but everyone else would, too, in an incredible variety of styles and approaches, everywhere and anywhere. Musicians didn't have to migrate to the big cities with their expensive studios anymore. If they were careful, they wouldn't get themselves in hock to the record companies either. As the costs of recording dropped precipitously, emerging musicians all over the world were increasingly on an equal footing with professional and well-funded Western pop/alt/urban musicians. Amateur musicians have always been equal as far as playing and writing go, but now more and more of them will be taken seriously—the quality of the recordings will be virtually indistinguishable.

OLD WAYS

I recently had an interesting experience with long-distance recording, in which I was asked to read a short story for a theater piece. Young Jean Lee, the author and director, was out of town, so we passed the takes back and forth electronically. For some projects, that kind of collaboration—which worked so well with Annie Clark, Fatboy Slim, Brian Eno, and many others I've worked with—has been convenient and efficient. For others, it doesn't work at all.

With this particular assignment, I'd do a reading, send it off, and then later get some notes via email: "Lighter, stick to the text, don't add any drama." Taking these into account, I'd try again. The whole process would then repeat—more notes would come back, I'd do another take, on and on. Eight takes later, I finally got it. I wasn't annoyed at all, really, but I realized that if we'd done this in a conventional manner—with me in a recording booth, and the director responding instantaneously—we might have accomplished in one afternoon what took weeks to do electronically. Sometimes the old ways work best.

HOMEMADE

I first saw a performance by Ultima Vez, the Belgian dance-theater group led by Wim Vandekeybus, in Seattle in 1991. I was knocked out. They were inspiring and inventive right down to the sets—I think that piece featured a backdrop of thrift-store dresses all stitched together.

Wim, the dancers, and I spoke after their show, and we more or less kept in touch after that. Some years later we talked about me doing music for a film that Wim had in mind based on a Paul Bowles short story. The film didn't happen, but the project managed to get us back together. I went to Brussels, where I watched an early rehearsal of the piece that would become *In Spite of Wishing and Wanting.* I liked what I was seeing and I offered to try to do as much music as possible, even the whole piece. I said that if Wim and company would like a trial, I would send them rough musical sketches as test material.

By now I had started getting the hang of recording with my home gear all by myself. I did almost all the recording for this project in my apartment. We recorded the strings, horns, and a few other instruments in a studio, but those sessions were generally fairly short. This was another big step away from where I had begun— that horrible feeling of not being in control of how things sounded, the clock ticking, being at the mercy of strangers. The mixing, however, was still done in a "real" studio. A fresh set of ears at that stage can be useful, as one tends to fall in love with parts for reasons that no one else can actually hear.

In Spite of Wishing and Wanting, recorded in 1998, was the first record I owned completely, so I began to sell copies at my concerts. I didn't sell very many, but it was satisfying to know that even that limited income helped offset some of the production costs, and it was equally satisfying that I had done so much of it myself. A new kind of music economy was coming into being, mostly facilitated by new recording technology.

I go about my business, mostly here in New York, traveling from midtown to my office downtown and back up again. Often I go to Brooklyn, less often to Hoboken or Queens. I live in an industrial neighborhood, but there's a family that lives across the street from me, and a sweatshop across the street, too. There's a police station next door, and farther down the block is a halfway house, a Chinese/Mexican take-out, and an off-Broadway theater center.

Sometimes it seems as if writing a group of songs is like getting groceries, or doing the laundry—banal things I do more or less on a day-to-day basis. We deal with the issues involved in our mundane activities as they come up, and songwriting might be viewed similarly, as the response to specific and even pedestrian needs. It might seem that in our day-to-day activities there is no overall plan at work, no consideration of where things are ultimately going. So, too, sometimes, with the process of writing songs. Little decisions are made invisibly every minute, and the cumulative effect, and the often unspoken principles that have guided them, define what appears to be, in retrospect, a conscious plan, with an emotional center and compass. What begins as a random walk often ends up taking you somewhere, somewhere that you later realize was exactly where you wanted to go.

During the time I was writing the songs for the record that became *Grown Backwards,* there was love, anger, sadness, and frustration in my life. There were two wars: one begun out of revenge and the second seemingly to consolidate oil interests. Huge amounts of money were expended in what seemed to be obviously futile and counterproductive efforts that many felt would not only bring death to many innocent people, but would end up making us, as a nation, less admired and certainly less safe, both physically and economically, for the foreseeable future. Along with many others, I felt angry—alienated, even—and I did my best to stop the rush into the second conflict, but it was inevitable. It seemed like a misdirected legacy of a nation still stunned, hurt, reeling—a fighter ready to strike out at anything that could be accepted as an enemy. I blogged, and began a campaign that resulted in full-page ads in the *New York Times* and *Rolling Stone* urging restraint. You can see an example of one of those ads on the next page.[K]

"If we go into Iraq unilaterally, or without the full weight of international organizations behind us, if we go in with a very sparse number of allies…we're liable to supercharge recruiting for Al-Qaeda."
—Wesley Clark, former NATO Supreme Commander

UN inspectors have destroyed more Iraqi weapons than all the bombs used in the '91 Gulf War — without the loss of a single life.

WAR ON IRAQ IS
WRONG
AND WE KNOW IT

DON'T LET BUSH, CHENEY, AND RUMSFELD DROWN OUT THE VOICES OF REASON!

DISARM IRAQ WITH TOUGH INSPECTIONS

Musicians United to Win Without War
www.moveon.org/musiciansunited

Autechre	Fugazi	Pharoahe Monch
Eric Benet	Emmylou Harris	Lou Reed
T-Bone Burnett	Natalie Imbruglia	REM
Busta Rhymes	Jay-Z	Raphael Saadiq
David Byrne	Donnell Jones	Ryuichi Sakamoto
Capone & Noreaga	K-Ci & Jo Jo	Russell Simmons
Rosanne Cash	Angélique Kidjo	Sonic Youth
George Clinton	Kronos Quartet	David Sylvian
Sheryl Crow	Massive Attack	Tweet
Ani DiFranco	Dave Matthews	Suzanne Vega
Steve Earle	Natalie Merchant	Caetano Veloso
Missy Elliott	Mobb Deep	Wilco
Brian Eno	Nas	Lucinda Williams
Fat Joe	Outkast	Zap Mama

☐ YES! I want to help stop the rush to war with Iraq.
Your contribution will be used to fund additional efforts to get the word out and to help avert a war.

Name

Address

City/State/Zip   E-mail

Make checks payable to MoveOn.org
Mail to MoveOn.org, 336 Bon Air Center #354, Greenbrae, CA 94904

"War is not the answer."
—Marvin Gaye

K

But it was hopeless. Recent studies have shown that people ignore facts that contradict what they want to believe. Even "smart" people I knew, and many others I respected, were convincing themselves we had to invade. It made me feel like I didn't know my country and its people, or even my own friends, anymore. How does one react and respond to that? I felt lost and adrift in my home. What kind of music would emerge from living with those feelings? These were not simply abstract political ideas. I felt angry and fucked up every day.

Protest songs? They can express what folks are already feeling, what they sense but have not yet been able to articulate, but they're maybe not the best way of changing people's minds—or even encouraging a second look. Ultimately, it's an act of hubris to try to do so. Maybe, I was thinking, songs and music should instead present an alternative path. Maybe songs can make an emotional case for inclusiveness and openness instead of just being critical. Maybe songs can *be* that possibility, rather than just a rational argument for it. I didn't know if I could write songs like that, but I was thinking about it.

I'd had a wonderful time performing the songs from my previous record, *Look Into the Eyeball*, so my instinct was to refine that approach and continue down that road. Musician and composer Stephen Barber had rearranged many of the string parts for the touring group, and I suggested that he do all the new arrangements on this next record. The string players on those North American dates were from Austin, Texas, like Barber, so he could work with them and iron out any issues on the next set of songs before we went into the studio. In keeping with the idea of presenting an alternative to what I saw as lies and the ugliness we were being dragged into, this set of songs was even more lush than what I had recorded a couple of years earlier. The opera arias I'd been hearing and had been moved by not long before were signposts, in a way. I sensed that I wanted something that could be unashamedly pretty and full-on, so I covered a couple of those tunes as a way of making that point. I didn't try to sing with the typical opera voice—I wanted the songs to be understood as the proto-pop songs they once were. People used to sing the catchy arias as they worked and played; everyone knew them. The closest I came to making an actual protest song was a cover of a Lambchop tune, but the lyrics for that came from an Egyptian poem dating back thousands of years—a cry against violence and alienation. Not a lot has changed.

I recorded my demos of the songs at home, and now I was getting more accustomed to yet another technology that once again changed the way I worked and recorded. Bulky machines were no longer needed to record demos; even at home you could now record into your laptop (or a regular desktop computer) using music software and some fairly modest gear.

I'd had a revelation about a year previously, after I'd been asked by British DJs X-Press-2 to write a tune and sing over a track they had. I had previously admired their work, so I said I'd give it a try. They sent me a track that I loaded onto my laptop (a black plastic Mac G3). It took a little time to learn the software and the audio connections, but once I figured them out, I recorded a vocal on the laptop and sent it back to them. They then made further changes to the music under my vocal. Whereas at first what they sent me sounded vaguely Talking Heads—like (hence their desire to approach me, I suspected), now it was the same song, same tempo, same key, but as a stripped-down house track. The resulting song, "Lazy," was released to club DJs in the UK, and ever so gradually became hugely popular. (In the UK and anywhere but in the United States, club songs can cross over and become radio hits.) I was delighted, and no one ever complained that the vocal sounded like it had been recorded on a laptop. The homemade recording had quietly passed the litmus test. Now I knew that I didn't have to use real recording studios for my work unless I was working with a sizable group of musicians, or with strings or live drums.

Not only were the demos for my newer songs all recorded at home, as they had been for years, but now various vocals, instruments, and electronic sounds could all be recorded at home too—often serving as the framework over which additional instruments were recorded in "real" studios. This did not signal the end of the recording studio—lots of artists still use them exclusively—but most emerging artists do exactly what I've been doing: they use studios more sparingly than bands used to, and only when the need arises. The big-studio era has ended; most of the ones in New York have closed down. (Although, in a weird reversal, the few that are left are now booked solid.) There are still times when I need to use a fully equipped studio for a project, but increasingly we keep the costs down by doing much of the initial work at home. We still need the studios—we'd be in trouble if they all vanished—but we're not held captive by their costs and the prevailing recording orthodoxies anymore.

These changes have had a pretty big financial impact on the recording process. The cost of making records can now be so low—if you don't count the rare trans-atlantic flights I took for my recent record with Brian Eno, of course—that average musicians can pay for it out of their own pockets. This means that when the time comes to think about a distribution arrangement, you aren't beholden to anyone. You don't come to the table already in debt. In effect, the ease and facility of home recording made me rethink how one might survive in the music business, given the ongoing collapse of the old system.

It's sad that just as it has gotten easier for anyone to make a record exactly in the way they envision, the traditional means of selling and distributing music are becoming less viable. Increasingly, recordings are the loss leaders for merchandise, live-performance tickets, and licensing opportunities. Recording, which used to be basically the most important thing one did as a professional musician, is increasingly just part of a larger package. That doesn't mean everyone except a few pop stars will stop recording, but it does mean that the way a musician survives is no longer primarily via sales of recordings. The era when all the various ways in which we hear and enjoy music are secondary to the most well-known recording of that music might be over. We soon might begin to view recordings as they were perceived when they came into being, as fixed versions of compositions—but not as the only or even the primary way the music is supposed to sound.

CHAPTER SIX

Collaborations

The online music magazine Pitchfork once wrote that I would collaborate with anyone for a bag of Doritos.[1] This wasn't intended as a compliment—though, to be honest, it's not that far from the truth. Contrary to their insinuation, I am fairly picky about who I collaborate with, but I am also willing to work with people you might not expect me to. I'll risk disaster because the creative rewards of a successful collaboration are great. I've been doing it my whole life.

I discovered early on that collaborating is a vital part of music's essence and an aid to creativity. Unless you're a solo folk singer or a laptop jockey, live performance usually involves playing with other musicians. A successful ensemble inevitably requires a certain amount of push and pull and creative compromise. Although there's usually a hierarchy and often assigned parts and arrangements, the idiosyncrasies of each player's interpretations make the sound of every group unique. And when an ensemble is also involved in the creation and/or recording of a piece of music, those individual expressive tendencies are that much more apparent. Even if I wrote a song myself, then played and sang it for Talking Heads or some other group of musicians on my guitar, their individual interpretations, abilities, and ensemble skills would make their collective version and performance of that song different from anyone else's.

Players inevitably add things that the songwriter might not have thought of, so you often end up with something very different from what a solo musician would have arrived at on his own. Sometimes this new thing is restricted by the players' abilities and sensibilities, but rather than being a liability, these restrictions can actually be liberating. Odd that I'm more focused on the limitations than the fact that some musicians might be able to play something better than anyone else. One adjusts to both the limitations and particular talents of a given set of musicians. Writers and composers learn to anticipate what is and is not likely to happen musically. Over time you internalize the tendencies and playing approaches of your fellow players, and after a while you don't even consider writing certain parts or in certain styles, because the musicians you're working with wouldn't naturally go that way. You play to their strengths. You don't try to reverse the river or get it to jump over a mountain, you harness its flow and energy to gently urge that it join up with other tributaries.

One might assume that having better players, with a higher level of musicianship, means that a composer can be more adaptable, free, and wide-ranging in what he writes. One might also assume that this would be a good thing, but the conventional hierarchy of musical skills is deceptive. Classically trained players often can't get the feel of what may seem like a simple pop or funk tune, and a great rock drummer may play in time but never learn to swing. It's not that technical abilities are beyond some players; it's more the sharpening of the ear and brain that happens over time. We learn to hear (or not hear) certain things, different things. The classical players who think all popular music is simple tend not to *hear* the nuances involved, so naturally they can't play very well in that style. Simplicity is a kind of transparency in which subtle nuances can have outsize effects. When everything is visible and appears to be dumb, that's when the details take on larger meanings.

There is really no hierarchy in music—good musicians of any given style are no better or worse than good musicians of another. Players should be viewed as existing across a spectrum of styles and approaches, rather than being ranked. If you follow this reasoning to the end, then every musician is great, a virtuoso, a maestro, if only they could find the music that's right for them, their personal slot in the spectrum. I'm not sure I'm actually willing to go *that* far, but there may be a little bit of truth in the idea.

Many songwriters write in teams: Lennon and McCartney, Jagger and Richards, Bacharach and David, Leiber and Stoller, Holland-Dozier-Holland, Jobim and De Moraes, Rodgers and Hammerstein. One person might write the words and the other the music, which is the division of labor I've often followed in my own collaborations. But just as often, the division of labor is less clear—ideas may get passed back and forth, collaborators may work on specific sections of a song. With some songwriting teams, the equality between the collaborators is less than obvious, and it can seem as though one of the partners was more of an instigator on a particular song than the other. But the fact that there have been so many of these teams, and that they have achieved such heights, seems significant.

There are obvious benefits to working in a team. Your weaker ideas might get corrected. My original concept for "Psycho Killer" was to play against type and do it as a ballad, but when the other band members joined in, it took a more energetic direction, which proved to be popular with our audience. There's a good chance you might be inspired by ideas that originate outside yourself.

Music written by teams makes the authorship of a piece indistinct. Could it be that when hearing a song written by a team, a listener can sense that they aren't hearing an expression of a solitary individual's pain or joy, but that of a virtual conjoined person? Can we tell that an individual singer might actually represent a collective, that he might have multiple identities? Does that make the sentiments expressed more poetically ambiguous and therefore more potentially universal? Can eliminating some portion of the authorial voice make a piece of music more accessible and the singer more empathetic?

PLAYING WELL WITH OTHERS

Many of my songs were written without songwriting partners. Are they less good than the ones where the job was split, or where a partner modified, added to, or rejected my ideas, or I theirs? I can't answer that, but certainly musical partnerships have often led me to places I might not otherwise have gone.

With Talking Heads we always collaborated on the interpretation, realization, and performance of the music, even if I brought a finished song to the table. We all had similar things in our record collections—O'Jays, Stooges, James Brown, Roxy Music, Serge Gainsbourg, King Tubby—so regardless of the limitations imposed by our playing abilities, there was another set of limitations—good ones, we felt—shaped by our collective musical tastes. As much as we wanted to sound like something entirely new, we communicated by referencing music that we all loved. An early Talking Heads song, "The Book I Read," had a middle section that to my ears sounded like KC and the Sunshine Band, whom I liked, so that reference was, for us, a good thing. No one else seemed to hear it, though. Perhaps my yelping vocal and other factors obscured those influences and touchstones? Though we may have combined those influences in a skewed and mangled manner, we could hear bits of the music that had preceded us all over our material. In the absence of any formal training, this mostly unspoken set of references was how we communicated. It's probably what made communication and collaboration possible for us in the first place.

After some years of a more or less traditional songwriting process—words and music completed by one person, or finished words by one set to music by another—Talking Heads evolved a kind of collaborative music-writing system based on collective improvisations. Sometimes these jams would happen in a rehearsal loft—the song "Life During Wartime" began as a one-chord jam with no lyrics based on a riff I'd brought in, which was wedded to a second chord that became the chorus. Sometimes these improvisations and jams wouldn't happen until we were in a recording studio. In such instances, the writing and recording were simultaneous. Jazz players, of course, respond fluently to one another by improvising in their live performances and in their recordings. We, however, were fairly minimal about what we would contribute. The aim of our improvising, probably inspired by our R&B heroes, was for each person to find a part, a riff, or even just a freaky honking accent, and then stick with it, repeating it over and over. So by improvisation I don't mean long meandering guitar solos. Quite the opposite. Ours were more about hunting and pecking with the aim of "finding" short, sonic, modular pieces. These pieces were intended to interlock with whatever was already there, so the period of actual improvisation would be short. It would end as soon as a satisfactory segment was found. Then we would shape those accumulated results into something resembling a song structure.

In this system, one person's response to another's contribution could shift the whole piece in a radically different direction—harmonically, texturally, or rhythmically. Pleasantly unexpected surprises would occur, but just as often they could seem like rude and arrogant impositions that missed the significance and integrity of the preexisting material. The guitarist Robert Fripp added a part to the Talking Heads song "I Zimbra," overdubbing a weird harmonic ostinato that he played through the whole song. The whole song! Initially that destroyed the song, and seemed like someone was being willfully perverse. But, as it turned out, when used sparingly it added a little psychedelic swirl to our Afro-pop groove, which put everything in a new perspective. Is this disruption and destruction a risk worth taking? Did the piece just get ruined, or did it really need to get radically rethought in order to go somewhere new and exciting? You can't be too precious in this process. For us, this method resulted in music in which the authorship was to some extent shared among a whole group of people, though I still usually wrote the vocal melody and eventually the words. The musical bed was, in these instances, very much collaborative.

NOTATION AND COMMUNICATION

There are not a lot of languages for describing and passing on music outside of traditional notation—and even that method, though almost universally accepted, sacrifices a lot. The same piece of written music can sound completely different depending on who plays it. If Mozart could have described in notation exactly how he intended every aspect of his compositions to sound, there would be no need for multiple interpretations. When musicians play together and record, they come up with terms—real and invented—to try to communicate musical nuance. Funkier, more legato, more holes and spaces, less pretty, spikier, simpler, pushed hard, more laid-back—I've said all of those things when trying to describe a musical direction or the feel I was looking for. Some composers resort to metaphors and analogies. You could use food, sex, texture, or visual metaphors; I've heard that Joni Mitchell described the kind of playing she wanted by naming colors. Then there's the shorthand of referring to other recordings, as Talking

Heads did. So, interpreting a written score, reading music notation, is itself a form of collaboration. The performer is remaking and in some ways rewriting the piece every time he plays it. The vagueness and ambiguities of notation allow for this, and it's not an entirely bad thing. A lot of music stays relevant thanks to the opportunities for liberal interpretation by new artists.

To encourage this kind of collaboration, to make the interpretive aspect more overt, some composers have written their pieces as graphic scores. This is a way of granting a generous degree of freedom in the interpretation of their work, while simultaneously suggesting and delimiting the organization, shape, and texture of their pieces across time. Below is one example, a graphic score by the composer Iannis Xenakis.[A]

This approach isn't as crazy as it might seem. While these scores don't specify

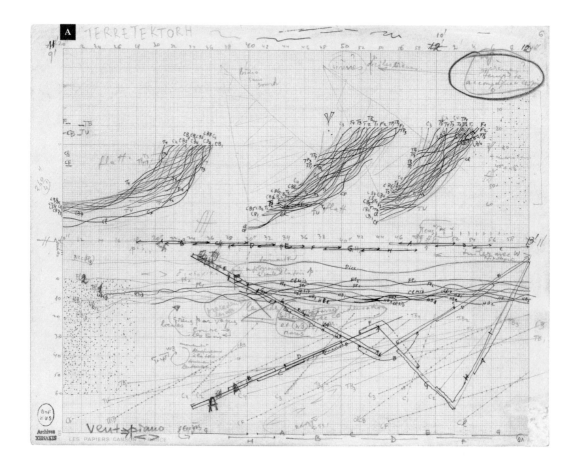

which notes to play, they do suggest higher or lower pitches as the lines wander up and down, and they visually express how the players are to relate to one another. This type of score views music as a set of organizing principles rather than a strict hierarchy—the latter viewpoint usually ends up with melody at the top of the pile. It's an alternative to the privileged position melody is usually given—it's about texture, patterns, and interrelationships.

Robert Farris Thompson, a professor of art at Yale, pointed out that once you let yourself see things this way, lots of things become "musical scores"—although they might never have been intended to be played. He argued that in a lot of African weaving, one can sense a rhythm. The repetition in these fabrics doesn't consist of a simple looping of mirror images and patterns; rather, modular parts recombine, shift position, and interact over and over with one another, aligning in different ways over time, recombinant. They are scores for a funky minimalist symphony. This musical metaphor implies a kind of collaboration as well. While each color module in a quilt or textile is essential, no one part defines the whole the way we might define many Western compositions by their dominant melody. Western compositions can often be picked out—the melodies, at least—with one finger on a piano. How would one pick out the "score" below in that way? There's no dominant motif or top line, though that doesn't stop it from having a distinct identity. It's a neural network, a personality, a city, the Internet.

Below, on the left, is an African textile.[B] No surprise that later versions of these patterns, like the one pictured on the right, originated in the New World.[C]

B

C

There are musical breaks, fugues and stanzas, inversions and recapitulations here. It's not that crazy to believe that some part of the vast African musical sensibility was carried across the oceans and reconstructed using visual means—that these fabrics functioned as a structural mnemonic aid. Perhaps they functioned as metaphors for how music could be organized, which is also a lesson that can be applied to other parts of life. I'm not suggesting that musicians sat down and "played" a quilt, but some of the organizing sensibility might have been kept alive and transmitted by such means.

If music can be regarded as an organizing principle—and in this case one that places equal weight on melody, rhythm, texture, and harmony—then we start to see metaphors everywhere we look. All kinds of natural phenomena are "musical." And I don't mean they make sounds, but rather that they organize themselves, and patterns become evident. Forms and themes arise, express themselves, repeat, mutate, and then become submerged again. The daily street ballet that Jane Jacobs wrote about, and the hustle and bustle of an outdoor market, are each a kind of music. Stars, bugs, running water, the chaotic tangle of vegetation. Musicians playing together find a kind of symbiotic relationship between one another and an interplay between their parts, so that the interlocking and interweaving create a sonic fabric.

How does this work? Let me share a few very different examples.

STANDING ON THE SHOULDERS OF GIANTS

A recent record of mine, *Everything That Happens Will Happen Today*, was pretty typical, as far as the collaborative process goes. Brian Eno, whom I hadn't worked with in more than twenty-five years, had a slew of largely instrumental tracks on his shelf that seemed to want to become songs rather than ambient tracks or film scores, but he was unhappy with his own attempts at completing them. He didn't have much to lose by passing them to me—they were just gathering dust (although I was told one did get passed to Coldplay), so unless I did something horrendous, which we agreed he could veto, it was a win-win situation.

As might be obvious by now, most contemporary collaborations, at least the ones I do, don't take place face-to-face anymore. They are the result of digital music files being shuttled back and forth via email or other Internet-based file-transfer formats. Does something get lost when the live aspect of collaboration disappears? Simple miscommunication can certainly spiral out of control without the subtle signals we send through our facial expressions and body language. And the encouragement, coaching, hyping, and prodding that tends to happen in person—"Why not try this?" or "That's great, but what if you play it on a different instrument?"—may not happen, and certainly not as spontaneously.

That said, there are big advantages to the new protocol. If I can use a Ping-Pong analogy, with Internet exchanges one can wait overnight or longer to return the serve, planning out what addition might work best, with no pressure to come up with something brilliant on the spot. The breathing space is a luxury you don't have when your collaborator is looking over your shoulder.

From Eno's studio in London, I was sent stereo mixes of his musical ideas, to which I added my vocal melodies and (eventually) lyrics without altering his music beds in the least. Sometimes this made for some odd lyrical structures. On the song "The River," Brian had a portion of what became a verse repeat quite a few times—as if the song had gotten stuck and couldn't move on. I accepted the challenge to write without straightening this peculiarity out—I knew that if it could be made to work, this unexpected variation in structure might prevent the song from being too predictable. It worked, and it added a kind of tension, as it delayed the musical resolution that came at the ends of verses. But just as often I slightly restructured his songs to bring them closer to a traditional form—repeating a section to create a place where a second verse could go, or nominating a "larger"-sounding section as a chorus, and then I might copy that, too, in order to make it recur again later in the song. However, I never even thought about requesting any substantial musical changes in the tracks, like key changes, or changes in groove or instrumentation. The unwritten rule in these remote collaborations is, for me, "Leave the other person's stuff alone as much as you possibly can." You work with what you're given, and don't try to imagine it as something other than what it is. Accepting that half the creative decision making has already been done has the effect of bypassing a lot of endless branching—not to mention a lot of waffling and worrying. I didn't ever have to think about what direction to take musically—that train had already left the station, and my job was to see where it wanted to go. This restriction on creative freedom turns out, as usual, to be a great blessing. Complete freedom is as much curse as boon; freedom within strict and well-defined confines is, to me, ideal.

I listened to Eno's instrumental tracks on and off, trying to get a sense of the story the music was trying to tell. These tracks weren't ambient, as one might have expected from him, and I sensed that song structures might emerge with just a little coaxing. "Emergence" is a popular term these days, but it almost perfectly evokes how musicians and songwriters cultivate the latent potential of a humble musical kernel. That's why writers and musicians often say they feel only partially responsible for the creation of the works they've nurtured. They claim that the song, painting, dance piece, or words they're working on "tells" them what kind of thing it wants to become. But when that thing that is speaking to you originated with someone else, it's sometimes even more of a puzzle. Does it necessarily speak the same language as you? Is it sincere? Could their version be ironic instead? Is that clunky section supposed to be funny, or should you try to "fix" it? Do they want it to remain as beautiful and pretty as it seems, or would a little grit help?

Well, I didn't exactly know at first what to make of Eno's tracks. Maybe I had some trepidation working in the shadow of *Bush of Ghosts*, which after thirty years had amassed kind of a weighty reputation. I knew we couldn't let ourselves do a *Bush of Ghosts II*. Music history is as much an influence on composition as anything else. After living with the tracks for almost a year, I eventually wrote Eno back. I told him the music inspired a sort of folk-electronic-gospel feeling, and suggested that my words and tunes might reflect this, and did that direction seem okay? Brian had discovered his love of gospel music years ago, and as he eventually wrote in the liner notes to *Everything That Happens*:

"Surrender to His Will," by Reverend Maceo Woods and the Christian Tabernacle Choir was the first gospel song I ever really responded to. I heard it on a distant South American radio station whilst in Compass Point, Nassau, working with Talking Heads on the album *More Songs About Buildings and Food*. Spending time with them, and becoming aware of their musical interests, opened my ears to genres and styles I hadn't really noticed up to that point, including gospel. So, it's fitting that the circle should close with this record.

As a foreigner in New York, where I ended up shortly after recording *More Songs*, I was surprised by how little attention Americans gave to their own great indigenous music. It was even slightly uncool, as though the endorsement of gospel necessarily implied support of its associated religious framework. Thanks to Reverend Woods however, I began to see gospel music as conveying the act of surrender more than the act of worship; and this, of course, intrigued me, and has informed my music ever since. Perhaps it's the reason I use modes and chords that are easy to follow and harmonize with. I want music to be inviting, to offer the listener a place inside it.

Though my trajectory as I described it to him was vague, Eno seemed fine with it, so I attacked the first song, which I think he had given the working title "And Suddenly." I'd just finished reading Dave Eggers's book *What Is the What*, which is about a young man named Valentino Achak Deng and his hallucinatory and horrific journey from his destroyed village in South Sudan to Atlanta, Georgia, and beyond. Valentino's story was harrowing but also beautiful, uplifting, and at times even funny. I think I may have been under the spell of his story when I sat down in front of my microphone. The result was "One Fine Day." I sang a few harmonies in the choruses to make it sound fuller, and emailed the result to Eno.

We were both thrilled: what the song—the whole album, really—was to become was fully articulated here, in this first piece. The words I had gravitated toward indeed had some biblical allusions (that would be the gospel connection I'd mentioned), but nothing too overt. We agreed to continue with the project.

I realized that the harmonic foundations of some of the tracks Eno had sent were simple, much like traditional folk, country, or old-school gospel songs before those styles evolved to become as sophisticated as some are today. Brian's chord structures were, in their apparent musical plainness, unlike anything I would have chosen myself. My music-geek side wouldn't have allowed me to write a song with essentially just three major chords in it, not anymore—I thought I was supposed to have outgrown that. However, the fact that this almost naïve directness was someone else's idea meant I could excuse myself—I could blame someone else, which made it okay. This pushed me in a new (old) direction, which, of course, was a good thing.

The lyrical challenge was more emotional than technical: how to respond to these harmonically "simple" (though texturally complex) foundations and write heartfelt words without drawing on the clichés that such chords and structures might bring to mind? I was surprised that the results that began to emerge were often hopeful and positive, even though some lyrics describe exploding cars, war, and similarly ominous scenarios.

There were some remnants of our previous work in these songs—no surprise there—but something new emerged as well. Where did this new sanguine and heartening tone come from, particularly in those troubled times? Every day, as the songs were emerging, I continued to be appalled by the cynical maneuvers of Dick Cheney, Donald Rumsfeld, Karl Rove, Tony Blair, and all the rest, as well as the disappointingly compliant manner in which they were reported by the media. By then, McCain was running for president and his minders had picked Sarah Palin to be his running mate—a move that was taken surprisingly seriously. A black man was running against them—a man who wrote inspiring speeches and held out a tiny bit of hope for some of us, though I think all politicians possess some amount of poison in their system. This was the political context in which I wrote these songs, and I found that my response was similar to that expressed on my previous solo records—hope and humanity as a force to counter cynicism and greed.

Some of the lyrics and the plaintive melodies I came up with were a response to what I sensed was already there, hinted at, but buried deep in Eno's music. I wanted to find a reason not to be cynical—to have some faith even when nothing around me seemed to justify it. Writing and singing seemed to be an attempt at a kind of musical self-healing.

DREAMWORLD

Red Hot, the AIDS charity organization founded in 1989, produces a series of benefit records in which they initiate collaborations between disparate musicians. Although he's not Portuguese, it was suggested in 1999 that the Brazilian composer and singer Caetano Veloso and I collaborate on a song for their *Red Hot + Lisbon* collection. I'm a huge fan of Veloso's, and we'd met a few times, so the idea of working together wasn't too insane. I happened to have a song in progress on which I was using a percussion loop taken from one of his songs—an aid in the writing process that I would typically replace with real musicians somewhere down the line. Though some composers appear to be able to write over forms they hear in their heads, I find that when the rhythms I'm writing over are audible and a little complex, when they swing a bit, then actually hearing them keeps me on the rails as far as the metric of potential melodic vocal lines. That I'd been writing over a loop from one of Veloso's songs meant that in a sense we'd already started collaborating and it made Red Hot's invitation seem fortuitous.

I already had a structure, too—guitar chords that had been inspired by a combination of the American standards and Brazilian songs I'd been learning from songbooks. They didn't sound much like rock chords. I also had a melody, but only a few words. The lyric fragments I had come up with were about a girl who spent all her time in nightclubs and discos, never really connecting with what most of us call daily life. Some called her a bad girl, but the lyrics defended her, saying there was nothing wrong with innocent sensual pleasure. Some of the lyrics reminded me of Neil Young, at least the way they fit with the melody, though I doubt anyone else noticed that. The piece had shape but was unfinished when I sent it to Veloso.

He bounced back with additional lyrics in Portuguese, but they were about Carmen Miranda. Outside of Brazil, most people think of her as the Brazilian with fruit on her head who went Hollywood. But Miranda was actually Portuguese, not Brazilian, so now we had a little Lisbon (or at least Portugal) connection after all. After Miranda's appearances in so many campy Hollywood movies, some people began to disparage her—she had previously been a respected and popular singer in Brazil. Her Hollywood manifestation was, for them, both something to be proud of and also somewhat dubious and confusing. Furthermore, her stage attire and even the big headdresses alluded to Afro-Brazilian culture—they mimicked, in a way that Brazilians would appreciate, the women of Candomblé, the Afro-Brazilian religion—so she represented more than just samba. There was some deeply profound shit secreted in those headdresses, and Veloso alluded to it obliquely in his lyrics. So we had my words talking about one girl and his referencing another, and they kind of worked together, juxtaposed. I rarely manage to collaborate on lyrics—I tend to mark my boundary as being between words and music, but maybe because we were also intercutting languages, it seemed natural.

STARTING WITH WORDS—OTHER PEOPLE'S WORDS

In 2005, I began working on a disco-musical project for the theater, collaborating with Norman Cook, aka DJ Fatboy Slim, about the former first lady of the Philippines, Imelda Marcos. Since it was based on a historical figure, I tried something I hadn't done in a very long time: I began the writing process with the words. While I was researching the characters and the period, I highlighted noteworthy and memorable passages and then assembled files of anecdotes, quotes from speeches, interviews, and conversations. I began to group these materials into potential episodes and plot points, which would ultimately link up to tell a story. The characters—all real people—and the story had precedence in this project, and each episode and its song had to convey something specific, so prioritizing the text made sense.

To begin writing a song, I would lay out all my notes on each scene—the quotes and oral testimony of Imelda Marcos and her family, for example—and simply try singing them, sometimes over chords I played simultaneously on guitar and sometimes over Cook's grooves. In my notes I'd kept track of the many peculiar, emotionally loaded, alliterative, repetitious, and original phrases that Imelda, her husband Ferdinand, and others were supposed to have said. For a songwriter, these things were a godsend. They were halfway to being lyrics already! I couldn't have made them up, and of course they always perfectly encapsulated what the people were thinking and feeling—or at least what they wanted the world to believe that they were thinking and feeling. Reading that Imelda had said she wanted the words HERE LIES LOVE inscribed on her tombstone was like being handed the title of the musical on a platter. Not only did it epitomize the fact that she often viewed herself as having unselfishly offered love and sacrificed herself for the Filipino people, but it gave me an opportunity to have her reflect on her life and accomplishments, along with some subtle ripostes she would throw at her detractors.

Other people have used such "found texts" as well. For example, Peter Sellars used congressional testimony as source material for the libretto of John Adams's opera about Robert Oppenheimer and the bomb, *Doctor Atomic*. Using these texts as source material for lyrics seemed to absolve me (at least in my own mind) of some responsibility for what the characters were saying, or singing, in this piece.

I could use a lyric that was, for example, way more sentimental or corny than anything I would ever have allowed myself to write, and it was okay because it was the character saying it, not me. In the song "Here Lies Love," Imelda sings, "The most important things are love and beauty," which is a quote from a speech she made. If I sang those lyrics, people would assume I was being ironic, but to have them come out of her character's mouth rings true. I found that the same thing applied musically: there were musical references—disco beats or, to my ears, a Kenny Rogers reference—and other genre quotations that were okay to include because they were what a character would have used as a vehicle for their feelings, if one imagined them being able to express themselves in song. Who wouldn't want to be able to "put on" the voice of Sharon Jones to express the jaw-dropping decadence, sense of fun, and abandon of first visiting a major dance club? Lastly, to me the words just seemed truer knowing that they were what someone had actually said—that I didn't put words in their mouths.

Was this process of lyric writing a sort of collaboration with the past? Although I reordered most of these found phrases, repeated some, and bent others to help them fit meter and rhyme, I tried to make my own writing embody the intentions of my invisible "collaborators."

Here Lies Love is a collaboration that is—like the score I did with Twyla Tharp, and like the film music I've done over the years—a collaboration not so much with another musician, but rather with the theatrical form itself (not to diminish Norm's contribution one bit). It is the stage production, not a person, that needs my music to accomplish specific dramatic, emotional, or rhythmic ends. There are exigencies and constraints in this kind of collaboration that make it very different from working alone or with another musician.

I don't know if stage, TV, and film composers think of themselves as collaborating with the directors, the medium, or the writers, but sometimes music and visuals work together so seamlessly that it's hard to imagine a theatrical work or a film without its score, and vice versa. Some film and stage music evokes the whole story, the characters, and the visuals every time one hears them. The constraints in these kinds of collaborations are not the tastes and proclivities of the other musician or songwriter, but the needs of the larger piece and its characters.

A book called *People Power: The Philippine Revolution of 1986, An Eyewitness*

History, about the four days of the People Power Revolution, was hugely helpful to me while I was working on *Here Lies Love*. It included not only testimony from generals, priests, and public figures, but the moving words of ordinary individuals—the real meat and potatoes of that movement. As in Tahrir Square, it was the presence of ordinary folks, manifesting daily, thousands and thousands of them, that tipped the scales in the Philippines. Their words allowed me to view events through their eyes, the mundane mixed with the sublime, and they made it come alive for me. Having visited Manila, I could picture the neighborhoods, the houses and streets these people described, the way their daily lives intersected with historical events. People tended to mention very specific details that swirled around and were folded into the onward rush of history. Joggers out for a morning run as tanks appeared on the streets. Going out for coffee to find hundreds of thousands gathered around the corner from your home.

Coincidentally, at this time I was also reading a book by Rebecca Solnit called *A Paradise Built in Hell*, about the almost utopian social transformations that sometimes emerge out of disasters and revolutions—citizens spontaneously and selflessly helping one another after traumatic events such as the San Francisco and Mexico earthquakes, the London blitz, and the 9/11 attacks. All these events have in common a magical and all too brief moment when class and other social differences vanish, and a common humanity becomes evident. These moments often last only a few days, but they have a profound and lasting impact on the participants, who witness a door cracked open a little to reveal a better world, one whose existence they never forget.

The Filipino People Power Revolution looked to me like one of those moments, and I hoped that a tiny bit of that feeling could be captured in songs and scenes. A theatrical piece that had previously struck me as a tragedy might also have a kind of happy and even inspirational ending, not simply by describing the overthrow of one dictator and his wife, but because the humanity of a people might allow itself to be revealed.

Being able to write songs in which I function as the conduit for the feelings and thoughts of others was hugely liberating and, well, easier than I thought. It's writing to order, but without too much vagueness in the intention, as the sources—the people—are as real as what happened.

Since the hardcover version of this book came out, the *Here Lies Love* musical has found its way to the stage. It's been well received, which is a great relief, and the material continued to evolve and change up until the opening.

I recently read a book by Jack Isenhour called *He Stopped Loving Her Today*, about the recording of a George Jones song that some call the best country song ever. A whole book about the recording of one song!

Well, that one song took eighteen months to record—not consecutive recording sessions, of course, but from beginning to end. That's a lot of time to persevere on one song. Part of the delay was due to Jones's infamous substance abuse—at one point, his friends had to hold him up to the mic to sing. Surprisingly, in that condition he could still produce; he even recorded huge hits during this period. But he would fall apart when he got to the spoken-word section at the end of "He Stopped Loving Her Today."

What really struck home for me was how collaborative the creation of that song was. Of course Jones gave every song he sang his own interpretation—the little vocal trills he typically added are not in the writing, for example. But it was Billy Sherrill, the legendary country producer, who had the vision of what that song could be. Sherrill had the crack songwriting team who wrote the initial version of the song rewrite it three times before he felt it was right. According to Jones's autobiography, *I Lived to Tell It All*, it was Sherrill who suggested that they do a verse where the woman comes to visit him one last time. That one is still in the song.

That process of rewriting, of being pushed and guided, reminded me of the way I worked with theater director Alex Timbers and Public Theater artistic director Oskar Eustis in the process of getting the musical *Here Lies Love* fit for the stage. As part of that process, Alex and Oskar would occasionally suggest not just where a new song might be needed, but they would, like Sherrill, get specific about what each proposed verse might say. Not how to say it—that was my job—but what emotions and information needed to be conveyed to advance the story and help us understand a character's motivations. For example, we already had songs and scenes where Imelda's husband, President Marcos, is caught having an affair; it's a turning point in her life. But in order for us to understand why it means something, we have to see them as a happy couple earlier. A new song was needed to accomplish that.

This was a new kind of collaboration for me. I've had plenty of experience writing words and melodies over someone else's music, but this was much more specific. Some of these songs evolved over many years, which beats Jones's record by quite a stretch.

These adjustments and ideas for new songs didn't occur all at once. The need for them and what they needed to do revealed themselves bit by bit. I remember about two years ago when we were doing a workshop, Alex thought we needed to have a song in which Imelda reacts to the revelation that her husband, the president, has cheated on her. The song should begin, Alex thought, with her in the depths of despair, then build in optimism as Imelda decides to dedicate her life and love to the Filipino people.

Luckily, I found some statements of hers that said almost exactly that—she had used the phrase "star and slave," which, while a bit self-dramatizing, expressed how she felt about her relationship to "the people" at that point. By the end of the song she has recovered from her despair and announces that she is going to forget about having any personal life. All of this she actually said, which was a huge help for me. I used "Stand by Your Man"—another Sherrill production, coincidentally—as a model, because its big chorus doesn't happen until the very end of the song. That might seem counterintuitive, as you usually want to hook the listener with the big theme expressed in a chorus as early as possible. But it worked for Tammy Wynette, and maybe, I thought, it could work for me. The verses would—step by step—lead you to the conclusion expressed in the final chorus. You needed to make the whole journey to get the full impact.

That worked, but Alex and Oskar wanted more. They felt we needed to see Imelda actually wrest command from her husband—both due to his illness and as revenge for having been betrayed. Luckily, again, the historical record proved helpful. In a half-joking way she'd taken over a cabinet meeting, entering with the complaint, "Poor me, now I have to do everything!"

Now I had a beginning and a title for the song ("Poor Me"). I wrote it by repurposing the music from an earlier song in which her husband molds her into the perfect political wife, and adding new words and melodies—it would be a good sonic flashback, I thought. I had the Philippine palace press agent announce that "the president's fine" when we could plainly see him lying sick in bed. All of this would be going on simultaneously, overlapping.

Two years later, we're in the final month of rehearsal, and Alex and Oskar feel that song and scene are good, but could be even better. They feel we need to see more clearly that Imelda's decision to assume power is absolute, fierce, and motivated by her husband's affair. I went home and wrote an additional verse for Imelda in which she curses the president out in the strongest possible way (in Tagalog) and ultimately announces, "It takes a woman to do a man's job." (This line often gets applause from a portion of the audience.) The narrative thread was therefore much clearer. The scene gets a great reaction, which of course is partly due to the performers and also to Alex's staging of the scene—the song alone doesn't do everything.

In retrospect, I wonder if it would have occurred to me to write the song in the first place, to say nothing of revising it to what it finally became. I'm glad we had the opportunity to let the piece evolve one insight at a time. This was a kind of collaboration I'd never experienced before—it was unlike soundtracks, for example, where the music has to fit the mood of a scene.

It wasn't always easy being pushed in this way. I had to swallow my pride sometimes, but I was partly helped by a "rule" in theater that the author (or songwriter) has absolute say—his or her words can't be changed. The text is considered sacred. So I knew that if I tried a suggestion and hated it, I could always demand, in the nicest possible way, that the song be returned to its original condition. This implicit power gave me a kind of freedom. I could be flexible and accommodating to all the suggestions, and I could try things I wasn't sure of, that I maybe even had doubts about, knowing that they weren't going to be set in stone. Instead of making me conservative, my hidden power encouraged me to take risks. As it turned out, most of those changes and additions really helped the piece—though some took a while to find their best expression.

EMERGENT STORYTELLING

Writing words to fit an existing melody and meter, as I did on *Everything That Happens* and many other records, is something anyone who writes in rhyme does naturally and intuitively—every rapper improvises or composes to a meter, for example. I had been encouraged to make this process, which is usually internalized, more explicit when I was writing the words for *Remain in Light*. That was the first time I tackled a whole record of lyrics this way. I found that, remarkably, solving the puzzle of making words and phrases fit existing structures often resulted, somewhat surprisingly, in words that have an emotional consistency and sometimes even a narrative thread, even though those aspects of the texts weren't planned ahead of time.

How does this happen? With *Remain in Light* and even before that, I would look for words that fit preexisting melodic fragments that I or others had come up with. After filling lots of pages with non sequiturs, I would scan them to see if a lyrically resonant group emerged. Phrases that would hint at the beginning of an actual subject often seemed to want to emerge. This might seem magical—claiming that a text "wants" to come into being (and we've heard this said before), but it's true. When some phrases, even if collected almost at random, begin to resonate together and appear to be talking about the same thing, it's tempting to claim they have a life of their own. The lyrics may have begun as gibberish, but often, though not always, a "story" in the broadest sense emerges. Emergent storytelling, one might say.

But at times words can be a dangerous addition to music—they can pin it down. Words imply that the music is about what the words say, literally, and nothing more. If done poorly, they can destroy the pleasant ambiguity that constitutes much of the reason we love music. That ambiguity allows listeners to psychologically tailor a song to suit their needs, sensibilities, and situations, but words can limit that, too. There are plenty of beautiful pieces of music that I can't listen to because they've been "ruined" by bad words—my own and others. In Beyoncé's song "Irreplaceable," she rhymes "minute" with "minute," and I cringe every time I hear it (partly because by that point I'm singing along). On my own song "Astronaut," I wrap up with the line "feel like I'm an astronaut," which seems like the dumbest metaphor for alienation ever. Ugh.

So I begin by improvising a melody over the music. I do this by singing non-sense syllables, but with weirdly inappropriate passion, given that I'm not saying anything. Once I have a wordless melody and a vocal arrangement that my collaborators (if there are any) and I like, I'll begin to transcribe that gibberish as if it were real words.

I'll listen carefully to the meaningless vowels and consonants on the recording, and I'll try to understand what that guy (me), emoting so forcefully but inscrutibly, is actually saying. It's like a forensic exercise. I'll follow the sound of the nonsense syllables as closely as possible. If a melodic phrase of gibberish ends on a high *ooh* sound, then I'll transcribe that, and in selecting actual words, I'll try to choose one that ends in that syllable, or as close to it as I can get. So the transcription process often ends with a page of real words, still fairly random, that sound just like the gibberish.

I do that because the difference between an *ohh* and an *aah* and a *B* and a *th* sound is, I assume, integral to the emotion that the story wants to express. I want to stay true to that unconscious, inarticulate intention. Admittedly that content has no narrative, or might make no literal sense yet, but it's in there—I can hear it. I can feel it. My job at this stage is to find words that acknowledge and adhere to the sonic and emotional qualities rather than to ignore and possibly destroy them.

Part of what makes words work in a song is how they sound to the ear and feel on the tongue. If they feel right physiologically, if the tongue of the singer and the mirror neurons of the listener resonate with the delicious appropriateness of the words coming out, then that will inevitably trump literal sense, although literal sense doesn't hurt. If recent neurological hypotheses regarding mirror neurons are correct, then one could say that we empathetically "sing"—with both our minds and the neurons that trigger our vocal and diaphragm muscles—when we hear and see someone else singing. In this sense, watching a performance and listening to music is *always* a participatory activity. The act of putting words down on paper is certainly part of songwriting, but the proof is in seeing how it *feels* when it's sung. If the sound is untrue, the listener can tell.

I try not to prejudge anything that occurs to me at this point in the writing process—I never know if something that sounds stupid at first will in some soon-to-emerge lyrical context make the whole thing shine. So no matter how many pages get filled up, I try to turn off the internal censor.[D]

Sometimes sitting at a desk trying to force this doesn't work. I never have writer's block, exactly, but sometimes things do slow down. At those times I ask myself if my conscious mind might be thinking too much—and it is exactly at this point that I most want and need surprises and weirdness from the depths. Some techniques help in that regard. For instance, I'll carry a microrecorder and go jogging on the West Side, recording phrases that match the song's meter as they occur to me. On the rare occasion that I'm driving a car, I can do the same thing (are there laws against driving and songwriting?). Basically, anything—driving, jogging, swimming, cooking, cycling—that occupies part of the conscious mind and distracts it, works.

The idea is to allow the chthonic material the freedom it needs to gurgle up. To distract the gatekeepers. Sometimes just a verse, or even a phrase or two, will resonate and be sufficient, and that's enough to "unlock" the whole thing. From there on, it becomes more like fill-in-the-blank, conventional puzzle solving.

This particular writing process could also be viewed as a collaboration: a collaboration with oneself, with one's subconscious as well as with the collective unconscious, as Jung would put it. As in dreams, it often seems as if a hidden part

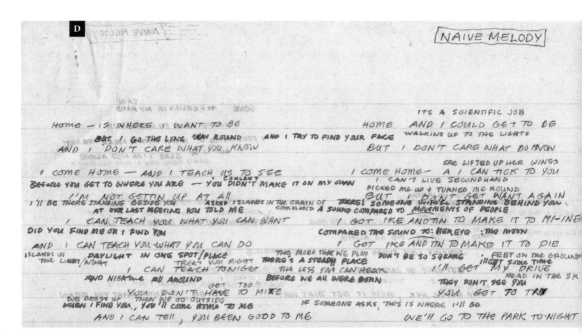

of oneself, a doppelgänger, is attempting to communicate, to impart some important information. When we write, we access different aspects of ourselves, different characters, different parts of our brains and hearts. And then, when they've each had their say, we mentally switch hats, step back from accessing our myriad selves, and take a more distanced and critical view of what we've done. Don't we always work by editing and structuring the outpouring of our many selves? Isn't the end product the result of two or more sides of ourselves working with one another? We've often heard this process described by creative folks as "channeling," or just as often people refer to themselves as a conduit for some force that speaks through them. I suspect that the outside entity—the god, the alien, the source—is a part of oneself, and that this kind of creation is about learning how to listen to and collaborate with it.

CHAPTER SEVEN

Business and Finances

Distribution & Survival Options for Musical Artists

A fter the studio work is finished, after the record has been mixed and pressed, how does a song or album get from the composer or the performer to the listener?

How important is that? How important is getting one's work out to the public? Should that even really matter to a creative artist? Would I make music if no one were listening? If I were a hermit and lived on a mountaintop like a bearded guy in a cartoon, would I take the time to write a song? Many visual artists whose work I love—like Henry Darger, Gordon Carter, and James Castle—never shared their art. They worked ceaselessly and hoarded their creations, which were discovered only after they died or moved out of their apartments. Could I do that? Why would I? Don't we want some validation, respect, feedback? Come to think of it, I might do it—in fact, I did, when I was in high school puttering around with those tape loops and splicing. I think those experiments were witnessed by exactly one friend. However, even an audience of one is not zero.

Still, making music is its own reward. It feels good and can be a therapeutic outlet; maybe that's why so many people work hard in music for no money or public recognition at all. In Ireland and elsewhere, amateurs play well-known songs in pubs, and their ambition doesn't stretch beyond the door. They are getting recognition (or humiliation) within their village, though. In North America, families used to gather around the piano in the parlor. Any monetary remuneration that might have accrued from these "concerts" was secondary. To be honest, even tooling around with tapes in high school, I think I imagined that someone, somehow, might hear my music one day. Maybe not those particular experiments, but I imagined that they might be the baby steps that would allow my more mature expressions to come into being and eventually reach others. Could I have unconsciously had such a long-range plan? I have continued to make plenty of music, often with no clear goal in sight, but I guess somewhere in the back of my mind I believe that the aimless wandering down a meandering path will surely lead to some (well-deserved, in my mind) reward down the road. There's a kind of unjustified faith involved here.

Is the satisfaction that comes from public recognition—however small, however fleeting—a driving force for the creative act? I am going to assume that most of us who make music (or pursue other creative endeavors) do indeed dream that someday someone else will hear, see, or read what we've made. Though Darger and some others might seem to be the exceptions, even they may have dreamed of sharing their work. An audience can be your family members or anonymous passersby on the street; just because you're not booked in a club or concert hall doesn't mean you're not a musician. Even conceptual artists and musicians who decided that to merely *think* about making something was enough—Yoko Ono, John Cage, and Sol LeWitt all made works that consisted solely of sets of instructions—have almost always documented their acts and presented them to their peers.

Many of us who do seek validation dream that we will not only have that dialogue with our peers and the public, but that we might even be compensated for our creative efforts, which is another kind of validation. We're not talking rich and famous; making a life with one's work is enough. So let's assume that you want to be a professional and get paid—although most of all you want to get your music to others' ears—then how does that work? Making great stuff is only half the battle.

When I was younger, it appeared to me that the whole process by which music got to my ears happened by magic. I'd hear a new band or a singer who seemed to have come out of nowhere expressly to blow my mind. It seemed to me as if my friends and I had "discovered" them. I wasn't aware of marketing—at least not the marketing of music. I was aware of celebrities shilling for cigarettes, laundry detergents, and cars on TV and radio, but I didn't know that cool music was being marketed in the same way. I must have felt that there existed a Republic of Peers and like-minded individuals who somehow got wind of what cool stuff everyone else was up to.

Now everyone has at least some understanding of the fact that they are being marketed to. Sometimes we still believe we have magically "discovered" something, but more often we are vaguely aware that someone made an effort to bring that artist or music to our attention. When I first noticed these hidden forces at work, I felt a little disillusioned. Realizing that something I really liked had been sold to me made me feel like some part of my free will had been usurped. I began to question the whole idea of free will and personal agency in my likes and dislikes—were they all manipulated according to someone else's plan? If we can do the mental gymnastics, separating this pragmatic knowledge from our enjoyment of music, then ideally this awareness of marketing campaigns might not spoil our enthusiasm.

My friends and I now have a better understanding of the fact that our tastes are always changing, that some musicians no longer seem relevant while others, in retrospect, seem prescient. We realize that there is an ebb and flow to what we are emotionally involved in, that there are no absolutes. But for a while the music business seemed like a utopian parallel universe.

As music fans and bystanders, we saw Elvis riding in a gold Cadillac, we saw Sting recording in a French château, we saw the Capitol Records building in LA shaped like a tower of 45s, and we heard the stories of lives lived in excess—drug binges, TVs thrown from hotel balconies, embroidered Nudie suits and painted Rolls Royces. We heard stories of Bruce Springsteen laboring in studios for more than a year on *Born to Run*, or D'Angelo haunting Electric Lady for four years to make *Voodoo*. Pragmatism seemed beside the point; the music world was about other things. Those tales of profligate spending and interminable recording sessions in expensive studios are almost unheard of now for the majority of artists, mainly for budgetary reasons. The music world then seemed glamorous and extravagant, and the practicalities of marketing and distribution seemed beside the point when one thought of the glory and the lifestyle. Much of that has changed.

Flaunting a luxurious lifestyle is now mainly the provenance of hip-hop artists, few of whom tour extensively—so someone must be buying some records if that's what pays for those bottles of Cristal, those music videos, those grills and chains. Or else their record companies feel that fronting the money for such things is a wise long-term investment. Many of those artists have cleverly diversified into perfumes, restaurants, shoes, and clothing; if music sales decline, if there are less and less profits from CDs, profile and income can presumably be maintained in other ways, like having your own line of perfume.

Over the years, I too have increasingly spent time working in forms that are not exclusively musical—art, books (like this one), films, and DVDs. None of those bring in anywhere near the income that a perfume deal would, or so I imagine— I really missed the boat in that department. With any extra-musical pursuit, my general financial rule is simply to try not to lose money; if a project covers costs and expenses, that's acceptable. One project is not supposed to bankroll another, though that ideal is hard to maintain. For me, diversification is about seeking out ways of stretching creatively. Diversity is not a business decision; it's a way of staying interested, alert. Though I don't want my creative decisions to be guided by profit and marketing—motivating criteria that inevitably end in disaster— I also don't want to be blissfully ignorant of budgets and business.

There's an adage often directed at easy-come, easy-go types: the musician who doesn't attend to his or her business pretty soon doesn't have any business. Decades ago, I took that warning to heart, and before signing to a record label I read books like *This Business of Music*. My limited research didn't guarantee all that much in the way of wisdom, and the lawyers who were hired to protect our baby band didn't really do much to guarantee us a truly fair deal. Although our initial record contracts weren't so great, to their credit, they did the best they could under the circumstances. At least we didn't do anything truly disastrous. In subsequent years we made an effort to learn a little each time out and make course corrections. Some business decisions I deeply regret; though I was never coerced, I was often told a given situation was the best I could hope for at the time. That line has been used to justify a lot of predatory deals, but I got off lightly. I have managed to incrementally improve my legal and contractual situation over the years, to avoid repeating mistakes and to protect myself. I've worked with companies big and small, and I've even owned my own record company.

That label, Luaka Bop, still exists, though I'm no longer involved in running it. Our first release was in 1990. I think one year in the early aughts I actually saw some income from the company, but the rest of the time, although it was hugely fun and the music we released was inspirational, it was also a drain on my time and finances.

I've also tried working without any record company at all. The *Everything That Happens* collaboration with Brian Eno was self-released, though various companies were involved in the distribution of the physical CDs. The *Here Lies Love* two-disc collaboration with Fatboy Slim came out through Nonesuch, a subsidiary of Warner Music Group. I have released music through indie labels like Thrill Jockey, and I have manufactured CDs of remixes and dance scores and sold them on tour at the merch table. I have, at one time or another, tried almost every form of music distribution.

These days, I tour every few years, and I no longer see it as simply a loss leader for CD sales. Touring used to be thought of mainly as a type of marketing—a way to get the public to buy more records by generating press and building an audience. It does do that, but it can also be a source of income and a creative endeavor all on its own. We've been told the old lie that losing money on tour is okay because you can make it up in record sales, but that really doesn't hold true for everyone anymore. Performing is psychologically and physically enjoyable for musicians, so cash is not the sole attraction. Sadly, that means it's relatively easy to tempt us to perform for peanuts. Being a musician is a good job, but that doesn't mean it's okay to go broke doing it.

I've made money and I've been ripped off (well, I've signed lousy contracts). I've had creative freedom and I've been pressured to make hits. I have dealt with diva behavior from crazy musicians and I have seen genius records by wonderful artists get completely ignored. I love music. I always will. It saved my life, and I know I'm not the only one who can say that. If you think success in the world of music is determined by the number of records sold, or the size of your house or bank account, then I'm not the expert for you. I am more interested in how people can manage a whole lifetime in music. Is that possible? And if so, how?

What is called the music business today, however, is nothing like what I researched before signing that first contract. In fact, the music business is hardly even in the business of producing music anymore. At some point, it became primarily the business of selling objects—LPs, cassettes, CDs in plastic cases—and that business will soon be over. Tower Records closed in 2006, and Virgin Megastores shut their doors in 2009. Borders declared bankruptcy in February 2011, and

HMV in the UK closed a massive number of branches in 2012. They're not coming back; this is not a "downturn." The few indie stores that have survived have staffs that are knowledgeable, and they love the music and the musicians whose work they sell. I stopped by a record shop in Nashville not too long ago where the staff picks are all worth considering, and I heard a band play there in the afternoon. Beers were passed out. I bought some records. But even those shops have to sell a critical mass of goods to pay the rent, so who knows how long such wonderful outlets will be around.

This changing landscape is not necessarily bad news for music, and it's not necessarily bad news for musicians, either. There have never been more opportunities for a musician to reach an audience, and that is what we have always wanted to do. Music, as far as this book is concerned, is the end, and as we have seen, the devices that deliver it come and go. Almost none of the myriad ways of currently making an audience aware of your work existed when I accidentally found myself with a music career. Though the current situation is rife with new possibilities, the industry itself is less flush with money, so you have to learn how to navigate some treacherous waters.

Lenny Waronker used to run Warner Bros. Records with Mo Ostin. I talked to him recently on the phone about their philosophy back when I signed with that label.

The music business was not as profitable then. It was run by entrepreneurs, and often the records they put out were based on their taste. Ahmet Ertegun was one, and Norman Granz, who specialized in jazz, was another. They were proud that the records they put out reflected their own taste. We at Warner had a philosophy. In the late sixties and early seventies, we could see that good songwriters learned as they went—one got a sense of their growth. They might not get it the first time around, but it might happen for them on their next record. So we tried to simply sign what we thought were the best artists. Artists who had an aesthetic. We eventually realized that what was important was our roster rather than our records. And sometimes what was right, what clicked, was also a good record. It was a bet, and sometimes you could bet on quality. It was a time of anything goes, artistically. We signed unsuccessful artists who made good records, and we eventually realized that these artists drew other artists (some of whom were successful) to the label. Randy Newman, Ry Cooder, Van Dyke Parks, and

Van Morrison were on the label, and other artists wanted to be on the label because they were there.

I remember Seymour Stein saying that he managed to sign Madonna because Talking Heads were on Sire Records at the time. Those days are gone for major labels, but smaller companies still follow some of that philosophy, though their finances and logistics might be different.

Take a look at this graph.

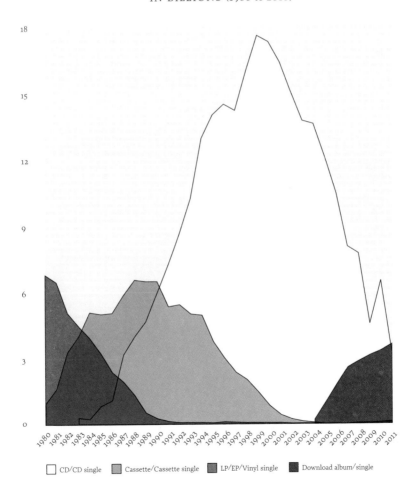

DOLLAR AMOUNTS OF UNITS SHIPPED—
IN BILLIONS (1980 to 2010)

☐ CD/CD single   ▨ Cassette/Cassette single   ▨ LP/EP/Vinyl single   ■ Download album/single

Wow. That looks pretty scary. See how much money CDs were bringing in at their peak? No wonder some bad decisions were made. Some say this picture depicts a dire trend. The fact that Radiohead left EMI not so long ago and debuted its 2007 album *In Rainbows* online, and that Madonna defected from Warner Bros. to sign with Live Nation, a concert promoter, are said to signal the end of the music business as we know it. Actually, these are just two examples of how musicians are increasingly able to work outside of the traditional label relationship. There is no single way of doing business these days. There are, in fact, six viable models, by my count, which I will review in this chapter. There are probably more, and one can mix and match, but these give a picture of the array of options. Having a variety of business choices is good for artists: it gives us more ways to make a living. And it's good for audiences, too, who will have the opportunity for more—and more interesting—music to listen to.

WHAT IS MUSIC?

First, a definition of terms. What is it we're talking about here? What exactly is being bought and sold? In the past, music was something you heard and experienced—it was as much a social event as an aural one. As I argued earlier in this book, before recording technology existed, you could not separate music from its social context. It was pretty much all tied to specific social functions. It was communal, and often utilitarian. You couldn't take it home, copy it, sell it as a commodity (except as sheet music, but that's not music), or even hear it again. Music was a singular experience, something connected to a specific time and place. It was part of the continuum, the timeline of your life, not a set of "things" that lived outside of it. You could pay to hear music by going to a concert or hiring musicians, but after you did, it was just a memory. Or, as many people did, you could make it yourself or with your family or friends.

Technology changed all that in the twentieth century. Music (or its recorded artifact) came to be regarded as a product—a thing that could be bought, sold, traded, and replayed endlessly in any context. You didn't have to go see a performance to hear music, and you didn't have to perform the music yourself, either.

Other people did those jobs. This was, of course, hugely convenient. Most of us grew up in an age when the existence of recorded music was a given. We heard music in other contexts as well, but at least half of what we heard had been pre-recorded or was played on the radio—and much of that was pre-recorded as well.

As record companies flourished, singers and songwriters began to earn additional income from the sale of recorded music, beyond their income from concerts. This must have seemed pretty exciting. Though there were lots of small record companies early on, the industry was soon dominated by a handful of large companies that signed artists (all of us were at least given the dignity of being referred to as artists), paid for their recordings to be made, and then promoted the hell out of them (sometimes). These companies would then get the records into any place that sold singles or LPs, and they'd also get them played on the radio. In return for this up-front and sometimes risky capital investment, most traditional record companies kept the lion's share of the income, passing on a relatively small percentage of the sales to the artists. The songwriter (if that person was different from the performer) got paid something too, as composers had with sheet music in the preceding decades.

These changes upended the function and use of music, transforming it from something we participated in to something we consumed. But our instincts remain intact: I spend plenty of time as a music consumer, with buds in my ears listening to recorded music, but I'll still go out to stand in a crowd as part of an audience. I also sing to myself, and, yes, I perform and play an instrument (not always well).

We'll always want music to be part of our social fabric. We gravitate to concerts and bars even if the sound sucks; we pass music from hand to hand (or via the Internet) as a form of social currency; we build temples where only "our kind of people" can hear our kind of music (opera houses, punk clubs, symphony halls); and we want to know everything about our favorite bards—their love lives, their clothes, their political beliefs. Something about music urges us to engage with its larger context, beyond the piece of plastic it came on—it seems to be part of our genetic makeup that we can be so deeply moved by this art form. Music resonates in so many parts of the brain that we can't conceive of it being an isolated thing. It's whom you were with, how old you were, and what was happening that day. Trying to reduce and package such a changeable and unwieldly entity is ultimately futile. But many try.

WHAT DO RECORD COMPANIES DO?

O r, more precisely, what did they traditionally do? As I outlined earlier, the record company not only has the capital to fund some of the recording and promoting, it presumably also has some skills, expertise, useful contacts, and access to the latest technology—more than a bank would have, for example. A bank would never give a kid with a guitar a loan; the kid has no collateral from a bank's point of view.

The idea used to be that the record company A&R folks all had good ears, and, as Lenny Waronker said, they could sense that these kids and their songs could, just maybe, become hugely popular and make a pile of money for the record company. At some point in the eighties these guys with the special ears began to disappear. Most of the major labels began to merge with one another, or even with non-music businesses. Warner Bros., where I was, got absorbed by Time, Inc. (Maybe we'd all get good reviews in *Time* from now on!) And then, to make it even more confusing, that entity merged with AOL. The new stockholders and boards soon demanded quarterly accounting, which pressured the labels to produce significant hits on a regular basis. The "ears" who spotted and nurtured talent were well paid, so to pay off the debts accrued by the recent mergers, these guys were let go. Then even the guys who managed and used to own the record labels were paid handsomely to go away. Other guys who didn't have a history of dealing with musicians thought they could do just as well or better by being more ruthless and efficient. Mostly, though, they didn't do any better. The smaller labels that survived still relied on their love of the form and their gut instincts, and because they were actually paying attention, sometimes they hooked a big one. They knew when something moved them, but they didn't have the same financial resources and marketing manpower as the big boys. Turning one's heart, ears, and love into cash could be a sometime thing.

Here's the traditional breakdown of what record companies used to do:

- Fund recording sessions
- Manufacture product
- Distribute product

- Market product
- Advance money for expenses (concert tours, videos, promotional events, hair and makeup)
- Advise and guide artists on their careers and recordings (managers are supposed to do this, but record companies do as well)
- Handle the accounting of all of the above and eventually funnel some of the leftover cash to the artist

This was the system that evolved in the twentieth century to market the product, which is to say the container—vinyl, tape, or disc—that carried the music. Can you imagine a business in which most of its investments prove to be bad? That was the record business before the collapse—the few massively successful acts were supporting the many who weren't exactly failures. So, in effect, Robert Palmer's sales funded the Pogues, and Madonna's income funded Randy Newman's idiosyncratic records. This system of corporate arts funding, however wacky, held up until the foundations began to crumble. Since 2000, many forces have conspired to reduce the value of the services those record companies offer to artists. The deals offered are no longer supported by the same a priori assumptions regarding what a label will do for an artist. Here are some of the things that have changed:

CHANGE 1: RECORDING COSTS
BEGAN TO APPROACH ZERO

Years ago, most artists simply didn't have the $15,000 (minimum) to pay for studio time, engineering fees, and mixing and mastering costs—the base investment needed for making a record. But now an album can be made on the same laptop you use to check email.

I still utilize proper studios fairly often, but I have come to realize that it isn't an absolute necessity anymore. The cost of a laptop and the gear that went into recording my vocals on "Lazy" (my collaboration with X-Press 2) might have come to a few thousand dollars, and though the laptop has been retired, it was also used for other recordings (as well as email and lots of other functions). Microphones, speakers, and other gear used for that project are still in use. So that "startup" cost gets amortized rapidly over a few years.

But what if you want to record a large band and not just yourself singing on a laptop? A company called ArtistShare, run by Brian Camelio, offers a new approach to funding recordings that require capital investment. I heard about them when an ArtistShare record by jazz composer Maria Schneider won a Grammy. (That put the lie to the argument that semi-self-funded recordings should be looked down on as vanity projects.) Schneider works with modest-size orchestras, a bit like Gil Evans did some decades ago. The cost of rehearsing with these ensembles and recording them is considerable—way beyond what would normally be available to jazz artists whose record companies anticipate fairly modest sales and adjust their funding accordingly. Camelio tried to solve this problem by initiating fan-funded recordings. Fans of Schneider's give money to ArtistShare before the record is made—an act of faith that won't necessarily work for everyone. The fans who can give just a little get a CD when it's done, and those who give a lot can get thanked on the CD, given free concert tickets, backstage passes, and all the rest. Kickstarter campaigns work in a similar way. Neither is a conventional investment, because the fans don't get a percentage of sales, but they are an investment in keeping artists working and recording at a high level. One might say these models facilitate investment in the continuation of our own culture. So one way or another it is sometimes feasible for musicians to find a way to record without going into serious debt—if they are careful.

CHANGE 2: MANUFACTURING AND DISTRIBUTION COSTS ARE APPROACHING ZERO

There used to be a break-even sales point below which it was impractical to distribute a recording. With LPs and CDs, there were base manufacturing costs, printing costs, shipping, warehousing of stock, and so on. It was essential to sell in volume, because that's how those costs got amortized. The costs per record came down the more records were pressed and potentially sold. If you sold less than a few thousand LPs or CDs, the initial costs of not only the recording, but of pressing the vinyl (or CDs) and making the covers and shipping to warehouses and record stores couldn't get paid back, so the record company would inevitably lose money. This meant that marginal music tended to remain marginal because of economics and technology, rather than the quality of the music. This also meant that for a record that only sold a few thousand copies, the percentage of each record sale that went back to the artist was lower than for those that sold millions, for which the percentage of the recording cost that is paid back by each record sold approaches zero. Records that sold well not only brought in more profit per copy sold, but a larger percentage of those profits per copy went to the record companies and the artists. Popular records could therefore be sold at a discount, which would undercut the little guys while still bringing in more money than the records the little guys put out. The music business was like Walmart that way.

No more: digital distribution is pretty close to being free. Digitally, it's no more expensive to distribute a million copies than a hundred. Well, one needs to use the services of a heftier server if larger quantities of music files are being downloaded at once and more credit-card payments are processed, but there are no more warehouses, trucks, damaged goods being returned, and pressing plants that consume natural resources. The big "stores" where digital downloads are available are few (iTunes, Amazon, and eMusic in the United States), and they do take a percentage of the digital sales—around 30 percent—which some people, including me, regard as unreasonable. So, to be fair, the distribution isn't really free. That percentage is often less than what old-school record stores took in as their percentage of the the retail price, though sometimes—surprise!—it works out the same for the artist in the end.

So, although distribution costs have dropped precipitously, there are still corporate gatekeepers who charge hefty tolls. The savings aren't passed on as fairly as one might hope in most cases, although, as we'll see, there are workarounds.

Due to the large percentage of each record sale kept, the record companies often broke even way before the artists began to see their own shares trickle in. Many bands lived off the money given them in advance of the estimated sales of their upcoming records, and these amounts were often based on an A&R person listening to rough demos or seeing a live show featuring new material. Most artists, however, never saw a cent from record sales after they got their advances. Their percentage of each record was still being used to pay off the recording and marketing costs and advances loaned to them by the record companies. The artists would then be obliged to write more songs in order to get an advance for another record—they'd be living record to record, advance to advance. The artists essentially went into debt—willingly, following the carrot of fame dangled before them. Making music and performing it is hugely enjoyable, so a reward was built in that the record companies didn't have to pay for. Artists would be having a pretty good time writing and playing music, making a name for themselves, but they'd be quietly getting deeper and deeper in debt. Most artists accumulated a debt that was hard to dig out of unless they managed to have record sales that stayed consistently high. The list of successful artists who at some point in their career went completely broke is astounding—TLC, the Ramones, Terence Trent D'Arby, Seal, Ron Wood, Meatloaf, MC Hammer, Michael Jackson, Sly Stone, and Toni Braxton, just to name a few. Some of these artists simply didn't manage their finances well and spent their money on drugs or limos, but some did nothing "wrong." They were just part of a business that wasn't designed to sustain them over the long term.

In 2011, the *New York Times* ran a story about the economic realities facing the musician Teddy Thompson:

Mr. Thompson, who has been struggling to succeed for more than a decade (he turns 35 on Feb. 19), has enjoyed only marginal success in the United States—his average record sales are 21,000—and is acutely aware of his dwindling shelf life in a business with a rapid turnover of talent. If his fifth album, *Bella*, to be released Tuesday on Verve/Forecast, doesn't break through, how many more chances will he get?

"My goal when I started out was to get to the point where I could tour a lot and make a living, which means getting paid enough to hire my own band, travel and end up with a bit of money, but I'm still nowhere near that point," he said. "Because I didn't have a band and fan base when I started, I did everything backward. I've ended up making five reasonably expensive records and not having a commensurate fan base." [1]

In another *Times* article, about singer-songwriter Nicole Atkins, Ben Sisario writes,

She was signed by Columbia Records and got the full star-in-the-making treatment, with a spread in *Rolling Stone* and even an American Express commercial in anticipation of her debut album, *Neptune City*. Critics began to fall for her darkly laced, almost sur-realistic songs and her soaring, dramatically powerful voice. Shortly before its release, however, the album was delayed—to be remixed by the label's new co-chairman, Rick Rubin—and when it came out, months later, its promotional momentum had evapo-rated. *Neptune City* sold a disappointing 32,000 copies, according to Nielsen Sound-Scan, and by 2009 Ms. Atkins and her label had "divorced," as she once put it. [*2]

It is important to keep in mind that the sales numbers described here as dis-appointing might have actually been okay if these artists could have held on to a larger percentage of that income. I know both these artists. Their records are good and they are plugging away, gigging around town and elsewhere, and I feel opti-mistic that the changes in the music-distribution landscape will help them find a way to make a life in music.

In the last decade things have changed. The big record companies have cut back, and they rarely offer generous advances to artists anymore. I have been paid sizable advances by Nonesuch, and though I could have tried to make a cheaper recording on my last record with them, and thereby pocketed the change, almost all of the money I received went into production costs. That was my choice. I did okay, but I don't recommend that to everyone.

---

* Sales quoted reflect United States numbers only. Overseas sales can, in fact, "save" deals for bands.

As the advances and marketing expenditures that record companies commit to projects continue to shrink, artists have naturally begun to seek other ways of funding their recordings, paying the rent, and marketing their music.

CHANGE 4: PERFORMING
IS NOW VIEWED AS A SOURCE OF INCOME

Live performances by artists were traditionally seen by record companies as a way to publicize their new releases—as a means to an end and not an end in itself. Bands would therefore ask for and often receive advances from record companies (called tour support) specifically to cover their touring losses: the cost of hiring musicians, hotel rooms, van rental, gas, and meals in strange cities. Bands would anticipate that they'd recover that advance from the record company, which they'd have to pay back later, through a subsequent increase in record sales. Sometimes the record sales would indeed increase as the result of a tour, and after a long time those loans could be paid off, but often they would not.

This, to be blunt, is all wrong. It's backward. First off, performing is a distinct skill, different from writing songs, singing, or making recordings. And for those who can do it, performing can be a good way to make a living. There are acts out there who don't sell all that many records, but whose excellent live performances can fill sizable halls. They don't need a record label's help to do that either.

Not everyone agrees with me. I spoke with Mac McCaughan, who co-runs the independent label Merge. He sees a continued value in bands touring to "support" their records. As he put it:

> The most old-fashioned way of doing things is still the best, which is touring. That really sells records more than anything else. It really does work. Most of what Merge puts out only gets played on college radio, non-commercial radio, KCRW, places like that. And that's great, but by the time you get to a record store two days later, you've kind of maybe forgotten what you heard. But if you see a band live, that stays with you. It's so memorable and it's so immediate. That, more than anything else, is gonna stay in your mind. And you can actually make money touring if you keep your budgets down.

So given all these changes, what is the purpose of record labels? Do they still have a place in this new world? Can we redefine what it is? Some will survive. Nonesuch, which has distributed several of my albums, has thrived under Warner Music Group ownership by operating with a relatively lean staff of twelve and staying focused on talent. "Artists like Wilco, Philip Glass, k.d. lang, and others have sold more here than when they were at so-called major labels, even during a time of decline," Bob Hurwitz, president of Nonesuch, told me. The label has had some unexpected successes recently, like Buena Vista Social Club and the Black Keys. Such successes, Hurwitz says, happen about 5 percent of the time. He says that things do a little better than hoped for about 10 percent of the time, exactly as expected about 60 percent of the time, and not as well as was hoped about 25 percent of the time. Without knowing how much each record costs to make and market, it becomes a little hard to know just how devastating the "not as well as hoped" records would be financially for that company. Similarly, a successful record is only a financial success if it didn't cost an arm and a leg in recording and marketing to make it happen. Hurwitz claims that Nonesuch, though prestigious, is not a vanity label for Warner Bros.

DISTRIBUTION MODELS

Do people need labels? Some bands don't, but some bands do just because they don't want to worry about what we do. They don't want to do what we do. They just want to make music and play shows and make records and write songs. They don't want to have to worry about finding a distributor and calling record stores and making sure they're stocking the record when they're coming through town.

—Mac McCaughan

Some big labels have disappeared, as these roles that Mac mentions get chopped up and delivered by more thrifty independent vendors. Brian Eno (who now produces Coldplay and is co-writing songs with U2) recently told me he was enthusiastic about ithinkmusic—an online network of indie bands, fans, and stores—and pessimistic about the future of traditional labels. "Structurally, they're much too large," he said. "And they're entirely on the defensive now. The only idea they have is that they can give you a big advance, which is still attractive to a lot of young bands just starting out. But that's all they represent now: capital."

So where do artists fit into this changing landscape?

Where there used to be one model, now I see six, ranging from the artists who put themselves entirely in the hands of the label to the artists who do nearly everything themselves. There could be more delineation along this spectrum, but the following will suffice for now. Not surprisingly, the more involved the artist is, the more likely it is that he or she will retain a bigger slice of the pie per unit sold. The totally DIY model is certainly not for everyone, but the point is that there are options.

SIX DISTRIBUTION MODELS WITH DIFFERENT LEVELS OF ARTIST CONTROL

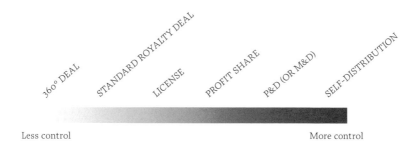

Less control   More control

1. THE 360° DEAL

At one end of the spectrum is the 360°, or equity, deal, where every aspect of an artist's career is handled by producers, promoters, marketing people, lawyers, accountants, and managers. Whew. The idea behind this model is that the artist can achieve wide saturation and massive sales because you are being boosted by a powerful machine working every angle—and they stand to profit from everything you do. That means, in some cases, they keep a major piece of every T-shirt, every bottle of perfume, every concert ticket, and of course every record sold. The artist in this model becomes a brand, owned and operated by the corporation, and in theory this encourages the company to adopt the long view because of enlightened self-interest. The company should have a strong incentive to nurture that artist's career because every aspect of it that makes money benefits them, too.

Pussycat Dolls, Korn, and Robbie Williams have made arrangements like this, selling equity in everything they touch. Jay-Z did a 360° deal as well, and one would assume that an astute, street-smart man like him would not get ripped off. It does vary, though. U2 did a deal with Live Nation in 2008 that lumped a percentage of their merchandise sales in with the concert income, but their CD (and download) sales were not included.[3] The artist often gets a lot of money up front in these deals. A *lot*. However, there's a trade-off. I doubt that every significant creative decision is left in the artist's hands. Too much is at stake. For an artist, kicking back and not promoting your product would not be an option. Making arty experimental records will be discouraged. As a general rule, as the cash comes in, creative control goes out.

Madonna just made a 360° deal with Live Nation. For a reported $120 million, the company—which until now has mainly produced and promoted concerts—will get a piece of both her concert revenue and her music sales. The following details were reported:[4]

- $17.5 million: A general advance—money Madonna gets just for being Madonna.
- $50 to $60 million: Advances for up to three new albums. As with a regular record deal, this money only gets handed over when Madonna delivers the music for each record. So it's possible that the company won't have to pay this out entirely. The Material Girl may not be moved to record another thirty-six to forty-five more songs, which is what it would take to fulfill that contract and get the entire advance.
- $50 million in cash and stock for the right to promote Madonna's concerts and license her name. Note that Live Nation still has to share concert and licensing revenue, which will give her 90 percent of concert sales (probably net) and 50 percent of the licensing money it collects.

I, for one, would not want to be beholden to Live Nation. They're a spinoff of Clear Channel, the radio conglomerate that turned much of the US radiospectrum into pabulum. But Madge is a smart cookie; she's always been adept at controlling her own stuff, so we'll see.

According to my manager, David Whitehead, "A new band, now at EMI, signed a deal like that. They didn't have a track record—no one had heard of them, so they had no negotiating leverage. EMI presumably negotiated a nice portion of album sales, merch, and a cut of touring."

One can see the logic in this model as record sales decline and the profits from downloads don't offset the loss. Record companies (and even concert promoters) feel that since they are the ones who helped create a popular artist/brand, they should naturally see a percentage of the profits from all possible revenue streams. And that seems fair, especially when the up-front investment is so high. If I'd spent millions bankrolling Lady Gaga's records, producing those elaborate videos and marketing plans (and I know nothing of her finances—she may have bankrolled it all herself), I'd sure want a piece of her live shows and any other lucrative sources of revenue that might come down the road.

All the major labels these days tend to want to sign artists to 360° deals. The question is whether the deal is "passive" or "active." In a passive deal, the label skims off some percentage of sales from the licensing income but isn't involved in an artist's business in other ways. As long as the label gets its money when it comes around asking, it won't be telling the artists how to run their careers.

Labels, however, tend to prefer an "active" deal. For example, since all the majors have affiliated publishing divisions, they solicit interest in the artist from them and the publishers, then make a separate offer to the songwriters alongside the record deal. If the artist resists and wants to retain publishing rights, the label will accept a passive participation in the publishing income and counter this less lucrative (for them) deal by offering lower rates on "mechanical" income as a tool to drive the artist to agree to the deal with their affiliated publisher.

Mechanical licenses, a mandatory requirement for any record deal, grant the right to mechanically reproduce a recording. This generally runs as high as 9.1 cents per song. The writer of a song, who is not necessarily the performer, receives that 9.1 cents per track for songs under five minutes (in addition to the royalties, if they are also the recording artist). Typically these songwriting cuts are negotiated—in favor of the record company—to be limited to ten tracks. Even if there are twelve or more songs on a CD, they agree to pay only on ten of them. Skits—like the short dramatic or comedic interludes on hip-hop records—don't count. If the artist writes his own songs, he has the option to negotiate this mechanical percentage, and often as a result it gets lowered to 7.1 cents. Mechanicals are an important source of income, as I'll discuss later.

Back to the active deal. If the company can manage to own a portion of the publishing of a song, then the label stands to reap additional income if that song is licensed by an ad or covered by another act. Typically the label will try to get a 10 percent passive participation in the publishing income, if they're not able to get an affiliated (active) publishing deal, which will therefore mean that they also get a piece of the mechanicals they are paying to the songwriter.

Touring is of course a big topic in these all-inclusive deals. Normally, touring falls under "passive" participation. The label doesn't actively promote the tours or help organize them; it's too much work. They just take a piece of the profit, although some labels try to exert more control and actually make deals directly with concert promoters. The tour participation in 360° deals are all over the place, ranging from those that take 5 to 15 percent of gross tour income to even higher amounts of net income. "Shelters" are often built into the deals so that the label only starts to participate above a certain net-income threshold. If, for example, you aren't netting more than a certain amount on your tour—if you're only playing clubs, for example—the label won't be terribly interested and won't commission your income. This benign neglect can be contractually formalized, and the artist is therefore "sheltered" somewhat.

Understandably, labels don't want to be stuck with the "short" dollars (meaning the debt or losses that the artist might incur while on tour), which will only increase the artist's tour-support demands. To get their act into the venues that will pull in serious money, and therefore be worth commissioning, the labels that sign artists to 360° deals aim for blockbuster hits—just like movie studios. If a song is a hit, then the performance venues tend to increase in size, and the act will actually make money on the tour—which will then be commissioned by the label.

Labels offering 360° deals also like to participate in sponsorship and endorsement deals, whether tour-related or not. Sometimes those deals can be limited to ones brought to the table by the label, but often not. Again, the company's commission on these deals ranges from 15 to 20 percent of net income. Labels are bolstering their staffs in this area, since they believe relationships with advertisers and corporate sponsors will be key to future profitability.

Needless to say, this means artists signed to these deals will be pressured into associating themselves with sponsors and the products they're selling. The line between music as a creative act and music as a means of getting you to buy something will become even fuzzier. As more artists sign these deals, we will have a hard time knowing whether or not we are listening to a song or a commercial—or whether there is any difference between the two.

2. STANDARD ROYALTY DEAL

This is more or less what I lived with for many years as a member of Talking Heads, and even as recently as 2004, when I released *Grown Backwards* with Nonesuch. In this model, the record company bankrolls the recording and handles the manufacturing, distribution, press, and promotion. The artist gets a percentage of record sales. The label does not a have financial stake in live shows, T-shirts, or endorsements.

In a typical deal of this type, the record label owns the copyright to the recording. Forever. This doesn't mean they own the "song," though. This distinction is confusing for many people—we tend to think of a recording as being the same as the song. However, the song itself and the version that the artist recorded are not always the same thing. It could be someone else's song, for example. In that case, the song copyright is shared by the writer(s) and the publisher(s) of the song. This goes back to the era before recordings, when sheet music was the published version of a "song." With the advent of the recording industry, sheet music now brings in a minuscule amount of income, but the recording of a song—particularly one that becomes a hit—is a valuable commodity. Since the record company in this model typically finances the recording, they claim 100 percent ownership of it, with an agreed-upon percentage of record sales going to the artist.

Obviously the cost of all the services a record company provides, along with their overhead, accounts for a big part of the price of a CD. You, the buyer, are paying for all those trucks, all those CD-pressing plants, all those warehouses, and all that plastic. Only a small percent of the retail price is for the music. Theoretically, as digital distribution increases and much of that overhead goes away, those costs should no longer be passed along to the consumer—or to the artist. Theoretically!

Much of the income for songwriters like myself doesn't come from record sales, though we do get the mechanical and publishing income before expenses like video budgets, recording costs, and tour support are repaid. However, I'm going to focus on sales of recordings for now, because the other sources of income—like touring and licensing songs to films or commercials—are optional. I could make a *lot* more money if I decided to license songs to commercials. Here is the breakdown of how I did on a record that was made under a more or less standard distribution deal.

Talking Heads spent many years with Warner Bros., and in 2004 I released *Grown Backwards* through their boutique Nonesuch label. Part of the attraction of Nonesuch was that we felt in good company with their eclectic roster of acts, like John Adams, the Black Keys, Laurie Anderson, Caetano Veloso, Wilco (until they left to start their own label, dBpm Records), Buena Vista Social Club, and the Magnetic Fields. Like the Warner Bros. of old and indie labels today like Warp, 4AD, Tomlab, Daptone, and Thrill Jockey, Nonesuch's taste is reflected in their roster of artists. If you like one record on the label, you just might like another.

Trusting that I'd sell some records, Nonesuch offered me an advance of $225,000. If I had recorded with just myself and a few other musicians, my expenses would have been lower and I could have pocketed the left-over money. Instead, after my recording studio and musician costs, all that was left over was about $7,000. Was I crazy? That's not much to live on for all the time that writing and recording takes, which in this case amounted to almost a year, though not of continuous work. That record did cost a significant amount to make, because I mixed a rhythm section with strings, winds, and horns on a lot of the tracks. There were lots of arrangements, players, and big studios for recording them. When you do a record like that with a corporate-owned label, you have to pay at least union rates for musicians. Though high, those rates are generally fair. In this case, recording costs (all the musicians, studio time, technicians, and arrangements) were $218,000, which seems like a sizable sum. I was glad Nonesuch was covering those expenses with their advance, but still, what was I to live on? Was I being foolish and naïve?

Presumably they didn't give me that advance knowing or even caring what the record would cost. Rather, for them the amount was based on projected sales. Needless to say, this "loan" would need to be paid off—it wasn't a gift for signing with them! I would begin to see income from my record only after that sizable sum was repaid.

There are two ways of handling a royalty deal, but they both come out more or less the same for the artist. In one form of accounting, artists get their percentage only after a lot of others get to the feed trough first. The other standard model involves the retailer and record company taking a lump sum off the top, with the artist receiving a fixed royalty on what's left. I'm going to focus on the first form of accounting, since it's more transparent.

A big chunk of the price a consumer pays goes to the retailer—either the physical store (those that are left) or to iTunes or Amazon. Then the record's producer gets some percentage (3 percent is common). Any tour support the record company advanced to the artist gets paid back, as do video costs, which can be as high as the cost of making a record and are often higher, like a million dollars for a really big-budget video. Then promotional costs are shared, including payola—which is essentially bribes of one form or another to radio stations. So half of what the record company pays to get your record played and marketed is your own money—you just don't have to front it. (To be fair, they usually ask at each step along the way.) It goes on and on. Returns (meaning the records that are pressed and shipped out but remain unsold and need to be returned), limos, those dinners they bought you that you thought were such a nice gesture—this all gets deducted before the artist's percentage kicks in. A lot of accounting work is required if an artist decides he or she wants to actually investigate where all that money went.

PHYSICAL ROYALTY BREAKDOWN

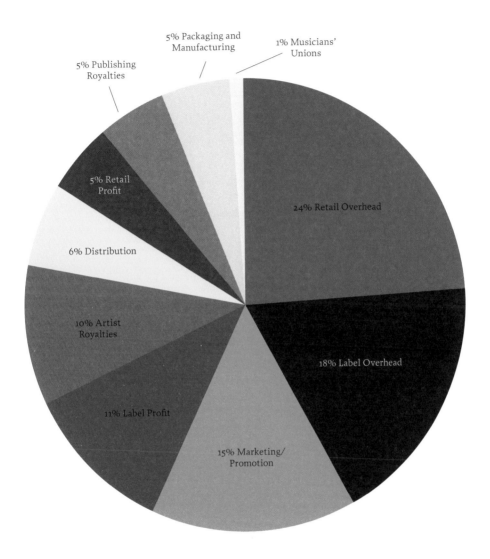

5% Packaging and Manufacturing

1% Musicians' Unions

5% Publishing Royalties

5% Retail Profit

6% Distribution

10% Artist Royalties

11% Label Profit

15% Marketing/ Promotion

18% Label Overhead

24% Retail Overhead

Here are the figures that show the cost of making my *Grown Backwards* record versus the advance I got from Nonesuch.

EXPENSE BREAKDOWN FOR *GROWN BACKWARDS*
($225,000 ADVANCE)

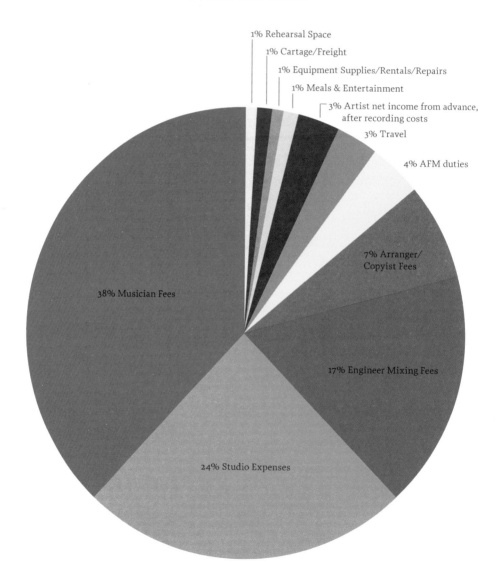

1% Rehearsal Space
1% Cartage/Freight
1% Equipment Supplies/Rentals/Repairs
1% Meals & Entertainment
3% Artist net income from advance, after recording costs
3% Travel
4% AFM duties
7% Arranger/Copyist Fees
17% Engineer Mixing Fees
24% Studio Expenses
38% Musician Fees

This was an expensive, and therefore risky, record to make in the current economic climate. The record business was heading down a slippery slope, so betting that I'd make that hefty advance back was in no way a sure thing. I felt lucky just to be able to make a record with strings, winds, and the host of great musicians I loved, and I was prepared not to reap much in the way of profits as a result. We all knew that records were costing more, but relative to what my record sales were at that time, this was really pushing it a bit. I've talked recently to some emerging musicians who are still watching the industry tank, and when I asked them why they even wanted to make a record, their feeling was, "I want to do it while they still exist." I may have been operating under a similar impulse: *Let me sneak under the wire before the whole game is over.*

How many copies of that record would I have to sell to actually make money? The record retailed for $18 (before inevitable discounts, but for the sake of this exercise let's use the full price). Eight dollars of that goes straight to the retail store selling physical CDs, which leaves $10. If my royalty percentage were a not-uncommon 14 percent, I'd get $1.40 from that wholesale price. If my royalty rate were a fairly high 19 percent I'd get $1.90 per CD sold. If I had a big-name producer on the record then I'd typically be obliged to give 3 percent to him or her, because producers get paid off the top—not after I go into profit. Really big producers get advances, too. T Bone Burnett often gets an advance in the six figures, which comes off the artist's royalty share, though many artists would say that he is worth the price.

Some producers also demand a share of the publishing, essentially claiming they co-wrote the songs. This might in fact be the case at times: the beats and sounds they contribute are often so integral to the success of the song that they could legitimately be classified as composition. There's no law that says beats are composition, though, so this demand is completely negotiable.* In a typical situation, I might be paying off my recording debt (and tour support money, if I took any) with that $1.40

---

* This isn't a new situation. One could argue that a song produced by Phil Spector back in his sixties heyday is almost a different song from a version he had no hand in. More recently a song with beats—not words or melody—by Timbaland is identifiable and sometimes catchier because of his unique way with samples. Are these guys then automatically co-writers of the songs? Technically and legally, no. But either the producer demands credit or the artist, recognizing the value of the producer's contribution, gives it.

per record, minus the 30 cents the producer would be getting from the very first record sold. So I'm left with $1.10 per record sold.

Foreign sales work a little differently. My royalty in this deal was 75 percent of the US dealer price in Europe and 50 percent in the rest of the world. So even if I were hugely popular in Japan, it would take me twice as long to recoup my recording costs using those record sales as it would in the United States. This seems completely arbitrary and unfair to me, especially when downloads are increasingly the way folks buy music. But this is the standard offer on such deals.

If I wrote every song on a CD (which I didn't on *Grown Backwards*), I would get, from the mechanical income mentioned above, 91 cents (9.1 cents per song multiplied by the ten songs the labels usually limit these mechanicals to), in addition to the sales royalty percentage and my publishing income. If my sales royalty was 14 percent of the $10 dealer price and I wrote all the songs, then I would get $1.40 + 91¢ = $2.31 per record sold. Things are looking a little better.

I believe it was the Beatles and other singer-songwriters of the sixties who realized that recording your own songs was far more lucrative than doing record after record covering other people's songs, as had often been the norm in pop music. This incentivized songwriting, and it was partly due to this insight that there was suddenly an explosion of creativity and innovation in pop music in the sixties. But it also made a few too many musicians feel more or less obliged to consider themselves songwriters. I'm as guilty as many others in feeling that I, or my bandmates, "had" to write every last song on a record, even though covering an underappreciated gem might have been a better choice than recording one of our not-so-stellar writing efforts. However, even not-so-good songs generate income from album sales, as long as there are a couple of hits on there that motivate folks to buy the whole album. The "filler" goes along for the ride and still generates money for the artists and publishers.

In the case of my Nonesuch record, the math is pretty simple: if I had written all the songs on that record, then I would have had to sell almost 100,000 records to break even on that $225,000 advance. (But remember, if I had recorded that album for a fraction of the actual cost, I would essentially have had that advance as income.) That might not have seemed a huge number of records to sell back in the day for a popular act, but it's far more than most records sell now. Few acts sell millions of copies anymore, and the artists who do tend to have more debts to pay off than just the recording costs—massive promotional budgets, percentages to managers and video producers. Say a top pop act does a video that costs half a million dollars (which is not unusual). They've then got to sell way more than my 100,000 records to break even; they've got to sell more like 750,000. Not all do, of course, and their debts begin to mount up quickly.

Here are some sobering facts from SoundScan via *Billboard*: only thirty-five albums released in 2006 sold more than one million copies within the calendar year; twenty-seven in 2007; twenty-two in 2008; twelve in 2009; and ten in 2010. Only 2,050 of the 97,751 albums released in 2009, or 2.1 percent, sold over 5,000 copies. That sort of puts a different spin on the dream of living large off of record sales. If that hypothetical record with its expensive video isn't successful, the artist is suddenly about a million dollars in the hole. The pressure to have a hit with the next record is then immense.

What about downloads? Aren't they picking up some of the slack as CD sales dwindle? Nope. Typically an album downloads for $10, and Apple's iTunes Store, for example, takes 30 percent of every sale. The record label applies the artist's royalty percentage to that $10 retail price, so if the artist is getting the traditional 14 percent, he or she is left with $1.40 per album download. So an artist isn't better off, especially when you think about the way people buy music online—they tend to buy songs, not entire albums. Artists are understandably trying to negotiate better royalty percentages for downloads, arguing that the record companies don't have the same overhead and expenses and nor do the "stores"—therefore the royalty given to artists should be higher. But there is, of course, a lot of resistance from the record companies.

In the end, how did I end up doing on that record? I asked my business manager, who had this to say:

With *Grown Backwards*, you have, as of 2010, sold approx. 127,000 physical albums, 53,000 digital singles, and 8,000 digital albums, for total revenues to you of approximately $276,000 (which does include some licensing money). This was a straight-up master deal. Total revenues of $276,000, less the cost of making the record, which was $218,000, means you have made $58,000 on the record deal. However, this amount doesn't include your publishing income (mechanicals and performance royalties).

REVENUE BREAKDOWN FROM WHOLESALE EARNINGS ON *GROWN BACKWARDS*
(140,000 UNITS SOLD)

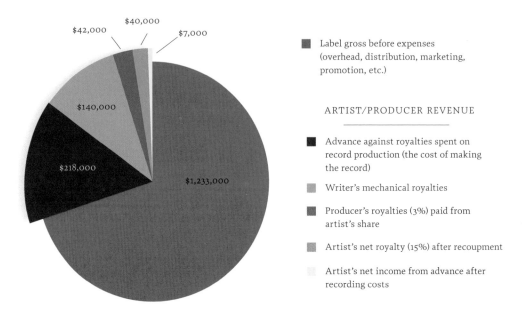

$40,000

$42,000

$7,000

$140,000

$218,000

$1,233,000

■ Label gross before expenses
(overhead, distribution, marketing,
promotion, etc.)

ARTIST/PRODUCER REVENUE
—————————————————————

■ Advance against royalties spent on
record production (the cost of making
the record)

■ Writer's mechanical royalties

■ Producer's royalties (3%) paid from
artist's share

■ Artist's net royalty (15%) after recoupment

■ Artist's net income from advance after
recording costs

Now, $58,000 doesn't sound too bad. That's what an elementary school teacher makes in New Jersey. But you also have to factor in the time it takes to write the songs, the time it takes to record them, and the lag before any of that money comes in. What's more, those figures my business folks provided are for six years' worth of sales—six years! It would be pretty tough to live on $58,000 for six years; I would be out of house and home and looking for other employment if I was hoping to rely on record sales to live. And that record sold okay. Luckily I work on more than one project or record sequentially, so while I'm waiting for possible income from one project, I'm already working on the next one. I might spend, on a record I have high hopes for, a couple of years on writing, recording, and performing. That's not six years, but it's a long time to hang on before the check comes in.

Of course, if I'd sold millions of records, I would have made more money—my income per record sold would have increased. My debt to the record company would have been easily paid back early on, and then I could have pocketed nearly *all* the royalty income rather than having to pay back the advance and other costs. Note that Nonesuch didn't make a whole pile on this record either—though they did go into profit. (I don't know their overhead costs, so I can't factor those in.) I am happy to be able to make the records I want to make, and I realize that those records don't always sell in the millions. Though sometimes we are pleasantly surprised: that "Lazy" single I co-wrote and sang sold a *lot*!

My point is that you have to sell an awful lot of records to expect to live off record sales alone, and maybe you shouldn't count on that happening. However, if you keep the recording and marketing costs down, you might squeak by.

So how is a mid-level artist—someone who sells more than 5,000 copies of a record but less than a million, supposed to live, given this scenario? Naturally, some of our records sell better than others—our careers have hills and valleys— but how can you sustain a career over time? The answer seems to be by supplementing your royalty income with other sources or by looking at the other distribution options I'll discuss next.

For decades, the standard royalty model made a lot of money for the record companies—and for a few artists. When sales were good, everyone was satisfied and the artists didn't feel they had to concern themselves with business matters too much. But that very lack of concern might explain why this model also led many artists to go bankrupt. Like real estate and home loans, it only works well when sales are booming and growth looks like it will continue upward forever.

Over the last decade, many of the services traditionally provided by record labels under that standard deal began to be farmed out. Press and publicity, digital marketing, graphic design—all are now often handled by independent firms. Even record companies that used to have departments dedicated to that stuff no longer provide such services in-house. It became cheaper to hire a graphic designer working out of her apartment in Brooklyn than to have a slew of designers taking up precious office real estate. However, record companies still try to make the same kinds of deals with the artists, as if they were still incurring all those expenses. The record companies still cover the payment and supervise these services, and he who pays the piper calls the tune. If the record company pays those subcontractors, then that company ultimately decides which artists have priority. If they "don't hear a single," they can tell you that your record isn't coming out. Or maybe they'll say it can come out, if you insist, but it won't get any promotion or publicity, which amounts to the same thing as not coming out at all.

So what happens when online sales eliminate many of these collateral expenses? Look at iTunes: $10 for an album download reflects the cost savings of digital distribution, which seems fair—at first. It's certainly better for consumers. But after Apple takes its 30 percent, often the same old royalty percentage is applied and the artist is no better off, and maybe even worse.

iTUNES' ALBUM REVENUE
BREAKDOWN ($10 RETAIL PRICE)

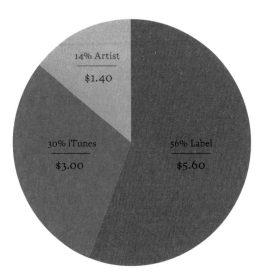

14% Artist

$1.40

30% iTunes

$3.00

56% Label

$5.60

I smell another revolution in the works.

Not coincidentally, these issues regarding the royalty rates for downloads are similar to those raised in the Hollywood writers' strike of 2007–2008. Would recording artists ever band together and go on strike like the writers who provide the content for films and TV shows did? Will book authors do the same when the majority of books are purchased via ebook downloads and publishers can no longer claim many of their costs as deductions? As these factors converge, things are going to get very interesting.

3. LICENSE DEAL

The license deal is similar to the standard deal, except that in this case the artist retains the copyright and ownership of the master recording. The right to exploit the recording is licensed to the label for a limited period of time—usually seven years. After that, the rights (and income) from licensing those masters to TV shows, commercials, and the like revert to the artist. During the period of the license, income from those sources is split between the artist and record company. If the members of Talking Heads held the master rights to our catalog today, we'd be earning twice as much from licensing songs to movies and TV shows as we do now. I'm doing fine as it is, but for emerging artists this can make a huge difference.

If artists can make a record by themselves and don't need creative or financial help doing so, then this model is worth looking at. A band that has a licensing deal is expected to pay their own recording costs. They're expected to deliver a finished product, more or less. Not being in debt to the record company right off the bat allows for a little more creative freedom, since you get less interference from the guys in the suits when the music is being created—they might not even be around. The advance from the record company is necessarily lower, because the company won't end up with the rights to the master recording in perpetuity. The income from this model is more or less structured the same as the royalty deal discussed previously, but the artist may see significantly more income down the line because they will retain ownership of their masters.

The downside to this model is that the label may have less incentive to spend money to ensure that the record is a success. They're being asked to take a risk without having as many guaranteed sources of income, so they have to feel quite strongly about the recording to go this route or they will temper their offer accordingly. If the artistic freedom that the artist gains here results in a more "difficult" record, then the odds of it being licensed by a film for a hefty chunk of change might be lower, too. Basically, you can be radical, you can be wild and free, but it will probably cost you.

With the right label, the license deal can be a great way to go. Arcade Fire has a license deal with Merge Records, an indie label that's done great for its bands by avoiding the big-spending, big-label approach. Mac McCaughan explained this approach to me:

Part of it is just being realistic and not putting yourself in the hole. The bands we work with, we never recommend that they make videos. I like videos, but they don't sell a lot of records. A company like ADA [Alternative Distribution Alliance] really changed the landscape [for indie labels]. It meant that we can get our records anywhere that Warner Bros. can get their records. That's huge. It presents its own issues, though. If you're gonna want your record in a Target, they're gonna want $25,000 from you.

What Mac is referring to is a kind of legalized bribery that the big chains—Target, Walmart, Best Buy—all participate in. They require a record label to pony up a flat fee in order to be "featured" in a given "program." A program might imply that the record will be included in an in-store display, or it might mean the record will be placed at the end of a rack (yes, those CDs are not there by accident; every position is paid for), listed in their flyers, or included in their print ads. But the fact is they charge the labels even if the records aren't going to be included in one of these programs. This flat fee is not refundable; even if the record isn't successful, you still have to pay to get your record into their store in order to find out if they will sell serious numbers or not. Not only that, but those stores have price ceilings. They force the label to sell records to them for less than they would to the record store on Main Street. Hence the mom-and-pop stores go out of business, and the record labels get squeezed even harder. Big labels can afford this shakedown, because a hit record—one that sells in massive numbers and basically starts promoting itself—cancels out the losses incurred by the ones that don't sell.

ADA, which Mac says is leveling the playing field, is an indie distribution network. It and others like it (Red is another) won't, one hopes, go bankrupt like some of the other small distribution services have in the past. When those businesses go bankrupt, they don't return your stock—your records are stuck in their warehouses. In a weird arrangement that only the record business could get used to, though, ADA is owned by Warner Bros. and Red is owned by Sony. How indie can they really be? Says Mac:

If we'd done *Funeral* [Arcade Fire's first record] fifteen years ago, I don't know that we could have handled the next record. But we've grown. When Merge started out it was just Laura and me in her bedroom. There are twelve people who work here now, but that growth happened over a long period of time. We've always been super conservative about the way we spend money. We work with artists who are living in the real world. We do deals and advances and marketing budgets based on reality, not based on "I wish." It would be great if your next record sold five times as many as your last, but if it doesn't, we try to do things so that no one is in the poorhouse. We try to operate so that if someone does sell five thousand copies, they do make a little money off that.

The profit-sharing deal often comes in the form of a 50/50 shared ownership of the master recording. Unlike the licensing deal, *everything* is shared—all the costs and expenses of producing an album are divided between the artist and the label. The mechanical royalties are considered part of the artist's "profit" under this deal, so they aren't paid off the top. One advantage of this deal is that when the profits do come in, they are shared 50/50 as well, which may be higher than the standard percentage in the previous deals.

I did something like this with my soundtrack album *Lead Us Not Into Temptation*, which was the score for the 2003 film *Young Adam*. I got a minimal advance from the label, Thrill Jockey. This modest amount made sense partly because of the kind of record it was (it had only two vocal tracks), partly because the label was small, and partly because we were evenly dividing the income. I retained ownership of the masters. The recording costs were covered by the soundtrack budget (part of the deal with the movie's producers was that I got to walk away with the music in return for taking a low fee), and Thrill Jockey and I shared the profits from day one. In a profit-sharing deal, the mechanicals come out of the artist's share, which makes some sense because the artist owns the master recordings and will stand to see additional income from possible licensing fees down the line.

The artist retains ownership of the master in a license deal too, but profits from co-ownership with the label flow from day one. Thrill Jockey does do some marketing, promo, and press, and they have a staff to handle the day-to-day eventualities around a release. Because they are a small company, I may not have sold as many records as I would have through a larger company with more marketing muscle, but in the end I took home a greater share of each unit sold, and besides, I didn't think it was the kind of record that Walmart customers would be drawn to.

I didn't expect that particular recording to sell massively, so having a sensitive company like Thrill Jockey (which could target the folks who might actually like that record) handle it was appropriate. An expensive promotional push from a larger company probably wouldn't have resulted in a huge increase in sales anyway.

5. P&D (OR M&D) DEAL

In the manufacturing and distribution (M&D) deal (also known as a production and distribution deal, or P&D), the artist does everything except, well, manufacture and distribute the product. The artist pays for the recording, ads, marketing, and promotion—the record label or distribution entity isn't expected to pay for any of that. The companies that do these kinds of deals often offer other services, like marketing, but given the numbers, they don't stand to make as much, so their incentive to do a lot of extra work is limited. Big record labels traditionally don't make P&D deals.

In this scenario, the artist gets absolute creative control, but it's a bigger gamble. Getting the public to know about your record is almost entirely up to you. Aimee Mann does this, and it works really well for her. Mann's manager, Michael Hausman, told me, "A lot of artists don't realize how much more money they could make by retaining ownership and licensing directly. If it's done properly, you get paid quickly, and you get paid again and again. That's a great source of income." This arrangement is different than a profit-sharing deal because the label is essentially relegated to being a vendor, and the artist either pays them a flat fee or offers them a fixed, modest percentage of the income—a commission—in exchange for what will be more limited services.

Hausman and Mann started off trying to do it all by themselves (a final option that I'll discuss next), but they found they needed help with physical distribution. As Hausman explains:

> We can sell [the album] online through the website and send an email to everybody letting them know that it's out and we'll do the fulfillment [getting physical records to buyers] somehow. [Aimee told] me, "If I can just have one place where my fans can get it, they'll go there." And I said, "That's not really gonna sell a lot of records, but it's certainly a start." So we put it up on the website and we sent around an email and we started selling records.
>
> And in the back of my mind, I knew getting it into some real retail [outlets] was the key... and also in the back of my mind were conversations we had with the director Paul Thomas Anderson, who was putting a bunch of her songs in the movie *Magnolia*, and I

suspected that was gonna be kind of a big deal. We had some stuff going on, but [the movie deal] gave us the confidence to do it ourselves… I think we sold about twenty thousand copies just off of the website ourselves before we got the record into traditional retail.

To do that we hired a traditional distributor and paid them a percentage in order to get the CDs into regular retail outlets. Tower Records, Best Buy, etc. We also did a deal with Artist Direct to fulfill the orders from Aimee's website instead of us continuing to do it ourselves. This also enabled fans to purchase the CDs with a credit card. We didn't have that function at the beginning, believe it or not. PayPal was either not invented or not in common use at the time.

My manager, David Whitehead, on P&D deals:

Mac touches on it, but the P&D model really fails when you aim to put records into not just Target, but also [into the] remaining chains, [like] Barnes & Noble, Best Buy, Transworld, Walmart. The costs of buying into these stores for a CD that may sell anything between two and ten thousand CDs can be very prohibitive, between $1 and $2.50 per CD. So you never reach the tipping point where your costs are recouped and you start to earn back at the full margin level, between $4 and $5 per CD—which is what they would hope to get on one of these kinds of deals. And while digital sales help offset this disadvantage to some degree, physical is still the high-volume format.

This sounds like one of the ways to go if you don't hope or expect to sell too much of a given record. But you will see much more income from those units sold than you would from larger-scale distribution deals. Sometimes, then, this is the most practical and profitable choice.

6. SELF-DISTRIBUTION

Finally, at the far end of the scale, is the self-distribution model, where the music is self-written, self-played, self-produced, and self-marketed. Do it yourself, all the way. Well, you don't necessarily have to play every instrument yourself and design the cover graphics, but everything after that stays under the artist's control. In its humblest form, self-distribution means CDs are pressed in limited numbers, and then sold at gigs and often through a website. Promotion in this model is sometimes a MySpace or Bandcamp page, and the band buys or leases a server to handle download sales. Within the limits of what can be afforded, the artists have complete and absolute creative control—not just of their music, but of how it is sold.

For emerging artists, this can mean freedom (nice!) but without much in the way of resources, so it's a pretty abstract sort of independence. What good is freedom, many argue, if no one gets to hear your music because you can't afford to market it? For those who plan to take their material on the road and play it live, the financial constraints involved in DIY cut even deeper, depending on how elaborate the show is. Backup singers, musical gear, vans—it all costs money. Obviously, though, of all the models we've discussed, the profit percentage in self-distribution is the most favorable to the artist.

Though I have painted it as rather homemade and self-limiting in scale, this approach doesn't exclude cobbling together the DIY approach with other deals—doing a P&D or something similar to get the physical CDs out, for example, but handling digital yourself. You can mix and match. That combo platter concept is one of the best things about the current environment.

Radiohead adopted a DIY model to sell their record *In Rainbows* online, and then they went a step further by letting fans name their own price for the download. They weren't the first to do this. Issa (now known once again as Jane Siberry) pioneered the pay-what-you-will model in 2005, but Radiohead's move was much higher profile. It may have been less risky for them than it was for her, because they have a huge preexisting fan base that knows their music and is excited about their output. One of their managers pointed out to me that it wasn't entirely the altruistic gesture it might have seemed: so many of their fans were sharing files of their records immediately upon release (or sometimes even before) that they couldn't do worse than the pay-what-you-wish plan. If there were going to be so many illegal downloads, this option might generate at least *some* income from people who had previously paid nothing. As one of Radiohead's managers, Bryce Edge, told me, "The industry reacted like the end was nigh. 'They've devalued music, giving it away for nothing.' Which wasn't true. We asked people to value it, which is very different semantics to me."

Obviously, not every artist can risk this approach. Even Radiohead's subsequent record went back to having fixed pricing, but they're still partly going it alone (they do a P&D deal for distribution of physical CDs). For artists who aren't so well-known, however, there's a chance that without marketing and promotion no one will ever know they exist. Others will not find the DIY route attractive because they don't have the time or inclination to get involved in all aspects of the business. It isn't for everyone.

However, within this model are sub-models. DIY can be done on a relatively small scale. A local band can have their own CDs pressed, sell their downloads, and market themselves via their live shows. A larger percentage of fewer sales is a likely, but not inevitable, result. Artists doing it for themselves can actually make more money than the massive pop stars with a standard royalty deal, even though the sales numbers may seem minuscule by comparison. The debts accumulated paying off label advances and promotional expenses aren't there in the DIY model, for starters. Of course, not everyone is as smart as those Radiohead boys.

Many new companies have emerged to play various roles in this new DIY universe—Bandcamp, Topspin, and CDBaby all allow unsigned artists to sell their songs as downloads in ways that are less financially onerous than using iTunes or Amazon, both of which charge hefty percentages and have lots of rules. Topspin, which I have worked with, can also sell physical CDs and other things online. They're not the megastore that iTunes is, so fewer customers are randomly wandering around the shop, but with the help of links from music blogs, reviews, and elsewhere, fans do find their way to buy through these sites. I know I do.

Amanda Palmer of the band Dresden Dolls made a record on which she covered Radiohead songs on her ukulele. She released it on Bandcamp and made $15,000 in a few minutes. In 2012, Palmer raised money for her new orchestral recording project via the crowd-funding website Kickstarter and has raised over $800,000. That's a lot of money! Way more than was needed for the actual recording, so much of it will go toward touring, distribution, and special packaging expenses. Her video on the website claims, "This is the future of music." Sufjan Stevens's Bandcamp release got him onto the Billboard chart of top-selling albums.[5] So DIY can be profitable and can move numbers of recordings as well.

When Brian Eno and I were nearing completion of our collaboration *Everything That Happens Will Happen Today* in 2009, we decided to give this DIY model a try, though we didn't go as far as the pay-what-you-wish plan. We'd both been mouthing off about all the new opportunities for artists, and here, we thought, was a chance to find out the truth for ourselves. We had some things working in our favor:

- The recording and mixing of our record didn't cost all that much for a typical pop record (if one could call it that); besides, we had already covered those costs ourselves, so we didn't owe anyone anything.
- We have established names and reputations, and we assumed that some folks who like what we've done previously might like this record as well. Our sales probably wouldn't be zero. Beyond that, the curious might even seek out news of the project without us having to pay for a huge marketing and promotional budget. (I was curious about what would happen if there were almost no ads or marketing at all—I hoped the magic of the Web would take care of spreading the news all by itself.)
- Lastly, I have been frustrated by the increasingly long time that record companies say they need to "set up" a record release—the time between delivery of the finished mixes and the time the album lands in stores. This time lag is at least three months, often four. I understand that you've got to prime the pump for ages for a blockbuster movie, because if it doesn't do amazing business in the first weekend it will get pulled from the theaters. But records don't work like that anymore. With digital distribution one can, if one desires, have the record "out" almost as soon as it is done. The artist doesn't have to worry quite as much whether or not the distributor actually has the records in the stores. You don't have to wait for the trucks and the advance copies to arrive—there's always stock available in the digital store, and shipping is instant.

Our DIY experiment sort of worked. When we had nearly finished the record, I decided that I wanted to do a tour during which I'd perform some of the material. This might draw some attention to the record, as Mac pointed out, but I didn't think of the tour as a sales tool; I did it because I wanted to have the experience of singing the songs again. Singing them was, to some extent, its own reward. As it turned out, the tour made money.

We had to hire other companies to handle some of the ancillary work: Sacks & Co. in North America and Gareth Davies at Chapple Davies in the UK did publicity; Topspin built the web pages to sell the tracks online in various configurations; Tunecore handled administration when the digital files went to iTunes; Red Eye handled Amazon and other digital download vendors in North America, as well as physical CDs; Essential pressed and sold physical CDs to shops, chains, and online merchants in Europe. That's a lot of vendors to keep track of! You can see how it might be daunting to an emerging artist.

David Whitehead explained his philosophy toward some of these vendors: "I prefer to get accounted to monthly by Tunecore (as opposed to quarterly by Redeye), and for a onetime flat fee of twenty-five dollars rather than paying 10 percent monthly fees. The big advantage for anyone supplying the digital service providers [download stores like Amazon and iTunes] direct or via Tunecore is you get paid monthly. Over the last twelve months we've averaged over $3,000 per month in income from iTunes sales on that record."

Within three weeks of the digital files being available online on our own websites, we sold enough to cover our recording costs, which added up to $49,000, and included travel, the mixing engineer, graphic design, flights, and extra musicians. Based on my own experience, that seemed amazing to me. With a standard record deal, it would normally have taken six months to a year to recoup those costs. And then there would have been other miscellaneous costs to recoup—the music video (there wasn't one), that open bar after the concert, the car service to the airport.

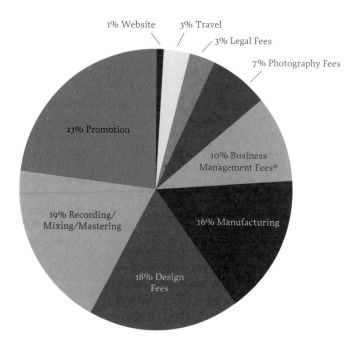

EXPENSE BREAKDOWN FOR SELF-RELEASED
EVERYTHING THAT HAPPENS
($315,000)

1% Website 3% Travel
3% Legal Fees
7% Photography Fees
10% Business Management Fees*
16% Manufacturing
18% Design Fees
19% Recording/Mixing/Mastering
23% Promotion

* Business Management traditionally retains a 5% commission on income generated. In this case, the 5% accrued by business management resulted in 10% of the total expenses related to self-releasing the album.

The charts on the next page give more detail on US and foreign sales. The one on top shows the percentage of total units each vendor sold. Below that is the income accounting for each of those vendors.

SALES BY DISTRIBUTOR FOR *EVERYTHING THAT HAPPENS*
(160,000 UNITS SOLD)

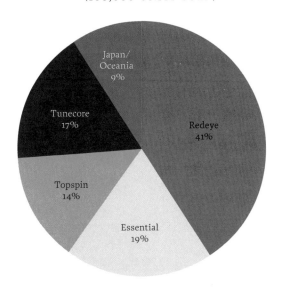

REVENUE BREAKDOWN FOR SALES OF
EVERYTHING THAT HAPPENS
($1.15 MILLION)

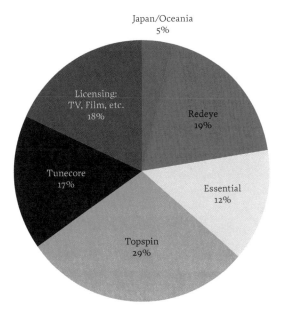

Note that although Redeye sold 41 percent of the total units, the income generated from those sales was only 19 percent of the total pie, which illustrates how expensive it is to sell records in stores. Conversely, Topspin only sold 14 percent of the total units, but they generated 29 percent of the total income, largely due to the fact that we were selling deluxe edition packages direct to consumers without having to give a percentage to retailers.

The $59,850 cost of making this record was only part of what it cost to prepare it for market. All told, the total costs to self-release the album were $315,000—building the website, paying for servers, design fees, promotion, manufacturing, etc. That's a lot more than any indie band could ever afford. We wound up generating $964,000 in total income. So minus the $315,000 in expenses, that left us with $649,000, 50 percent of which went to Eno, leaving me with $324,500. Since we were the record company, we paid our own mechanicals out of our profit.

I was elated. Here, finally, was the future. I made $324,500 on this "self-distributed" record, compared to the $58,000 I made on the standard royalty-deal record *Grown Backwards*—and the two sold nearly the same number of copies: 140,000 for *Grown Backwards*, and 160,000 for *Everything That Happens*. Wow, the writing is on the wall here! Well, that enthusiasm might be justified if you can afford the $315,000 that we paid to assemble the apparatus needed to make, sell, and market a record. (It should be pointed out that some of those costs were start-up, learning-as-you go costs. Presumably they wouldn't be as high down the road, as the infrastructure has been built.)

Whenever I get too excited about these figures, I need to remind myself that I splurged on the *Grown Backwards* recording costs, which came in at $218,000. I didn't have to front that money; it came out of the advance from Nonesuch. The recording costs for *Everything That Happens* were $49,000, so if I had kept the costs similarly low for *Grown Backwards*, then, redoing the math, I could have made $167,000 more than I ended up making on that album. My net for *Grown Backwards* would then have been about $225,000. So in this hypothetical scenario in which the recording costs were equal, I actually would have made only about $89,000 more on the somewhat self-distributed *Everything That Happens*. That's still quite nice, and if you amortize that $323,000 over the two years of writing and recording, it's a "salary" of about $160k a year. Way better than an elementary school teacher in New

Jersey. (For the record, I think most teachers are woefully underpaid.)

But if *Everything That Happens* had been a real solo record, if it had been just me like it was on *Grown Backwards*, then I would have walked home with the full $626,000 as my net income. Now we're talking! That's nearly three times what I made with *Grown Backwards*, even assuming that that record could have been made equally cheaply. Of course, *Grown Backwards* would have been a completely different record had I chosen to record with fewer musicians, and *Everything that Happens* wouldn't have been the same without the Eno collaboration. It's really hard to compare records, given all the variables, but you get my point. With this particular situation one could indeed imagine living off sales of one's recordings via self-distribution. It's even enough income to allow time for writing—or the occasional flop.

Can this distribution model eventually net enough so that even an emerging artist could live on their own music sales (excluding live performing income)? Could more musicians and composers have a life in music this way? There are no guarantees, but if you don't need a huge recording budget, tour support, and a big marketing effort, then this approach is worth exploring.

Self-distributing didn't work as well for me in Europe and in the UK as it did domestically. We didn't do extensive marketing. I did press, and we gave a free advance copy of one song as an exclusive to some music blogs, but there weren't the traditional ads and paid radio promotions. In North America, music blogs are replacing print music journalism. They respond faster to breaking news and to feedback from their readers, and they can link to video clips, streaming music, and websites provided by the artist. Music fans get more and more of their information from the Internet in North America, so there was a little bit of a viral effect that happened here without us having the usual expense of ads and conventional marketing. The Europeans in general aren't buying or reading as much stuff online as North Americans do. Digital sales are generally lower there, and they still seem to look to print as their main source of news. There are lots of countries with varying musical tastes and different languages, so one campaign can't blanket the whole region as it can in North America.

I toured for about a year after *Everything That Happens* came out, on and off through 2008 and 2009. The shows were super well received; we all had a wonderful time performing. I made some money from the tour as well, but it was expensive to mount. I examined the receipts when it was done, and if most shows hadn't sold out, I would have lost money. That's not a good omen for anyone who isn't sure they can fill seats. I am still not convinced the tour really helped sell records. Maybe it helped a little, but not, for example, like getting wide radio play would have. Some songs were played on NPR, and on indie and college stations, but the larger, more commercial stations never jumped on board. That's not a surprise; the record is what it is. However, well after the record came out, another way of getting the songs in front of people presented itself. And this opportunity highlights a few of the advantages of retaining some ownership and publishing rights.

LICENSING

Another source of income for recording artists is licensing. That means letting a movie, TV show, or commercial use your song in exchange for cash. I don't license songs to commercials, but I still see more money from licensing songs to films and TV than I do in actual record sales. Those who allow their songs to be used in ads can become instantly familiar to a wide audience overnight—or at least that one song does. This too is a form of marketing, one that is usually completely separate from and unreliant on the record company.

A few years after *Everything That Happens* came out, Oliver Stone included a substantial number of songs from it in his movie *Wall Street: Money Never Sleeps*. A fair number of people commented on the fine songs we'd written for that film, not realizing that the record they appeared on had been out for quite some time. That confirmed for me that while distribution is moving online relatively quickly, getting the word out still requires some traditional marketing effort and muscle—and money. For artists without recognizable names, that would have been even more true.

Eno and I might be exceptions, but films will often license a song from a record or band that isn't that well-known. I suspect that there's a cool-factor at work—many film directors are covert music geeks. The late singer-songwriter Nick Drake didn't sell a lot of records and wasn't that well-known, but whoever handles his publishing is doing okay. His songs have been used more than once in big ad campaigns, movies, and TV shows.

If you hold on to the rights, and your song is sampled, that, too, becomes a source of income. If a song is sampled by another artist, it's usually because of a musical or sonic quality, not because it was already a hit. In fact, sampling a hit is anathema, so the obscure artist has a better shot. Even a relative unknown can sometimes find himself with a surprise source of income if his song is sampled, but that income is always more significant for the writer if he has held on to a good percentage of those publishing rights.

The more a writer or band holds on to their publishing—or even, when possible, their master recording rights—the more they will benefit from income sources like these—though it might take a while. One licensing deal can provide more income than a whole tour, and certainly more than royalties from CD sales through a label. Often a band or songwriter will feel it is necessary to give away some of their publishing for the cash in hand that will get them through their struggling years, but if you can hold on to that stuff, it turns out much better for you pretty quickly. Musicians often don't have pension plans, sad to say, so planning ahead can be critical.

Some decades ago, when MTV was doing well, pulling in viewers and making money, the big record labels decided that the commonly held idea that MTV was providing free exposure for the labels' acts wasn't acceptable anymore. They began to see MTV reaping profits while the record labels were providing all the network's content for free. So the labels made deals with MTV to continue providing music videos, but now for a flat fee. The labels said that they would then funnel some of that considerable income back to their artists, but I don't think they ever did. Eventually MTV played fewer and fewer music videos, turning instead to cheap reality shows, which they could own and syndicate. Part of that change had to be motivated by not wanting to pay the record labels for content.

LAST NAIL IN THE COFFIN

In recent years, various companies have come forward with software applications and websites that stream music to listeners through the internet. Some have touted these as the "savior" of the music business—the idea is that consumers will pay a small fee to hear the music they like via a legal service. Most of these streaming services play music interspersed with commercials, and for a nominal subscription fee those ads go away. If enough listeners opt for the pay version of these services, then, it is argued, there might be a real source of income. One such service, Pandora, is a streaming personalized "radio" with a recommendation engine built in. If I tell them I like Led Zeppelin's second album, they won't play that album immediately, but they will play something similar. The result is sort of like a radio station that plays music within a genre you have created. You get surprised sometimes with a song or artist you didn't know about, which is a nice feature.

The owners of song copyrights (who are usually the record companies) get paid some small amount every time a song is played on one of these services and an even smaller percentage of that then goes to the artist. Pandora has been lobbying Congress to allow it to lower its payouts in recent months.

There are other services as well, but the one that currently seems to be the most significant to artists is Spotify—a streaming service that, unlike Pandora, plays exactly the songs or the album you want to hear. Quite quickly, Spotify has become the second largest source of income for major labels—preceded only by iTunes. Its catalogue is huge, though not comprehensive, and it has established itself deeply in some European territories. In Spain, it's the way most young people consume music. That means most young music fans in Spain don't pay for downloads—they either listen to the free, commercially sponsored version of Spotify, or they are among the 25 percent worldwide (6 million people total) who subscribe and pay a monthly fee.[6]

Like Pandora, Spotify pays the copyright owners (again, the record companies), who then toss out some crumbs to the artists. As you can imagine, these crumbs do not amount to much. I checked on some songs I had done some years ago that were pretty big hits, and that therefore get streamed fairly often by these services. My income over a number of years of Spotify streams on a hit song amounted to something like $490. Try living on that, Spanish artists. Meanwhile, Spotify has given "advances" to US record labels in the area of $90 million—which encourages the labels to allow Spotify to have access to their catalogues. In fact, Spotify is partly owned by some of these record labels, so they're giving advances to themselves! These advances were not shared with the artists; they were pocketed by the labels.

When I first heard about a service where you could hear whatever record you wanted instantly, I thought to myself, Why would anyone *ever* buy a record again? Of course, you don't own any of the music you are listening to on these services— you can't pass the songs to your children, and when you stop paying, or if Spotify goes bust, you end up with nothing at all. You have been licensing, not buying, the recordings.

In some way, it all seems lovely and idealistic that we are moving into a world where we don't own anything. No possessions—like John Lennon imagined. The Internet as a Marxist Utopia. But the fact is someone—some large corporation, probably—owns, or at least makes money off of, what you might consider to be your culture. And since you're licensing the work, not buying it, they can take it away from you. They end up with your money and you end up with nothing.

Amazon Kindle eBooks did just that. They famously took back copies of *1984* that they had sold by mistake. The book simply vanished from people's devices. I had an enhanced Jay-Z eBook, and all the video enhancements went away one day, with no explanation. I paid for those! When you click "agree" before setting up your account, you welcome Big Brother into your house.

iTunes, who made about $8.5 billion in 2012, works under the same rules. Consumers are paying to license the music they purchase, so Apple can in fact wipe your hard drive clean of every song you bought from iTunes, if it wants to. So far, thankfully, it has not wanted to. But shouldn't there be different laws and accounting for such a transaction, both for the consumer and the artist?

When artists license a song to a film or a commercial, they typically get half of that licensing income. The record company gets the other half. (If the artists self-release their recordings, then they get both halves.) But with iTunes purchases—which are, according to the iTunes agreement, licenses—the artist for some strange reason often gets the same royalty percentage as if it were a CD sale.

What's wrong here is twofold: the record company doesn't incur the same costs when selling songs through iTunes even though the royalty arrangement implies that it does, *and* it's paying close to physical-sales-level royalties on a licensing deal. A 50 percent share of this income would be fair, or so it seems to me. Same goes for Spotify income, and those mysterious Spotify advances—those should all be shared fifty-fifty as well, as I see it.

A few artists and their representatives have begun legal challenges to this licensing issue that leaves artists without much to live on. In 2010, the producers who discovered Eminem, F.B.T. Productions, successfully challenged Universal Music Group (UMG) on this issue when the Supreme Court failed to hear UMG's appeal to a lower court's ruling that digital music should be treated as a license. What that means for the larger issue isn't clear, although F.B.T.'s manager expressed the sentiment that "As of now it's worth $17 million or $20 million, but on a future accounting basis, five or ten years from now, it could easily be a $40 million to $50 million issue." UMG, not wanting to admit a precedent has been set, released a statement saying, "The ruling [on this case] has no bearing on any other recording agreement." A class action suit followed in 2011 by Rob Zombie, and representatives of the late Rick James went after UMG as well, and so far Universal has managed to stall and block discovery by the claimants.[7]

What's the answer, then? Did the Internet break recorded music? Are we going back to a time before recorded music provided an income for musicians and composers? Maybe so. Music has been around for a long time, and recorded music is maybe just a one-hundred-year blip. It's a shame if Big Digital and the various pirate sites—and not the artists—are the ones making money off that content. Maybe we're back to live shows as income. You can't download an experience—yet.

The immersive music-theater piece I wrote with Fatboy Slim some six or seven years ago is up and running now. It's selling out, and the ticket prices aren't cheap. The public is obviously craving music experiences and performances that move them. Is this an answer? The record that includes many of those songs had mediocre sales—it's the show itself that is doing great. But we're not even making any real money on that yet; mounting a musical is expensive! And we're one of the lucky few whose piece has been well received, so it's hardly a model to hold up in response to declining income. The number who rake in big income from successful shows is minuscule.

So, despite there being a host of business models from which artists can choose, it may all become irrelevant. The whole future of recorded music as a significant source of income for artists might be a thing of the past. That may or may not be inevitable—but even if it is, it's certainly not the end of music.

FREEDOM VERSUS PRAGMATISM

The models I've outlined are not absolute. They can morph and evolve. Aimee Mann and her manager initially went the 100 percent DIY route, but they eventually made deals with various distributors to get their records into retail outlets.

In the future we will see more artists mix and match elements of the models I've described to create hybrid deals. The business is more flexible than it used to be, which is a good thing for both veteran and emerging artists. We read over and over that the music business is going down the drain, but this is actually a great time to be making music—full of possibility. A life in music—which is what we're actually talking about, not just fame and glory—is indeed still possible.

The wealth of options can be paralyzing, though. Many who take a good amount of cash upfront will never know the benefits of long-range thinking. Hanging on to more rights in exchange for less money is usually the wiser course of action. Mega pop artists will still need that mighty push and marketing effort for their new releases, and that is something that only traditional record companies (or record companies in combination with concert promoters) can provide. For others, what we now call a record label could be replaced by a new entity, a small company that essentially funnels the income and invoices from the various entities and vendors and keeps all the different accounts in order. A consortium of mid-level artists who share the services of such an entity could make that model work—a kind of music business co-op.

United Musicians, the company that Michael Hausman founded, is one such example. He mentioned to me that there is a scale below which such an organization cannot support itself. One needs to have a number of artists on board to amortize the costs of staff, publicists, administration, and rent. But since most artists aren't in sync—one is often writing while another is recording—this can work. The administrative staff doesn't suddenly find itself without work or the business without a steady income when one artist decides that he or she needs to hole up to write new material.

No single model will work for everyone. There's room for all of us. Like a lot of people, I liked Rihanna's "Umbrella" and Christina Aguilera's "Ain't No Other Man." Sometimes corporate pop is what I want, but I don't want it at the expense of everything else. At times it has seemed that we have been offered a Hobson's choice: corporate pop or nothing. But perhaps that's no longer the case.

This is exciting. Ultimately, all these scenarios have to satisfy the same human urges: What do we need music to do? How do we visit the land in our head and the place in our heart that music is so good at taking us to? Isn't *that* what we really want to buy, sell, trade, or download? We can't, though, not really. No matter what format music is delivered in, the experience we treasure, the thing we value, is still ephemeral and intangible. Advertisers have always tempted us with the idea that the pleasurable sensations, the joy and surprise of music, can be bottled or affixed to some tangible artifact, like perfume, shoes, jeans, or a car—but it can't be. It's a slippery beast, and that's part of its appeal.

BRAVE NEW DIGITAL WORLD

I did a promotional tour after this book came out in hardcover last year, though instead of readings, I participated in conversations with folks in various towns across North America and the UK. The people with whom I conversed generally had some special insights into an aspect of music covered in this book, and several had something to say about this chapter.

In LA, I discussed this chapter with Trent Reznor of Nine Inch Nails, because he was one of the first to try a DIY model for putting out his own music—specifically his soundtrack work. That worked well for him financially, and offering free tracks also functioned as a way to get his fans to hear those scores. Though now, for a larger project, he is going back to getting some label support. As I mentioned earlier, the new model isn't dogmatic or singular—it's not even a fixed model. It's more about mixing and matching according to one's needs.

I found myself at various points along that book tour talking to folks whose viewpoints on digital rights and copyright are pretty much diametrically opposed to each other, and I began to wonder if there might be some common ground between their positions—though I'm not sure I want to be the mediator in that debate. In Toronto, I chatted with Cory Doctorow, an author and activist who prioritizes internet freedom over the rights of musicians and artists, sometimes to their financial detriment. Like some others—Larry Lessig and the late Aaron Swartz—he feels (I believe rightly) that in the last century copyrights have been extended way too long, and that an unfortunate parallel trend has been for copyrights to be owned and controlled by large media companies. This is not simply music copyrights, but all sorts of intellectual property: books, movies, and research, academic, and technical papers—it's all increasingly under lock and key.

The result is that access to our own culture—which includes the work of artists like myself—is controlled not by us but by giant media corporations. These advocates of a looser kind of copyright argue that we need to have more free circulation and access to culture in order to be able to build upon the work of our predecessors. I agree with this, but I only partly agree with the oft-proposed remedy—i.e., "Just make everything free." I think there might be some middle ground between the odious "permission society," as Lessig calls it, and artists, musicians, and writers not getting compensated for their work. The solution, in my opinion, to the increasingly overmediated and controlled world of media and intellectual property isn't necessarily piracy. The way I see it, downloading music using Napster was not a political statement—it was just getting stuff for free.

Writer Chris Ruen—my converser in New York, who is part of a growing response to advocates of "free"—has some valid points in his book *Freeloading*. He suggests that it is the artist who should decide how accessible his or her work should be, at least within a limited time period. He suggests that if a creator wants to limit access for the period during which one may do so, then that is his or her right. If the artist wants to have his or her work distributed and managed by a big media company, then that is also their decision. Conversely, it should also be the artist's decision to give his or her music away. Free access is not an option most artists would choose as an ongoing way of permanently "getting their work out there." Many artists have offered tracks as free downloads, but Ruen's distinction is that in these cases it is the artists—not Mega Upload, YouTube, or Pirate Bay—who have been the ones deciding to give the track away. Besides, those other sites derive advertising dollars from the free stuff they offer and that they themselves don't create—artists may or may not want to do that. Ruen is essentially saying that if you enjoy music—if it means something to you, if you value it—then maybe it's time to think about compensating the artists for their work.

Ruen's book begins with a wonderful personal insight. He, like many others, filled up his computer with free music while at college. After college, he was working as a barista in Brooklyn, at a place where lots of band members came in for coffee and conversation. He was shocked to see that his musical heroes were barely getting by financially. They weren't doing much better than him, and yet many of them were on national TV, doing tours, and were critically acclaimed. Unless they were to jump to the level of arena and stadium shows, they were doing about as well as one could hope to do as a working musician. Then it occurred to him that he hadn't paid for any of their music. He realized that freeloading, as he calls it, wasn't just something big bands like Metallica complained about: it was directly affecting the potential and longevity of the local bands he loved, too.

In a recent *New York* magazine article, the band Grizzly Bear revealed that they were faring worse than you would expect for a band that just sold out Radio City Music Hall. Some of the band don't have medical insurance, and many of them live in the same places they always have. It's not horrible, but if such a successful band is just making ends meet, what about all the rest?

At around the same time, in June 2012, a young NPR intern wrote a blog post on All Songs Considered about how much she loves music, but mentioned that she hadn't paid for almost any of it in her lifetime. A musician, professor, and derivatives trader (!) named David Lowery wrote a passionate but reasonable response to her that went viral. I chatted with him in Washington, DC, and, like Ruen, he was amazed so many people assumed that the Internet gave us all the right to get whatever we wanted for free. The digitati—or the inevitabalists, as some call them—have managed to espouse the idea that the effects of new technology are deterministic, and all somehow for the best. So, for example, if artists and newspapers can't make it in the brave new digital world, it's simply because they didn't adapt. It's their own fault.

In an effort to increase transparency regarding how the sites that carry illegal files make money, Lowery and a group at the USC Annenberg Innovation Lab have initiated a study to see which corporate brands advertise on sites that everyone knows carry illegal content.[8] These brands, and the services that coordinate these ads (like Google), are essentially funding piracy, in Lowery's view. And there's a *lot* of money to be made—Mega Upload founder Kim Dotcom, who was recently busted in New Zealand, was living high on the hog. Lowery and others contend that big brands and online services could block or stop that support, but it seems there's too much money to be made. The tech industry isn't as clean as it might like to make out.

Sometimes the response to the decline of income for musicians is to say that artists should stop living in the past and seek out new forms of funding—be that corporate support, live concerts, Kickstarter, or licensing their songs to commercials. But not all the alternatives out there encourage a free, vibrant, and long-term life in the arts. Fan-supported Kickstarter campaigns are designed to fund a single project, not an ongoing career in music. I don't begrudge any artist playing corporate gigs or getting funded by Converse, Mountain Dew, Red Bull, or BMW—you do what you have to do—but ultimately I'm suspicious of the Medici-corporate-sponsorship model's effect on the actual music being made and what that model does to a person's life. In the end, it needs to be remembered that corporations exist to sell shoes or sugary drinks, not art.

CHAPTER EIGHT

How to
Make a Scene

I'm not referring to how best to insult your host at a dinner party. I'm referring to that special moment when a creative flowering seems to issue forth
from a social nexus—a clump of galleries, a neighborhood, or a bar that
doubles as a music club. I've often asked myself why such efflorescence
happens when and where it does, rather than at some other time, in some
other place.

The bar and music club CBGB that was located on the Bowery in New York
was one such place. Over the years people have asked me if I sensed that something special was going on there in the mid- to late seventies. I did not. It seems
to me that there is at least as much musical creativity going on around town now
as there was then—it just isn't focused on one particular bar or neighborhood.
I remember hanging out at the bar at CBGB watching other bands play, and sure,
sometimes I'd think, "Wow, that band is *really* good," but just as often I'd think,
"That band really sucks, too bad they're such nice guys." The exact same thing
happens now when I go out and hear music—sometimes I'm blown away, and
other times it's a wasted evening.

Back then, my bandmates and I would rehearse in our nearby loft and then play
at CBGB as often as was practical. But that was just what we did; it didn't seem in
any way special. We felt like a typical group of artists struggling to survive, as they

always have. Our days (and even nights) were often routine, boring. It wasn't like a movie, where everyone's constantly hopping from one inspirational moment or exciting place to the next and consciously making a revolution. Besides, CBGB was a dump in a part of town that was pretty much ignored—a factor I might have undervalued.

I was not aware of any revolution in the making—if one could even call it that. But I was conscious that I and many others were rejecting much of the music that had come before us, and that this sentiment was pervasive at that time. But so what? Everyone was doing that in their own way, rejecting things and moving on. It's just a part of discovering who you are; it's nothing special.

As I remember it, things kicked in at CBGB in 1974, when Tom Verlaine and a few others persuaded owner Hilly Kristal to allow them to play for the door at what was then a biker bar on the Bowery. "Playing for the door" meant that the bar charged a small admission fee, which went to the band, and Hilly in turn reaped the money from all the new patrons who had wandered in and were now buying beers. It was an equitable deal. Both sides benefited—the bar hadn't been drawing many customers at the time, so Hilly didn't really have a lot to lose. I will argue in the rest of this chapter that the venue and its policies make a music scene happen as much as the creativity of the musicians. So Tom and Hilly deserve a lot of credit, because with their simple agreement, they opened the door just a crack, and that allowed the emergence of a scene.

When my friends and I gravitated to New York City around 1974, I initially slept on the floor of a loft belonging to a painter who happened to live a block from CBGB. Patti Smith and Tom's band, Television, had just started playing there, and my friends and I realized that maybe, possibly, our project, which was about to become Talking Heads, might be able to play there too. That prospect spurred us all on. We began to rehearse in earnest. I was already writing songs in dribs and drabs on my own anyway, and I suspect (despite my wondering in the previous chapter if artists would even create without an outlet) that I would have been doing so with or without CBGB across the street. But knowing there was a possible venue for our songs focused my energies, and I began to churn out more of them, and the band that became Talking Heads eventually began to rehearse them.

CBGB was, from a structural point of view, a perfect, self-actuating, self-organizing system. A biological system, in a way: a coral reef, a root system, a termite colony, a rhizome, a neural network. An emergent entity governed by a few simple rules that Hilly established at the start, rules that made it possible for the whole scene to emerge, and, subsequently, to flow and flourish with a life all its own. Of course I didn't know that at the time—it's not like there was a policy statement or flyer with rules on it posted anywhere.

Later on I came to realize that you can sometimes tell in advance whether or not a given situation will develop into a vibrant scene. As I've said, it doesn't depend entirely on the inspiration and creativity of the individuals hanging out there. A confluence of external factors helps encourage the latent talent in a community to flower. In the rest of this chapter, I will elucidate some of those factors. This might not be definitive, but it's a start.

1. THERE MUST BE A VENUE THAT IS OF APPROPRIATE SIZE AND LOCATION IN WHICH TO PRESENT NEW MATERIAL

This sounds kind of obvious, but it's worth saying because not every space works for every kind of music. As I explained in chapter one, where music is heard can determine the sort of music created by the artists who perform there. It might seem dispiriting to acknowledge that humble brick and mortar can shape what pours out of a creative soul, but this reality doesn't take anything away from the talent or skill of composers or performers. Their songs and performances will be, one hopes, absolutely heartfelt, passionate, and true—it's just that we channel our ineffable creative urges, sometimes unconsciously, into figuring out what is appropriate for a given situation. The mere existence of CBGB facilitated the creation of the bands and songs that touched our hearts and souls. It was the right size, the right shape, and in the right place.

It was fairly intimate, but not quiet. There was always bar chatter and jukebox music, so it didn't have the aura of a concert hall or a vibe like the Bottom Line's, a few blocks away, where people felt compelled to sit quietly and listen. The room, its physical and social setting, proposed that if there were to be any theatricality employed by the performers, it would be of a type that used limited technical means. There was no space for elaborate facilities or high-tech creations, and everybody who was in the "wings," about to go onstage, was in plain view. That meant that no one would even consider staging theatrical spectacles that required elaborate lighting and sets—that sort of stuff just wasn't physically possible there. I've always liked creative restrictions, and here, happily, many were already in place.

A show using extremely modest means still left plenty of room for gesture, costume, and sound. "Poor theater," as Polish theater innovator Jerzy Grotowski called it. He wrote that theater is about "the discarding of masks, the revealing of the real substance: a totality of physical and mental reaction." He went on to write, "Here we can see the theater's therapeutic function for people in our present-day civilization. It is true that the actor accomplishes this act, but he can only do so through an encounter with the spectator."[1]

Taking Grotowski at his word, I would argue that some of the most innovative and viscerally moving theater in America at that time was not being made in proper theaters, but taking place on the stage of this grotty club on the Bowery and in the clubs that imitated it in the years that followed. There were some innovative theater groups that emerged downtown around that same period—the Wooster Group and Mabou Mines come to mind—and they were similarly direct, immediate, and real, despite being in no way naturalistic. But in CBGB a new theater was emerging that was both naked and confrontational. And you could dance to it—in a manner of speaking.

2. THE ARTISTS SHOULD BE ALLOWED TO PLAY THEIR OWN MATERIAL

This might seem obvious, too, but it's important. Hilly was open to original music, and much of what happened there flowed from that stance. There were very few outlets then for bands and musicians who didn't already have record deals (and the promotional and financial support that used to go with them) or who weren't willing to cover other people's songs. There were some folk clubs over on Bleecker Street, but they didn't seem to be interested in rock music as a serious musical form (by "serious" I don't mean difficult or virtuosic). Jazz clubs could be found in some nearby lofts and lounges, but they wouldn't work as venues for a rock band either. To most club owners, it must have been inconceivable that any sane person would be interested in hearing a band they'd never heard on the radio before—or heard of at all, for that matter.

When Hilly and a few others took the tentative step of letting bands play their own material for small groups of friends and beer drinkers, it was therefore a big deal. When Talking Heads eventually made our first record and began playing outside of New York City, no such network of open-minded club owners existed. As a result we played in whatever ridiculous venue would let us play our own material—like a student center at a university where some kid thought we could amplify our music through his home stereo, a pizza parlor in Pittsburgh, and a kid's birthday party in New Jersey. However, over the course of a few years, a network of small clubs established itself, and bands like ours could connect the dots and play all across North America and Europe. But that came later.

The fact that there came into existence a forum within which anyone with a band and some songs could broadcast their insights, fury, and lunacy did not just get the water flowing, it actually helped bring the water into existence.

3. PERFORMING MUSICIANS MUST GET IN FOR FREE ON THEIR OFF NIGHTS (AND MAYBE GET FREE BEER TOO)

There wasn't much camaraderie among the bands at CBGB. Not that there was antagonism, but everyone wanted to stake out their own creative territory, and aligning oneself with others might have created the risk of dilution. Nevertheless, Hilly let many musicians in for free once they'd played there, so it soon became a de facto hangout. None of us complained that our fellow musicians weren't paying to see us—we weren't paying to see them, either. There were always a few local band members leaning on the bar with a beer in hand, a precursor to the way, years later, club and restaurant owners would ply models with free drinks to get them to linger at downtown lounges and thus draw more (mostly male) customers. At CBGB, this was a more organic process, less calculated and cynical. It also meant that there was always an audience for whatever band was playing. They might not be paying all that much attention, but at least there were bodies there. So even a band that had no following had some folks listening—sort of.

4. THERE MUST BE A SENSE OF ALIENATION FROM THE PREVAILING MUSIC SCENE

A successful scene presents an alternative. Some of us eventually came to realize that we wouldn't feel as comfortable anywhere else, and that the music in other places would probably be terrible. The hangout, then, is the place for the alienated to share their misanthropic feelings about the prevailing musical culture.

That didn't mean we all reacted to this alienation in the same way. If you were to believe the press, the CB's scene was only made up of a handful of bands—but that just wasn't true. Despite being lumped under the punk-rock moniker, all sorts of bands played there. There were progressive-rock bands, jazz-fusion acts, jam bands, and folk singers who seemed as if they'd strayed to the wrong end of Bleecker Street. The Mumps were power pop, and one might even say that the Shirts were the precursors to the musical *Rent*. We were all disaffected and dissatisfied with the rock dinosaurs who roamed the earth back then. We expressed that disaffection in different ways, but here was a place where we could commiserate and plot a new course.

The glam acts that already existed—New York Dolls, Bowie, Lou Reed, and a few others—were considered cool and provocative, but almost everything associated in any way with the mainstream seemed hopelessly irrelevant. The radio was dominated by the Eagles and the "California sound," hair bands and disco—all of which seemed to exist in another universe. We liked a lot of disco, but the prevailing rocker attitude was that dance music was "manufactured" and therefore not authentic or heartfelt.

The highest ideals of live performance at the time seemed irrelevant to us as well. Arena rock and the mega-R&B ensembles were legendary for their elaborate shows—enormous spectacles with pyrotechnics and spaceships. These shows were light years away from any connection to our reality. They were an escape, a fantasy, and hugely entertaining, but they had no relationship to any sense of what it felt like to be young, energetic, and frustrated. Those artists sure didn't speak to or for any of us, even if they did have some good songs. If we wanted to hear music that spoke directly to us, it was clear that we'd have to make it ourselves. If no one else liked it, well, so be it—but at least we would have some songs that meant something to us.

Meanwhile, the art world in SoHo, just a few blocks west of the Bowery, was dominated by the twin poles of conceptualism and minimalism. Pretty dry stuff, for the most part, but the drones and trance-inducing repetition emanating from the avant-garde composers associated with that scene (such as Philip Glass and Steve Reich) somehow took that minimalist aesthetic and made it engaging, and aspects of it found their way into punk rock. You can trace connections from Tony Conrad's one-note compositions to the Velvet Underground, Neu!, and Faust, and from there to bands like Suicide and onward. The trance sound made its way onto the club stages as well, with the volume and distortion turned way up.

Pop art from the sixties lingered on as a movement, mutating and becoming more ironic as it drifted further from its origins. Compared to some of the dour work of the conceptualists and minimalists, one felt that at least these artists had a sense of fun. Warhol, Rauschenberg, Rosenquist, Lichtenstein, and their kin were about embracing, in a peculiar, ironic way, a world with which we were familiar. They accepted that pop culture was the water in which we all swam. I think I can speak for a lot of the musicians in New York at that time and say that we genuinely liked a lot of pop culture, and that we appreciated workmanlike song craft. Talking Heads did covers of 1910 Fruitgum Company and the Troggs, and Patti Smith famously reworked the über-primitive song "Gloria" as well as the soul song "Land of 1,000 Dances." Of course, our cover tunes were very different from those we would have been expected to play if we had been a bar band that played covers. That would have meant Fleetwood Mac, Rod Stewart, Donny & Marie, Heart, ELO, or Bob Seger. Don't get me wrong, some of them had some great songs, but they sure weren't singing about the world as we were experiencing it. The earlier, more primitive pop hits we'd first heard on the radio as suburban children now seemed like diamonds in the rough to us. To cover those songs was to establish a link between one's earliest experience of pop music and one's present ambitions—to revive that innocent excitement and meaning.

If I were to diagram the art/music connections, I might say that the Ramones and Blondie were pop-art bands, while Talking Heads were minimalist or conceptual art with an R&B beat. Suicide was minimalism with rockabilly elements. And Patti Smith and Television were romantic expressionists, with a sometimes slightly surrealist slant. Of course it isn't as simple as that—you can't really align everything and anything with art movements. One thing the bands did have in common was that we were all working within the framework of a popular form we loved, and had in recent years become alienated from. As a result, we would all occasionally look for inspiration elsewhere—in other mediums like fine art, poetry, art actions, drag performances, and circus sideshows. All served as points of reference for us. Being forced to look outside of music was a good thing. It may have been done out of desperation, but it pushed everyone to make something new.

5. RENT MUST BE LOW—AND IT MUST STAY LOW

CBGB was in a rough neighborhood. Now[A] there are gourmet-food shops and fancy restaurants nearby, but at that time[B] the Lower East Side and the area around the Bowery were in pretty bad shape. Winos were everywhere. It wasn't romantic to see one of them pull down his pants in the Associated Supermarket and take a dump in the aisle; it was just disgusting and depressing, as was much of what we had to deal with around there. But the rents were cheap—$150 a month for the place that Tina, Chris, and I shared on Chrystie Street, though there was no toilet, shower, or even heat. You get what you pay for.

A

B

In the winter it was sometimes hard to tell whether someone you'd see passed out in the snow was merely drunk or high, or if that comatose body on the sidewalk was a dead person. Our apartment was near an area with the cheapest, skankiest hookers in town. Further east, heroin was sold pretty much openly on the street corners, and the clientele used the abandoned buildings nearby as shooting galleries. Empty glassine envelopes marked with the logos of the various "brands" could be seen all over the sidewalks. Succeeding in this world, becoming a downtown star, was not exactly "making it" in the music business in any conventional sense. We might feel we were making it because we were being accepted by our peers, but all our parents and other outsiders could see was that we were still living in squalor.

But surviving and creating here meant you were part of a place where you could have a tiny sense of community. Even though by today's standards the rents in the area were insanely cheap, the three of us who began Talking Heads all shared a loft to save money, like everyone else was doing. The Blondie loft was just a little south of CB's on the Bowery, and Arturo Vega, who guided the Ramones' style, had a place just around the corner.

A certain romanticism about the cultural history of the area did linger in our minds. People who were huge inspirations to us were still neighborhood fixtures—William Burroughs lived nearby, as did Allen Ginsberg—and we imagined that we were in some ways continuing their legacy. Though not musicians per se, they were as inspirational as the best music that had come before us. And though neither Ginsberg nor Burroughs could be classified as "romantics," they, and their attitude toward life and art, were part of a funky mystique that gave the squalor a kind of glamour in our eyes.

Cheap rent allows artists, musicians, and writers to live without much income during their formative years. It gives them time to develop, and it gives creative communities that nurture and support their members time to form. Everybody knows that when these neighborhoods get gentrified, both the locals and the struggling creative types get pushed out. But not every neighborhood with cheap rents gives rise to a scene. I recently lived in the West Thirties in Manhattan, where the rents used to be cheap, but no community ever arose there. Affordable rent alone is not enough.

6. BANDS MUST BE PAID FAIRLY

At CBGB, bands got either the entire door or a pretty good percentage of it, while Hilly continued to get the profits from the bar—which improved considerably as bands began to draw an audience. Talking Heads had day jobs early on, but after about a year we were able to devote ourselves to music full-time. Once we began packing the place, which meant a modest 350 paying customers, that door percentage was enough to pay our bills. Try that policy at a club today. CBGB was our safety net, both creatively and financially.

When I later heard about bands actually paying to play in certain clubs, I knew things had been perverted in a terrible way. The desperate, innate desire to create and perform had been exploited rather than supported. It was like taking a basic human need, like wanting to love and be loved, and then finding a way to make money from it. Sick. It was a sign of the times. The me-first decade had begun.

7. SOCIAL TRANSPARENCY MUST BE ENCOURAGED

At CB's there were small dressing rooms without doors, so any passerby could watch you unpacking your gear and tuning up. There was no privacy—annoying sometimes, but maybe a good thing. Junkies and lovers managed to find places to hide elsewhere, but performers had to be transparent. Diva behavior was rendered difficult or impractical—the physical situation would have made it look silly. The performers were obliged to interact and mingle with their audience. There was no VIP area. The toilets were legendarily nasty—I'm pretty sure that for a while they didn't have seats. One might have been smashed. This was not a factor that helped the scene; it was not charming or romantic. While being forced to put on a show with limited means and having to mingle might have actually been productive, busted toilets in clubs are just sad and mean.

There was always a jukebox playing when the bands weren't. Hilly filled much of it with 45s by the local bands who played there, so if a band had paid for a song to be recorded and pressed up as a 45, you knew at least one jukebox in town where it could find a home. Of course, there were also plenty of talismanic 45s by other inspirational bands on that jukebox—the Stooges, the Mysterians. Lenny Kaye's *Nuggets* compilation could have taken up the whole jukebox and everyone would have nodded in recognition. Oddly, as musically disparate as the performers of CBGB were, we drew inspiration from a lot of the same songs and bands. Every night we received these aural reminders of where we all came from, where we were at that moment, and where we were going. This insular selection might seem a little dogmatic in retrospect—God forbid someone snuck a jazz or folk 45 in there!—but it provided a sense of solidarity, something rare for New Yorkers whose monstrous egos often stood in the way of forging a community. The jukebox was, in a certain way, crowd-sourced, and it served as a kind of sonic adhesive, a social glue. The jukebox leveled the playing field as much as the lack of privacy in the dressing rooms.

Plenty of music clubs are set up like movie theaters: when the show is over, everyone is asked to pay their bar and snack bills and leave. You can't go to most of these clubs just to hang out, because they have a schedule of specific showtimes, and if you show up before the show you came to see and there's an earlier set, you're not allowed in to see it. Needless to say, no one hangs out in these places. There is no community of musicians, and a scene can't begin to develop. There is, I am told, a community of waitresses and bartenders—the few people who are allowed to be there all night. Bill Bragin booked a terrific few years at Joe's Pub in New York, but as much as I enjoyed attending those shows, I also realized that the evenings were very structured. After a performance, I usually went right home. The music might have been excellent, but there was no possibility for casual or chance encounters—people only saw what they bought a ticket to see. Places like this make more money in the short run, because they can charge a separate admission for every show and have two, sometimes three acts a night, each with their own paying crowd. But there's also no loyalty, nor any customers to fall back on who trust the place as much as the music. You know a scene is developing when you hang out at a place and you have no idea who's going to be playing.

There are a few places like this in New York, still, though they tend to be small, like Nublu in the East Village and Barbès in Park Slope and Zebulon in Williamsburg. By the time this book comes out, they might not be around.

8. IT MUST BE POSSIBLE TO IGNORE
THE BAND WHEN NECESSARY

CBGB originally had a long bar, and you had to walk past it and then past the little bandstand in order to reach a pool table located farther back.[c] You could pass the time playing pool while watching the band (sort of—they'd be facing away from you) or while waiting for the next band to go on. CBGB was long and narrow, and only a small group of fans could actually stand in front of the stage. Most of the audience would end up at the bar, or hanging around the pool table, and those people behind the bands were often barely paying attention. It doesn't sound ideal, but maybe *not* having to perform under intense scrutiny (it always seemed as if only the few folks in front were really paying attention) is important, even beneficial. This odd, relaxed, and even somewhat insulting arrangement allowed for more natural, haphazardly creative development.

Later, Hilly resituated the stage (I am avoiding the word "remodeled") and improved the sound system, which made CBGB one of the best-sounding rooms in town.[D] This seems incredibly enlightened—the sound system part, anyway. Most club owners are loath to make technical improvements. As long as drinkers are congregating at the bar, why should they? I think Hilly had ulterior motives. I think he pictured a whole series of live recordings being made there that could have been another potential source of income for him. But who knows? Maybe he was just being a decent guy!

In a way, the casual setup reminded me of busking. When playing on the street, it was never hard to get one or two curious folks to stop and listen, but if you could get the ones who were walking purposely on their way somewhere else to pay attention, then you'd really made a breakthrough. Sometimes the person who seemed to have been playing pool all night was the one who came up to you afterward and said something that proved that they were the one who had really been listening.

THE LEGACY OF A SCENE

After some of the bands that emerged from CBGB were signed, they played there less and less. They went on the road or holed up writing and rehearsing new material, becoming a tiny bit more professional. Talking Heads was one of those bands. I remember writing in my East Village loft in the late seventies and then heading to CBGB's after I'd gotten something down. Going out was some kind of reward for me. CB's even found its way into a song we wrote, "Life During Wartime," in which the club was imagined from the point of view of a member of a North American version of the Baader-Meinhof gang—urban guerrillas who missed being able to go to the clubs where they used to hang. Being out in the world more, we all came to miss hanging out in an old familiar place.

I kept returning to the club throughout the following decades. The bands of the post-punk era—which, as I write this, are being rediscovered—filled the gap left by those of us who were on tour. They pushed their music and performances further, too. Some of them really took the ball and ran with it, making bands like ours seem tame by comparison. DNA, Bush Tetras, and the Contortions brought newer and sometimes more radical musical approaches to the club. In a way they kept the promise we had made. They continued to make raw and innovative music, and for years, the club remained a place to catch waves of emerging musicians.

As time went on, you could hear new bands at a variety of venues. CBGB hung in there, and Hilly never entirely renovated or turned the place into a tourist trap or a theme restaurant, bless his heart. (Though there were rumors of a faux East Village to be built in Vegas that would include a re-creation of CB's.) The place used to shock visitors and tourists who expected some kind of imposing rock palace. CBGB doesn't have grandeur, but it was a place to hear what was bubbling up for quite a while. I remember seeing a wonderful band there in the mid-nineties, Cibo Matto, and then a few weeks later seeing Chocolate Genius (Mark Anthony Thompson) in the CBGB lounge next door. The club remained a vital place for a surprisingly long time.

There was a period after that when I didn't go there much, because the music I was interested in was elsewhere. And then there was the whole transformation of the Bowery and the surrounding area into a chic boho zone—a change that spelled

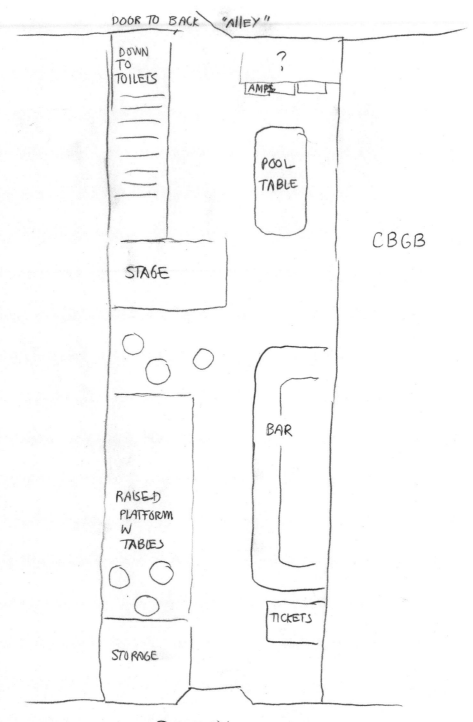

DOOR TO BACK "ALLEY"

DOWN TO TOILETS

?

AMPS

POOL TABLE

CBGB

STAGE

RAISED PLATFORM W TABLES

BAR

STORAGE

TICKETS

BOWERY

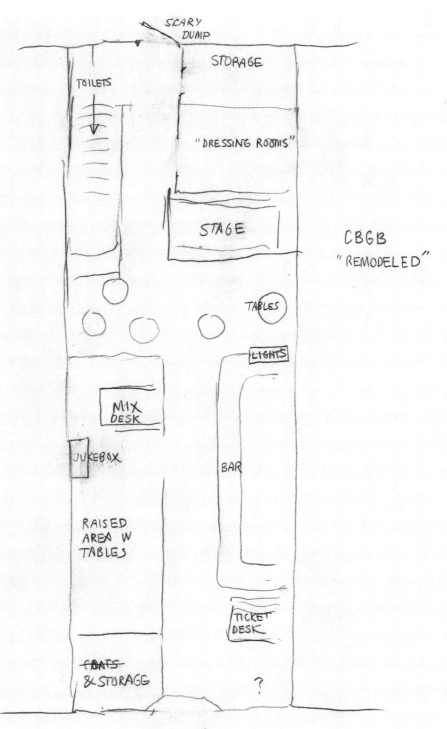

the end of those old places that weren't pulling in lots of cash (except from the souvenir T-shirts). I didn't miss CB's when it shut down—it wasn't a vital place anymore, and the waves of nostalgia that were being whipped up as its closing approached were a little obnoxious. There were other clubs that had also fostered scenes, but that weren't mourned quite as strenuously—the original Knitting Factory, El Mocambo, Area, Don Hill's, and Hurrah's, to name a few. I guess CB's had a grittiness that made for a better story. I tried to help broker a deal between the building's owner (a charity focusing on the homeless) and CB's, but I could sense that nostalgia was overriding reason and that there would be no compromise.

The rules I've enumerated aren't hard and fast. Think of them as guidelines that can steer you away from what might at first seem like obvious or logical moves. One might, for example, think that making patrons pay rapt attention to the bands is key, but maybe it's the exact opposite that fosters devotion to bands and musicians. What's important is that local talent of whatever type is given an outlet. Newer places in the New York area have spawned scenes recently. I don't know if the new venues follow all of my rules, but they are certainly relaxed places—you can hang out, and musicians come to hear other musicians. It's a real testament to how much creativity we all harbor that scenes emerge the way they do. People and neighborhoods that were never suspected of being huge creative hubs—Detroit, Manchester, Sheffield, Seattle—exploded when folks who didn't even know they had it in them suddenly blossomed and inspired everyone else around them.

HORIZONTAL AND VERTICAL BOOKING

Earlier in this chapter I name-checked Bill Bragin, who used to book Joe's Pub here in New York and now books the excellent music series at Lincoln Center, *Out of Doors*. I talked with him recently and, while flattered to be mentioned, he seemed slightly stung by the fact that I held Joe's up as a place that has had wonderful music (sometimes), but never managed to nurture a scene.

What follows is an email from Bill explaining his career—past and current—curating music and audience experiences, making cultural connections and cross-overs, and generally trying to make a scene:

I started at Joe's Pub at the Public Theater a week before 9/11. When the economy started tanking in the period immediately following, the Public, like many arts organizations and nightclubs, had to look at layoffs and other austerity measures, and Joe's Pub was at risk. We needed to find ways to stabilize the program and come up with a plan to turn the finances around.

In November 2001, Sandra Bernhard came to us looking for dates to workshop a new show. The format of Joe's Pub at the time was to present one ticketed show and then open up into more of a late-night lounge. Since we were already booked, we added a 10:30 set [in order to make room for Bernhard's show in progress], and voila—we realized that we could double our virtual capacity without doubling our fixed costs. We started presenting two shows a night as a matter of course starting in January 2002, and through a combination of high-quality booking, really controlling costs, and the easing of the immediate post-9/11 trauma, we were able to turn things around. We eventually learned how to make the two-shows-a-night turnaround work on a tight time frame, but at the expense of encouraging the kind of cross-fertilization of our audiences that would have been ideal to create the kind of scene you describe. One of the ideas behind global-FEST [a nonprofit, one-day world music festival], which started at the Public before it moved to Webster Hall, was to create an event using three stages simultaneously, which could allow musical grazing and encourage chance connections in the audience.

One point about intermingling: while the audiences generally didn't cross over, many of the artists did (and still do). Because of the tight quarters backstage, musicians often had a chance (and really no choice) to meet, and catch one another's sets, sound checks, and/or shows. We were generally pretty open with comps for other artists to check out music of all types, and invited them to shows we thought they'd be especially interested in. So I'd say that there were opportunities for intersecting scenes of musicians created through Joe's Pub that continue to this day.

Backing up to before my time at Joe's Pub—a lot of my programming approach came from two inspirations: Hal Willner's programming of *Night Music* and Joe Killian's programming in the early days of Central Park SummerStage, which is where I spent a lot of my spare summer afternoons starting in college. Shows like the July 4 Sun Ra/ Sonic Youth double bill, or earlier shared bills with Tito Puente and Koko Taylor, and Ntozake Shange with Jean-Paul Bourelly, were personally influential examples of how audiences could be cross-fertilized—making both aesthetic and cultural connections. When I eventually went to work at SummerStage, that strategy became a key part of my approach, and SummerStage producer Erica Ruben and I spent a lot of time crafting multiple-artist bills in that tradition.

I had very much started to look at the idea of mixing artists and audiences on a single bill as a central part of my approach. It was certainly an approach I missed when I started programming Joe's Pub—that's why your brief mention in the book struck home. It was something I was quite aware of, but I was able to look at the overall lineup of the club horizontally over time, rather than vertically on a single night, and find the diversity I sought. When we programmed Joe's Pub in the Park at the Delacorte Theater in Central Park, we were able to create multiple-artist bills (like a triple bill with Antibalas, Greg Tate's Burnt Sugar, and Butch Morris conducting the Nublu Orchestra, or Patty Griffin, Allen Toussaint, and a Country Music Association songwriters' circle) that were more consistent with my past.

When I made the move to Lincoln Center, I thought a lot about what it would mean to be back curating summer outdoor events and how I could make the experience different for me so it wouldn't feel like I was programming either Joe's Pub or SummerStage again. I started off immediately working on some programs that were of a scale I couldn't begin to conceive at Joe's Pub: Rhys Chatham's *A Crimson Grail for 200 Electric Guitars*, and an Ethiopiques-inspired double bill featuring Getatchew Merkurya with Dutch postpunk band the Ex, and Mahmoud Ahmed and Alemayehu Eshete with jazz big band Either/Orchestra. The ability to go back to curating and producing large-scale events that would help make artistic connections, develop audiences, and build community that were beyond the possible scope at Joe's Pub was definitely a large part of the attraction.

And I thought a lot about the physical environments—the relative formality of Lincoln Center's urban plazas versus the informality of Central Park, the presence of multiple sites (both official venues and spaces that could be transformed into new performance spaces), the far broader generational diversity at Lincoln Center, the classical "high art" resonances and institutional trappings.

I came to Lincoln Center in the midst of a physical redevelopment process that was designed to make the institution more open and welcoming, in part through the creation of new green spaces and public plaza. With that redevelopment largely completed, I also started playing with how the renovated campus itself could be used as an alternative to traditional onstage presentations. I continue to focus a lot on creating mixed bills—live music and contemporary dance on shared programs, adding pre-mainstage plaza-based performances, etc., all with an eye to bringing multiple audiences together for artistic revelations, and as a way to build community by bringing sometimes fragmented audiences together for a shared experience.

I don't know what more I can add to what Bill has written here. Throughout this chapter I have written about my own experience as a musician and how certain clubs and policies fostered creative interaction among us performers. Bill focuses more on the audience experience. Now, I'm an audience member too, but he rightly puts that first and points out how booking interesting and unexpected combinations of acts playing on the same bill can make musical connections happen in the listener's head. He calls that vertical booking.

Bill refers to what he did at Joe's as horizontal booking. An audience member had to frequent the club over a number of nights throughout a season to really understand what was going on with this kind of booking. He's right. Over time, if there is a real coherent sensibility behind the selection of acts, you eventually begin to sense that pattern, and you start to develop a kind of trust in the place. You might even (and I have done this) go to a club to hear whoever is playing there, partly because you trust the often invisible person who is making the selection. You don't know who that person is, but they are what gives an identity to a place, as much as the factors I have mentioned previously.

The process Bill revealed to us above happens in other clubs and venues as well, though not as often as one might like. Bill's taste is pretty eclectic, and most places tend to think of themselves as a "jazz club," a "rock club," a "singer-song-writer club," or a "hip-hop club." What's really energizing and exciting is when those definitions start to break down. The Afro Punk festival I went to in Brooklyn recently was a good example of that. Most musicians don't think of themselves in restrictive ways, and an enlightened booker can help make that explicit—and in the process allow something creative to happen.

CHAPTER NINE

Amateurs!

Music is made of sound waves that we encounter at specific times and places: they happen, we sense them, and then they're gone. The music *experience* is not just those sound waves, but the context in which they occur as well. Many people believe that there is some mysterious and inherent quality hidden in great art, and that this invisible substance is what causes these works to affect us as deeply as they do. This ineffable thing has not yet been isolated, but we do know that social, historical, economic, and psychological forces influence what we respond to—just a much as the work itself. The arts don't exist in isolation. And of all the arts, music, being ephemeral, is the closest to being an experience more than it is a thing—it is yoked to where you heard it, how much you paid for it, and who else was there.

The act of making music, clothes, art, or even food has a very different and possibly more beneficial effect on us than simply consuming those things. And yet for a very long time, the attitude of the state toward teaching and funding the arts has been in direct opposition to fostering creativity among the general population. It can often seem that those in power don't want us to enjoy making things for ourselves—they'd prefer to establish a cultural hierarchy that devalues our amateur efforts and encourages consumption rather than creation. This might sound like

I believe there is some vast conspiracy at work, which I don't, but the situation we find ourselves in is effectively the same as if there were one. The way we are taught about music, and the way it's socially and economically positioned, affect whether it's integrated (or not) into our lives, and even what kind of music might come into existence in the future. Capitalism tends toward the creation of passive consumers, and in many ways this tendency is counterproductive. Our innovations and creations, after all, are what keep many seemingly unrelated industries alive.

EATING CANNED SALMON BY A TROUT BROOK

In his book *Capturing Sound: How Technology Has Changed Music*, Mark Katz explains that prior to 1900, the aim of music education in America "was to teach students how to make music."[1] The advent of the record player and recorded music in the early twentieth century changed all that. I know what you must be thinking—I am someone who to a large extent has made his living off the sale and dissemination of my recordings; is it really possible that I believe that the way technology changed how we receive music wasn't entirely a good thing for creative individuals like myself, or for us generally as a culture?

Of course people have always been able to go hear professional musicians performing in big cities. Even in small towns, paid entertainers played at dances and weddings, as they still do in many parts of the world. Not all music was played by

A

amateurs. But a hundred years ago most people didn't live in big cities, and for them music was made locally, often by friends and family. Many people likely had never heard an opera or a symphony. Maybe a traveling group would pass through, but for the most part people outside big cities had to be somewhat self-reliant when it came to musical performance. (By the 1920s, a network of ten thousand regional performance centers called Chautauquas had been established to serve as a way for people to hear music and lectures brought in from other places.)[A]

Ellen Dissanayake, a cultural anthropologist and author

of *Homo Aestheticus*, says that early on—she means *prehistorically* early on—all art forms were communally made, which had the effect of reinforcing a group's cohesion and thereby improving their chances of survival. In other words, writing (storytelling), music, and art had a practical use, from an evolutionary perspective. Maybe, like sports, making music can function as a game—a musical "team" can do what an individual cannot. Music making imparts lessons that reach well beyond songwriting and jamming.[2]

In the modern age, though, people have come to feel that art and music are the product of individual effort rather than something that emerges from a community. The meme of the solitary genius is powerful, and it has affected the way we think about how our culture came into being. We often think that we can, and even must, rely on blessed individuals to lead us to some new place, to grace us with their insight and creations—and naturally that person is never us. This is not an entirely new idea, but the rise of commercially made recordings accelerated a huge shift in attitudes. Their promulgation meant that the more cosmopolitan music of folks who lived in the big cities (the music of professionals), and even the professional musicians in far-off countries, could now be heard everywhere. Amateurs and local music makers must have been somewhat intimidated.

As explained in chapter four, the first record players could record as well as play, so for a short while, every amateur had the possibility of becoming a recording artist. The quality of those recordings wasn't great, so there was a lot of spoken word—a lot of talking into the recorders. Audio letters. Audio postcards. The rough sounds of local singers and parlor players coexisted for a while with the recordings of professionals that the record-player manufacturers were distributing. But fairly soon, the companies realized that more money could be made if the flow of music was one-way, so the recording feature was eliminated. Much technology in contemporary culture, in which creative tinkering by non-professionals has been crippled by the efforts of computer and software companies, and by the enforcers and lobbyists behind copyright and intellectual-property laws, displays this same tendency. Amateur music makers have had to take a backseat. So much for the market catering to the will of the people!

John Philip Sousa felt strongly about the value of amateurs making music. Here is what he wrote in his 1906 essay "The Menace of Mechanical Music":

This wide love for the art springs from the singing school, secular or sacred; from the village band, and from the study of those instruments that are nearest the people. There are more pianos, violins, guitars, mandolins, and banjos among the working classes of America than in all the rest of the world... [but now] the automatic music devices are usurping their places.

For when music can be heard in the homes without the labor of study and close application, and without the slow process of acquiring a technic, it will be simply a question of time when the amateur disappears entirely...

The tide of amateurism cannot but recede, until there will be left only the mechanical device and the professional executants.

Then what of the national throat? Will it not weaken? What of the national chest? Will it not shrink?

I love those phrases—the national throat, the national chest! They're kind of Whitmanic.

The country dance orchestra of violin, guitar, and melodeon had to rest at times, and the resultant interruption afforded the opportunity for general sociability and rest among the entire company. Now a tireless mechanism can keep everlastingly at it, and much of what made the dance a wholesome recreation is eliminated.

This is an interesting point, and it isn't made very often. Sousa is saying that the gaps between performances might in some ways be just as important—socially, at least—as the performances themselves. The times when we're *not* being entertained are as important as the times when we are. Too much music, or too much continuous music, might not be a good thing. It's a little counterintuitive, but I'd be inclined to agree. To Sousa, the prospect of recorded music was "a thought as unhappy and incongruous as [eating] canned salmon by a trout brook."[3]

He might have been a bit alarmist and cranky, but he wasn't entirely wrong about amateur music making. I myself didn't start out as a musical professional. For years I only had ambitions to be an amateur who made music with friends for fun. Some of the most satisfying music I've made has come about as a result of naïve enthusiasm rather than from professional considerations. Music making always involved socializing, so in the process I've met people I wouldn't have otherwise. Music was a handy cover for my social awkwardness, and I learned a thing or two about getting along. Those are a lot of useful by-products that have nothing to do with dexterity or virtuosic skills.

The "don't give a shit" attitude of the amateur is another precious commodity. The Spanish film director Fernando Trueba claims that many directors' best films are the ones they didn't care all that much about. These films, he says, have more soul than the films those same directors made when they intentionally set out to create their masterpiece. Amateurism, or at least the lack of pretension associated with it, can be liberating.

According to Mark Katz, many teachers believed that recorded music would encourage children to take up music. When the phonograph was new, and schools were a little leery of adopting it, several prominent pedagogues argued in its favor. J. Lawrence Erb, for one, asserted that "the total effect of mechanical players has been to increase interest in music and stimulate a desire to make music on one's own account." But if there was such an increase in the percentage of amateur musicians, it soon subsided.[4]

Though what the elite listened to prior to 1900 was certainly different from what the masses enjoyed, there was always some overlap between the two. The catchy tunes that littered popular Italian operas—music that we would consider high art today—were sung by farmers and played by brass bands in town squares. These arias were the pop music of their time. This popularity was not a result of capitulation, of ordinary folks being obliged to like music that was endorsed by their "betters"; it was genuinely popular music. And yet it's probably true that as long as there has been an aristocracy or an elite, they have promulgated the idea that certain kinds of music and art are somehow better, more refined, more sophisticated, and can only be appreciated by the few.

Recordings, however tinny or scratchy, made it possible for everyone to hear these sophisticated and accomplished artistes. Music education boomed, and soon the emphasis shifted: it became about learning and understanding musical forms, rather than making them. The new pedagogical goal was to expose students to all kinds of music, in genres that were previously unavailable to them. Not only was the emphasis on listening; the expressed goal was to get the kids to appreciate the superiority of a certain kind of music over what some declared to be coarser, more popular forms.

WHAT IS MUSIC GOOD FOR?

Is some music really better than other music? Who decides? What effect does music have on us that might make it good or not so good?

Like Ellen Dissanayake, many believe that music must be useful to humanity, even if you can't fix a leaky sink with it—if it wasn't, it wouldn't have survived to play as prominent a role in our lives as it does. Furthermore, it is presumed that certain kinds of music have more beneficial effects than others. Some music can make you a "better" person, and by extension other kinds of music might even be detrimental (and they don't mean it will damage your eardrums)—certainly it won't be as morally uplifting. The assumption is that upon hearing "good" music, you will somehow become a more morally grounded person. How does that work?

The background of those defining what is good or bad goes a long way toward explaining this attitude. The use of music to make a connection between a love of high art and economic success and status isn't always subtle. Canadian writer Colin Eatock points out that classical music has been piped into 7-Elevens, the London Underground, and the Toronto subways, and the result has been a decrease in robberies, assaults, and vandalism.[5] Wow—powerful stuff. Music can alter behavior after all! This statistic is held up as proof that some music does indeed have magical, morally uplifting properties. What a marketing opportunity! But another view holds that this tactic is a way of making certain people feel unwelcome. They know it's not "their" music, and they sense that the message is, as Eatock says, "Move along, this is not your cultural space." Others have referred to this as "musical bug spray." It's a way of using music to create and manage social space.[6]

The economist John Maynard Keynes even claimed that many kinds of amateur and popular music do in fact reduce one's moral standing. In general, we are indoctrinated to believe that classical music, and maybe some kinds of jazz, possess a kind of moral medicine—whereas hip-hop, club music, and certainly heavy metal lack anything like a positive moral essence. It all sounds slightly ridiculous when I spell it out like this, but such presumptions continue to inform many decisions regarding the arts and the way they're supported.

John Carey, an English literary critic who writes for the *Sunday Times,* wrote a wonderful book called *What Good Are the Arts* that illustrates how officially sanctioned art and music gets privileged. Carey cites the philosopher Immanuel Kant: "Now I say the beautiful is the symbol of the morally good, and that it is only in this respect that it gives pleasure... The mind is made conscious of a certain ennoblement and elevation above the mere sensibility to pleasure."[7] So, according to Kant, the reason we find a given work of art beautiful is because we sense—but how do we sense this, I wonder?—that some innate, benevolent, moral essence is tucked in there, elevating us, and we like that. In this view, pleasure and moral uplift are linked. Pleasure alone, without this beautiful entanglement, is not a good thing—but packaged with moral uplift, pleasure is, well, excusable. That might sound pretty mystical and a bit silly, especially if you concede that standards of beauty just might be relative. In Kant's Protestant world, all forms of sensuality inevitably lead to loose morals and eternal damnation. Pleasure needs a moral note to be acceptable.

When Goethe visited the Dresden Gallery,[B] he noted the "emotion experienced

upon entering a House of God." He was referring to positive and uplifting emotions, not fear and trembling at the prospect of encountering the Old Testament God. William Hazlitt, the brilliant nineteenth-century essayist, said that going to the National Gallery on Pall Mall was like making a pilgrimage to the "holy of holies... [an] act of devotion performed at the shrine of art."[8] Once again it would appear that this God of Art is a benevolent one who will not strike young William down with a bolt of lightning for an occasional aesthetic sin. If such a punishment sounds like an exaggeration, keep in mind that not too long before Hazlitt's time, one could indeed be burned at the stake for small blasphemies. And if the appreciation of the finer realms of art and music is akin to praying at a shrine, then one must accept that artistic blasphemy also has its consequences.

A corollary to the idea that high art is good for you is that it can be prescribed like medicine. Like a kind of inoculation, it can arrest, and possibly even begin to reverse, our baser tendencies. The Romantic poet Samuel Taylor Coleridge wrote that the poor needed art "to purify their tastes and wean them from [their] polluting and debasing habits." Charles Kingsley, a nineteenth-century English novelist, was even more explicit: "Pictures raise blessed thoughts in me—why not in you, my brother? Believe it, toil-worn worker, in spite of thy foul alley, thy crowded lodging, thy thin, pale wife, believe it, thou too, and thine will some day have your share of beauty."[9] Galleries like Whitechapel in London were opened in working-class neighborhoods so that the downtrodden might have a taste of the finer things in life. Having done a little bit of manual labor myself, I can attest that sometimes beer, music, or TV might be all one is ready for after a long day of physically demanding work.

Across the ocean, the titans of American industry continued this trend. They founded the Metropolitan Museum of Art in New York in 1872, filling it with works drawn from their massive European art collections in the hope that the place would act as a unifying force for an increasingly diverse citizenry—a matter of some urgency, given the massive number of immigrants who were joining the nation. One of the Met's founders, Joseph Hodges Choate, wrote, "Knowledge of art in its higher forms of beauty would tend directly to humanize, to educate and to refine a practical and laborious people."[10]

The late Thomas Hoving, who ran the Met in the sixties and seventies, and his rival J. Carter Brown, who headed the National Gallery in Washington, DC, both felt that democratizing art meant getting everyone to like the things that they liked. It meant letting everyone know that here, in their museums, was the good stuff, the important stuff, the stuff with that mystical aura. Below, left, is a promotion the Met did in the sixties in *Life* magazine.^{C} The idea was that even reduced to the size of a postcard, reproductions of verified masterpieces could still enlighten the American masses. And so cheap!

Music was (and is) presented in the same way. Below, right, is an ad that appeared in the *New York Times Book Review* not too long ago.^{D} This ad isn't about learning to play for your own enjoyment or self-expression—it's purely about learning to value the classics more than any music you and your pathetic friends might make. It's a little more expensive than the $1.25 the Met was asking for back in the day, but times have changed. The effect, however, is the same: to make you feel anxious and insecure about what you know and might already like, and to show you how to fix the situation.

This line of thinking led Hoving and others to create the now ubiquitous blockbuster museum show. The first one famously brought King Tut to the masses—or, more precisely, it brought the masses to Tut. These shows "reached out" and made the Met and other like-minded museums into temples where all were welcome. Hard to remember, but the Met was once a fussy, dusty old place, and that show set it on its way to becoming super popular.

Here are some blockbuster-exhibit attendance figures from the Met:[11]

- *Treasures of Tutankhamun* (1978—79), 1,360,957 visitors
- *The Mona Lisa by Leonardo da Vinci* (1963), 1,077,521 visitors
- *The Vatican Collections: The Papacy and Art* (1983), 896,743 visitors
- *Painters in Paris: 1895-1950* (2000—01), 883,620 visitors
- *Origins of Impressionism* (1994—95), 794,108 visitors
- *The Horses of San Marco* (1980), 742,221 visitors
- *Picasso in the Metropolitan Museum of Art* (2010), 703,256 visitors

Hoving did ride a bike, so he can't have been all about fancy art.[E] In fact, his stint as parks commissioner, before he joined the Met, was incredibly fruitful and changed the lives of many ordinary New Yorkers. He had been offered the job with no prior experience, so his success belies the idea that we should only put our trust in experts. It was he who closed Central Park to cars on Sundays, and he who established more than one hundred pocket parks around the city, on vacant lots and in weird, unused parcels of real estate.

And now add to the list of blockbusters the 2011 Alexander McQueen show, which had folks waiting in line in the sweltering heat for hours.[F] To be honest, I can understand the McQueen show's popularity; the others are a bit more of a mystery to me. The presentation of the McQueen frocks involved a slightly more transgressive aura: they were presented as if they were part of a sci-fi opera, or a sexier version of a sword-and-sorcery world like *Game of Thrones*. The display created a slightly creepy alternative universe; it was much more than a parade of well-designed dresses on mannequins. That freaky otherworld that was hinted at seems genuinely populist, much more so than, say, *The Horses of San Marco*.

John Carey pretty much demolishes the idea that appreciating high art—and I am going to assume we can transfer his arguments concerning fine art to

E F

music—is inherently good for you. How, he asks, can anyone believe that art (or music) encourages moral behavior? He concluded that assigning moral acuity to those who like high art is generally class-based. "Meanings," he writes, "are not inherent in objects. They are supplied by those who interpret them. High art is that which appeals to the minority whose social rank places them above the struggle for mere survival."[12] The fact that such art has no practical use—or none that is acknowledged—heightens its appeal.

This line of reasoning leads him to the following conclusion about the art-builds-character attitude:

> One is saying, "What I feel is more valuable than what you feel." In assuming that high art makes life worth living, there is an inherent arrogance toward the masses of people who don't partake of such forms... and an assumption that their lives are not worth as much, not as full. The religion of art makes people worse—because it encourages contempt for those considered inartistic.[13]

Although the idea is continually espoused that art is for all and that all can benefit from it, I wouldn't say that the presentation of art is entirely democratic. Though seemingly benign, too often it's a top-down version of culture. We want you all to look at it, and listen to it, and appreciate it, but don't even think you could ever make it yourselves. Moreover, what has been deemed "real art" has nothing in common with the reality of your daily life. Twentieth-century British art critic Clive Bell wrote, "To appreciate a work of art we need to bring with us nothing from life, no knowledge of its ideas and affairs, no familiarity with its emotions."[14]

"Quality" works are said to be timeless and universal. People like Bell think that they would be good in almost any context. The Scottish Enlightenment philosopher David Hume insisted that an unvarying standard exists, and that "[it] has been universally found to please in all countries and in all ages."[15] The implication is that great work should, if it is truly great, *not* be of its time or place. We should not be aware of how, why, or when it was conceived, received, marketed, or sold. It floats free of this mundane world, transcendent and ethereal.

This is absolute nonsense. Few of the works that we now think of as "timeless" were originally thought of that way. Carey points out that Shakespeare was not universally favored; Voltaire and Tolstoy didn't care for him much, and Darwin found him "intolerably dull."[16] For many decades his work was derided as low and popular. The same could be said for a "great" painter like Vermeer, who was "rehabilitated" only recently. As a society, we change what we value all the time. When I was working with the UK trip-hop band Morcheeba, they extolled the virtues of an American seventies band called Manassas. I had dismissed that band when I was growing up—I thought they were great players but not in any way relevant to me—but I could see that a younger generation of musicians, without my prejudices, might see them in a different light. I don't think that particular band ever got elevated to the "timeless" pedestal, but many others have been. I discovered Miles Davis's electric jams from the seventies relatively late—for the most part, they were critically frowned upon when they came out—but there might now be a whole generation who looks on those records as founding gospel, hugely inspirational.

The artist Alex Melamid satirized beliefs about the mystical and moral power of art in a slideshow I saw, in which he showed photos of himself holding up reproductions of well-known masterpieces by such artists as Van Gogh and Cézanne in front of folks in rural Thailand. He was proposing, with tongue firmly in cheek, that exposure to these "spiritual" works would elevate these "heathens," and that the artworks might even have some healing properties. It was hilarious, partly because Melamid kept a straight face throughout, but the point was clear: out of context, the great Western masterpieces simply are not the transformative icons they are considered to be back home.

FUNDING

Opera halls, ballets, and large art museums receive more funding—and not all from the government—than do popular art and what might be considered popular music venues. This is because of the edifying value ascribed to such institutions by people of a privileged economic and social class throughout much of the twentieth century.

This arrangement has become a little hard to parse in America, where much of the sponsorship and audience for these institutions no longer comes from old money. Class and wealth were not always synonymous here, but maybe now they are becoming so. Joining the club that supports these venues is a way for a Texas oilman or an arms dealer to seem like a more cultured person. The image is so common as to be a cliché. Jett Rink, James Dean's character in the film *Giant*, starts off as oil-field trash, but when he strikes it big he tries to be a society sophisticate. For the most part, the new rich do try to behave and appreciate the same things as the old rich. (Interesting that the titans of tech, the nerdopoly, didn't follow this pattern—they seem to have little interest in joining those clubs.)

Funding well-established institutions that play "quality" music isn't only about a search for status; it is also about keeping many kinds of music or art out of the temple, and discouraging amateurism in general. Hazlitt wrote that "Professional art is a contradiction in terms... Art is genius, and genius cannot belong to a profession."[17] That would seem to imply that no amount of aid or support could possibly do much good—so why fund the arts at all? But I think he means that we should support these geniuses, and let the rest—the ungifted and the unprofessional—fall by the wayside. Marjorie Garber, in her book *Patronizing the Arts*, responded to this idea, writing, "By this logic, [arts] funding was, in a sense, doomed by paradox: the training, schooling, and fostering of professional artists could only support the *wrong* artists, the nongeniuses."[18] It's a bit of a catch-22. The work that has been approved, and that appears in the institutions, *must* be good, because it's already been included in those institutions. Sort of a closed system, but I guess that's the idea.

Outside of his work as an economist, Lord Keynes was involved in an organization called the Council for the Encouragement of Music and the Arts (CEMA), a government arts-funding agency that later morphed into the Arts Council of Great Britain. It was established during World War II to help preserve British culture. Keynes, however, didn't like popular culture—so some things were deemed outside the provenance of the agency's mission. Keynes "was not the man for wandering minstrels and amateur theatricals," observed Kenneth Clark, the director of London's National Gallery and later the host of the popular television series *Civilisation*. Mary Glasgow, Keynes's longtime assistant, concurred: "It was standards that mattered, and the preservation of serious professional enterprise, not obscure concerts in village halls."[19]

If we subscribe to the nineteenth-century view that professionally made classical music is good for you and good for the ordinary man, then it follows that supporting it financially is more like funding a public-health measure than underwriting entertainment. The funding of "quality" work is then inevitable, because it's for the good of all—even though we won't all get to see it. The votes came in, and the amateurs lost by a landslide. (The Arts Council did, however, modify their brief after Keynes's death.) There seemed to be no way, meanwhile, to teach folks how to develop their own talent—one was either born with it or not. Hazlitt, Keynes, and their ilk seem to discount any knock-on effects or benefits that amateur music making might have. In their way of thinking, we should be happy consumers, content to simply stand back and admire the glorious efforts of the appointed geniuses. How Keynes's friends like Virginia Woolf or his wife, the ballerina Lydia Lopokova, learned their own skills is not explained.

Elitism is not the sole reason that the "temples of quality" are lavishly funded. There is also the undeniable glory of seeing your name on a museum or symphony hall. David Geffen may have gotten his start managing popular folk rockers, but now his name is on art museums (and AIDS charities). I'm not criticizing this philanthropy, just noting that it's not being done with the aim of building a thriving network of folk-rock clubs across the nation. Museums and symphony halls encourage this trend by offering more and ever-smaller spots on which to chisel your name. I've seen donor names on hallways, cloakrooms, and even on the vestibule as you enter the toilets. Pity the poor donor who proudly points that one out. Soon every chair and doorknob will have someone's name on it.

The writer Alain de Botton wonders why our residences and offices are often so enervating:

> I met a lot of people in the property business [developers, as they are called in the United States], and asked them why they did what they did... They said it was to make money. I said, "Don't you want to do something else? Build better buildings?" Their idea of doing something better for society was to give money to the opera.[20]

This kind of compartmentalizing—separating one's livelihood from one's social aspirations—is part of the reason David Koch, the hidden hand behind a lot of ultraconservatives and, reportedly, the Tea Party movement in the United States, transforms himself into a respected arts patron by funding a theater at Lincoln Center, or why a Swiss bank that helps US depositors avoid paying taxes generously supports symphony halls and the ballet. It's almost as if there are moral scales, and by tossing some loot on one side, you can balance out the precarious situation your reputation might be getting into on the other.

Industry titans have long directed a good amount of their wealth to the acquisition of the artifacts of high culture. After accumulating a collection, they need to find somewhere to park it. Henry Clay Frick was a coke and steel manufacturer and railway financier before he became the founder of the jewel-box museum on the Upper East Side that bears his name. The core collection of American art at the de Young Museum in San Francisco was donated by John D. Rockefeller III, whose wealth was originally generated by his grandfather, the founder of the energy monopoly Standard Oil. In 1903, Isabella Stewart Gardner used an inherited industrial fortune to build a Renaissance palace in the swamps outside Boston to house her own collection. Referring to oil magnate John Paul Getty, Carey writes,

> In his view, artworks are superior to people. His art collection was viewed as an external or surrogate soul. These spiritual values attributed to the artworks were transferred to the owner. That owner can be an individual or a nation. It applies to theaters and concert halls as well as paintings. The artworks or performance spaces become like spiritual bullion—underwriting the authority of the possessor.[21]

Such industrialists, whose wealth was sometimes brutally obtained or whose moral judgment was entirely questionable (Getty felt that women on welfare should be denied the right to become parents), thus engaged in a kind of reputation laundering. Someone who supports "good" music must be a good person, too. (I have no idea why the Mafia dons and the narco-gangsters haven't wised up to this fact. Wouldn't you love to see the Joey Bananas opera hall?) Reputation laundering works because it's assumed that the folks who support fine music would be less likely to commit heinous crimes than the human flotsam that frequent a honky-tonk or a techno club. Participating in the scrums and mosh pits at pop concerts must be less morally and psychologically uplifting than sitting stock-still in complete silence at the ballet.

What if, in an imaginary country, a hypothetical king preferred house music to Mozart? Would that confer high status on raves? Would we then see buckets of funding being allocated for dance venues, and witness top-flight architects vying to build pop-music clubs out of titanium and imported marble? I don't think so. But seriously, why not? Why does the idea of equal funding for popular music seem ridiculous? Granted, pop music is supposed to stand on its own two feet financially—"pop" stands for "popular," after all—so by definition it shouldn't need help. High-art music is not nearly as popular, so it needs financial support to stay afloat, to continue to have a presence in our culture.

But there are plenty of innovative musicians who now work in a vaguely pop idiom (though that definition has been stretched a lot lately) who have had as much trouble surviving as symphony orchestras and ballet companies. For years, pop music was considered crassly commercial—a place where most musical choices were made solely in order to pander to the lowest common denominator and rake in more cash. Now, though, many would agree that there is a lot more than money behind all the work and innovation that falls within the increasingly fuzzy boundaries of the form. There is still plenty of soulless work being churned out, but I would argue that for sheer quantity of innovative output, there is more going on within pop music than in any other genre. The mere use of electric guitars, laptops, or samples, for example, doesn't mean the intentions of the composer or performer are any less serious than anything traditionally deemed high art. Much of it is done for the joy of it, with no hope of having a commercial hit. (Though some hit songs can be innovative, too.) Why not fund the venues where these young, emerging, and semi-amateur musicians can make and perform their own music? Why not invest in the future of music, instead of building fortresses to preserve its past?

Take pity on popular music. Leftist critics like the late Theodor Adorno felt that popular music worked like a drug, pacifying and numbing the masses so that they could be easily manipulated. Adorno felt that the public in general had bad taste, but he generously maintained that it was not their fault; it was the wily capitalists and their marketing folks who conspired to keep the plebes stupid by *making* them like pop music. People liked pop, he believed, because it was cynically tailored to mirror their sad, mass-produced world. The mechanized rhythms of popular music echoed the industrial production process. One can certainly imagine metal or techno evoking an assembly line or a giant pile driver; the feeling of surrendering to such a sonic machine might even have a sublime aspect to it as well. Surrendering feels good. But Adorno doesn't credit us with the ability to enjoy industrial-sounding music without actually becoming a cog in the capitalist machine. In his view, capitalist societies produced both workers and music via a kind of assembly line. That criticism is still leveled at a lot of contemporary pop music—it's called "cookie cutter" now, or formulaic. But did Adorno really think that the music made by the giants of classical music didn't adhere to any tried-and-true formulas? I hear formulas in almost every genre—it's rare when something really shatters the rules and appears to be completely sui generis. Besides, you can be a headbanger without accepting your horrible factory job. Any kid will tell you that, yes, their music is both an escape and a survival mechanism, and that sometimes the music gives them hope and inspiration. It doesn't just placate and pacify.

Adorno's ideal was Beethoven, and he felt that subsequent trends in German music were corrupted. "It is this lack of experience of the imagery of real art," he wrote, "which is at least one of the formative elements of the cynicism that has finally transformed the Germans, Beethoven's people, into Hitler's people."[22] Here we go again, linking music with moral and ethical values. Adorno maintained that such music—the work of corrupted popular composers—no longer attempted to suggest something greater than itself; it was content to be a utilitarian product, a diversion, a hummable tune. God forbid a tune should be hummable!

Adorno argued that by reminding the dehumanized masses of their humanity, classical music—classical music, mind you!—threatens the capitalist system, and it was therefore this music that was discriminated against and discouraged. But wait—wasn't classical music encouraged by Hitler? And isn't classical music, as evidenced by the symphony halls and opera houses that are proudly displayed in the center of many of the world's cities, fairly well supported by those very same capitalists? If that's discrimination, I'll have some.

It is easier to find evidence of the overt persecution of pop music by the totalitarian left. In 1928, the Soviets announced that the playing of American jazz was punishable by six months in jail. Jazz jail. Hip-hop is still an underground phenomenon in Cuba, and until recently pop music was narrowly circumscribed in China. The government of the former East Germany was worried about the subversive influence of rock and roll, so they attempted to "inoculate" their populace by introducing a fake popular dance called the Lipsi.^G These governments view pop, not classical music, as a potentially disruptive force. While Adorno's musical favorites might indeed inspire a transcendent look toward the stars, it's the social aspect of pop in the streets that really frightens totalitarian governments. Even in the United States, popular music has been banned when it seemed to encourage disreputable racial mixing or unwelcome sexuality.

The Brazilian composer Tom Zé, who has to some extent bridged the elite world of academic composition and popular music, proposes a theory in which, in a weird nod to Adorno, workers are (poorly) "manufactured" by the system—in other words, the capitalist project aims to create cogs in the machine. But Zé says that our manufacture is defective, and that our quirks and our innate humanity

make us, in effect, damaged goods. We'll never work the way we were designed to; our humanity is our saving defect. In a way, he's saying that while Adorno might be right about the system's intention, he's wrong about how things actually work out. Zé and his music prove that we will always fuck the system up in the most beautiful and unexpected ways.

The 2011 annual operating budget for the New York Metropolitan Opera is $325 million; a big chunk of that, $182 million, came from donations from wealthy patrons.[23] That these donors should choose to support this music at this institution is of course entirely their business. A 2010 Los Angeles Opera production of Wagner's *Ring Cycle* cost $31 million to produce.[24] Broadway shows don't usually cost that much, unless you're talking about the recent *Spider-Man* debacle. U2's last concert-tour budget might be in that range, but those were stadium shows attracting huge numbers of people. And in those latter two instances, the people who wrote the music are still alive, and presumably they get paid a piece out of every ticket sold, which is part of what keeps those production costs up. Wagner has been dead for a long time, so one assumes it's not his agent who is charging the moon and driving up the cost of these *Ring* productions. (Granted, it is a four-part epic.) The Los Angeles Opera ended up with a $6 million deficit due to "slack demand for expensive tickets."

Los Angeles is not known for its arts funding, public or private. The philanthropist Eli Broad and a few others might be trying to change that, but LA thinks of itself as a place that makes its own culture and entertainment—it tends to value things according to how popular they are and how much money they bring in. These values are completely the opposite of those espoused by the supporters of high-art music. Status in LA comes with having a huge hit, not by being seen at the opera.

What makes this situation notable is not the amount of money—movies, of course, often cost a lot more than $31 million to produce—but the fact that the audience for this production was, inevitably, fairly small, coupled with the fact that the state ended up footing part of the bill. A $31 million movie—a moderate budget by today's standards—has a chance of making back its investment and more, and there is the possibility that it will be seen by vast numbers of people. A new opera production is by nature limited from the start. Most of the time they are confined to one theater. Alex Ross, the music critic for the *New Yorker*, observes that some opera and symphony seats cost less than those at Broadway theaters, and less than those for some pop-music spectacles as well. So any charge of elitism doesn't hold if one uses ticket prices as a gauge. But in general, cheaper tickets are artificial—they are offered at a loss to support the idea that this good and uplifting medicine should be available to all. Like the early museums that were intended to be free for everyone. Private and state funding, in this business model, is supposed to pick up the shortfall. Even with this aid they often have a hard time covering the expense of running and maintaining these halls or mounting their productions, as the Los Angeles Opera *Ring* production proved.[H] In fact, since many high-art productions often lose money for their venues, to extend their runs and thereby increase attendance would be to risk going deeper into debt.

Is this any way to run a business? Opera companies have been trying to compensate for these unfortunate financial realities by looking for other income sources. The Met has set up satellite simulcasts in cinemas—live high-definition broadcasts of the productions for those who can't make it to the theater. Peter Gelb at the Met has been fairly successful with this kind of thing; the screenings brought in $11 million last year. That is hardly going to make a dent in that $325 million annual operating budget, but every little bit helps. David Knott, one of the Met's board members, echoes the Victorian sentiments when he endorses the simulcasts: "If we can't bring people to the opera let's bring opera to the people."[25] On an outside wall of the new Frank Gehry—designed symphony hall in Miami, a beautiful projection screen faces a park with outdoor seating.[I] This area effectively doubles the hall's size and makes symphony music available to those who can't afford a ticket.

But is it even right to think of classical music as a business? Or are we to believe it has a higher civic purpose? Even with all that private and governmental support, a lot of symphonies are struggling to hold on to their audiences and make ends meet. In October of 2010, the Detroit Symphony Orchestra wanted to require their players to work for community outreach programs: engagement, education, and chamber music services, among other adaptations to the financial squeeze they found themselves in. This would have brought an unprecedented number of symphony musicians into classrooms and art centers. The contract

would also allow for greater accessibility through streaming options, CD releases, and digital downloads. The musicians, however, wanted things to remain pretty much as they were, and they went on strike for twenty-six-weeks. Well, have you seen Detroit in the last couple of decades? The symphony lies on the edge of the center of downtown, beyond which lies a wasteland. From the symphony building one can see empty lots and crumbling, abandoned houses, formerly elegant hotels and boarded-up mansions. More than half the city population has left. Few of those who remain in the city center are symphony patrons. The tax base that would normally fund a symphony hall along with private donors isn't there anymore. In April of 2011, the Detroit Symphony Orchestra musicians agreed to the new terms and ratified the contract.

Other cities have followed the same pattern. The Philadelphia Orchestra filed for bankruptcy in the spring of 2011. Joseph Swensen, a violinist and conductor, wrote in to the *New York Times* with his thoughts on this state of affairs.

> [The big orchestras] have become symbols not only of Western civilization at its best, but of prosperity and the quality of life in the cities, which they serve. But these huge institutional orchestras are like imperialist armies that have over-extended themselves... [Their musicians are] overworked, fanatically dedicated, highly trained and highly paid people... [They are confronted with] the realities of absurdly limited rehearsal time, an abysmally limited repertoire, incredibly high expectations for consistent technical perfection and little possibility for anything one could call personal or individual creativity and what do you get? Well, in addition to very low job satisfaction, you get performances which inspire the phrase: "Once you've heard one major American symphony orchestra's Beethoven 5 these days, you've pretty much heard them all!"[26]

In his recent books, Alex Ross has been delicately pointing out that a lot of North American orchestras are indeed stuck in the mud as far as their repertoire goes. His unspoken assumption is that some more adventurous fare might draw a younger generation of listeners and keep some of these places from going under as their subscription audience ages into oblivion. I'm not sure it would work, not in those traditional venues anyway. The venues are physically and acoustically

I

made for a particular kind of music and a very specific way of enjoying it. To this end, the New York City Opera that used to be based in the Koch Theater at Lincoln Center tried doing some wonderful and adventurous programming that I really enjoyed—I saw a John Zorn piece there! But the noble intentions of the director may just be swimming against the tide. The $3 million generated in ticket sales didn't come anywhere near covering the annual $31 million budget for the opera series in that building. They have moved out now, and are looking for somewhere else to mount their productions. These kinds of venues also have a well-established reputation for being staid and conservative, while the programming of adventurous fare in funkier and smaller venues like Le Poisson Rouge, Merkin Concert Hall, and elsewhere have, in a limited way, been more successful as far as getting a new generation in the door to hear something other than pop songs in a club setting. These programmers feel free to mix and match with complete disregard for any idea of high and low music. I saw tUnE-yArDs do a show at Merkin that consisted of Merrill Garbus accompanied by a ten-piece a cappella group called Roomful of Teeth. The walls really are coming down—a little.

THE BILBAO EFFECT

New concert halls and museums went up like crazy all around the world during the economic bubble. It was not the programming that was drawing audiences in many cases, but the buildings themselves. That's what happened when the Guggenheim Museum opened in Bilbao, Spain: tourists had a reason to visit a place that many had never heard of before. It was truly amazing to behold how a new museum and a Calatrava bridge could change a whole town. The museum recently had a show of Frank Lloyd Wright's work (which had been previously exhibited in New York's own Guggenheim), along with a permanent-collection hodgepodge—not exactly reasons to make a special trip. But people do. The city was a port and industrial backwater that had seen better days, and now

the whole town has enjoyed a revival thanks to high-end culture. Other cities tried to copy this model—if you build it, they will come.

Based on the Bilbao experience, one answer to the question "What good are the arts?" seems to be, "They can revitalize a whole town." LA's Walt Disney Concert Hall looks almost exactly like the Bilbao Guggenheim. New York almost built one in lower Manhattan, a place that hardly suffers from a shortage of tourists. Everybody wanted one. Famous architects drew up plans for wild new edifices in Dubai, Abu Dhabi, Dallas, Ft. Worth, and St. Petersburg. Alice Walton (an heiress to the Walmart fortune) just opened a massive museum to show off her collection in Bentonville, Arkansas; and Russian "businessman"-in-exile Roman Abramovich has funded his girlfriend Dasha's new contemporary art museum in Moscow. This is all fine. If the oligarchs of the world want to build their own culture palaces, symphony halls, and opera houses and fund the work that goes in them, great—who could possibly complain? It's their money, and why shouldn't they spend it on what are largely harmless showcases for their newfound good taste? I was surprised to learn that the amount of state support for a place like Lincoln Center—the whole complex of which has an annual operating budget of close to half a billion dollars—is relatively small. Twenty million or so. The place is open to the public, and there are reasonably priced seats for all, but it is still essentially a massive clubhouse for a certain set.

Since the crash, most cities know that their hopes for new culture palaces will have to be deferred, but the ideal of a museum, symphony hall, or similar showcase as a symbol of the soul of a city remains potent and popular. A bunch of LA museums were given a bailout by real estate king Eli Broad, but not every city has a Broad who can come to the rescue.

NURTURING AMATEURS

In Guadalajara, Mexico, there's a former movie theater called the Roxy that has just reopened as a combination bar, gallery, and performance space. It's a pretty raw, dusty, bare-bones space, but if the walls could talk they would speak of some pretty memorable days when Radiohead or local punk bands played there.

The culturally dispossessed felt welcome at the Roxy. Rogelio Flores Man-ríquez, who ran it, wrote in a press release celebrating the reopening of the space, "Culture is formed by *tortas ahogadas*, Mickey Mouse, television, advertising, pop music, opera and the expressions, traditions, and customs that embody and provide a sense of identity to a given community."[27] This inclusive approach to culture can not only make more people happy than the traditional models, but it can act as an insurance policy against all kinds of alternatives. Kids who have nowhere else to channel their pent-up energy often turn it against their own communities, or even against themselves. If they are culturally excluded and don't feel like a part of society, then why obey its rules?

We should broaden our idea of what culture is. In Japan, there used to be no word for art. There, the process of making and drinking a pot of tea evolved into what we in the West might say is an art form. This ritualized performance of a fairly mundane activity embodied a heightened version of a ubiquitous atti-tude—that utilitarian objects and activities, made and performed with integrity, consciously and mindfully, could be art. The Zen philosopher Daisetz Suzuki said, "Who would then deny that when I am sipping tea in my tearoom, I am swallow-ing the whole universe with it, and that this very moment of my lifting the bowl to my lips is eternity itself transcending time and space."[28] That's a lot for a cup of tea, but one can see that elevation of the mundane in a lot of areas and daily activi-ties in the East. The poets, writers, and musicians of the Beat generation were inspired by this Eastern idea. They too saw the transcendent in the everyday and saw nobility in the activities of ordinary people. This is an almost Cagean view of the arts—that it's all around you if you merely adjust the way you look and listen.

Ellen Dissanayake tells us that some African societies have the same word for "art" and "play." Even in English, we "play" an instrument. This attitude toward art and performance is in complete opposition to the Western idea of monuments and great works. It views culture as ephemeral and fleeting, like music. It's an experience (again, like music), not an unchangeable fixed image. Music, in this view, is a way of living, a way of being in the world, not a thing you hold in your hand and play on a device.

Dissanayake writes that art that engages the mind and hands, that is not just passive connoisseurship, can act as an antidote for our contentious and alienated relationship to our own societies. She sees art making as capable of instilling self-discipline, patience, and the ability to resist immediate gratification. You invest your time and energy in your future. This all reminds me of the recent rise of "maker" culture—Etsy and a host of other popular companies and fairs around the world that encourage amateur creation. There's a growing movement, a real turning away not just from the passive absorption of culture, but from art and music as mere vehicles for expressing concepts. The hand has been brought back into the lives of a new generation. The head is still there, but there is an acknowledgment that part of our understanding and experience of the world comes through and from our bodies.

In some communities, music and performance have successfully transformed whole neighborhoods as profoundly as the museum did in Bilbao. In Salvador, Brazil, musician Carlinhos Brown established several music and culture centers in formerly dangerous neighborhoods. In Candeal, where Brown was born, local kids were encouraged to join drum groups, sing, and compose songs and stage performances in homemade costumes.[K]

The kids, energized by these activities, began to turn away from dealing drugs. Being *malandros* was no longer their only life option—being musicians and playing together in a group looked like more fun and was more satisfying. Little by little, the crime rate dropped in those neighborhoods; the hope returned. And some great music was made, too.

A similar thing took place in the Vigário Geral favela located near the airport

in Rio. It had been the scene of a massacre in which a police helicopter opened fire and killed scores of kids during a drug raid. Life in that favela was about as dead-end as you could get. A cultural center eventually opened under the direction of José Junior and, possibly inspired by Brown's example, they began to encourage the local kids to stage musical events, some of which dramatized the tragedy that they were still recovering from. The group AfroReggae emerged out of this effort, and, as with the Brown projects in Salvador, life in the favela improved. The dealers left; their young recruits were all making music. That, to me, is the power of music—of making music. Music can permanently change people's lives in ways that go far beyond being emotionally or intellectually moved by a specific composition. That happens too, then it passes, and often something else lingers. Music is indeed a moral force, but mostly when it is part of the warp and woof of an entire community.

I visited José Junior's center and, to be honest, the music I heard was not always among the best stuff I've ever heard in Brazil. That's not the point, though. I worked with Junior recently on music for a documentary about alternatives to the war on drugs. Maybe the specific work, the individual song, isn't always what's most important. Maybe it's not essential that the music is always of the very top-most quality, as Keynes insisted. Music as social glue, as a self-empowering change agent, is maybe more profound than how perfectly a specific song is composed or how immaculately tight a band is.

In San Francisco, a former elementary school teacher named David Wish became frustrated when the music curriculum was canceled in some Bay Area schools. He started a program called Little Kids Rock that encourages children to learn how to play songs they already like, usually on the guitar. "The first thing I eliminated was the canon," he said. No more following the ingrained program that made kids learn "Little Brown Jug" before graduating to more complicated, often classical pieces. Only the few kids who had extraordinary abilities and stamina or parental encouragement have persevered with the traditional approach. The rest abandoned learning an instrument. Another radical thing Wish did was "eliminate the use of musical notation."[29] I have to admit that I do often wish I could read music way better than I do. But I, too, was thrilled when I first began to pick out tunes and riffs by ear based on the pop songs I loved.

That rapid and profound feedback—hearing myself playing something cool that I loved—was exciting, and it spurred me to continue playing. Wish's next innovation was to add two elements that had never even been considered as part of the music curriculum before—improvisation and composition. The kids were encouraged to make up solos and to eventually write their own songs, sometimes alone and often collaborating.

Critics complained that teaching kids simple pop tunes was dumbing down their repertoire and would spell the death of classical music, which they'd never discover otherwise. The justification for this argument is that pop music is everywhere, kids will hear it anyway, and alternatives that they might not otherwise encounter need to be introduced. However, this seems to be a fallacy—as one LKR teacher and classical guitar player in LA said, "Rock music turned me on to classical music, not the other way around."[30] Wish showed that most kids have a vast reservoir of creativity just waiting for permission to come out, waiting for a forum, a context—just like when someone opens a music club!—within which their feelings and ideas can be expressed. It seems to me that *here* is where funding should go.

Maybe the most successful music education program in the world originated in a parking garage in Venezuela in 1975. It's called El Sistema (the system), and it was begun by economist and musician José Antonio Abreu with just eleven kids. Having now produced high-level musicians, two hundred youth orchestras, 330,000 players, and quite a few conductors (Gustavo Dudamel was a product of this program), it is being adopted by countries all over the world. When Sir Simon Rattle first witnessed El Sistema, he said, "I have seen the future of music."[31]

This program starts with kids as young as two or three years old, and though they don't play instruments at that age, they begin to learn rhythm and body coordination. There is no testing or admissions policy—all are welcome. The focus, though, is mainly on kids from disadvantaged backgrounds. Ninety percent of the students in the Venezuelan branch of El Sistema are poor, and the program is entirely free. If the kids get to be really good, to the level where they can play professionally, then they begin to receive a stipend so they don't have to miss classes because of work.

Of course, this system has a huge effect on the lives of the kids and their communities, far beyond their enjoyment of music. As Abreu says, "Essentially this is a system that fights poverty... A child's physical poverty is overcome by the spiritual richness that music provides." When asked if his music program was a vehicle for social change, he replied, "Without a doubt that is what is happening in Venezuela." The kids who might otherwise feel that their options in life are extremely limited are passionate about the program. "From the minute a child is taught how to play an instrument, he is no longer poor. He becomes a child in progress, heading for a professional level, who'll later become a citizen."[32]

Much of the music the kids learn in El Sistema is classical, so I have to temper my bias toward pop music here, as the program has achieved its goals many times over. In the smaller villages they might play guitars, drums, and a marimba, so it's not all classics, but it's the classical repertoire, the youth orchestras, that are the main focus of El Sistema.

Abreu is now retired, but he guided the system through ten administrations—right and left wing—in Venezuela. I'd venture that this nonpartisanship is essential to the survival of these programs, as well as the fact that El Sistema falls under the Ministry of Family, Health and Sports, not the cultural or educational departments. This designation might have helped make the program immune to the arts biases that crop up here and everywhere—I know I have some. Hugo Chávez increased the funding for this program, and naturally he would have liked to take some credit for its success, but it started long before he was on the scene. But it was smart of him to invest in the future of his country, rather than cutting it off at the knees as the No Child Left Behind program did to the arts in US schools. As a result of No Child Left Behind's emphasis on test scores, US schools gutted their arts programs by more than half in most states. If Venezuela can find the means to fund music programs, why can't we?

A similar program in the UK is called Youth Music, but the kids learn pop, jazz, and rap—not just the classics. In one depressed district, Morecambe, where there had been territorial gang conflict for years, it was suggested that the kids use rap to express their frustrations and to talk about their situation. A local bricklayer named Jack says, "When I was sixteen, [I wrote] my own songs about my attitude and gun and knife crime, and how to stop it." The neighborhoods eventually declared a kind of truce, though tensions remain—but it's a start.

In Liverpool, Youth Music is associated with the Liverpool Philharmonic and has been adopted by a school called St. Mart of the Angels. Peter Garden, the director of the project, said, "The percentage of children who improved their reading by at least two levels in 2008–9 was 36 percent. For 2009–10, it was 84 percent. The figure for mathematics increased from 35 percent to 75 percent." In Northern Ireland, kids have turned away from joining loyalist or paramilitary groups to play music—the effects of these programs go way beyond music and even beyond improving overall academic achievement.[33]

Statistics like these really put an end to the argument questioning the utility of learning to play music, and they make a strong case for the importance of the arts remaining part of a school curriculum.

Recent programs that nurture creativity don't all focus exclusively on school kids. A program called the Creators Project is funded by Intel, the computer chip manufacturer, and *Vice*, a magazine and media company. Intel provides funding and *Vice* decides who gets it. Their support is sometimes thrown to established artists and musicians to help them manifest or realize a project that otherwise would have been beyond their financial and technical means. I recently saw theatrical pieces by Björk and Karen O that were funded by the Creators Project. They're also seeking out emerging and unknown artists, and their pockets are fairly deep, their support wide-ranging (with projects in China, Buenos Aires, Lyon, and around the Cern atom smasher). Significantly, they are supporting artists and musicians who are working on the fringes of popular culture. So while I might have wondered earlier why Silicon Valley hasn't shown support for the arts, here is a big exception—and they're not funding symphony halls or museums, they're funding live shows in warehouses and in other oddball venues.

THE FUTURE

I have nothing against the music performed in opera houses or much of the art in the spectacular new museums that have been thrown up in the last couple of decades—in fact I like quite a lot of it. The 1 percent are certainly entitled to their tasteful shrines—it's their money after all, and they do invite us to the party sometimes. I wonder, however, if those places and what they represent, along with their healthy budgets, hint at some skewed priorities that will come back to bite us in the ass before too long.

I'm not the only one who believes that future generations will view our present arts budgets with bafflement. The slashing of state and federal budgets for teaching music, dance, theater, and visual arts in grades K–12 will have a profound effect on the financial and creative future of the United States and other countries that are following our example. In California, the number of students involved in music education dropped by half between 1999 and 2004. Participation in music classes, many of which are now no longer available anyway, dropped 85 percent. The other arts have had similar fates, and the humanities have suffered as well.

A study done by the Curb Center at Vanderbilt University (Mike Curb is, among other things, a songwriter and record producer who dropped Frank Zappa and the Velvets from MGM, claiming they advocated drug use!) found that arts majors developed more creative problem-solving skills than students from almost any other area of study. Risk taking, dealing with ambiguities, discovering patterns, and the use of analogy and metaphor are skills that are not just of practical use for artists and musicians. For example, 80 percent of arts students at Vanderbilt say that expressing creativity is part of their courses, while only 3 percent of biology majors and about 13 percent of engineers and business majors do. Creative problem solving is not taught in those other disciplines, but it is an essential survival skill.[34] If one believes, as I do, that creative problem solving can be learned, and is something that can be applied across all disciplines, then we're chopping our children's legs off if we slash the budgets for classes in the arts and humanities. There's no way these kids will be able to compete in the world in which they are growing up.

In his book *Musicophilia*, Oliver Sacks described an interesting experiment conducted by Japanese scientists:

[They] recorded striking changes in the left hemisphere of children who have had only a single year of violin training, compared to children with no training... The implication of all this for early education [in the arts] is clear. Although a teaspoon of Mozart may not make a child a better mathematician, there is little doubt that regular exposure to music, and especially active participation in music, may stimulate development of many different areas of the brain—areas which have to work together to listen to or perform music. For the vast majority of students, music can be every bit as important educationally as reading or writing.[35]

Roger Graef, who has written about the effectiveness of arts programs in UK prisons, believes that violence, like art, is actually a form of expression. Prisons, he says, are therefore ideal arenas for art creation and expression. Art can serve as an outlet for the violent feelings of inmates in a way that does not harm others, and that actually enhances their lives. Making art, Graef writes, "can break the cycle of violence and fear."[36]

He claims that the remedy for violence is an agency that will defeat feelings of impotence. Historically, religion has successfully done this, and the rise of fundamentalism might be viewed as a reaction to increasing feelings of alienation and inconsequentiality around the world. Making music might act as an antidote to those feelings too, as those cultural and music centers in the Brazilian favelas attest. In those UK prisons, the quality of the work is beside the point, as it was in Brazil. And, unlike religion, no one has ever gone to war over music.

However, grant-giving organizations often take the opposite view. Most arts grants focus on the work, rather than on the process that the work comes out of. The product seems to be more important than the effect its production process has. Sadly, Graef learned that it is hard for many of the inmates he worked with to continue making art outside of prison. They find the professional art world elitist and its "posh buildings" intimidating. Without a support system, and with their work being judged by criteria that are foreign to them, they lose the outlet for frustration that they had discovered.

Education advisor Sir Ken Robinson points out that every educational system on the planet was designed to meet the needs of nineteenth-century industrialization. The idea, as Tom Zé implied, was to "manufacture" good workers. What the world needs now are more creative thinkers and doers, more of Zé's defective humanoids. But the educational system hasn't evolved to do that. As Robinson writes:

I've lost track of the number of brilliant people I've met, in all fields, who didn't do well at school. Some did, of course, but others only really succeeded, and found their real talents in the process, once they'd recovered from their education. This is largely because the current systems of public education were never designed to develop everyone's talents. They were intended to promote certain types of ability in the interests of the industrial economies they served.[37]

Canadian composer and music teacher R. Murray Schafer originated the concept of the soundscape. The soundscape, as he defines it, can be thought of as our sonic surroundings and involves the study of how that acoustic environment gives us a sense of place. A soundscape that is out of whack, he says, makes us feel impotent. The soundscape of a bureaucratic office building's lobby tends to make you feel small and insignificant. Schafer's pedagogy begins with trying to create awareness, to help students hear their sonic environment:

What was the last sound you heard before I clapped my hands?
What was the highest sound you heard in the past ten minutes? What was the loudest?
How many airplanes have you heard today?
What was the most interesting sound you heard this morning?
Make a collection of disappearing or lost sounds, sounds that formed part of the sonic environment but can no longer be heard today.

Schafer writes, "For a child of five, art is life and life is art. Experience is a kaleidoscopic and synesthetic experience, but once the child is in school they get separated—art becomes art and life becomes life." He proposes a radical solution: that we abolish all study of the arts in a child's first years at school. This seems counterintuitive to me—isn't that precisely when we're supposed to encourage children's creativity? "In their place," he suggests, "we substitute subjects that encourage sensitivity and expression." He says that the focus should not be on anything specific, but on general awareness of the world around us. This might be admirable, but it seems unlikely that it would be adopted widely.[38]

Funding future creativity is a worthy investment. The dead guys won't write more symphonies. And the output of a creative generation doesn't confine itself to concert houses; it permeates all aspects of a city's life. Creativity is a renewable resource that businesses can and do tap into. By this I don't mean that businesses are looking for painters and composers, but that the habit of creative problem solving translates to any activity we find ourselves engaged in. If the talent and skills are not there, if they're not nurtured, then businesses will be forced to look elsewhere. The arts are good for the economy, and their presence makes for more interesting living as well. Cutting those school arts budgets makes economic recovery harder, not easier. It will leave us with a generation that isn't as used to thinking creatively or in collaboration with others. In the long run there is a greater value for humanity in empowering folks to make and create than there is in teaching them the canon of great works. Nothing against those great works, but maybe they have been prioritized out of proportion to their lasting value. I have discovered many of them at various points in my life, and yes, they have had a profound impact. In my opinion, though, it's more important that someone learn to make music, draw, photograph, write, or create in any form, regardless of the quality, than it is for them to understand and appreciate Picasso, Warhol, or Bill Shakespeare—to say nothing of opera as it is today.

There are some classical works that I do genuinely enjoy, but I never got Bach, Mozart, or Beethoven—and I don't feel any worse for it. There's plenty left to love and enjoy. I have gradually come to appreciate a wide variety of music that didn't have to be forced on me. I resent the implication that I'm less of a musician and a worse person for not appreciating certain works. Sometimes the newest thing on the block is indeed five hundred years old, and sometimes the way forward is through the past—but not always! We certainly don't have to stay back there. By encouraging the creativity of amateurs, rather than telling them that they should passively accept the creativity of designated masters, we help build a social and cultural network that will have profound repercussions.

I know it's not exactly the same as learning the skills involved in mounting a multidisciplinary work like opera, but I would say: show someone three chords on the guitar, show them how to program beats, how to play a keyboard, and if you don't expect virtuosity right away, you might get something moving and affecting. You as a listener, or as a creator, might be touched in a way that is every bit as deep as you would be by something that demands a more complicated skill set. Everyone knows you can make a song with almost nothing, with really limited skills. Beginners can enjoy that, it's a source of instant positive feedback, and they don't feel inadequate because they're not Mozart. I wish I'd learned to play a keyboard, but I gravitated to where my interests (and abilities) took me. I didn't take guitar lessons. Over time (a lot of time) I learned a lot more chords and I began to be able to "hear" harmonies and tonal relationships. And, of course, I learned a lot more grooves over the years, and how to instinctively feel and enjoy them. I *learned* these things; I wasn't born knowing them. But even at first, playing only a few notes, I found I could express something, or at least have fun using my extremely limited means and abilities. When I made something, even something crude, I would momentarily discredit and ignore the nagging feeling that said that if I couldn't match the classical or high-quality model then I was somehow less of an artist. My gut was telling me that what I was doing was just fine.

CHAPTER TEN

Harmonia Mundi

"You are the music, while the music lasts."
—*T.S. Eliot*

So far, we've covered how music is distributed, how it's affected by architecture, and a lot more, but why do we need music? Does it even matter? Where did it come from?

Far from being merely entertainment, music, I would argue, is a part of what makes us human. Its practical value is maybe a little harder to pin down, at least in our present way of thinking, than mathematics or medicine, but many would agree that a life without music, for a hearing person, is a life significantly diminished.

Everything started with a sound. "In the beginning was the Word," the Bible tells us. We are told that it was the *sound* of God's voice that caused the Nothing to become Something. I'm not given to being literal about such things. I doubt that "Word" here means a syllable or an actual utterance. I can more easily picture this "Word," this sonic event, referring to a celestial vibration than to an actual *word*. Maybe we could go a step further and imagine that this ancient metaphor reflects some kind of intuition regarding the Big Bang, which one can view as a kind of really, really big "sound," one that still radiates out from its theoretical beginning and from which was made our world and all the others. If *that* was the "Word" God was shouting, then we're all in agreement. At any rate, it seems significant that

A

B

the chosen metaphor was a word and not a drawing, a text, or even a dance.

Though sound could conceivably be, in this scenario, *the* key to creation, the Big Bang wasn't exactly music. Lots of theories attempt to explain how music first came into being. Some say music originated with the non-verbal sounds mothers make to their children, while others connect music to sounds in nature or animal utterances, or as a means of inducing warriors into a trance state. The musicologist Joseph Jordania suggests that complete silence is often perceived as a sign of danger, so humming and whistling were used to fill those scary empty spaces. The jury is still out on which of these theories is correct, but all agree that music emerged at the same time people did.

The earliest evidence we have of early man actually making music dates back about 45,000 years. Neanderthals and other "cave dwellers" were playing flutes that seem to have been based around what we now call diatonic scales. The diatonic scale is the musical scale familiar to most of us today—seven notes, the eighth note being the octave of the first one. If you play the white notes of a piano from C to C, you are playing a diatonic scale. To the left is a photo of one of these flutes that was found in Divje Babe, in what is now Slovenia.

A Canadian musicologist, Robert Fink, proposes that the notes produced by the holes in this bone flute are the start of a diatonic scale—do, re, mi, fa.[1] Fink suggests that if one imagines an extended version of the flute,[B] then the rest of the diatonic scale we use could be played on it. Not everyone buys this, but there is strong evidence that the Sumerians (c. 3100–2000 BCE) and the Babylonians (c. 2000–1600 BCE) used this same scale. A diatonic scale on cuneiform tablets found in Nippur (present-day Iraq) dates from 2000 BCE. Musical instruments have been found at Mesopotamian burial sites, and pictures of musicians at ceremonies playing lyres, drums, and flutes are on a mural in the Tomb of the Harpists in Egypt that dates to 1200 BCE. The prevalence of relationships and intervals between notes that produce fifths, fourths, and sixths on these instruments correspond to consonant harmonies we still recognize. "Consonant," in this case, means harmonies that are felt to be "stable" and settled, while dissonant harmonies are felt to be unstable, temporary, and "want" to move on to something else. Consonant, according to these discoveries, is what we as humans generally find harmonically comfortable to listen to, and this has led scientists to believe that we might have an innate biological predisposition toward certain musical relationships.

Here is a reproduction of a tablet found in Ugarit, present-day Syria, with the oldest bit of complete written music on it, from 1400 BCE. It is described as a hymn to Nikkal, the goddess of orchards. There are instructions for the singer, and for the accompaniment music to be played on a lyre. Other cuneiform fragments describe how to tune the lyre, which is how we know they were using a diatonic scale. To my surprise, some of these hymns even cite the name of the composer. Already some individuals were recognized as being good at this thing called music.

What did ancient music sound like? Though we can figure out the notes that the flutes and lyres played—we can either play them or reconstruct them—it's a little harder to know what singers sounded like or how their songs were structured. Did the singers holler or whisper? Did they sing with chest tones or whine through their noses? Musicologist Peter van der Merwe suggests that Mesopotamian singers sang with intense but inwardly directed emotion, somewhat like contemporary Assyrian musicians do. They sing as if listening to themselves. It's

a gesture that conveys intensity, and implies that you are communicating with your interior feelings, as if the song were a message from someplace deep inside rather than simply being the manifestation of the ego of the person performing. The implication is that the singer is not so much a performer as a conduit, a vehicle. There's a pretty direct connection between this kind of singing and contemporary flamenco vocalizing. Not much has changed.

There are 9,000-year-old flutes in China that can play scales very similar to these Mesopotamian ones, which begs the question: Did we evolve to prefer certain notes more than others? Have we developed a neurological "ear" that is predisposed to enjoy the structured sounds that humanity has come to call music? Even infants prefer the harmonies we think of as consonant, and they can distinguish different scales. Infants can also hear what are called "relational pitches," which means that you can sing "Happy Birthday" to a baby starting on any note you choose, and if the child knows the song, there's a good chance she will still recognize it. That might not sound so special, but it's actually quite difficult, because the absolute notes will change completely if the singer starts on a different key. The third note in the melody will no longer be A, for example, but what we think of and recognize as a melody will be the same. Machines can't do this yet—they can only compare melodies to an absolute reference. To present-day machines, a song that starts in the key of C is different from one that starts in B, even though the melody might be identical. We have evolved many extremely specialized skills—physical and neurological—that seem to be related to music making. It's something that must be important to our being homo sapiens, and despite cultural differences, musical forms and structures are often shared. We've been asking ourselves why we have this special relationship for a long, long time. What larger patterns in the universe make us gravitate to specific musical relationships and forms?

THE MUSIC OF THE SPHERES

The followers of Pythagoras (around 590 BCE) were called Acousmatics because they listened to his talks while he remained hidden behind a curtain. Maybe this was intended to help them focus on his words rather than on what might have been distracting gestures. Pythagoras surmised that there might be a divine reason behind our tendency to find specific harmonies and note intervals more pleasant to the ear than others. He pointed out that there were mathematical congruencies behind these notes—a phenomenon he first observed when he passed by a blacksmith's shop and noticed that the pings of the various hammers fell along common musical intervals. Why? It was the proportions of the varying weights of the hammers—a twelve-pound hammer and a six-pound hammer produced pings an octave apart. Similarly, a string stopped at 3/4 of its length produces a note that is 1/4 above the octave—the sound of the full-length string. This fourth harmony is extremely common, and we find it pleasant. If the stop is 2/3 the length of the string, then the note is a perfect fifth. A stop at half the length produces a note that is an exact octave higher than the full length of the string. Needless to say, this is somewhat uncanny. Spooky, even. Why should this be?

Pythagoras surmised that the gods generally prefer small numbers such as occur in these fractions, because simplicity is always more profoundly elegant. Pythagoras was a bit of a numbers nut, so the fact that there were mathematic underpinnings to the most common musical harmonies was very exciting for him. It was like unlocking a key to the universe. He further identified three kinds of music: instrumental, human, and celestial. Music played on instruments by mortals was viewed as a pale echo of the "original" celestial music, an idea that seems to presage Plato's shadows-in-the-cave metaphor. The celestial music, the music we attempt to imitate—where the divine harmonies emanate from—actually does exist, Pythagoras said, and this music has its source in the spheres that "hold" the planets. He believed that the planets were attached to revolving crystal spheres (how else could they stay up?), and that each planet, along with its crystal sphere, produced its own unique tone as it whistled through the cosmic ether. Hence the Music of the Spheres. The distances between the spheres (and their planets) were, of course, based on a series of relationships that followed these same "harmonic" and mathematical ratios, or relatively simple combinations of them. So the whole universe, or what was known of it at the time (the stars were thought to lie on these crystal spheres as well), was like a giant mechanical instrument producing a shifting and ever-morphing chord as the spheres creaked through the ether. The implication was that all earthly harmonies—the harmonies of all things, dead and alive, both inside and out—were based on those same ratios.

This idea lingers still. NASA recorded inaudible electromagnetic signals—not even what we would call sound waves—as the probes *Voyager* and *Cassini* passed by a number of planets. Then these signals were processed and converted into sonic vibrations that fell within the range of human hearing. A collection of these sounds was released as an album with the title *Symphony of the Planets*. It's basically a collection of ambient drones—quite nice ones, too, though Mercury is a little scary sounding. One online reviewer of these recordings credits the solar system with being a composer of ambient trance music. "As if creation were performing for you," he wrote.

Not surprisingly, these notes, as Pythagoras conceived them, produced the most divine harmony imaginable—a great cosmic chord that created us and everything else. The sound was so perfect, he said, that ordinary people like you and me couldn't hear it. Pythagoras could hear it, though. It was claimed by his followers that Adam and Eve heard it, too, as God imparted to them the means to hear this perfect chord. Like links in a mystic chain, the Zoroastrians then passed the way of listening down to their disciples. It was said that Moses also heard it when he received the tablets of the ten commandments. According to St. Augustine (around 400 CE), all men would hear this sound just before they died, at which point the secret of the cosmos would be revealed—which is very exciting, although just a little late to be of much use. This secret was passed down through the ages, from prophet to prophet, although at some point, according to Renaissance philosophers, it was lost. Oops.

Pythagoras was convinced that each musical scale, the varieties of that cosmic mode, have profound, specific, and unique effects on people. The Hypophrygian mode is one of the many variations of the diachronic scale where the intervals between notes have been altered. For example, a C scale (all white keys) and a C-minor scale are two different modes. According to Pythagoras, a tune in the Hypophrygian mode could totally sober up a drunk young man. In his day, the power of music was commonly accepted, and there were music-based healing centers throughout Greece. The notes of the basic scale were associated with the Muses, and each tone had its own attributes and temperament. The seven planets that the Greeks could see had associations with the seven vowel sounds of classical Greek, which were also considered sacred. The various names of God were formed out of recombinations of these vowels and harmonies—like Ho Theos, or God, Ho Kurios, or Lord, and Despotes, which means master, and is the root of our word *despot*. The cosmic harmonies informed every aspect of life—our speech, our bodies, and our state of mind. The weather, the cycles of crops, disease and health.

These musical and mathematical correspondences among all things were out there, and the idea was that we needed only to discover them. God, or the gods, put them there, and in the emerging Western tradition, the goal of science and the arts was to decode what the gods had written. The belief that the goal of science is to unearth preexisting patterns forms the basis of much of scientific practice today. Even in the periodic table of the elements, where all the materials that make up our world are ordered according to atomic weight, there are "harmonies." John Newlands, who worked on the table, discovered in 1865 that "at every eighth element a distinct repetition of properties occurs"—a pattern which he called the Law of Octaves.[2] Newlands was ridiculed, and his paper on the subject wasn't accepted. But when his prediction that "missing" elements should therefore exist was later proven to be true, he was recognized as the discoverer of the Periodic Law. "Musical" relationships, it seems, are still viewed as governing the physical world. The Music of the Spheres idea is, in slightly altered form, still with us.

The astronomer and astrologer Johannes Kepler published his book *Harmonices Mundi* in 1619. In it he proposed that it was the Creator who "decorated" the whole world, using mathematical and musical harmonic proportions. The spiritual and the physical are united. In a search for these proportions, Kepler first suggested that the varieties of polyhedral shapes—three-dimensional figures made of pentagons, octagons, etc., and each nested inside a sphere and inside each other—might have guided the Creator's plan.[D]

Kepler wasn't satisfied with its accuracy, so he looked at the musical and mathematical harmonic proportions. He wrote: "The Earth sings Mi, Fa, Mi: so that even from the syllable you may guess that in this home of ours *misery* and *famine* hold sway."[3] His calculations seemed to imply that the orbits of the planets had some wobble in them, and the resulting vibrato was sometimes unsettling and even discordant. This was not good.

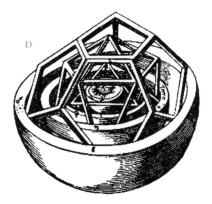

D

However, it did seem that they sometimes fell into perfect harmony—and one of these moments, he believed, was the moment of creation.

On the following page is a simple chart from Stanley's *History of Philosophy*, published in the 1600s, that shows the musical intervals that would naturally occur on an imaginary string stretched from the highest heaven, through Earth, and via the orbits of the various planets (which included the sun in the midst of the others rather than at the center, as that was where we, on Terra, were thought to reside).[E]

The great seventeenth-century alchemist and scientist Robert Fludd made further elaborate renderings. He called the imaginary string the Mundane Monochord. "Mundane" refers to the whole world in this case, not to something banal and ordinary. At the top in his drawing, God's hand is reaching in to "tune" the universe.[F]

In both Fludd and Stanley's view, seven musical modes—which are sort of the equivalent of scales—correspond to the seven planets. Each planetary orbit and its mode had a character, such as saturnine (gloomy) or mercurial (fickle). Each musical key, as it were, was therefore associated with personality traits we might find in our fellow humans. Astrology—the influence of the heavens on our personalities—was in this way being given some "scientific" basis.

This idea of a universe ordered according to musical harmony fell into disrepute and was more or less forgotten for hundreds of years, but recently it has been picked up by, of all people, the movie editor and sound designer Walter Murch. I saw Murch give a talk, and though he did discuss sound in films and his

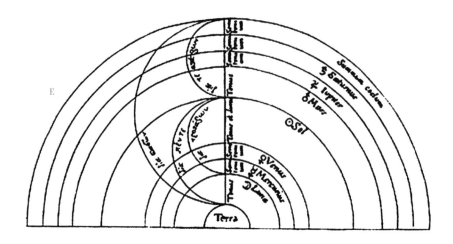

thoughts on editing, what he was really excited about was reviving the idea of cosmic ratios. Murch wondered why Copernicus, who gets credit for proposing the sun-centric solar system, would make such an unintuitive and dangerous statement. A heliocentric system was unintuitive because, from our point of view, it really does seem like the stars and sun revolve around us. It was dangerous, because it was assumed that God made the universe the way the church said he made it—Earth-centric—and to question God's plan and wisdom was heresy. Murch theorized that the explanation might lie in the fact that Copernicus knew about a Greek astronomer named Aristarchos of Samos (c. 310–230 BCE), who had proposed his own sun-centric system. Aristarchos even suggested that the moon revolved around the Earth, but by Copernicus's time, his theories had been forgotten.

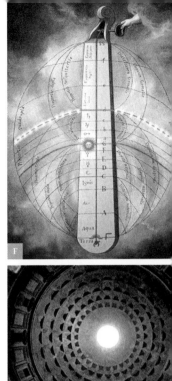

Here is Murch's theory of how Copernicus revived Aristarchos's idea. Copernicus visited Rome after completing his studies, where he surely went to see the dome of the Pantheon, which was one of the wonders of the age.[G] Murch suggests that upon viewing that ceiling, Copernicus put two and two together and sensed that here, in this architecture, was encoded the secret order of the solar system. This sounds very *Da Vinci Code*, but read on.

To the right, Copernicus's sun-centric system.[H] Below it is a superimposition that Murch did, placing Copernicus's solar system over the concentric circles of the Pantheon's dome.[I]

In the sun-centric system, the ratios (the distances between the planetary orbits) are still not absolutely "correct," so we're not in perfect celestial harmony just yet.

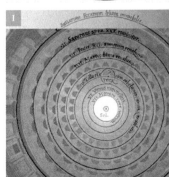

In the 1760s, the director of the Berlin observatory, Johann Daniel Titius, published a paper that contained what came to be known as Bode's Law. It proposed some mathematical formulas and constants that, Titus claimed, not only described where the orbits of the planets were relative to the sun, but also predicted where new planets would be found—and therefore where the next "harmony" should be. Shades of the periodic table! One can predict musical overtones in much the same way.

As you can see in the diagram below, it all worked fine until the discovery of Neptune, which didn't fit the pattern. In 1846, Bode's Law was therefore abruptly abandoned and thrown into the pile of discarded and lost science. Murch said:

> So it seemed more logical (to me) to abandon the Astronomical Unit and just concentrate on the ratios. Once you do that, the formula gets much simpler: it doesn't have to do two things at once. This new formula is not only simpler, but it's also lost its "Earth-centricity." Now you can apply it equally to other orbital systems—the miniature "solar systems" of the moons around Jupiter, Saturn, Uranus, and Neptune, for instance—and you find the same set of ratios cropping up! Underlying all the orbits of these moons and planets, there is a pattern of ratios, like the musical ratios underlying a keyboard. Just as you are restricted to playing certain musical ratios on many instruments, so it seems

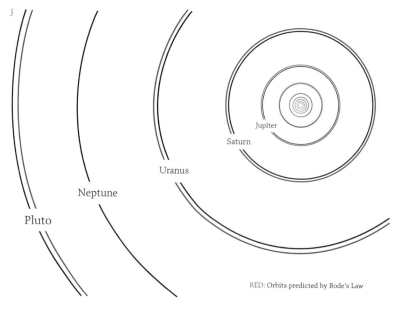

RED: Orbits predicted by Bode's Law

BLACK: Actual average distances of planets

to be with the arrangements of these moons. Some systems "play"—or *occupy*—certain orbits, while others are left blank. By *playing* different orbits these systems generate a variety of chords. Chords we recognize. If I wrote the simplified Bode formula down on a piece of paper and showed it to music theorists, they would ask: "Why are you showing us the formula of the overtone series...?" In other words, Bode's Law gives a series of orbital ratios, which are mathematically identical to the common intervals in musical theory. They're primarily variations on what we call the 7th chord: C, E, G, B flat.[4]

You might say that the universe plays the blues.

We've come back around to Pythagoras and the other Music of the Spheres and universal harmony proponents. Pythagoras's computations were slightly off and didn't quite match true musical ratios. It was Galileo's dad, Vincenzo Galilei, who figured out the formula that generates a musical scale as we know it. The Renaissance architect Leone Battista Alberti said:

[I am] every day more and more convinced of the truth of Pythagoras's saying, that Nature is sure to act consistently... I conclude that the same numbers by means of which the agreement of sounds affect our ears with delight, are the very same which please our eyes and our minds. We shall therefore borrow all our rules for the finishing of our proportions from the musicians... and from those things wherein nature shows herself most excellent and complete.[5]

Alberti went on to develop the formula for perspective in painting—a way of mathematically organizing our vision.

Andrea Palladio, another, rather more famous Renaissance architect, used these same ratios in the buildings that he built in the sixteenth century, which have been emulated all over the world as designed of harmonic visual and spatial relationships that are pleasing to the eye. Jefferson's Monticello, hundreds of museums and monuments all over the world—they all owe their proportions to Palladio, and to the cosmic musical ratios that he and others believed gave structure to all things.

Vitruvius was a Roman engineer and writer (born 70 BCE) whose ideas were revived during the Renaissance, particularly by Daniele Barbaro, who was also Palladio's patron. Vitruvius espoused the ideas of symetria (symmetric objective beauty) and eurythmia (which is more about arrangement, and is subjective and experiential). It was to illustrate a reappraisal of Vitruvius's book *On Architecture* that Leonardo da Vinci drew his famous Vitruvian man (as you can see below, he was somewhat emasculated by NASA) that elucidated the divine proportions of the human body.[K]

Barbaro wrote that what harmony is for the ear, beauty is for the eye, and this was made explicit in Palladio's work. In the Villa Malcontenta (who would give such a name to their house?), there is a room that he describes as the "most beautiful and proportionate," which is musically a major sixth. This room can be subdivided into smaller rooms, which work out to be a fourth and a major third.

THE EAST

In the ancient Far East it was also thought that sound played an essential role in the formation of the universe. In Tantric Buddhism there is a "sonoriferous" ether called the *akasha*, and from that ether flows the primordial vibrations. The *akasha* is self-generative—it didn't come from something else, it made itself. But according to Tantric philosophy, this cosmic sound, which is sometimes referred to as Nāda-Brahman, actually comes from the vibrations that emanate when Shiva and Shakti have sex.[L]

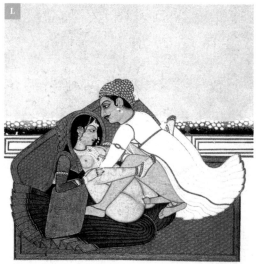

It is referred to as the Cosmic Orgasm, and from it the entire material universe was formed. A little more than a hundred years ago, Madame Blavatsky, who developed a mystical system called Theosophy that was for a while very popular, referred to this Nãda as the "soundless sound" or the "voice of silence." Discreet, silent, true, esoteric, and momentous.

The idea that vibrations permeate everything is indisputable—you don't have to be a Tantric Buddhist or an Acousmatic to accept it. The Venn diagrams that contain spiritualist ideas, religious myths, and what we consider scientific fact do indeed overlap. Molecules vibrate at one hundred times per second, atoms faster than that. These vibrations produce what could be considered sound, albeit sound that we cannot hear. The composer John Cage said:

> Look at this ashtray. It's in a state of vibration. We're sure of that, and the physicist can prove it to us. But we can't hear those vibrations... It would be extremely interesting to place it in a little anechoic chamber and listen to it through a suitable sound system. Object would become process; we would discover... the meaning of nature through the music of objects.[6]

None of these divine or ancient scientific theories really explains the *why* part—why we gravitate to the specific harmonies we do—unless you accept "God made it that way, end of discussion" as an explanation. However, in our world of little faith, we ask for proof.

BIOLOGY AND THE NEUROLOGICAL BASIS FOR MUSIC

The question, then, is not only why do we like the harmonies we do, but also does our enjoyment of music—our ability to find a sequence of sounds emotionally affecting—have some neurological basis? From an evolutionary standpoint, does enjoying music provide any advantage? Is music of any truly practical use, or is it simply baggage that got carried along as we evolved other more obviously useful adaptations? Paleontologists Stephen Jay Gould and Richard Lewontin wrote a paper in 1979 claiming that some of our skills and abilities might be like spandrels—the architectural negative spaces above the curve of the arches of buildings—details that weren't originally designed as autonomous entities, but that came into being as a result of other, more practical elements around them.

The linguist Noam Chomsky proposed that language itself might be an evolutionary spandrel—that the ability to form sentences might not have evolved directly but might be the by-product of some other, more pragmatic evolutionary development. In this view, many of the arts got a free ride along with the development of other, more prosaic qualities and cognitive abilities.

Dale Purves, a professor at Duke University, studied this question with his colleagues David Schwartz and Catherine Howe, and they think they might have some answers. First they describe the lay of the land: pretty much every culture uses notes selected from among the twelve that we typically use. From one A to another A an octave above it, there are usually twelve notes. This is not a scale, but there are twelve available notes, which on a piano would be all the black and white keys in one octave. (Scales are generally a smaller number of notes chosen from within those twelve.) There are billions of possible ways to divide the increments from A to A—yet twelve gives us a good start.

Traditional Chinese music and American folk music usually employ five notes selected from among those twelve to create their scales. Arabic music works within these parameters too. Western classical music uses seven of the twelve available notes (the eighth note of the Western scale is the octave). In 1921, the composer Arnold Schoenberg proposed a system that would "democratize" musical composition. In this twelve-tone music, no note is considered to be more important than any other. That does indeed seem like a fair and democratic approach, yet people often call music using that system dissonant, difficult, and abrasive. Dissonant sounds can be moving—either used for creepy effect or employed to evoke cosmic or dark forces as in the works of Messiaen (his *Quartet for the End of Time*) or Ligeti (his composition *Atmospheres* is used in the trippy stargate sequence of the movie *2001*). But generally these twelve-tone acts of musical liberation were not all that popular, and neither was free jazz, the improvisational equivalent pioneered by Ornette Coleman and John Coltrane in his later years. This "liberation" became, for many composers, a dogma—just a new, fancier kind of prison.

Very few cultures use all twelve available notes. Most adhere to the usual harmonies and scales, but there are some notable exceptions. Javanese gamelan music, produced mainly by orchestras consisting of groups of gong-like instruments, often have scales of five notes, but the five notes are more or less evenly spread between the octave notes. The intervals between the notes are different from a five-note Chinese or folk-music scale. It is surmised that one reason for this is that gongs produce odd, unharmonic resonances and overtones, and to make those aspects of the notes sound pleasant when played together, the Javanese adjusted their scales to account for the unpleasantly interacting harmonics.

Harmonics are the incidental notes that most instruments produce above and below the principal (or "fundamental") note being played. These "ghost" notes are quieter than the main tone, and their number and variety are what give each instrument its characteristic sound. The harmonics of a clarinet (whose vibrations result from a reed and a column of air) are different from those of a violin (whose vibrations result from a vibrating string). Hermann von Helmholtz, the nineteenth-century German physicist, proposed that it is qualities inherent in these harmonics and overtones that lead us to line up notes along common intervals in our scales. He noticed that when notes aren't "in tune," you can hear beating, pulsing, or roughness if they are played at the same time. You can hear this beating if you play the same note on more than one instrument, and if they are ever so slightly different, if they aren't *exactly* the same note, you will hear a throbbing or beating that varies in speed depending on how similar they are. An instrument that is out of tune produces beating tones when the octaves and harmonics don't line up. Helmholtz maintained that we find this beating, which is a physical phenomenon and not just an aesthetic one, disturbing. The natural harmonics of primary notes create their own sets of beats, and only by placing and choosing notes from the intervals that occur among the usual and familiar scales can we resolve and lessen this ugly effect. Like the ancients, he was claiming that we have an inherent attraction to mathematical proportions.

When a scale is made up of fifths and fourths that resonate perfectly and mathematically (this is referred to as "just intonation"), all is well unless you want to change key, to modulate. If, for example, the key (or new scale) you want to move to in your tune begins with the fourth harmony note of your original key—a typical choice for a contemporary pop tune—you will find that the notes on the new key don't quite line up in a pleasant-sounding way anymore—not if you are using this heavenly and mathematical intonation. Some will sound fine, but others will sound markedly sour.

Andreas Werckmeister proposed a workaround for this problem in the mid-1600s. Church organs can't be retuned, so they presented a real difficulty when it came to playing in different keys. He suggested tempering, or slightly adjusting the fifths, and thus all the other notes in a scale, so that one could shift to other keys and it wouldn't sound bad. It was a compromise—the perfect mathematical harmonies based on physical vibrations were now being abandoned ever so slightly so that another kind of math, the math of counterpoint and the excitement of jumping around from key to key, could be given precedence. Werckmeister, like Johannes Kepler, Barbaro, and others at the time, believed in the idea of divine harmonic proportion described in Kepler's *Harmonia Mundi*, even while—or so it seems to me—he was in some ways abandoning, or adjusting, God's work.

Bach was a follower of Werckmeister's innovations and used them to great effect, modulating all over the keyboard in many keys. His music is a veritable tech demo of what this new tuning system could do. We've gotten used to this tempered tuning despite its cosmic imperfections. When we hear music that is played in just intonation today, it sounds out of tune to us, though that could be because the players might insist on changing keys.

Purves's group at Duke discovered that the sonic range that matters and interests us the most is identical to the range of sounds we ourselves produce. Our ears and our brains have evolved to catch subtle nuances mainly within that range, and we hear less, or often nothing at all, outside of it. We can't hear what bats hear, or the sub-harmonic sound that whales use. For the most part, music also falls into the range of what we can hear. Though some of the harmonics that give voices and instruments their characteristic sounds are beyond our hearing range, the effects they produce are not. The part of our brain that analyzes sounds in those musical frequencies that overlap with the sounds we ourselves make is larger and more developed—just as the visual analysis of faces is a specialty of another highly developed part of the brain.

The Purves group also added to this the assumption that periodic sounds—sounds that repeat regularly—are generally indicative of living things, and are therefore more interesting to us. A sound that occurs over and over could be something to be wary of, or it could lead to a friend, or a source of food or water. We can see how these parameters and regions of interest narrow down toward an area of sounds similar to what we call music. Purves surmised that it would seem natural that human speech therefore influenced the evolution of the human auditory system as well as the part of the brain that processes those audio signals. Our vocalizations, and our ability to perceive their nuances and subtlety, co-evolved. It was further assumed that our musical preferences evolved along the way as well. Having thus stated what might seem obvious, the group began its examination to determine if there was indeed any biological rationale for musical scales.

The group recorded ten-to-twenty-second sentences by six hundred speakers of English and other languages (Mandarin, notably) and broke those into 100,000-sound segments. Then they digitally eliminated from those recordings all the elements of speech that are unique to various cultures. They performed a kind of language and culture extraction—they sucked all of it right out, leaving only the sounds that are common to us all. It turns out that, sonically, much of the material that was irrelevant to their study were the consonants we use as part of our languages—the sounds we make with our lips, tongues, and teeth. This left only the vowel sounds, which are made with our vocal cords, as the pitched vocal sounds that are common among humanity. (No consonants are made using the vocal cords.)

They eliminated all the S sounds, the percussive sounds from the P's, and the clicks from the K's. They proposed that they would be left with universal tones and notes in common, having stripped away enough extraneous information so that everyone's utterances would now be some kind of proto-singing—the vocal melodies that are imbedded in talking. These notes, the ones we sing when we talk, were then plotted on a graph representing how often each note occurred, and sure enough, the peaks—the loudest and most prominent notes—pretty much all fell along the twelve notes of the chromatic scale.

In speech (and normal singing) these notes or tones are further modified by our tongues and palates to produce a variety of particular harmonics and overtones. A pinched sound, an open sound. The folds in the vocal cords produce characteristic overtones, too; these and the others are what help identify the sounds we make as recognizably human, as well as contributing to how each individual's voice sounds. When the Duke group investigated what these overtones and harmonics were, they found that these additional pitches fell in line with what we think of as pleasing "musical" harmonies. "Seventy percent… were bang on musical intervals," he continued. All the major harmonic intervals were represented: octaves, fifths, fourths, major thirds, and a major sixth. "There's a biological basis for music, and that biological basis is the similarity between music and speech," said Purves. "That's the reason we like music. Music is far more complex than [the ratios of] Pythagoras. The reason doesn't have to do with mathematics, it has to do with biology."[7]

I might temper this a little bit by saying that the harmonics our palates and vocal cords create might come into prominence because, like Archimedes's vibrating string, any sound-producing object tends to privilege that hierarchy of pitches. That math applies to our bodies and vocal cords as well as strings, though Purves would seem to have a point when he says we have tuned our mental radios to the pitches and overtones that we produce in both speech and music.

MUSIC AND EMOTION

Purves took his interpretation of the data his team gathered one step further. In a 2009 study, they attempted to see if happy (excited, as they call it) speech results in vowels whose pitches tend to fall along major scales, while sad (subdued) speech produces notes that tend to fall along minor scales. Bold statement! I would have thought that such major/minor emotional connotations must be culturally determined, given the variety of music around the world. I remember during one tour, when I was playing music that incorporated a lot of Latin rhythms, some (mainly Anglo-Saxon) audiences and critics thought it was all happy music because of the lively rhythms. (There may also have been an insinuation that the music was therefore more lightweight, but we'll leave that bias aside.) Many of the songs I was singing were in minor keys, and to me they had a slightly melancholy vibe—albeit offset by those lively syncopated rhythms. Did the "happiness" of the rhythms override the melancholy melodies for those particular listeners? Apparently so, as many of the lyrics of salsa and flamenco songs, for example, are tragic.

This wasn't the first time this major/happy, minor/sad correspondence had been proposed. According to the science writer Philip Ball, when it was pointed out to musicologist Deryck Cooke that Slavic and much Spanish music use minor keys for happy music, he claimed that their lives were so hard that they didn't really know what happiness was anyway.

In 1999, musical psychologists Balkwill and Thompson conducted an experiment at York University that attempted to test how culturally specific these emotional cues might be. They asked Western listeners to evaluate Navajo and Hindustani music and say whether it was happy or sad—and the results were pretty accurate. However, as Ball points out, there were other clues, like tempo and timbre, that could have been giveaways. He also says that prior to the Renaissance in Europe there was no connection between sadness and minor keys—implying that cultural factors can override what might be somewhat weak, though real, biological correlations.

It does seem likely that we would have evolved to be able to encode emotional information into our speech in non-verbal ways. We can instantly tell from the tone of someone's voice whether he or she is angry, happy, sad, or putting up a front. A lot of the information we get comes from emphasized pitches (which might imply minor or major scales), spoken "melodies," and the harmonics and timbre of the voice. We get emotional clues from these qualities just as much as from the words spoken. That those vocal sounds might correspond to musical scales and intervals, and that we might have developed melodies that have roots in those speaking variations, doesn't seem much of a leap.

YOU FEEL ME?

In a UCLA study, neurologists Istvan Molnar-Szakacs and Katie Overy watched brain scans to see which neurons fired while people and monkeys observed other people and monkeys perform specific actions or experience specific emotions. They determined that a set of neurons in the observer "mirrors" what they saw happening in the observed. If you are watching an athlete, for example, the neurons that are associated with the same muscles the athlete is using will fire. Our muscles don't move, and sadly there's no virtual workout or health benefit from watching other people exert themselves, but the neurons do act as if we are mimicking the observed. This mirror effect goes for emotional signals as well. When we see someone frown or smile, the neurons associated with those facial muscles will fire. But—and here's the significant part—the emotional neurons associated with those feelings fire as well. Visual and auditory clues trigger empathetic neurons. Corny but true: if you smile you *will* make other people happy. We feel what the other is feeling—maybe not as strongly, or as profoundly—but empathy seems to be built into our neurology. It has been proposed that this shared representation (as neuroscientists call it) is essential for *any* type of communication. The ability to experience a shared representation is how we know what the other person is getting at, what they're talking about. If we didn't have this means of sharing common references, we wouldn't be able to communicate.

It's sort of stupidly obvious—of course we feel what others are feeling, at least to some extent. If we didn't, then why would we ever cry at the movies or smile when we heard a love song? The border between what you feel and what I feel is porous. That we are social animals is deeply ingrained and makes us what we are. We think of ourselves as individuals, but to some extent we are not; our very cells are joined to the group by these evolved empathic reactions to others. This mirroring isn't just emotional, it's social and physical too. When someone gets hurt we "feel" their pain, though we don't collapse in agony. And when a singer throws back his head and lets loose, we understand that as well. We have an interior image of what he is going through when his body assumes that shape.

We anthropomorphize abstract sounds, too. We can read emotions when we hear someone's footsteps. Simple feelings—sadness, happiness, and anger—are pretty easily detected. Footsteps might seem an obvious example, but it shows that we connect all sorts of sounds to our assumptions about what emotion, feeling, or sensation generated that sound.

The UCLA study proposed that our appreciation and feeling for music is deeply dependent on mirror neurons. When you watch, or even just hear, someone play an instrument, the neurons associated with the muscles required to play that instrument fire. Listening to a piano, we "feel" those hand and arm movements, and as any air guitarist will tell you, when you hear or see a scorching solo, you are "playing" it too. Do you have to know how to play the piano to be able to mirror a piano player? Dr. Edward W. Large at Florida Atlantic University scanned the brains of people with and without music experience as they listened to Chopin. As you might guess, the mirror neuron system lit up in the musicians who were tested, but somewhat surprisingly, they flashed in non-musicians as well. So playing air guitar isn't as weird as it sometimes seems. The UCLA group contends that *all* of our means of communication—auditory, musical, linguistic, visual—have motor and muscular activities at their root. By reading and intuiting the intentions behind those motor activities, we connect with the underlying emotions. Our physical state and our emotional state are inseparable—by perceiving one, an observer can deduce the other.

People dance to music as well, and neurological mirroring might explain why hearing rhythmic music inspires us to move, and to move in very specific ways. Music, more than many of the arts, triggers a whole host of neurons. Multiple regions of the brain fire upon hearing music: muscular, auditory, visual, linguistic. That's why some folks who have completely lost their language abilities can still articulate a text when it is sung. Oliver Sacks wrote about a brain-damaged man who discovered that he could sing his way through his mundane daily routines, and only by doing so could he remember how to complete simple tasks like getting dressed. Melodic Intonation Therapy is the name for a group of therapeutic techniques that were based on this discovery.

Mirror neurons are also predictive. When we observe an action, posture, gesture, or a facial expression, we have a good idea, based on our past experience, what is coming next. Some on the Asperger spectrum might not intuit all those meanings as easily as others, and I'm sure I'm not alone in having been accused of missing what friends thought were obvious cues or signals. But most folks catch at least a large percentage of them. Maybe our innate love of narrative has some predictive, neurological basis; we have developed the ability to be able to feel where a story might be going. Ditto with a melody. We might sense the emotionally resonant rise and fall of a melody, a repetition, a musical build, and we have expectations, based on experience, about where those actions are leading—expectations that will be confirmed or slightly redirected depending on the composer or performer. As cognitive scientist Daniel Levitin points out, too much confirmation—when something happens exactly as it did before—causes us to get bored and to tune out. Little variations keep us alert, as well as serving to draw attention to musical moments that are critical to the narrative.

These emotional connections might help explain why music has such a profound effect on our psychological well-being. We can use music (or, for better or worse, others can use it) to regulate our emotions. We can pump ourselves (or others) up, or calm others (or ourselves) down. We can use music to help integrate ourselves with a team, to act in concord with a group. Music is social glue—it holds families, nations, cultures, and communities together. But it can tear them apart as well. As much as music sometimes seems to be a force for good, it can be harnessed to swell nationalistic pride and stoke belligerent warmongering, too. Beyond these applications for communities and nations, it's also a cosmic telegraph that links us to a world beyond ourselves, to an invisible realm of spirits, gods, and maybe even to the world of the dead. It can make us physically well, or horribly ill. It does so many things to us that one can't simply say, as many do, "Oh, I love all kinds of music." Really? But some forms of music are diametrically opposed to one another! You can't love them *all*. Not all the time, anyway.

MUSIC AND RITUAL

Music features in most religious and social ceremonies around the world. Ethnomusicologist Alan P. Merriam points out that social organization is marked at almost every point in the lives of communities by song—birth songs, lullabies, naming songs, toilet-training songs (I want to hear those!), puberty songs, greeting songs, love songs, marriage songs, clan songs, funeral songs. A Sia Indian who lives in a pueblo in northern New Mexico said, "My friend, without songs you cannot do anything." Without music, the social fabric itself would be rent, and the links between us would crumble.

Ritualistic music has to be repeated in the same way, in more or less identical circumstances every time that ritual is performed. If you get it right, you are, it is assumed, in accordance with the patterns and order of the universe, but woe unto you if you screw it up. According to Hindu scripture, the inaccurate singing of a raga can be fatal to the singer. Apache shamans ran the same risk if they sang off-key. In Polynesia, a careless performer might be executed. In the context of a ritual, there is no concept of an "original" creation of a piece of music, a composer, or a first performance. Such music is thought to have always been there, that it exists outside history, like a myth. Our task as performers and participants is simply to keep it alive. In this sense, music and the rituals it is part of keep the world going.

The urge to notate music, especially music that was going to be used in rituals, emerged naturally from a need to get it absolutely right before performing for the gods—the music being played had to be correct, and the same each time. Written music is thus a useful means of maintaining continuity, but it can also stifle change and innovation. The strict ordering of music was originally a by-product of theocratic and even political control. Written notation is fairly accurate, but it's also imperfect; it's not an exact "recording" of a piece of music. Lots of expressive, textural, and emotional nuances are lost with any kind of notation—they simply are not transcribable. However, as long as the written symbols and notes are accompanied by oral instruction and some modeling and physical demonstrations, one can imagine that this ritual music would stay the same and get passed on largely intact. It's presumed to be healing; spiritual and social agency would be maintained. But if that instructional thread gets broken, if all that's left is the written music, then there will be a lot of guesswork involved, and what gets passed down might bear little resemblance to the original. This inaccuracy isn't all that bad for music, but it's not good for serving the interests of the powers that be. For all we know, the sound of a performance of Mozart's music in his time might be somewhat intolerable to our own ears—we can play the same notes, but we have modernized his pieces and many other musical forms so that they are palatable to contemporary sensibilities. Even the instruments themselves have changed—and in many ways that is what has allowed the music to stay alive and somewhat popular. Similarly, moving liturgical music away from its original Latin—a language almost no one understands anymore—diminishes some of its power and mystery. The Church inevitably loses some of its deep cosmic power when the hymns are written in languages everyone speaks.

Penelope Gouk of the University of Manchester wrote a wonderful essay called "Raising Spirits and Restoring Souls: Early Modern Medical Explanations for Music's Effects." By "early modern," she means the late seventeenth century. At that time, a more modern, scientific conception of the universe was beginning to take hold. The scientific method, with its experiments and proofs, had—or so they claimed—no place for the Music of the Spheres and ethereal harmonic spirits. Music was now to be explained by science; it was a symptom of something greater, something scientific that would describe how the physical world works. Music was no longer viewed as the motor that drives everything. It was the physics of the universe that drove music. The universe was no longer enchanted, and music's all-powerful place was usurped by science.

Those religious rituals that had provided a reason for music to be written down in the first place began to be looked down on, too. The Protestant ethic and the Enlightenment viewed ritual—both social and religious—as superfluous. A lot of rituals were therefore tossed out, and much music went with them. But people like and even need rituals. Humanity's unmet needs demanded satisfaction, and people eventually found an outlet in newly emerging secular and social rituals that also involved music. The first public concert was in London in 1672. It was organized by a composer and violinist named John Banister shortly after he was fired from the royal band. The price was one shilling, and the audience could make requests. Who could say that music performances—in opera halls, cabaret bars, rock clubs, and outdoor festivals—are not rituals? They all have their own very special sets of prescribed behaviors associated with them, they heal and consecrate community bonds. The ritual was preserved under another name.

VISUAL CULTURE VS. ACOUSTIC CULTURE

Marshall McLuhan famously proposed that after the Enlightenment and the Scientific Revolution, we shifted from an acoustic culture to a visual one. He said that in acoustic culture, the world, like sound, is all around you, and comes at you from all directions at once. It is multilayered and non-hierarchical; it has no center or focal point. Visual culture has perspective—a vanishing point, a direction. In visual culture an image is in one very specific fixed spot: it's in front of you. It isn't everywhere at once.

McLuhan claims that our visual sense began to get increasingly bombarded by all the stuff we were producing. It began to take precedence over our auditory sense, and he said that the way we think and view the world changed as a result. In an acoustic universe one senses essence, whereas in a visual universe one sees categories and hierarchies. He claims that in a visual universe one begins to think in a linear fashion, one thing following another along a timeline, rather than everything existing right now, everywhere, in the moment. By blocking your sight, a wall can erase the existence of a man shouting on the other side, but you can hear things happening all around you—left, right, front, and back—even things that are happening behind the wall, like that shouting man. We tend to downplay the influence of some of our senses, especially our sense of smell, partly because it can work on us subconsciously and partly because we don't have the words to describe the myriad smells that affect us every day.

The way we imagine what our senses do is affected by our cultural biases as well as by the way our language limits our perception. What we refer to simply as the sense of touch actually includes separate sensors for vibration, texture, temperature, and movement—each of which could have qualified as a separate sense, should our culture have deemed them important. The Hausa in Africa identify only two senses: seeing and experiencing. The experiencing sense includes intuition (why don't we include that as a sense?), emotion, smell, touch, and hearing. The Ivilik Inuit, who live in northeast Labrador, don't think of space in visual terms the way we do (possibly because their visual environment is almost devoid of features and landmarks); they think of space by referencing their other senses.

I read a short piece in the *New York Times* recently about a nine-year-old named Matthew Whitaker who was born twenty-three weeks premature, weighing just under two pounds. He has never been able to see. Every Saturday, he travels to New York from his home in Hackensack, New Jersey, for a full day of music lessons. He plays seven instruments.

"He hears everything as music," said his father, Moses Whitaker. "The fax machine sounds like an A. The copy machine is a B flat. The jackhammers are making the drum beats that he likes." When the subway rumbles, Matthew taps his cane on the ground to re-create the noise. He hums along with the city—the fast cars and fast talkers. When asked to describe New York, he stands and pivots a full 360 degrees, pointing his fingers in front of him. "New York City is a circle of sounds," he says. "There is music everywhere. Everybody has a smile on their face. It's musical, it's dark and so beautiful."[8]

What Matthew describes is a kind of re-enchantment of the world. Of course those magical and unexplainable parts of the world didn't just go away; as both Freud and Jung argued, they burrowed into our unconscious, knocking around in there and affecting everything we do, and they emerge from time to time in different forms. This might happen via urban myths, goth-inspired fashion shoots, folk tales, horror movies, Japanese anime monsters, experimental music, or the power of pop songs and the somewhat theatrical and ritualized ways that singers perform them. We're fascinated and drawn to stuff that science can't explain—the transcendent, the uncanny, things that affect us without words—and music both touches on and emanates from those mysteries. It reconnects us to that lost time of enchantment.

I think that this semi-mystical sense of the world has also begun to reemerge explicitly as music over the last fifty years or so. A lot of post-war musicians and composers began to think of music in completely new, or maybe in completely old, ways. John Cage is maybe the most famous of them. He likened his view of music to what was then contemporary architecture. Those modern buildings and houses had lots of massive glass walls and windows, and in Cage's view this meant that the outside world was being allowed in, was being considered part and parcel of the architecture, instead of being shut out. Compartmentalization, the difference between inside and outside, between the environment and oneself, was breaking down. Art, too, was being made of junk from the street—Cage's friends Jasper Johns and Robert Rauschenberg were making art out of everyday stuff, as did Duchamp before them. Couldn't music, Cage reasoned, be similarly inclusive? He answered the question in a fairly literal way—by including street sounds, speech, accidents, and thumps in his compositions. This might not have been what Pythagoras had in mind, but still, Cage was inviting the universe in.

Erik Satie might have been one of the earliest to imagine that music could be something more than what it had been relegated to in Western culture. "We must bring about a music which is like furniture, a music which will be part of the noises of the environment... softening the noises of the knives and forks, not dominating them, not imposing itself."[9] He wrote some pieces that he referred to as furniture music, which weren't exactly the proto-ambient music you might imagine, but they're pleasant, if fairly repetitious, and soon, as he hoped, one begins to ignore them. This was a radical idea—that you would write music with the idea that some of it might *not* be heard. But things went further than that.

Bing Muscio (his real name!) of the Muzak corporation said that the music his company produced should be *heard* but not *listened to*. At one point, Muzak was the largest music network in the world. It had at least 100 million listeners—or non-listeners, if you prefer. Though we don't have traditional Muzak to complain about anymore, its concept was ingenious. Its inventors noted that the efficiency experts who had insinuated themselves into the American workplace were concerned that workers were alert at some points in their work day and, typically, had an energy slump in the mid-to-late afternoon. The bosses wanted a flat graph—constant and efficient workflow all day long. This brings us back to Ken Robinson and Tom Zé's ideas of industrial capitalism as a producer of human machines. The technologists at Muzak thought they had a solution to this productivity problem: they would smooth out those curves using music. Calm music would be played during energetic hours, and slightly more energetic music was programmed later to pull workers out of a slump. People believed it worked.

Rather than licensing existing recordings to play in shops and workplaces that subscribed to their service, as is usually done now, Muzak hired musicians to replay familiar songs and instrumental pieces in ways so that the music intentionally *wouldn't be listened to*. The dynamics (the changes in volume level), and even the higher and lower pitches, were ironed out. It seemed as if Muzak had sucked the soul out of the songs, but in fact they had created something entirely new, something close to what Satie imagined: furniture music, music that was clearly a useful and (to their subscribers) functional part of the environment, there to induce calm and tranquility in their shops and offices. Why is it that Satie's compositions, Brian Eno's ambient music, or the minimal spaced-out work of Morton Feldman all seem fairly cool, while Muzak is deemed abhorrent? Is it simply because Muzak alters songs that are already familiar to everyone? I think it's something else. The problem is that this music is intended to dull your awareness, like being force-fed tranquilizers. Of course, not everyone objected—Annunzio Paulo Montovani recorded a series of lush, string-heavy albums billed as "beautiful music," and he was the first artist to sell a million stereo records.

The concept of a musical soporific doesn't work across the board, though. Not every activity is improved by adding a soundtrack. I can't listen to music while I write this, though I have friends who have music playing constantly in their studios while they paint, do Photoshop work, or design web pages. But my attention is always drawn to music. One recent study claims that analytical work is hindered by music, while creative work can get a boost. I guess it depends on the creative work, and on what kind of music you're talking about.

NO MUSIC

In 1969, UNESCO passed a resolution outlining a human right that doesn't get talked about much—the right to silence. I think they're referring to what happens if a noisy factory gets built beside your house, or a shooting range, or if a disco opens downstairs. They don't mean you can demand that a restaurant turn off the classic rock tunes they're playing, or that you can muzzle the guy next to you on the train yelling into his cell phone. It's a nice thought, though—despite our innate dread of absolute silence, we should have the right to take an occasional aural break, to experience, however briefly, a moment or two of sonic fresh air. To have a meditative moment, a head-clearing space, is a nice idea for a human right.

Cage wrote a book called, somewhat ironically, *Silence*. Ironic because he was increasingly becoming notorious for noise and chaos in his compositions. He once claimed that silence doesn't exist for us. In a quest to experience it, he went into an anechoic chamber at Bell Labs, which was a room isolated from all outside sounds, with walls designed to inhibit the reflection of sounds. A dead space, acoustically. After a few moments he heard a thumping and whooshing, and was informed those sounds were his own heartbeat and the sound of his blood rushing through his veins and arteries. They were louder than he might have expected, but okay. After a while, he heard another sound, a high whine, and was informed that this was his nervous system. He realized then that for human beings there was no such thing as true silence, and this anecdote became a way of explaining that he decided that rather than fighting to shut out the sounds of the world, to compartmentalize music as something outside of the noisy, uncontrollable world of sounds, he'd let them in: "Let sounds be themselves rather than vehicles for manmade theories or expressions of human sentiments."[10] Conceptually at least, the entire world now became music.

Others used length and duration to create music that more closely resembled phenomena in the world. In the mid-1980s, Morton Feldman wrote a string quartet that lasts six hours. "My whole generation was hung up on the twenty- to twenty-five-minute piece. It was our clock. We all got to know it, and how to handle it... Before my pieces were like objects; now they're like evolving things."[11] Music, in this way of thinking, became a space you inhabited rather than a discrete object. There's a similarity here to the Chinese musical tradition that sees each tone as a musical entity in itself. This is a very different approach from the classical Western view, which says that music is about relationships between pitches and notes rather than about the sound of the notes themselves. Chinese composer Chou Wen-chung wrote an essay in 1971 in which he seems to agree when McLuhan says that in the West, *how* things are organized is more important than *what* those things are. Newer Western composers seem to be moving toward some meeting place in the middle; their compositions ask us to see music and notes as form, as things, as an environment and a place of deep listening. In a way this is reminiscent of the cosmic monochord. They have heightened their work by making very little happen—nothing goes on or changes, often for very long periods of time. The repetition and stasis force you—if you don't turn off your stereo or leave the perfomance—to sink deeper into the piece. It becomes a part of your surroundings, or similar to a natural sound like waves or wind. Things change just like they do in the natural world, but very slowly.

In 1977, composer Alvin Lucier made a piece using one string—a monochord. By listening and focusing on different parts of it as it vibrated, one could hear a whole range of sounds when these overtones were amplified via microphonic pickups. Like Lucier, composer Ellen Fullman also works with long strung wires as her instruments, turning the entire interior of a building into an instrument by running the "strings" from one side to the other. As with Lucier's piece, she lets the natural overtones determine what the mode or scale will be.

In 2005, I, too, turned a building into an instrument, by using an old pump organ's keys essentially as a set of switches that activated machines clamped to various parts of a big old industrial space. Motors would vibrate girders, which would resonate according to their length. Little hammers would strike hollow cast-iron columns, and they'd act like xylophones or gongs. Skinny air tubes would blow into the plumbing, which would become like lovely resonant alto flutes. You'd think it would be noisy and "industrial," but it was actually quite musical. The general public was invited to play the building via this contraption. Everyone got a chance to sit at the organ and do whatever they wanted.

Was this a piece of music? A composition? Who knows? What was more important to me was that this device democratized music. Given that this wasn't an instrument on which anyone could be a virtuoso, the playing field was leveled. Kids who played it were technically as good as trained and experienced composers, and even as good as the musicians who sometimes sat at the thing, and *knew* it, instinctively. The kids' usual fear and trepidation about playing an unfamiliar instrument in front of others vanished. Like Lucier's wire and Fullman's strings, there was no composition involved in the creation of this music—the music was absolutely determined by its environment and by the players. A lot of this cosmic music has no beginning and no end. It's music that proposes that it exists, like myriad other elements that surround us, as a constant element in the world, rather than as a finite recording or performance.

Last year, I saw a performance by composer John Luther Adams. It took place at the cavernous Sixty-seventh Street Armory in Manhattan and featured, for more than an hour, at least sixty percussionists playing mallet instruments like xylophones and wind-effect machines. There was a score, of sorts. I looked at one that was resting on a music stand and saw that it consisted of a series of short, unconnected two- or three-note phrases. The idea was to play a phrase, not necessarily in unison with the other players, and then gradually the players would move on to the next phase. One by one the players would begin playing the next group of notes on their charts on whatever instrument it was written for. And so on, until everyone reached the end, which was when everyone had exhausted all the little parts. It took about an hour. The result was textural, a landscape, and not melodic. A wash of one kind of sound would surround you, its nature specific to whatever instruments were being played, and then slowly the sound environment would segue into a new texture, as players here and there decided to move on. The audience was free to wander around, and the players were spread all over—there was no "stage," and therefore no central focus. I'd compare the experience to watching weather, to seeing clouds build up on the horizon, come closer, and gradually grow darker, take on an ominous texture, and then burst, releasing a torrent of water, and then just as quickly they would move on and the sky would become clear again. It wasn't like Cage, but it was also a way of sensing and experiencing that the world is music, a composition of sorts, and not a predetermined one.

In the sixties, composer Terry Riley used to give all-night concerts in which he'd create sonic environments by improvising (within strict parameters) to tape loops. The audiences would often bring sleeping bags and doze through parts of the "concert." (Shades of Bing Muscio and Satie with their ignorable music.) When Riley needed a bathroom break, he'd let the loops continue without him. Rhys Chatham and Glenn Branca created similar soundscapes for massed guitars—wonderful experiences that evoke the thrum of a highway overpass or a steel foundry. In 2006, I saw the band SunnO))), who theatricalized this experience—they played a concert in a former church. Their music consists of monstrously loud drones that swell and roll over the audience while the performers stand with their guitars in front of a wall of stacked guitar amps, dressed as a group of hooded Druids. There are no drums and no songs, not as we know them. Ritual was back or maybe it never went away. The sound of SunnO))) is amazing—the beautiful dark side of ambience.

SELF-ORGANIZING MUSIC

Maybe there's a logical end to the path I'm going down here. If music is inherent in all things and places, then why not let music play itself? The composer, in the traditional sense, might no longer be necessary. Let the planets and spheres spin. Musician Bernie Krause has just come out with a book about "biophony"—the world of music and sounds made by animals, insects, and the nonhuman environment. Music made by self-organizing systems means that anyone or anything can make it, and anyone can walk away from it. Cage said the contemporary composer "resembles the maker of a camera who allows someone else to take the picture."[12] That's sort of the elimination of authorship, at least in the accepted sense. He felt that traditional music, with its scores that instruct which note should be played and when, are not reflections of the processes and algorithms that activate and create the world around us. The world indeed offers us restricted possibilities and opportunities, but there are always options and more than one way for things to turn out. He and others wondered if maybe music might partake of this emergent process.

A small device made in China takes this idea one step further. The Buddha Machine is a music player that uses random algorithms to organize a series of soothing tones and thereby create never-ending, non-repeating melodies. The programmer who made the device and organized its sounds replaces the composer, effectively leaving no performer. The composer, the instrument, and the performer are all one machine. These are not very sophisticated devices, though one can envision a day when all types of music might be machine-generated. The basic, commonly used patterns that occur in various genres could become the algorithms that guide the manufacture of sounds. One might view much of corporate pop and hip-hop as being machine-made—their formulas are well established, and one need only choose from a variety of available hooks and beats, and an endless recombinant stream of radio-friendly music emerges. Though this industrial approach is often frowned on, its machine-made nature could just as well be a compliment—it returns musical authorship to the ether. All these developments imply that we've come full circle: we've returned to the idea that our universe might be permeated with music.

I welcome the liberation of music from the prison of melody, rigid structure, and harmony. Why not? But I also listen to music that does adhere to those guidelines. Listening to the Music of the Spheres might be glorious, but I crave a concise song now and then, a narrative or a snapshot more than a whole universe. I can enjoy a movie or read a book in which nothing much happens, but I'm deeply conservative as well—if a song establishes itself within the pop genre, then I listen with certain expectations. I can become bored more easily by a pop song that doesn't play by its own rules than by a contemporary composition that is repetitive and static. I like a good story and I also like staring at the sea—do I have to choose between the two?

CHEESECAKE!

As part of my book tour last year, I spoke onstage in Boston with cognitive scientist Steven Pinker, the man who had referred to music as "auditory cheesecake." Maybe I can paraphrase what he meant by that: he suggests that cheesecake is pleasurable because of the human propensity for liking sweet and fatty flavors, which at an earlier point in our evolution were good for us, much sought after, and harder to come by. Music, he suggests, is attractive to humans because several adaptations have combined to make our brains receptive to its qualities. Music synthesizes different, evolutionarily evocative stimuli, but it may not, he suggests, be something that we have evolved to like or enjoy for its own sake, since it's not clear how a specific taste for music would have caused our ancestors to have more surviving children (any more than a specific taste for cheesecake could have had that effect). It's the evolutionary version of spandrels—a concept proposed by Gould and Lewontin that I mentioned earlier in this chapter, and illustrated below.

Pinker refers to the arts in general as machines for refining and heightening stimuli in our brains. Music synthesizes different, long-evolved stimuli, but it is not, he suggests, something we have evolved to like or enjoy for its own sake. Like cheesecake. Pinker mused in an email to me as we were planning our conversation, "I wonder whether music might be innate, not as a self-contained mental organ but rather as a consequence of the way that language, rhythm, emotion, and acoustic analysis are packed into the brain."

What are these adaptations and agreeable stimuli that Pinker thinks music has latched on to?

Social status is one. Like many other arts, being affiliated with certain kinds of music might give one a boost in social standing. That might mean the status conferred in being an opera aficionado, but it could just as well mean someone who is aware of all the references dropped in the latest hip-hop mixtape. This of course depends on whose acceptance means something significant to you. It's easy to see how gaining acceptance into a group might be an adaptation that would have evolved a long time ago—before there was opera or hip-hop. It is, in this view, the partaking of group membership that gives more pleasure than the music itself. We think we like the music, but what we really like is the company it puts us in. The fact that this argument degrades music into a mere membership badge, and that the qualities of the music itself seem irrelevant, seems a bit hard to swallow, but maybe coupled with the following it becomes a little less crazy sounding.

There is another adaptive tendency linked to music that is mentioned in the book *Keeping Together in Time: Dance and Drill in Human History*. William McNeill, the author, proposes that "muscular bonding" is something that dance, military drill, and music all have in common. When we move, perform, or play music in unison, we lose ourselves in a way that is psychologically pleasurable. This even happens when one isn't participating—when one listens to music or watches dance. Maybe that's due to the mirror neuron phenomena I mentioned earlier.

In sync we become less individual and more part of a group. Our differences—personal, political, physical—become less significant and we can (or feel like we can) do things as a group that we could never do as individuals. As participants, when we act in unison we feel we're now affecting a superorganism—a very heady sensation. It seems we have evolved a neurological sense that rewards this syncing propensity by triggering a pleasurable feeling when it happens.

Obviously, this adaptation has great uses for large military troops or for small hunting groups, as well as for a group of dancers or even for a social agency working toward a cause. But, as Pinker says, this adaptation has also, in his view, been usurped by music. Music—played or enjoyed—physically brings us together to the extent that even our physiological processes come into sync; our heartbeats and breathing begin to align when we are all involved in the same piece of music. McNeill goes further and proposes that partaking in the adaptations of music and dance may have been essential in the process that makes us the social animals that we are. In his view, we don't dance because we're human as much as we are human because we dance.

An associate of Pinker's, Adena Schachner, thinks that there is an unexpected neurological correlation between the ability to mimic sounds and an innate sense of rhythm—a sense that McNeill thinks we find very socially and psychologically seductive. Schachner says that most animals can produce only a small repertoire of barks and calls, though it's entirely possible that their vocal apparatus could physically do more. However, other animals, like the cockatiel and some elephants, can also hear, imitate, and learn new sounds. Only animals with this ability, Schachner says, can respond to rhythms in music. So maybe the part of the brain that allows one to analyze a sound and then mimic it is the same part that can sense and physically respond to a rhythm. We apparently seek and identify rhythms for good reasons; repetitive sound more than likely implies that an animal, person, or natural phenomenon that created it is close enough to warrant attention.

In a related area, Pinker suggests that music also partakes of an innate tendency for humans to seek all kinds of pattern recognition. It's obviously useful for us to be able to discern sounds that matter to us among the chaos of the soundscape: a voice, a warning of danger, an animal. Music, he says, is sound conveniently pre-distilled for us. The confusing sonic clutter of the soundscape has been filtered out, and for the most part what we have left are pure tones, in fairly easily discernible rhythms.

Then there's the emotionality of music. It can move us as nothing else can, but how does it do this? One theory, similar to Purves's dissection of speech into often-occurring pitch intervals, is that even musical effects—crescendos and sudden changes, for example—partake in some parallels with purely emotional vocal effects like whimpering, shouting, sighing, moaning, and laughing. So not only do the intervals of music mimic the intervals common in emotional speech, but these dramatic musical effects might mimic emotive vocal effects as well.

This idea that music may be an expanded and abstracted version of sounds we are familiar with is not uncommon, but being a musician I have to feel that the vast number of variations in music has wandered fairly far from speech (except for maybe the musical speech of gospel sermons and Lou Reed's vocals). Not sure I'm buying this one.

Last, there is culture—a large part of what it means to be human. Beyond social status, music also helps us participate in that part of ourselves. Though we do have adaptations that encourage us, from an early age, to absorb and extract certain things from the culture around us, it's hard to know if there are specific musical adaptations. Do we not have the kind of built-in ability to "understand" music from an early age, similar to the way we have an innate ability to clock relationships between people? Don't toddlers rock out to music? Are they merely cockatiels? Is there more to loving the sound of a mother humming a lullaby to her baby than just a mother's soft voice? If it's just the sound of a soft voice and soothing harmonic intervals, then speech might be enough to calm a baby—but somehow the song seems to have come into being, too.

Music, according to this idea, is part of the "geometry of beauty"—a phrase coined by biologists, though it's strangely reminiscent of a phrase from one of J.G. Ballard's dystopian novels. This geometry, when we spot it, is a visible—or in this case audible—signal that something might be valuable and important to us: it's good to eat; it's safe; it's fertile; it's related to us and our people. Music has that geometry of beauty, and for that reason, so these thinkers say, we love it. The specific gene for music is an illusion, or so Pinker suggests—though our love for it is real.

ACKNOWLEDGMENTS

————————

Many years ago, while on tour, I sent Dave Eggers some journal entries from the road for his amusement—from Eastern Europe, I believe it was. They were possibly sent by fax; it was that long ago. Dave thought they shed light on what a touring musician's life was really like—a peek into a world he felt hadn't been revealed previously. This was encouraging and exciting feedback, but it was also before the era of blogging, so my missives remained unpublished, though a few anecdotes managed to sneak into my previous book about bikes and cities. Dave's enthusiasm planted a seed that I might write about music someday. But I had many trepidations about going down that road—the "aging rocker bio" is a crowded shelf—and I resisted for a long time, but it seems the day is here. I think I managed to give a sense that the world of music is wider than my personal experience, but my experience figures in here too.

Scott Moyers, who is now at Penguin Press, did the first rough edit and helped restructure this thing. Then it moved on to the McSweeney's team: Ethan Nosowsky has been the principal editor. Adam Krefman, Dave Eggers (cover design), Chelsea Hogue, and Walter Green all helped with content, design (Walter did most of the interior layout), and the time-consuming image licensing. My own office, Todomundo, has kept this project on track over quite a few years—LeeAnn Rossi has been involved in overall coordination, and Frank Hendler helped with the music business research in chapter seven, as did my manager, David Whitehead. My business managers, Lia Sweet, Nan Lanigan, and Illene Bashinsky, were also hugely helpful in our attempts to decode and present the finances of musicians and to explain as clearly as possible a transparent accounting history of a couple of my own projects.

My literary agent, Andrew Wylie, was understanding when I explained that this book was going to be neither an autobiography nor a series of think pieces—but a little bit of both. Now that it's done, it's a little easier to explain.

Thanks to Sally Singer for insisting I go through it one more time. Thanks too to the folks who have allowed use of their photos, quotations, and diagrams, and to the rights holders of the music snippets included in the e-book.

NOTES

Chapter One

1. *Folk Song Style and Culture*, by Alan Lomax, Transaction Publishers, 1978.
2. "Why So Serious?" by Alex Ross, *The New Yorker*, September 8, 2008.
3. "Bird Songs," by Gareth Huw Davies, in David Attenborough's program *The Life of Birds*, PBS. *www.pbs.org/lifeofbirds/songs/index.html*.
4. "The relation of geographical variation in song to habitat characteristics and body size in North American Tanagers," by Eyal Shy, *Behavioral Ecology and Sociobiology* vol. 12, Number 1, p. 71–76.
5. "How City Noise Is Reshaping Birdsong," by David Biello, *Scientific American*, October 22, 2009.
6. *Survival of the Beautiful: Art, Science and Evolution*, by David Rothenberg, Bloomsbury Press, 2011, p. 6.
7. "Was Maya Pyramid Designed to Chirp Like a Bird?" by Bijal P. Trivedi, *National Geographic*, December 6, 2002.
8. "Ancient Maya Temples Were Giant Loudspeakers?" by Ker Than, *National Geographic*, December 16, 2010.

Chapter Two

1. "Creativity and psychopathology: A study of 291 world-famous men," by Felix Post, *The British Journal of Psychiatry* (1994) 165: p. 22–24.

Chapter Three

1. "The Heleocentric Pantheon: An Interview with Walter Murch," by Geoff Manaugh, *BLDG Blog*, April 2007. *http://bldgblog.blogspot.com/2007/04/heliocentric-pantheon-interview-with.html*.
2. *Capturing Sound: How Technology Has Changed Music*, by Mark Katz, University of California Press, 2010, p. 13.
3. *Perfecting Sound Forever: An Aural History of Recorded Music*, by Greg Milner, Faber & Faber, 2010, p. 14.
4. *Capturing Sound: How Technology Has Changed Music*, by Mark Katz, University of California Press, 2010, p.60.
5. "The Menace of Mechanical Music," by John Philip Sousa, originally published in *Appleton's Magazine* vol. 8, 1906, p. 278. *www.phonozoic.net/n0155.htm*.
6. *Capturing Sound: How Technology Has Changed Music*, by Mark Katz, University of California Press, p. 17.
7. *Perfecting Sound Forever: An Aural History of Recorded Music*, by Greg Milner, Faber & Faber, 2010, p. 60.
8. *Si sos brujo: A Tango Story*, Caroline Neal, Cinemateca, 2005. DVD.
9. *Perfecting Sound Forever: An Aural History of Recorded Music*, by Greg Milner, Faber & Faber, 2010, p. 78.
10. *Capturing Sound: How Technology Has Changed Music*, by Mark Katz, University of California Press, p. 74–75.

11. "Wiring the World: Acoustical Engineers and the Empire of Sound in the Motion Picture Industry, 1927–1930," by Emily Thompson, in *Hearing Cultures: Essays on Sound, Listening and Modernity*, Veir Erlmann, ed., Berg Publishers, p. 198.
12. Ibid, p. 201.
13. Ibid, p. 202.
14. "The Prospects of Recording," by Glenn Gould, in *High Fidelity* vol. 16, no. 4, April 1966, p. 46–63.
15. Ibid.
16. "Thanks for the Memorex," by Hua Hsu, *ArtForum*, February 2011.
17. *Capturing Sound: How Technology Has Changed Music*, by Mark Katz, University of California Press, 2010, p. 12.

Chapter Four

1. *Perfecting Sound Forever: An Aural History of Recorded Music*, by Greg Milner, Faber & Faber, 2010, p. 258–261.
2. Ibid, p. 268.
3. Ibid, p. 207–208.
4. "Thinking About Sound, Proximity, and Distance in Western Experience: The Case of Odysseus's Walkman," by Michael Bull, in *Hearing Cultures: Essays on Sound, Listening and Modernity*, Veir Erlmann, ed., Berg Publishers, p. 174.
5. Ibid, p. 176.

Chapter Five

1. "The Prospects of Recording," by Glenn Gould, in *High Fidelity* vol. 16, no. 4, April 1966.

Chapter Six

1. "N.A.S.A: The Spirit of Apollo" by Tom Breihan, *Pitchfork*, February 18, 2009. *www.pitchfork.com/reviews/albums/12686-the-spirit-of-apollo*.

Chapter Seven

1. "The Artistry Is Apparent, So Where's the Audience?" by Stephen Holden, *The New York Times*, February 6, 2011.
2. "Musical Survivor Hustles for a Second Chance," by Ben Sisario, *The New York Times*, February 8, 2011.
3. "U2 Signs 12-Year Deal with Live Nation," *Billboard. www.billboard.com/news/article_display.jsp?vnu_content_id=1003782687#/news/article_display.jsp?vnu_content_id=1003782687*.
4. "Live Nation's $120 Million Bet: Breaking Down Madonna Deal," by Peter Kafka, *Business Insider*, October 10, 2007. *http://articles.businessinsider.com/2007-10-10/tech/30040635_1_madonna-deal-live-nation-material-girl*.
5. "Bandcamp Powers Online Sales, Aims to Fill Myspace 'Vacuum,'" by John Tozzi, *Bloomberg*, November 01, 2011. *www.bloomberg.com/news/2011-11-01/bandcamp-powers-online-sales-aims-to-fill-myspace-vacuum-.html*.
6. "Spotify hits 6 million paid users as market for music streaming heats up" by Jeff John Roberts, *paidContent*, March 12, 2013. http://paidcontent.org/2013/03/12/spotify-hits-6-million-paid-users-as-market-for-music-streaming-heats-up/
7. "Eminem Lawsuit May Raise Pay for Older Artists" by Ben Sisario, *New York Times*, March 27, 2011. http://www.nytimes.com/2011/03/28/business/media/28eminem.html?pagewanted=all&_r=0

8. "USC Annenberg Lab Ad Transparency Report, Fourth Edition" May 8, 2013.

Chapter Eight

1. *Toward a Poor Theater*, by Jerzy Grotowski, Routledge, 2002, p. 255.

Chapter Nine

1. *Capturing Sound: How Technology Has Changed Music*, by Mark Katz, University of California Press, 2010, p. 61.
2. *What Good Are the Arts?* by John Carey, Faber & Faber, 2005, p. 34–36.
3. "The Menace of Mechanical Music," by John Philip Sousa, originally published in *Appleton's Magazine* vol. 8, 1906.
4. *Capturing Sound: How Technology Has Changed Music*, by Mark Katz, University of California Press, 2010, p. 70.
5. "What's Wrong with Classical Music?" by Colin Eatock, 3 *Quarks Daily*, October 4, 2010. *www.3quarksdaily. com/3quarksdaily/2010/10/whats-wrong-with-classical-music.html*.
6. Ibid.
7. *What Good Are the Arts?*, by John Carey, Faber & Faber, 2005, p. 11.
8. Ibid, p. 97.
9. Ibid, p. 97–99.
10. Ibid, p. 101.
11. The Blockbuster attendance figures can be found here: *http://blogs.artinfo.com/ realcleararts/2011/08/08/wait-a-minute-further-thoughts-on-two-blockbuster-shows*.
12. *What Good Are the Arts?* by John Carey, Faber & Faber, 2005, p. 20–32.
13. Ibid, p. 25.
14. Ibid, p. 90.
15. Ibid, p. 60.
16. Ibid, p. 61.

17. *Criticisms on Art*, by William Hazlitt, Nabu Press, 2011, p. 110.
18. *Patronizing the Arts*, by Marjorie Garber, Princeton University Press, 2008, p. 52.
19. Ibid, p. 54.
20. "Design for Living," by Paul Goldberger, *The New Yorker*, April 4, 2011.
21. *What Good Are the Arts?* by John Carey, Faber & Faber, 2005, p. 132–133.
22. *Perfecting Sound Forever: An Aural History of Recorded Music*, by Greg Milner, Faber & Faber, 2010, p. 119.
23. "A Metropolitan Opera High Note, as Donations Hit $182 Million," by Daniel J. Wakin, *The New York Times*, October 10, 2011. *www.nytimes.com/2011/10/11/arts/music/ metropolitan-operas-donations-hit-a-record-182-million.html?pagewanted=all*.
24. "L.A. Opera's 'Ring' cycle may be in the red," by Mike Boehm, *Los Angeles Times*, May 29, 2010. *http://articles.latimes. com/2010/may/29/entertainment/la-et-ring-tickets-20100529*.
25. "A Metropolitan Opera High Note, as Donations Hit $182 Million," by Daniel J. Wakin, *The New York Times*, October 10, 2011. *www.nytimes.com/2011/10/11/arts/music/ metropolitan-operas-donations-hit-a-record-182-million.html?pagewanted=all*.
26. "Reader Response: Orchestras Are Overextended," by Daniel J. Wakin, *The New York Times*, April 22, 2011. *http://artsbeat. blogs.nytimes.com/2011/04/22/reader-response-orchestras-are-over-extended*.
27. "Los galeones en el siglo XXI. El Roxy, un ejemplo de art deco tapatio," in *Replicante* vol. 3, No. 12, Summer 2007.
28. *What Good Are the Arts?* by John Carey, Faber & Faber, 2005, p. 40.
29. "Beyond Baby Mozart: Students Who Rock," by David Bornstein, *The New York Times*, September 8, 2011. *http://opinionator.blogs. nytimes.com/2011/09/08/beyond-baby-mozart-students-who-rock*.

30. "Rock Is Not the Enemy," by David Bornstein, *The New York Times*, September 13, 2011. *http://opinionator.blogs.nytimes.com/2011/09/13/rock-is-not-the-enemy*.

31. "Strings Attached: What the Venezuelans Are Doing for British Kids," by Ed Vulliamy, *The Observer*, October 3, 2010.

32. Ibid.

33. Ibid.

34. "Let's Get Serious About Cultivating Creativity," by Steven J. Tepper & Georde D. Kuh, *The Chronicle of Higher Education*, September 4, 2011. *www.chronicle.com/article/Lets-Get-Serious-About/128843*.

35. *Musicophilia: Tales of Music and the Brain*, by Oliver Sacks, Knopf, 2007, p. 102.

36. *What Good Are the Arts?*, by John Carey, Faber & Faber, 2005.

37. "Transform Education? Yes, We Must," by Sir Ken Robinson, *The Huffington Post*, January 11, 2009. *www.huffingtonpost.com/sir-ken-robinson/transform-education-yes-w_b_157014.html*.

38. *The Thinking Ear: Complete Writing on Music Education*, by R. Murray Schafer, Arcana Editions, 1986, p. 246–48.

Chapter Ten

1. *Selected Essays and Readings: On the Origin of Music*, by Robert Fink, Greenwich Publishing, 2003.

2. *The Secret Teachings of All Ages: An Encyclopedia Outline of Masonic, Hermetic, Qabbalistic and Rosicrucian Symbolical Philosophy*, by Manly P. Hall, Jeremy P Tarcher/Penguin, 2003, p. 252.

3. *The Harmony of the World*, by Johannes Kepler, American Philosophical Society, 1997, p. 440.

4. "The Heliocentric Pantheon: An Interview with Walter Murch," by Geoff Manaugh, *BLDG Blog*, April 2007. *http://bldgblog.blogspot.com/2007/04/heliocentric-pantheon-interview-with.html*.

5. *The Music of Pythagoras: How an Ancient Brotherhood Cracked the Code of the Universe and Lit the Path from Antiquity to Outer Space by Kitty Ferguson*, Walker Publishing Company, 2008, p. 239.

6. "Ether Ore: Mining Vibrations in American Modernist Music," by Douglas Kahn in *Hearing Cultures: Essays on Sound, Listening and Culture*, Veit Erlmann, ed., Berg Publishers, 2004, p.127.

7. "In Search of Music's Biological Roots," by Ker Than, *Duke Magazine* vol. 94, No. 3, May–June 2008. *www.dukemagazine.duke.edu/issues/050608/music1.html*.

8. "A Sonorous, Smiling City," by Kerri MacDonald and Béatrice de Géa, *The New York Times*, March 16, 2011.

9. "Cage's Place in the Reception of Satie," by Matthew Shlomowitz, 1999. *www.satie-archives.com/web/article8.html*.

10. "Experimental Music," by John Cage, statement given as an address to the convention of the Music Teachers National Association in Chicago in 1957. *www.kim-cohen.com/seth_texts/artmusictheorytexts/Cage%20Experimental%20Music.pdf*.

11. *Outsider: John Rockwell on the Arts, 1967–2006*, 2006, Limelight Editions, p. 210.

12. "Experimental Music," by John Cage, statement given as an address to the convention of the Music Teachers National Association in Chicago in 1957. *www.kim-cohen.com/seth_texts/artmusictheorytexts/Cage%20Experimental%20Music.pdf*.

SUGGESTED READING

Chapter One

Campbell, Joseph, *The Hero with a Thousand Faces*, New World Library, 2008.

Lomax, Alan, *Folk Song Style and Culture*, Transaction Publishers, 1978.

Lomax, Alan; Paulay, Forrestine, directors, *Rhythms of Earth: The Choreometrics Films of Alan Lomax and Forrestine Paulay*, NTSC, Media-Generation, 2008.

Chapter Two

Tanizaki, Junichiro, *In Praise of Shadows*, Leete's Island Books, 1977.

Rouget, Gilbert, *Music and Trance: A Theory of the Relations Between Music and Possession*, University of Chicago Press, 1985.

PAJ: A Journal of Performance and Art, originally called *Performing Arts Journal*, often featured interviews with "experimental" theatrical artists such as Mabou Mines and Bob Wilson.

Artaud, Antonin, *The Theater and Its Double*, Grove Press, 1938.

Thompson, Robert Farris, *African Art in Motion*, University of California Press, 1979.

Canetti, Elias, *Crowds and Power*, Farrar, Straus and Giroux, 1984.

Goodman, Felicitas D., *Speaking in Tongues: A Cross Cultural Study in Glossolalia*, University of Chicago Press, 1972.

Young, Neil; Crazy Horse, *Rust Never Sleeps*, LP, Reprise Records 1979.

Country Legends, VHS, Hallway Entertainment Inc., 2000.

Chapter Three

Eisenberg, Evan, *The Recording Angel*, Yale University Press, 2005.

Erlmann, Veit, ed., *Hearing Cultures: Essays on Sound, Listening and Modernity*, Berg Publishers, 2004.

Emmerson, Simon; Wishart, Trevor, ed., *On Sonic Art*, Hardwood Academic Publishers, 1996.

Katz, Mark, *Capturing Sound: How Technology Has Changed Music*, University of California Press, 2010.

Milner, Greg, *Perfecting Sound Forever: An Aural History of Recorded Music*, Faber & Faber, 2010.

Jones, George, *Anniversary: Ten Years of Hits*, CD, Sony, 1982.

Chapter Five

Emerick, Geoff; Massey, Howard, *Here There and Everywhere: My Life Recording the Music of the Beatles*, Gotham, 2007.

Davis, Miles; Troupe, Quincy, *Miles: The Autobiography*, Simon & Schuster, 1990.

Chernoff, John Miller, *African Rhythm and African Sensibility*, University of Chicago Press, 1981.

33 1/3 (Thirty-Three and a Third) is a series of books written about music albums, featuring one author per album, published by Bloomsbury Publishing.

Godard, Jean-Luc, director, *Sympathy for the Devil*, film, 1968.

Chapter Six

Jacobs, Jane, *The Death and Life of Great American Cities*, Modern Library, 2011.
Eggers, Dave, *What Is the What*, Vintage, 2007.
Mercado, Monina Allarye, *People Power: The Philippine Revolution of 1986: An Eyewitness History*, Writers & Readers, 1987.
Solnit, Rebecca, *A Paradise Built in Hell: The Extraordinary Communities That Arise in Disaster*, Viking, 2010.
Veloso, Caetano, *Tropical Truth: A Story of Music and Revolution in Brazil,* Da Capo Press, 2003.

Chapter Seven

Krasilovsky, M. William; Shemel, Sidney; and Gross, John M., *This Business of Music*, Billboard Books, 2007.
Dannen, Fredric, *Hit Men: Power Brokers and Fast Money Inside the Music Business,* Vintage, 1991.
Stokes, Geoffrey, *Starmaking Machinery: The Odyssey of an Album*, Bobbs-Merrill, 1976.

Chapter Eight

Wilson, E.O., *On Human Nature, Harvard University Press*, 2004.
Guillermoprieto, Alma, *Samba*, Vintage, 1991.
Tiger, Lionel, *Men in Groups*, Transaction Publishers, 2004.

Chapter Nine

Carey, John, *What Good Are the Arts?*, Oxford University Press, 2010.
Robinson, Ken, *Out of Our Minds: Learning to be*
Pontynen, Arthur, *For the Love of Beauty: Art*

Creative, Captone, 2011.
The Trips Festival, DVD, directed by Eric Christensen (2008; Trips Festival).
Ross, Alex, *Listen to This*, Farrar, Straus and Giroux, 2011.
Friedman, B.H., ed., *Give My Regards to Eighth Street: Collected Writings of Morton Feldman,* Exact Change, 2004.
Roberts, John Storm, *The Latin Tinge: The Impact of Latin Music on the United States,* Oxford University Press, 1999.
Krich, John, *Why Is This Country Dancing?: A One-Man Samba to the Beat of Brazil,* Cooper Square Press, 2003.
Schafer, R. Murray, *The Thinking Ear: Complete Writing on Music Education*, Arcana Editions, 1986.
Dissanayake, Ellen, *Homo Aestheticus: Where Art Comes from and Why*, University of Washington Press, 1995.
Kuh, George D.; Tepper, Steven J., "Let's Get Serious About Cultivating Creativity," *The Chronicle of Higher Education*, September 4, 2011 *http://chronicle.com/article/Lets-Get-Serious-About/128843.*

Chapter Ten

Walter Murch interview by Geoff Manaugh, "The Heliocentric Pantheon: An Interview with Walter Murch," BLDG Blog, April, 2007. *http://bldgblog.blogspot.com/2007/04/heliocentric-pantheon-interview-with.html.*
Wittkower, Rudolf, *Architectural Principles in the Age of Humanism*, W.W. Norton & Company, 1971.
Blesser, Barry, *Spaces Speak, Are You Listening?: Experiencing Aural Architecture*, the MIT Press, 2009.
Mitrovic, Branko, *Learning from Palladio*, W.W. Norton & Company, 2004.
History and the Moral Foundations of Aesthetic

Judgement, Transactions Publishers, 2006.

Cage, John, "Experimental Music," an address given at the convention of the Music Teachers National Association in Chicago in the winter of 1957. *http://www.kim-cohen.com/seth_texts/ artmusictheorytexts/Cage%20Experimental%20 Music.pdf*

Gill, Kamraan Z.; Purves, Dale, "A Biological Rationale for Musical Scales," Duke University Center for Cognitive Neuroscience and Department of Neurobiology, as published on plsone.org, December 3, 2009. *http://www.plosone.org/article/ info:doi%2F10.1371%2Fjournal.pone.0008144*

Molnar-Skazaks, Istvan; Overy, Katie, *Social Cognitive and Affective Neuroscience,* "Music and Mirror Neurons: From Motion to 'e' motion," Oxford University Press, 2006.

Balkwill, Laura-Lee; Thompson, William Forde, "A Cross Cultural Investigation of the Perception of Emotion in Music: Psychophysical and Cultural Cues," *Music Perception: An Interdisciplinary Journal,* vol. 17, Fall 1999.

Bowling, Daniel L.; Choi, Jonathan D.; Gill, Kamraan; Prinz, Joseph; and Purves, Dale, "Major and Minor Compared to Excited and Subdued Speech," *Journal of the Acoustical Society of America,* Volume 127, Issue 1, 2010.

Levitin, Dan, *This Is Your Brain on Music: The Science of a Human Obsession,* Plume/Penguin, 2007.

Sacks, Oliver, *Musicophilia,* Knopf, 2007.

Cardew, Cornelius, *Stockhausen Serves Imperialism,* Latimer New Dimensions, 1974.

Zimmermann, Walter, *Desert Plants: Conversations with Twenty-three American Musicians,* A.R.C. Publications, 1976.

Coitt, Jonathan, *Stockhausen: Conversations with the Composer,* Pan Books, 1974.

DISCOGRAPHY

Chapter One

Talking Heads, "A Clean Break (Let's Work) Live at CBGB's, 10/10/1977,"Bonus Rarities and Outtakes, 2006, Sire Records.

HeyBale, "Honky Tonk Mood," The Last Country Album, 2008, Shuffle 5 Records.

Various Artists, "Wenlega (a Mossi Dance)," Burkina Faso / Savannah Rhythms, 1981, Nonesuch Records.

Thomas Tallis, "Spem in Alium," Tallis: Spem in Alium, Etc., 1985, Gimell Records.

Johann Sebastian Bach (Author: Bernard Legace), "Fantasia super Jesu, Meine Freunde. Chorale BWV 713," Complete Organ Works & Other Keyboard Works 2: Toccata Adagio & Fugue in C Major BWV 564 And Other Early Works. Vol.2, 1998, Analekta.

Wolfgang Amadeus Mozart; Authors: Hansgeorg Schmeiser & Ingomar Rainer, "Sonata in F KV.13: Allegro," Mozart — The Early Sonatas, 2006, Nimbus Records.

Richard Wagner; Authors: New York Philharmonic Orchestra, "Lohengrin / Act 3 — Prelude to Act III," Twilight of the Gods: The Essential Wagner Collection, 1998, Deutsche Grammophon GmbH.

Gustav Mahler; Author: Mari Anne Haggander; Composer: Johann Wolfgang Von Goethe, "Symphony No. 8 in E flat major ('Symphony of a Thousand'): Veni, creator spiritus," Mahler — Symphony No. 8, 1995, BIS Records.

Clarence Williams and Spencer Williams; Author: Ethel Waters, "Royal Garden Blues," Ethel Waters 1921-1923, 1994, Classics Records.

Lorenz Hart and Richard Rogers; Author: Chet Baker, "My Funny Valentine," My Funny Valentine, 1954, Golden Stars / Back Up / Delta Distribution.

Sugarhill Gang; Composer: Bernard Edwards and Nile Rodgers, "Rapper's Delight," Sugarhill Gang, 1980, Sugar Hill Records.

U2, "I Still Haven't Found What I'm Looking For," Joshua Tree, 1987, Mercury Records.

Lil Jon & The East Side Boyz, "Who U Wit," Get Crunk, Who U Wit: Da Album, 1997, Mirror Image Records.

John Williams; Authors: London Symphony Orchestra, "Main Title," Star Wars: Episode IV: A New Hope, 1977, 20th Century Records.

Bernard Hermann; Author: London Symphony Orchestra, "The Murder," Psycho, 1960, Soundstage Records.

Chapter Two

The Who, "I Can't Explain," "I Can't Explain" Single, 1964, Decca Records.

Crosby, Stills & Nash, "Suite: Judy Blue Eyes," Crosby, Stills & Nash, 1969, Atlantic Records.

The Kinks, "Waterloo Sunset," Something Else by the Kinks, 1967, Reprise Records.

Chuck Berry, "Maybellene," *Maybellene" Single*, 1955, Chess Records.

Eddie Cochran, "Twenty Flight Rock," "Twenty Flight Rock" Single, 1957, Liberty Records.

Bing Crosby, "Pennies from Heaven," Pennies from Heaven, 1936, Hallmark Recordings

Benny Goodman ft. Helen Ward, "The Glory of Love," Original Benny Goodman Trio and Quartet Sessions: After You've Gone, Vol. 1, 1936, Pair Records.

? & The Mysterians, "96 Tears," 96 Tears, 1966, Cameo Records.

Grin, "Slippery Fingers" and "White Lies," 1+1, 1972, Spindizzy Records.

Dr. John The Night Tripper, "I Walk on Guided Splinters," Gris-Gris, 1968, Atco Records.

Rahsaan Roland Kirk, "Dance of the Lobes," Natural Black Inventions: Root Strata, 1971, Atlantic Records.

Sun Ra, "Space Probe," Space Probe, 1978, Saturn Records.

Al Green, "Love and Happiness," I'm Still in Love With You, 1972, Hi Records.

Talking Heads, "Psycho Killer," Talking Heads: 77, 1977, Sire Records.

David Bowie, "5 Years," The Rise and Fall of Ziggy Stardust and the Spiders from Mars, 1972, Virgin Records.

Nancy Sinatra, "Some Velvet Morning," Movin' with Nancy, 1968, Sundazed Records.

Shangri-Las, "Remember (Walking in the Sand)," Single, 1964, Red Bird Records.

The Jackson 5, "Dancing Machine" Get It Together, 1973, Motown Records.

KC and the Sunshine Band, "Get Down Tonight," KC and the Sunshine Band, 1974, TK Records.

Television, "See No Evil," Marquee Moon, 1977, Elektra Records.

The Modern Lovers, "Girl Friend," The Modern Lovers, 1976, Beserkeley Records.

David Byrne and Brian Eno, "Regiment," My Life in the Bush of Ghosts, 1981, Sire Records.

Talking Heads, "Once in a Lifetime," Remain in Light, 1980, Sire Records.

Talking Heads, "This Must Be the Place (Naïve Melody)," Speaking in Tongues, 1983, Sire Records.

Margareth Menezes, "Elegibò (Uma História de Ifá)," Elegibò, 1990, Mango Records.

Willie Nelson, "Stardust," Stardust, 1978, Columbia Records.

Jorge Ben, "Ponta de Lanca Africano (Umbabarauma)," África Brazil, 1976, Philips Records.

Caetano Veloso, Livro, 1998, Nonesuch Records.

Chapter Three

Duke Ellington, "East St. Louis Toodle-oo," Duke Ellington (1956), 1956, Charly Records.

Max Bruch and Wolfgag Amadeus Mozart; Author: Jascha Heifetz, "Concert for Violin & Orchestra No. 4 in D major, K. 218" Bruch: Violin Concerto No. 1 in G minor; Mozart: Violin Concerto No. 4; Violin Concerto No. 5, 2011, RCA Red Seal

Alessandro Moreschi; Composer: Ignace Leybach, "Pie Jesu," The Last Castrato, 1984, OPAL Records.

The Philadelphia Orchestra; Conductor: Leopold Stowkowski, "The Sorcerer's Apprentice (L'apprenti Sorcier)," Walt Disney's Fantasia: Original Soundtrack, 1942, Walt Disney Records.

Louis Armstrong & His Hot Five, "Skid-Dat-De-Dat," Louis Armstrong & His Hot Five No. 2, 1958, Philips Records.

Lead Belly, "Rock Island Line," Rock Island Line: Original 1935-1943 Recordings, 1951 Naxos Nostalgia Records.

Darius Milhaud; Author: William Bolcom, "Trois Rag-Caprices Op. 78: Precis Et Nerveux," Milhaud: Piano Music, 1975, Nonesuch Records.

Orchestra Baobab, "Pape Ndiaye," Made in Dakar, 2007, World Circuit Records.

Glenn Gould, "The Idea of North," Glenn Gould's Solitude Trilogy - 3 Sound Documentaries, 1992, CBC Records.

Clara Rockmore, composed by Stravinsky, "L'oiseau de Feu (The Firebird): Arr. For Theremin," The Art of the Theremin, 1987, Delos Records.

Benny Goodman Sextet featuring Charlie Christian, "Shivers," Benny Goodman Sextet Featuring Charlie Christian: 1939-1941, 1991, Columbia Records.

The Jimi Hendrix Experience, "Purple Haze," Are You Experienced?, 1967, Sony Legacy Records.

Various Artists, "Hawaiian Wedding Song," World of Music: Songs of Hawaii, 2000, Blue Music Records.

Les Paul and Mary Ford, "Lover," The Best of Capitol Masters: Selection from the Legend and the Legacy, 1992, Capitol Records.

Turtles, "Happy Together," Happy Together, 1967, Sundazed Records.

Ki Nartosabdho, "Jula Juli Suber," Identitas Jawa Tengah, 1989, Fajar Records.

Chapter Four

David Byrne and Fatboy Slim, "Here Lies Love," Here Lies Love, 2010, Nonesuch Records.

Serge Gainsbourg, "Ford Mustang," Initials B.B., 1968, PolyGram Records.

Crystal Waters, "Gypsy Woman (She's Homeless)," Surprise, 1991, Mercury Records.

Talking Heads, "Sugar on My Tongue," Once in a Lifetime, 2003, Sire & Warner Bros Records.

Trick Daddy (feat. Cee Lo, and Ludacris), "Sugar (Gimme Some)," Thug Matrimony: Married to the Streets, 2004, Slip-N-Slide Records.

Grace Jones, "Feel Up," A One Man Show, 1978, PolyGram Records.

Pet Shop Boys, "Opportunities (Let's Make Lots of Money)," Disco, 1986, EMI Records.

Chapter Five

Simon and Garfunkel, "The Sound of Silence," Wednesday Morning, 3 A.M., 1964, Columbia Records.

John Cage, "Roaratorio: Pt 1," Roaratorio: An Irish Circus on Finnegan's Wake, for voice, tape & Irish musicians, 1992, Mode Records.

Philip Glass, "Victor's Lament," Philip Glass: North Star, 1977, Virgin Records.

Steve Reich, "Pulses," Music for 18 Musicians, 1998, Nonesuch Records.

Terry Riley, Terry Riley: In C, 1968, Sony Music Distribution.

Velvet Underground, "Heroin," The Velvet Underground & Nico, 1967, Polydor Records.

The Stooges, "1969,"The Stooges, 1969, Elektra Records.

Captain Beefheart & The Magic Band, "She's Too Much For My Mirror," Trout Mask Replica, 1969, Reprise Records.

Talking Heads, More Songs About Buildings and Food, 1978, Sire Records.

Talking Heads, Fear of Music, 1979, Sire Records.

St. Vincent, Actor, 2009, 4AD Records.

Prince Danurejo VII, "Langen Mandra Wanara. Opera de Danuredjo Debut" Langen Mandra Wanara, 1988, Ocora Records.

Pete Seeger, "Risselty-Rosselty" With Voices Together We Sing, 1956, Folkways Records.

Fela Kuti, "Expensive Shit," Expensive Shit/He Miss Road, 1975, PolyGram Records.

Farid al-Atrache, "Hebbina Hebbina," Forever, Vol. 2, 2000, EMI Records.

Holger Czukay, "Persian Love," Movies, 1979, Electrola Records.

Konono Nº1, "Kule Kule Reprise," Congotronics, 2005, Crammed Discs Records.

Swedish House Mafia (feat. Pharrell), "One (Your Name)," Until One, 2010, Virgin Records.

James Brown, "Funky Drummer," In the Jungle Groove, 1986, Polydor Records.

Talking Heads, "Burning Down the House," Speaking in Tongues, 1983, Sire Records.

David Byrne, "Leg Bells," The Catherine Wheel, 1981, Warner Bros. Records.

Talking Heads, "Cool Water," Naked, 1988, Fly Records.

David Byrne and Celia Cruz, "Loco de Amor," Rei Momo, 1989, Luaka Bop/Sire Records.

Rodolfo y su Tipita RA7, "La Colegiala," Cumbia Cumbia, 1989, World Circuit Records.

Zeca Pagodinho, "Samba Pras Moças," Zeca Pagodinho, 1997, PolyGram Records.

The Meters, Look-Ka Py Py, 1970, Josie Records.

David Byrne, "Something Ain't Right," Uh-Oh, 1992, Luaka Bop/Sire/Warner Bros. Records.

Chapter Six

Serge Gainsbourg, Histoire de Melody Nelson — 40ème Anniversaire, 1971, PolyGram Records.

King Tubby, "A Truthful Dub," Dub from the Roots, 1975, Jamaican Records.

Joni Mitchell, Blue, 1971, Reprise Records.

Iannis Xenakis, "Concret Ph," Electronic Music, 1997, EMF Records.

David Byrne and Brian Eno, "The River," Everything That Happens Will Happen Today, 2008, Todo Mundo Records.

Reverend Maceo Woods, "Surrender to His Will," Maceo Woods and the Christian Tabernacle Baptist Church Choir, 1969 Volt Records.

David Byrne and Caetano Veloso, "Dreamworld," Onda Sonora: Red Hot + Lisbon, 1999, Bar/None Records.

Carmen Miranda, "Diz Que Tem," Brazilian Recordings, 1993, Harlequin Records.

John Adams, composer; David Robertson, conductor; St. Louis Symphony Orchestra, orchestra; Doctor Atomic Symphony, 2009, Nonesuch Records.

David Byrne & Fatboy Slim, "Here Lies Love," Here Lies Love, 2010, Nonesuch Records.

Sharon Jones & The Dap-Kings, "How Long Do I Have To Wait For You?," Naturally, 2005, Daptone Records.

Chapter Seven

D'Angelo, "Send It On," Voodoo, 2000, Modern Classics Records.

Randy Newman, "Louisiana 1927," Good Old Boys, 1974, Warner Bros. Records.

Maria Schneider, Sky Blue, 2007, Artistshare Records.

Jay-Z (feat. Kanye West and Rihanna), "Run This Town," The Blueprint 3, 2009, Roc Nation Records.

U2, "Beautiful Day," Beautiful Day, 2000, PolyGram Records.

Madonna, "Candy Shop," Hard Candy, 2008, Warner Bros. Records.

David Byrne, Grown Backwards, 2004, Nonesuch Records.

David Byrne, Lead Us Not Into Temptation, 2003, Thrill Jockey Records.

Aimee Mann, "How Am I Different," Bachelor No. 2 Or, The Last Remains of the Dodo, 2000, SuperEgo Records.

Radiohead," Weird Fishes/Arpeggi," In Rainbows, 2007, XL Recordings.

Amanda Palmer, Amanda Palmer Performs the Popular Hits of Radiohead on Her Magical Ukulele, 2010, self-released on Bandcamp.

David Byrne & Brian Eno,"My Big Nurse," Everything that Happens Will Happen Today, 2008, Todo Mundo Records.

Rhianna, "Umbrella," Good Girl Gone Bad, 2007, Def Jam Records.

Christina Aguilera, "Ain't No Other Man," Back to Basics, 2006, RCA Records.

Chapter Eight

Television, "Little Johnny Jewel," Marquee Moon, 1977, Warner Music Records.

The Mumps, "Muscleboys," Fatal Charm,1994, Eggbert Records.

Neu!, "Hallogallo," Neu!, 1972, Groenland Records.

Faust, "Krautrock," Faust IV, 1973, Virgin Records.

1910 Fruitgum Company, "1, 2, 3 Red Light," 1, 2, 3 Red Light, 1968, Buddah Records.

Patti Smith, "Gloria: In Exelsis Deo," Horses, 1975, Arista Records.

Ramones, "Beat on the Brat," Ramones, 1976, Rhino Records.

Blondie, "Hanging on the Telephone," Parallel Lines, 1978, Chrysalis Records.

Various Artists, Nuggets: Original Artyfacts from the First Psychedelic Era, 1965–1968, 1972, Elektra Records.

DNA, "Egomaniac's Kiss," No New York, 1978, Antilles Record.

Cibo Matto, "Know Your Chicken," Viva! La Woman, 1996, Rhino / Warner Bros. Records.

Chocolate Genius, "My Mom," Black Music, 1998, V2 Records.

Chapter Nine

Manassas, "The Love Gangster," Manassas, 1972, Atlantic Records.

Tom Zé, "Toc," Estudando o Samba, 1976, Continental Records.

tUnE-yArDs, "Bizness," W H O K I L L, 2011, 4AD Records.

Café Tacuba, "No Controles," Avalancha de Éxitos, 1996, WEA Latina/WM Mexico.

Chapter Ten

Fairuz, "Ya Tayr," The Very Best of Fairuz, 1987, Digital Press Hellas Records.

David Habba, "Iraq-Al Ted Ag Leche Avar y Avo Ha-go El," Hazanout: Chants Lithurgiques Juifs, 2008, MCM Records.

Liu Fang, "Hautes Montagnes Et Eaux Ruisselantes (High Mountains and Rippling)," Silk Sound, 2006, Accords-Croises Records.

Arnold Schoenburg, composer; Berlin Philharmonic Orchestra/Herbert von Karajan, performers, "5 Orchestral Pieces: IV. Peripetie - Sehr Rasch," Schoenberg, Berg & Webern: Orchestral Works, 2003, EMI Classics Records.

Olivier Messiaen, Quartet for the End of Time, 1972, Candide Records.

"Rangda Mesolah," Tabuh Anaklung Terbaru, Aneka Stereo Records.

Ornette Coleman, "Beauty is a Rare Thing," This Is Our Music, 1961, Warner Jazz Records.

John Coltrane, "Sun Ship," Sun Ship, 1965, Impulse! Records.

Bernard Desgraupes & Ensemble Ereawtung, "Musique d'ameublement: I. Tenture de cabinet prefectoral," Essential Satie, 2012, EMI Classics Records.

Brian Eno, "Lux 1," Lux, 2012, Warp Records.

Mantovani & His Orchestra, "Theme From 'A Summer Place,'" The World of Mantovani, 2009, Decca Records.

Morton Feldman, "Movement 2," Rothko Chapel; Why Patterns?, 1991, New Albion Records.

Alvin Lucier, "Music on a Long Thin Wire," Alvin Lucier: Music on a Long Thin Wire, 1980, Lovely Music Records.

John Luther Adams, John Luther Adams: Winter Music, 2004, Wesleyan University Press.

Terry Riley, "Persian Surgery Dervishes: Performance 2, Part 2," Terry Riley: Persian Surgery Dervishes, 1972, Shanti Records.

Sunn O))), "Big Church," Monolith & Dimensions, 2009, Sun Lord Records.

ILLUSTRATION CREDITS

Chapter One

A. CBGB interior by Joseph O. Holmes
B. Rancid at CBGB by Justin Borucki
C. Tootsies Orchid Lounge "House Band" by Henry Horenstein
D. Tootsies Orchid Lounge "Last Call" by Henry Horenstein
E. Photo by Eric Ashford, courtesy of *Ethnomusicology Review*
F. Ely Cathedral by Walt Bistline, 2010
G. Arnstadt Church by Piet Bron
H. Photo by Marianne Haller, courtesy of Bundesmobilienverwaltung, Hofmobiliendepot, Möbel Museum Wien
I. Hall of Mirrors by Jenson Z. Yu
J. La Scala by Blake Hooper, Hooper & Co. Photography
L. Carnegie Hall by Peter Borg, Westminster Choir College of Rider University
M. Buddy Bolden's band, from the personal collection of trombonist Willie Cornish
O. Shure Brothers model 55S microphone by John Schneider
P. Graetz Melodia radio
Q. WE LOVE Sundays, at Space, Ibiza, by Harry Sprout
R. Roseland Ballroom by Joe Conzo
S. Photo by Eric W. Beasman
T. Photo by Olaf Mooij
V. Scarlet Tanager by Joe Thompson
W. Spectrogram by Bernie Krause
X. Photo by Daniel Schwen
Y. Photo by Thor Janson, first printed in *Revue Magazine*
Z. Photo by Silvia Rodriguez Kembel
AA. 3D Map by Silvia Rodriguez Kembel

Chapter Two

A. Courtesy of David Byrne
B. Photo by Patti Kane
D. Photo by Barbara A. Botdorf
E. Courtesy of The Estate of Karlheniz Weinberger, care of Patrik Schelder, Zurich, Switzerland. Courtesy of Artist Management, New York
F. Photo by Andrej Krasnansky
G. Photo by Maria Varmazis
H. Drawing by David Byrne
I. Photo by Rick Wezenaar Photography, *http://www.wezenaar.org*
K. Robert Wilson performance by Stephanie Berger
L. Courtesy of Hiro
M. Photo by Clayton Call
N. Photo by Tony Orlando
O. Hoola Hoope Dancer, Sufjan's BQE show, by Lawrence Fung
P. Photo by Anne Billingsley

Chapter Three

B. Illustration from *The Case of the Cottingley Fairies* by Joe Cooper
C. Courtesy of Georg Neumann GmbH
D. Courtesy of Pavek Museum of Broadcasting
E. Photo from the Museum of Making Music

Chapter Four

A. Early 1970s transistor vocoder custom built and used by the pop duo Kraftwerk
B. Courtesy of David Byrne

Chapter Five

A-B. Courtesy of Record Plant Remote
C-D. Photos by Hugh Brown

E. Electric Boogaloos, courtesy of Vicki Stavrinos
F-J. Courtesy of David Byrne
K. Ad originally appeared in the *New York Times*

Chapter Six

A. Courtesy of Bibliothèque Nationale de France
B. Kente Prestige Cloth, on display at the British Museum, London
D. Courtesy of David Byrne

Chapter Seven

The charts within this chapter were created from statistics and figures provided by the following publications:
p. 209: Recording Industry Association of America
p. 220, 226, 233: *Wired* magazine
p. 227, 231, 242, 243: RZO Music Ltd.

Chapter Eight

C-D. Drawing by David Byrne

Chapter Nine

C. Originally printed in *Life* magazine
D. Originally printed in the *New York Times*
H. Photo by Monika Rittershaus
I. Photo by Claudia Uribe
K. Carlinhos Brown from *A Tarde Online*

Chapter Ten

M. Photo by Einar Einarsson Kvaran

Uncredited images are public domain.

ABOUT THE AUTHOR

Known as the force behind Talking Heads and later as creator of the highly regarded record label Luaka Bop, David Byrne also works as a photographer, film director, author, and solo artist; he has published and exhibited visual art for more than a decade. Among Byrne's more recent works are *Playing the Building*, an interactive sound installation at New York's Battery Maritime Building and London's Roundhouse; *Everything That Happens Will Happen Today*, Byrne's first collaboration with co-writer Brian Eno since 1981's *My Life in the Bush of Ghosts*; a series of unique bike racks installed throughout New York City in conjunction with the New York City Department of Transportation; and *Bicycle Diaries*, a chronicle of his travels on his bicycle. *Here Lies Love*, his song cycle in collaboration with Fatboy Slim about the life of Imelda Marcos, made its theatrical debut at New York's Public Theater in the spring of 2013.

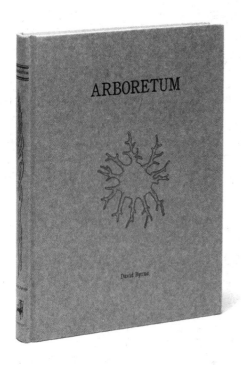
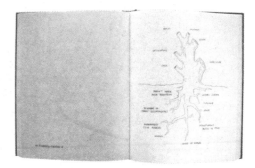
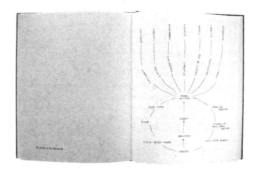